ACROSS EAST AFRICAN GLACIERS.

AN ACCOUNT OF
THE FIRST ASCENT OF KILIMANJARO.

BY

Dr. HANS MEYER.

TRANSLATED FROM THE GERMAN

BY

E. H. S. CALDER.

With Forty Illustrations and Three Maps.

THE FRONTISPIECE AND EIGHT PHOTOGRAPHS PRINTED IN GERMANY.

LONDON:
LONGMANS, GREEN, AND CO.
AND NEW YORK: 15 EAST 16th STREET.
1891.

General view of Kilima-njaro from the S.E.

PREFACE.

IN the matter of geographical exploration, which may be said to constitute the groundwork of the successful development of all countries, German East Africa has not hitherto shared the advantages enjoyed by our colonies on the western side of the continent. There, and more especially in our Protectorate of the Cameroons, the work of geographical research has been systematically carried out under Government supervision and at Government expense, whereas the exploration and exploitation of East Africa have been left entirely to the more limited resources of commercial companies.

In all the expeditions which have penetrated the region since the first delimitation of the various spheres of interest, the interests of Geography and of Science in general have been of secondary importance to the making of treaties and the establishment of stations. It seemed to me, therefore, that, since Government showed no signs of moving in the matter, the work of geographical research in East Africa must be taken up by private individuals. I resolved to devote myself and my means to it forthwith; and in the course of three expeditions I have done my best to make known the districts geographically the most interesting and colonially the most valuable. First in importance in both these respects is Kilimanjaro, a mighty mountain mass, which attains an altitude of nearly 20,000 feet, and upon which every imaginable shade of climate is represented. After it comes the mountain ranges of Usambara, Paré, and Ugweno, which run inland from the coast to Kilimanjaro, rising like island oases from the surrounding barrenness of the steppes.

Kilimanjaro was discovered by a German—the missionary, Rebmann; it was first explored by a German—Baron von der Decken; and it seemed to me to be almost a national duty that a German should be the first to tread the summit of this mountain, probably the loftiest in Africa, and certainly the highest in the German Empire. Notwithstanding the efforts of the numerous travellers who had visited the region, many problems still lay awaiting solution. The geological structure of the mountain, the causes of the prevailing climatic conditions, the nature of the snow and ice in equatorial Africa, were all matters of universal interest which yet remained to be determined.

Tempted by these many attractions, I quitted Europe for Africa in the autumn of 1886, proceeding first to South Africa with a view to obtaining some experience of African life and methods of working. Although this was my first visit to the Dark Continent, I was already a past master in the art of travel. I had climbed the Alps and the Himalayas, and in Ceylon and Southern India had become familiar with all the details of tropical agriculture; I had gazed into the craters of the volcanoes of Java, and penetrated the recesses of the forests of the Philippines; I had sailed up the rivers of China and Japan, and had traversed Mexico and California in all directions, and thus little by little I had become accustomed to travel in all climates and under all conditions. In South Africa I passed through Cape Colony, and spent some time at the diamond fields of Kimberley and the goldfields of the Transvaal, afterwards making a sojourn in the Drakenberg mountains, whence I gradually made my way northwards along the coast, and reached the island of Zanzibar in April 1887.

From Zanzibar I set out on my first East African expedition. It was the rainy season—the most unfavourable time of year for an expedition of the kind—and the extraordinary scarcity of porters, due to the great demand recently occasioned by the setting out of the Emin Pasha Relief Expedition and Count Teleki's expedition to Lake of Samburu, increased in no small degree the difficulty I had in raising a caravan. I was next confined to bed for some weeks with a bad attack of malaria, but by the month of June I was so far recovered as to be able to start, and set out from Mombaza accompanied by a caravan of a hundred men, and by Baron A. von Eberstein, who, in his official capacity as a representative of the German East Africa Company, was about to visit Jagga with a view to selecting a site suitable for a station. A fourteen days' march across the arid steppes brought us, after the usual hardships, to the forest fastness of Taveta at the foot of Kilimanjaro. Here we met Count Teleki and his companion, Lieutenant von Höhnel. They were now on their return journey, and, as the result of their experiences, were able to give us much profitable advice. A few days later we reached Marangu, one of the small states forming part of the district of Jagga, the cultivated zone which runs round the southern half of the mountain at an altitude of between 4000 and 6000 feet. Here I left the main body of my caravan under the care of the chief, Mareale, and accompanied only by Herr von Eberstein and a small picked body of men, proceeded to ascend the mountain. Five days were spent in crossing the belt of primeval forest and the wide stretch of pasture land above. The latter terminates at the small barren plateau at the saddle (14,400 feet) between the two peaks of Kilimanjaro—Kibo and Mawenzi.

Here Herr von Eberstein and I took up our quarters alone. After a day's rest we set out to attempt the ascent of Kibo, the western and higher of the two peaks, which towered upwards above our camp for another 5000 feet. Soon we had reached the first patches of snow, across which we continued to make tolerably rapid progress, until at length, at an altitude of 16,400 feet, it began to snow, and shortly afterwards my companion sank down exhausted. For some time I pressed forward alone, but at last found myself confronted with a solid wall of ice, 150 feet high, which effectually barred the way. It was the lower edge of the ice-cap that rests on the rim of the Kibo crater, and I saw that without the aid of the usual alpine climbing-tackle it would be impossible to scale it. The snow beginning to fall more heavily, I hastened to rejoin Von Eberstein, and together we made our way back to camp with all possible speed. The rest of the day was spent in taking observations and photographs, and in making various measurements in the neighbourhood of the base of the cone. Next morning we set out to return to Marangu. Although, on this journey, we did not succeed in reaching the summit of the mountain, I thus got as far as the ice-cap (18,000 feet), and found that it was composed of a compact mass of ice. We also explored the saddle-plateau and the series of hills which rise from it; and besides taking the photographs and measurements above - mentioned, made large collections— geological, botanical, and zoological—in the upper zones as well as in the lower. The results of the expedition are briefly sketched in the work entitled *Zum Schneedom des Kilimandscharo*, Leipzig, 1888, which I published shortly after my return to Europe.

Taking leave of Von Eberstein, who had the more immediate object of his mission to attend to, I proceeded from Taveta through the district of Kahe and Arusha to the south of Kilimanjaro, following the course of the Rufu all the way to the coast. In the course of the journey I visited the German stations of Mafi and Korogwe, which seemed to be in anything but a flourishing condition. I was struck with the same impression at the stations of Dunda, Madimola, and Usungula, which I visited later on in the course of a run from Bagamoyo through Usaramo. These unproductive, poorly peopled districts in the midst of the steppes are alike unsuitable for trade and agriculture; the colonial future of East Africa lies in the coast and mountainous regions, a remark, the truth of which is illustrated by the fact that the above-named stations have all recently been abandoned.

I had not long returned to Europe when I resolved to organise a second expedition, with a view to exploring the German sphere of interest throughout its entire breadth. My plan was to proceed from the coast to Kilimanjaro by way of Usambara, Pare, and Ugweno, and, provided with more suitable equipments, once more to attempt the ascent of the mountain. From Kilimanjaro it was my intention to penetrate westward to the south end of the Victoria Nyanza, and thence to the Albert Edward Nyanza and the neighbouring mountain regions lately explored by Stanley. The journey, I calculated, would extend over two years.

My companion on this occasion was the Austrian geographer, Dr. Oscar Baumann, who had a large experience of travel in West Africa. After spending several months in making our preparations, we landed at Zanzibar in July 1888, and immediately set about raising a caravan of 230 men. A hundred loads of all sorts of articles of barter were sent on to the south end of the Victoria Nyanza in advance, under the charge of the well-known agent and carrier, Mr. Stokes. From these I expected to be able to replenish my stores when I should have got so far on my way.

Before we left Pangani for the interior in the end of August, there had been considerable friction between the Europeans and the Arabs all along the coast, but as yet no one dreamed of anything like an open insurrection. The caravan being too cumbrous to accompany us on our projected mountain tour, at Lewa Dr. Baumann and I separated from the main body, which was sent on by the usual caravan route along the Pangani, with instructions to await us at Gonja, among the mountains of Pare. Accompanied by sixty men, Dr. Baumann and I then set out from the mission station of Magila, and made our way into Usambara, which in the course of the next three weeks we traversed from north to south, profiting by the trip to make all manner of observations and collections. We were the first Europeans who had thoroughly explored the district, which is, I should say, eminently suited for cultivation. It is only a day's march inland from the coast, and is easily accessible in all parts along the broad valleys by which it is intersected. The average elevation is about 4250 feet, the country is well wooded, the climate temperate, and the inhabitants industrious and peaceful.

Our little excursion over, we hastened on to Gonja, where we were to overtake the rest of our caravan. When we arrived at the appointed meeting-place, no caravan was to be seen, and we were told that it had been detained in Masinde by the chief Semboja. Here it had been broken up, and the porters one and all had returned to the coast, leaving their loads behind them. Without delay I set out for Masinde, but on the way my porters deserted in a body, and I arrived at my destination accompanied only by Dr. Baumann, two Somál, and one or two Asikari. At Semboja's I learned that the caravan had ostensibly acted upon orders received from the Sultan of Zanzibar, by whom the men were said to have been recalled on account of the rebellion which had just broken out at the coast. Leaving the loads to the care of Semboja, I and my faithful few started off in pursuit. For eight days we hastened on without meeting with any adventure worth mentioning. At the end of that time, however, we were joined by a gradually increasing rabble of armed natives, who did not keep us long in doubt as to their intentions. A day's march from the coast we were overwhelmed and made prisoners, loaded with chains, and thrown into a dark hut, where we were left to lie for some days, ignorant of what fate might be in store for us. At the end of that time the Arab Sheik Bushiri, the leader of the insurrection, made his appearance, and it was agreed that we should be allowed to go free on payment of a heavy ransom. The stipulated sum having been paid through the medium of an Indian, Bushiri himself conducted us to Pangani, and after several hairbreadth escapes we reached Zanzibar, and finally Europe, thankful to have got off with bare life. The expedition was totally ruined, and all our European equipments, with the goods intended to last a caravan of 230 men for two years, were lost.

A graphic account of our journey through Usambara, and of the other adventures of the expedition, has been given by my companion, Dr. O. Baumann, in his charming book. *In Deutsch-Ostafrika während des Aufstandes :* Vienna, 1889. As for myself, undaunted by the mischances which had already befallen me, I at once set about preparing for a third expedition, which, however, I resolved should be confined to the Kilimanjaro region. As I was bent not only on making a thorough geographical survey of the mountain, but on ascending to its highest peak, I considered myself happy in securing as a companion Herr Ludwig Purtscheller, a name well known in European alpine circles. Events proved that my expectations were amply justified. As is shown in the following pages, we were successful almost beyond what I

had dared to hope, all that had been left unfinished on my
first and second expeditions being fully completed on the
third. Kilimanjaro is now an open secret; the great crater
of Kibo has been discovered, the summit of the mountain has
been attained, and the scientific material collected is such as
to afford a tolerably complete picture of the most interesting
region of equatorial East Africa.

In sitting down to recount my experiences, with the conquest of the "Ethiopian Mount Olympus" still fresh in my
memory, I feel how inadequate are my powers of description
to do justice to the grand and imposing aspects of Nature
with which I shall have to deal. It is easier to make a
journey than to tell the story of it, and it seems to me that all
I can do is to transport myself in thought to Africa once
more, and retrace my wanderings step by step and day by day,
narrating events as they occurred and as they impressed me at
the moment. In this way and by the help of the illustrations
it is hoped that the reader will gain a full and vivid idea
of the characteristics of the region. The plates have been
executed by the master-hand of Mr. E. T. Compton, and have
been selected from a series of 240 photographs taken by myself. They reproduce not only the main features of the
mountain scenery with remarkable fidelity, but are equally
true to the "local colour" of East Africa in general.

In recalling here and there my experiences on my two
former journeys, I have to express my thanks to my companions, Herr von Eberstein and Dr. Oscar Baumann, to
whose kindly and sympathetic assistance the satisfactory
results achieved were largely due. I am equally indebted
to Herr Ludwig Purtscheller, who accompanied me on my
third journey, and stood by me on every occasion with the
greatest discretion and the most indomitable zeal. I have no
hesitation in saying, that the success of the expedition is

largely to be attributed to his untiring efforts, as may be seen from almost every chapter of this book. It also affords me much pleasure to have this opportunity of acknowledging my indebtedness to the German and English Governments, and to the British East Africa Company, whom I have to thank for allowing my expedition to pass through their territory while the war was still going on.

To my other friends, Adolph Bastian, Herr von Danckelmann, Paul Güssfeldt, Bruno Hassenstein, Wilhelm Junker, Pechuel-Loesche, Friedrich Ratzel, E. G. Ravenstein, Gerhard Rohlfs, Colonel Euan-Smith, Erich Steifensand, Justus Strandes, and Major von Wissmann—to all of whom I am indebted for much friendly advice and assistance both at home and abroad—I tender my most hearty thanks. To Messrs. Hassenstein and Ravenstein I am especially grateful; to the former for the arduous labour he has had in constructing the maps, and for his assistance in compiling the bibliography; to the latter for the valuable information he afforded me on the subject of the Mountains of the Moon, on which my remarks in the introductory chapter are based.

Last, but not least, I have to thank all those who have so kindly co-operated in classifying my collections and working out my astronomical and meteorological data within such an exceedingly short space of time. The conclusions at which they have arrived are briefly stated in the Appendices, and will be published more fully elsewhere. If from the latter, as well as from the text, the reader gathers that we have done something more than merely " travel," I shall feel amply rewarded for the time, the toil, and the means I have spent in the exploration of German East Africa.

HANS MEYER.

LEIPZIG, *Autumn* 1890.

CONTENTS.

CONTENTS.

CHAPTER VIII.

CHAPTER IX.

APPENDICES.

b*

xviii   CONTENTS.

ILLUSTRATIONS.

FULL-PAGE ILLUSTRATIONS.

ILLUSTRATIONS IN THE TEXT.

MAPS.

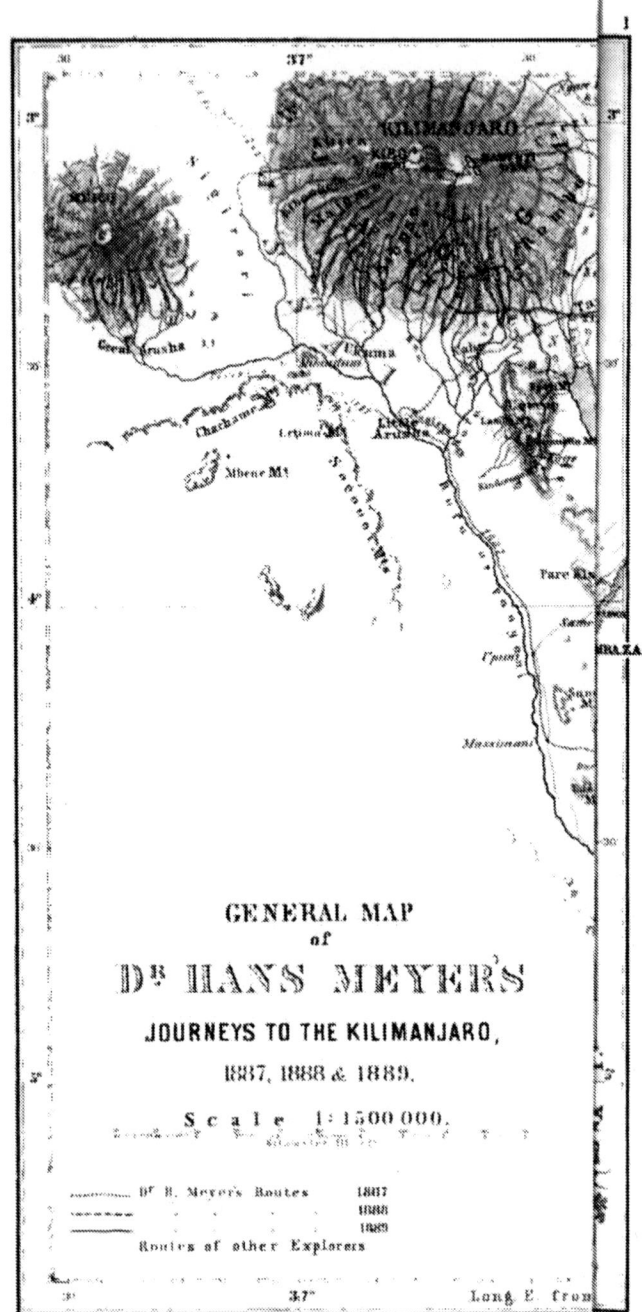

GENERAL MAP
of
DR HANS MEYER'S
JOURNEYS TO THE KILIMANJARO,
1887, 1888 & 1889.

Scale 1:1500000.

.... Dr H. Meyer's Routes   1887
--------------   1888
————————   1889
Routes of other Explorers

Long. E. from

ACROSS EAST AFRICAN GLACIERS.

INTRODUCTORY.

KILIMANJARO IN THE PAST.

GALLEON OF THE MIDDLE AGES.

In the whole history of African travel and discovery there is no more interesting chapter than that which deals with the exploration of Mount Kilimanjaro, the story of which we have briefly endeavoured to sketch in the following pages.

At a very early date we find the classical geographers intent on penetrating the mystery which enshrouded the equatorial regions of inner Africa and the undiscovered sources of the Nile; and by the time of Ptolemy they had got the length of placing the fountains of the great river some distance south of the equator, among the streams and lakes of the mysterious snow-clad Mountains of the Moon.

A

And here arises the interesting problem, What are the modern representatives of those lakes and mountains of the ancient cartographers, with Ptolemy at their head?

If we follow the more generally accepted opinion, we must either, with Dr. Beke, look upon the snow-clad mountain masses of Kenia and Kilimanjaro as the true representatives of Ptolemy's Lunar Mountains, or we must seek them farther in the interior, identifying the Victoria, Albert, and Albert Edward Nyanzas with the lakes of the ancients and of their successors the Arabs, and accept Stanley's Ruwenzori as the mountain whose snows feed the Upper Nile.

On the other hand, if we adopt the view entertained by other geographers, and notably by Mr. E. G. Ravenstein, we arrive at another and much more probable result.

Up to the time of Ptolemy, as is shown by the map of Eratosthenes, it was believed that the Nile had its origin in a number of lakes in the vicinity of the Indian Ocean, if not indeed in the Indian Ocean itself. The latter absurdity was strongly condemned by Ptolemy, in whose map, as we have already said, the Nile is shown to rise among the so-called Mountains of the Moon, its head-waters combining to form two lakes.

It would be interesting to learn in what way Ptolemy came by his information at this early date. His knowledge was certainly not derived from the north, for it is highly improbable that either conqueror or explorer ever advanced from that direction into the distant regions lying beyond the equator. No record of such an achievement has ever reached us, and Ptolemy, who gives such an unsatisfactory delineation of the "island of Meroë," which was easily within reach, cannot be presumed to have possessed a more accurate knowledge of the Nile far, far to the south of it. Such information as he had must have reached him from the east coast, with which commercial relations were maintained from the most ancient times. We cannot, however, assume that this information was based on the reports of persons who had actually visited the interior, for in that case Ptolemy, according to his wont, would have laid down their itineraries on his map, or described it in one of his introductory books. On the contrary, we may very safely conclude that he had merely the hearsay evidence of coast-traders to go upon.

On Ptolemy's map the Nile in Meroë is formed by the junction of three rivers, namely, an unnamed river which flows past Axum; the Astapus, which rises in Lake Coloë; and the Nile proper, which is fed by the lakes lying to the south of the equator. Ptolemy knew nothing of the Hawash river, or of the lakes nearer the coast, already referred to by Strabo; and thus, considering how little the former knew of a region comparatively accessible even in his time, are we justified in assuming that his knowledge of the distant sources of the Nile was more precise?

As regards Ptolemy's delineation of the course of the Nile, we learn from the anonymous Periplus of the Erythrean Sea that Coloë was an ivory mart only three days distant from the coast-town of Adulis; that thence to Axum was a five days' journey; that the "Nile" (that is, Ptolemy's Astapus) was crossed beyond; and that on the farther side of this river were situated the passes (*pylæ*) in modern Samen. Coloë, consequently, instead of lying five hundred miles in the interior, must be sought for close to the coast, and may safely be identified with the Kolô of the Abyssinian chroniclers and the Halai (Kalai) of modern maps.

Ptolemy further places the "Catadupi" on that branch of the Nile which flows directly from the south; but as the Cataracts really occur on what is now known as the Blue Nile, the river which Ptolemy represents as flowing out of the equatorial lakes must be the Blue, and not the White Nile. We are thus enabled to identify the river which passes Axum with the modern Mareb, whilst the Astapus, rising in Lake Coloë, is the Takaze, and the "Nilus," rising in the traditional distant lakes, is the Blue Nile. Ptolemy's Lake Coloë can be no other than Lake Tana, and was supposed by him to give rise to the Takaze (Atbara), just as was believed to be the case by the early Portuguese explorers of Abyssinia. But if it be granted that the Nile of Ptolemy is the Blue Nile, it follows that the Mountains of the Moon are not Ruwenzori, but the mountains of Abyssinia, among whose snows the most easterly branch of the great river has its origin.

It has likewise been attempted to connect the "Mountains of the Moon" with Unyamwezi, supposed to mean "Land of the Moon." There is, however, no justification for this, as "Unyamwezi" has probably no connection whatever with the word "*mwesi*" (moon), but, through its first root-syllable *nyam*, is rather related to such terms as *Unyamyembe, Unyambangu, Unyambewa, Unyamwenda*, &c. According to the rules of the Bantu languages, the "Land of the Moon" would be U-mwezi.

The Arab geographers faithfully repeated the errors of their great predecessor, Ptolemy. Like him, they placed the lakes of the Nile and the Mountains of the Moon in the heart of Africa, but they added a third lake (Kura or Kawar), close upon the equator, from which flowed not only the Nile proper, but also the "Nile" of Makadosho (Webbi Shabeela) and the "Nile" of Ghana (Niger). That their knowledge even of the regions nearer the coast was of the vaguest is abundantly proved by such statements as that the "Mountains of the Moon" (Jebel el Kuamar) are opposite the coast of Serendib (Ceylon); and that "the sources of the Sindh (Indus) and of the Nile are in one place." If they ever succeeded in reaching the interior from the east coast — their caravans undoubtedly penetrated from the north to the Niger and Lake Tsad—there is no trace of any such enterprise in their writings. We leave it to the reader to judge, therefore, whether their Lake Kura or Kawar is to be identified with Tana, the Ptolemaic Coloë, or with Lake Tsad. It was not until early in the present century that their caravans first penetrated far into East Central Africa, and returned with trustworthy information regarding the snow-mountains and lakes of the interior. In short, it is not too much to say, judging from the nomenclature of most of the geographers from Ptolemy downwards through the Middle Ages, that the lakes and mountains they described as occupying Equatorial Africa were in reality those of Abyssinia.

Of one thing we may oe almost certain, namely, that the ancient " Mountains of the Moon " are not to be identified with any equatorial snow-mountain, whether it be Ruwenzori or Kilimanjaro. The first undoubted reference to the latter occurs in the works of one Fernandez de Encisco, a Spanish writer of the sixteenth century. This traveller had made a voyage to Mombaza, which had been occupied by the Portuguese since 1507, and from native caravans he obtained some information regarding the topography of the interior. In his *Suma de Geographia*, published in 1519, he says that " west of this port (Mombaza) stands the Ethiopian Mount Olympus, which is exceeding high, and beyond it are the Mountains of the Moon, in which are the sources of the Nile " —the latter names plainly a reminiscence of Ptolemy. But Encisco's bald assertion was supported by no confirmation, and in succeeding maps the " Ethiopian Mount Olympus " appears and disappears according to the fancy of the carto-

grapher. It was not until the year 1848 that its existence
and position were finally established.

It was reserved for a German missionary, by name Johann
Rebmann, first to set eyes on one of the most wonderful of
the many wonders of Africa—the mountain whose snows
defy the fierceness of the equatorial sun. In the year 1846,
along with his colleague, Dr. Krapf, Rebmann landed on the
east coast and founded the mission station of Rabai-mpia
(New Rabai) on behalf of the Church Missionary Society.
The house they erected is still occupied by their successors
in the mission-field.

Bent on carrying the Gospel inland to the distant region
of Jagga, in April 1848 Rebmann started on the first of his
memorable series of trips to the interior. On the 11th of
May, when still a day's journey from Taveta, he makes the
following simple entry in his diary:—"This morning, at
ten o'clock, we obtained a clearer view of the mountains of
Jagga, the summit of one of which was covered by what
looked like a beautiful white cloud. When I inquired as
to the dazzling whiteness, the guide merely called it 'cold,'
and at once I knew it could be neither more nor less than
snow. . . . Immediately I understood how to interpret the
marvellous tales Dr. Krapf and I had heard at the coast, of
a vast mountain of gold and silver in the far interior, the
approach to which was guarded by evil spirits."

Continuing his way towards the Jagga state, Kilema,
Rebmann, every time he raised his eyes, saw "the eternal
ice and snow of Kilimanjaro, apparently but a few miles
distant, but in reality separated from him by about a couple
of days' journey."

Content for the time being with this discovery, Rebmann returned to Rabai in June, but in November of the
same year set out again for Jagga. Proceeding through

Kilema to Majamé, he "came so close to Kilimanjaro" that at night the grand old head of the snow-capped mountain "could be seen gleaming like silver in the bright moonlight," and he thought that the foot of Kibo was "distant only some three or four miles. . . . There are two main peaks," the diary goes on to say, "which arise from a common base measuring some twenty-five miles long by as many broad. They are separated by a saddle-shaped depression, running east and west for a distance of about eight or ten miles. The eastern peak is the lower of the two, and is conical in shape. The western and higher presents the appearance of a magnificent dome, and is covered with snow throughout the year, unlike its eastern neighbour, which loses its snowy mantle during the hot season. . . . By the Swahili at the coast, the mountain is known as Kilimanjaro (Mountain of Greatness), but the Wa-Jagga call it Kibo, from the snow with which it is perpetually capped." All Rebmann's observations are correct, with the exception of his estimate of the extent of the mountain, and his interpretation of its name as "Mountain of Greatness." These errors we shall rectify later on.

Returning to Rabai in February 1849, the indefatigable missionary immediately set about preparations for a third and yet more extended journey "into the heart of Africa." Despite the approach of the rainy season, April saw him once more on the road to Jagga, "armed only with an umbrella," and accompanied by a caravan of thirty porters. Following his old route through Kilema and Uru to Majamé, he reached a point, in his opinion, "so close to the snow-line that, supposing no impassable abyss to intervene, I could have reached it in three or four hours." Unfortunately, illness and privation compelled him to turn back, but the unfinished work of exploration was taken up by his colleague, Dr. Krapf, and in some measure successfully accomplished.

In November 1849, Krapf organised an expedition to Ukamba, a district lying to the north-east of Kilimanjaro, and on the 10th of the month obtained from the mountains of Maungu "a magnificent view of the snow-mountain Kilimanjaro in Jagga, which loomed up from behind the ranges of Ndara and Bura. . . . Even at this distance I could make out that the white substance crowning the summit was certainly snow." On three other occasions, in the course of this journey, Krapf had an opportunity of assuring himself of the reality of the snow-cap, his testimony thus placing the accuracy of Rebmann's reports beyond a doubt. The altitude was estimated at 12,500 feet.

This confirmatory evidence notwithstanding, the late Mr. W. Desborough Cooley, a critical geographer of great merit, persistently cast doubts upon the assertions of the two missionaries, and even made unwarrantably fierce attacks upon the worthy men themselves. These attacks, combined with a subsequent passage at arms which he had with Von der Decken, won for this otherwise estimable *savant* a certain degree of unenviable notoriety. The controversy is here noted because it arose out of the interesting question as to whether snow-clad mountains did or did not exist in Equatorial Africa. According to Cooley, Rebmann's discovery was only "a most delightful mental recognition, not supported by the evidence of the senses," while Krapf was characterised as a man of vaulting ambition, whose taste for dealing with mighty problems was not accompanied by that mental acumen without which intellectual activity becomes to its possessor a highly dangerous endowment. Having thus more than hinted that the discoveries of the two simple missionary explorers were of a purely visionary

nature, Cooley and his partisans deemed they had disposed
for ever of the snow-mountains of Equatorial Africa. In
the course of a few years, however, events were to prove the
contrary.

In 1861, Baron Von der Decken, who a year earlier
had made an unsuccessful attempt to reach Lake Nyassa,
travelled as far as Jagga, accompanied by the English
geologist Thornton, the former associate of Livingstone. In
the month of August, they attempted the ascent of the
mountain, but, after three days spent in penetrating the
forest zone, they were compelled by stress of weather
to turn back at a height of only 8200 feet. Von der
Decken, like Rebmann before him, then proceeded to the
western side of the mountain, and was favoured with an unobstructed view of Kibo. "Bathed in a flood of rosy light,
the cap that crowns the mountain's noble brow gleamed
in the dazzling glory of the setting sun. . . . Beyond
appeared the jagged outlines of the eastern peak, which
rises abruptly from a gently inclined plain, forming, as it
were, a rough, almost horizontal platform. Three thousand
feet lower, like the trough between two mighty waves, is
the saddle which separates the sister peaks one from the
other."

On his return to Europe, Von der Decken added his
testimony to that of Rebmann, describing Kibo as a "mighty
dome, rising to a height of about 20,000 feet, of which the
last three thousand are covered with snow."

But Von der Decken was not content to rest here. In
the following year, along with Dr. Otto Kersten, he paid a
second visit to Kilimanjaro, and starting from Moji in the
month of December, succeeded in reaching an altitude of
14,000 feet. "During the night it snowed heavily," he says
in his account of the expedition, "and next morning the

ground lay white all around us. Surely the obstinate Cooley will be satisfied now."

As the result of observations made on this journey, the height of Kibo, the western peak, was estimated at 18,680 feet, that of Mawenzi at 16,250 feet. On Kibo, the snow-line was stated to be 16,400 feet; water was said to cease at 9000 feet; and all vegetation at 12,000 feet. Remarking on the appearance presented by this peak, Thornton adds that " on the north-east side the rim of the old crater can still be distinguished, but on the south-west, which is considerably lower, it seems to have been destroyed." As regards the geological structure of the mountain, the whole mass was found to consist of lava which had consolidated in the open air.

But the " obstinate Cooley " was not yet convinced, and hotly took up the glove thrown down to him. " So the Baron says it snowed during the night," he exclaims. " In December, with the sun standing vertically overhead ! The Baron is to be congratulated on the opportuneness of the storm. But it is easier to believe in the misrepresentations of man than in such an unheard-of eccentricity on the part of Nature. This description of a snowstorm at the equator during the hottest season of the year, and at an elevation of only 13,000 feet, is too obviously a ' traveller's tale,' invented to support Krapf's marvellous story of a mountain 12,500 feet high covered with perpetual snow."

This fierce onslaught did harm to no one but Cooley himself, and it hardly required Barth's warm defence to secure to Von der Decken and his companion the recognition they so richly deserved at the hands of geographical students. As a mark of its appreciation of his valuable services, the Royal Geographical Society of London presented the enterprising explorer with its much-coveted gold medal.

To the results of Von der Decken's explorations, as

recorded by Dr. Kersten, no material addition was made by later travellers till the Kilimanjaro region was visited by Mr. Joseph Thomson in 1883. Even Von der Decken's map remained practically unaltered until my own recent journey to the same district enabled me to supply a number of details.

A period of nine years elapsed before the work of exploration was resumed in the region. Then, in 1871, the missionaries Charles New and R. Bushell penetrated as far as Moji, the former also attempting the ascent of the summit. The season was unfavourable, and he was compelled to turn back, but a second attempt in August of the same year proved more successful. Making for the south-east of Kibo, where the ice-cap stretches down almost to the base of the cone, New crossed the snow-line, and so won for himself the distinction of being the first European to reach the equatorial snows. So far as can be made out from his somewhat vague description, the height he attained was a little over 13,000 feet. Perhaps the most interesting result of the expedition was the discovery that between the base of the mountain and the snow-line the vegetation is naturally divided into six distinct zones.

On his return journey, New discovered the beautiful little crater lake of Jala, lying at the foot of Kilimanjaro, on its south-eastern side. Carried away with the enthusiasm born of these successes, and charmed with the wonderful beauty of Jagga, he returned two years later to the scene of his former labours, but was stripped of all he possessed by Mandara, the rapacious chief of Moji, from whom he was glad to escape with his life. Utterly broken down in health and spirits, he hastened to quit Jagga, but died on his road to the coast.

This tragic termination to New's promising career seems for a time to have frightened Europeans from the region, and another ten years elapsed before Dr. G. A. Fischer, in the course of his expedition to Lake Naivasha in 1883, passed to the south of the mountain and visited its giant neighbour Mount Meru, and the adjacent range of Arusha. In the same year Kilimanjaro itself was visited by the young Scottish geologist, Mr. Joseph Thomson, who was then on his way to the Masai country, having already won his spurs among the knight-errantry of Africa, first as companion and afterwards as successor to Keith Johnston in the expedition to Lake Nyassa in 1878.

Starting from Moji, the kingdom of "the notorious thief" Mandara, Thomson was unable to do more than penetrate the forest region to a height of about 9000 feet; but in an excursion to the district of Shira, and subsequently, while pursuing his route towards Masai Land, he covered much new ground, and gathered the materials for a clear and comprehensive account of the probable origin and main geological and geographical features of the mighty volcanic mass. Thomson was the first to give us any information regarding the northern aspect of the mountain, which he describes as "a solitude, owing to its extremely precipitous nature," with "no projecting platforms and no streams;" and his sketch of its physical history—of Mawenzi as the original seat of eruption, the subsequent upheaval of Kibo during a later phase of volcanic activity, and the formation of the numerous parasitic cones and of the terrace of Jagga as the final manifestation of a gradually decaying volcanic energy—was a yet more important contribution to scientific knowledge.

As much can scarcely be said of Thomson's successor in the field, Mr. H. H. Johnston. Sent out by the British Association and the Royal Geographical Society for the immediate purpose of making a more exhaustive survey than had yet been possible of the flora and fauna of the region, Johnston, who had already distinguished himself on the

Congo, made a stay of some six months in Jagga and the neighbourhood; and though the extent and variety of his collections did not quite correspond to the length of time he spent in making them, his visit furnished him with the materials for a very charming book of travels, full of clever sketches and equally delightful word-pictures of man and Nature. Unfortunately these are in many instances over-drawn. In describing the difficulties and dangers he en-countered, the fights among the natives, and many other details, Mr. Johnston's facile pen has been completely at the mercy of his ardent imagination. His account of the com-mercial prospects of this region is full of exaggeration; whilst his map scarcely presents a single novel feature.

During the month of October, Johnston on two occasions attempted the ascent of the summit. On the first, starting from Moji, he penetrated the forest region to a height of 8600 feet. Here, in the beginning of the hot season, he tells us that in the evening "a white rime settled on the grass." The approach of a body of hostile natives prevented him from going farther.

On the second occasion he started from the Jagga state of Marangu, respecting the harmless chief of which, Mareale, and his yet more harmless mother, he treats us to a variety of startling legends. His route was the same as that which I myself followed several times later on, and reaching the upper limit of the forest zone, he formed a camp, at an alti-tude of nearly 10,000 feet, from which to pursue his explora-tions. From this point he made an excursion to the base of Mawenzi, covering the distance in a single day—a feat I cannot but consider herculean, seeing it took us double the time to traverse the same ground.

Dismissing Mawenzi with the remark that he doubts "if it be possible for any one to reach the summit, owing to the want of foothold," Johnston next turned his attention to Kibo. Starting from his camp, as before, after an "easy climb" of four hours and a half, he and his three attendants reached an elevation of 14,117 feet, and stopped to lunch at a spot a few hundred feet below the base of the small peak which rises midway from the edge of the plateau above. Climbing upwards by himself for about a thousand feet more, he reached the peak itself, and was now " on the central connecting ridge of Kilimanjaro, and could see a little on both sides."

I must confess I do not understand this description. In ascending from Johnston's camping-ground the view is entirely blocked by the southern edge of the plateau between Kibo and Mawenzi, and no outlook is possible over the country behind. Its comparatively even line is broken only by the tiny peak referred to above, which we, as well as Johnston, found such a useful landmark. But this peak does not lie " at an elevation of 15,150 on the central connecting ridge ; " it occurs at an altitude of only 13,780 feet, and the ground gradually rises from its base to the highest point of the saddle, which lies a considerable distance behind. Any view of the surrounding country " on both sides " is thus impossible.

From this point, however, which is described as "nearly as high as the summit of Mont Blanc," Johnston made his way along a narrow ridge, till by degrees he was completely overcome by the feeling of "overwhelming isolation," and was obliged to have recourse to "some brandy and water from his flask" in order to restore his sinking courage. By this time it was four o'clock in the afternoon, and having ascertained that, according to his calculation, the altitude was 16,315 feet, he made his way back again as fast as he could to the peak on the edge of the saddle, which he ultimately reached "in the waning daylight."

Again I fail to apprehend the drift of Mr. Johnston's

narrative. If he only stopped for half an hour to lunch at the peak in question, it must have been two o'clock when he started off to continue the climb by himself; and from the distance he had to traverse, it would be utterly impossible for him to get beyond the base of Kibo by four. For the first time, however, we begin to understand his remark that Kilimanjaro is "a mountain that can be climbed without even the aid of a walking-stick." He never reached a point at which a walking-stick would be necessary, let alone an altitude of 16,315 feet, and his mountaineering feats did not exceed those of the missionary New.

Towards the end of 1884 Johnston returned to England. Carried away by his glowing descriptions, the Church Missionary Society immediately resolved to found a mission station in Moji, and for this purpose sent out Bishop Hannington to visit the Jagga district. March of 1885 saw Hannington in the new field of missionary enterprise, where, in addition to his other work, he found time to make a most interesting botanical collection, which included several species of moss and lichen not observed by former travellers, and of great importance in relation to the geographical distribution of Alpine plants. (See Appendix.) Hannington was followed by a number of brother missionaries, whose efforts on behalf of the temporal interests of Britain, while nominally looking after the spiritual affairs of their flock, were rudely interrupted by the arrival of Dr. Jühlke and Lieutenant Weiss. These emissaries of the German East African Company concluded a treaty with Mandara, whereby he agreed to recognise the suzerainty of the Company, although, shortly before, he had concluded a similar treaty with General Matthews,* acting on behalf of the Sultan of Zanzibar. The final outcome of this agreement has been to hand over Kilimanjaro to Germany.

* An English officer, commander-in-chief of the Sultan's army.—*Tr.*

To the writings of Thomson and Johnston we may also trace the sudden irruption of English and American sporting caravans which has recently taken place in the district. On the whole, these pleasure parties have not come and gone without adding their quota to the scientific knowledge of the region ; notably the expedition under Willoughby and Harvey, who during the years 1886–87 made many excursions to different parts of the mountain, ascended as far as the saddle plateau, and returned with a valuable collection of zoological specimens. Their wholesale slaughter of the game, however, in the endeavour to swell the record of "big bags," cannot be too severely criticised. Other sportsmen have striven to emulate their achievements in this respect ; and if things are to continue as they have begun, it needs no seer to prophesy the ultimate result. The rich preserves of East Africa will share the fate of the vast hunting-grounds of South Africa and North America, and in the not far distant future will utterly cease to exist.

For the most important contribution to our knowledge of Kilimanjaro since the time of Von der Decken, we have to thank the Hungarian expedition under Count Teleki and Lieutenant Höhnel. Having broken much new ground towards the plains of Kahé and the neighbourhood surrounding Mount Meru, Teleki followed Johnston's route to the saddle plateau, and was the first seriously to attempt the ascent of Kibo, which he climbed to a height of 15,800 feet. His companion at the same time took a series of valuable observations for bearings and altitudes, and drew up a map which includes the northern side of the mountain—a district visited by the expedition at a later date. In August 1887, when on my way to Kilimanjaro for the first time, I met Teleki and Höhnel at Taveta. They were then on the way to Masai Land, and, following their advice, along with my companion, Herr von Eberstein, I made for the saddle plateau by way of Marangu, whence I succeeded in ascending Kibo to a height of about 18,000 feet. Here further progress was checked by the precipitous face of the ice-cap, and we were compelled to turn back. For farther particulars of this attempt I refer my readers to the preface.

On our return to Taveta, we met the expedition of the German East African Company, which afterwards founded a station in Moji and another in Lower Arusha, besides doing some good work in exploring the southern plains. The district was next visited by a number of Englishmen, in the wake of whom came the American naturalist Dr. Abbott. During a stay of a year and a half, Dr. Abbott thoroughly explored the whole of Jagga, and the flanks of the mountain as far as the saddle plateau, making most valuable additions to our knowledge of its flora and fauna.

In the autumn of 1888, while I was travelling with Dr. Baumann in Usambara, Abbott resolved to attempt the ascent of Kibo in company with Herr Otto Ehlers, the representative of the German East African Company in Moji. Ehlers' narrative of the expedition is worth repeating. Pitching their camp at an altitude of 9800 feet, Ehlers set off by himself for Mawenzi, and, according to his own account, reached a height of 16,400 feet, doing the distance there and back in a single forenoon! The camp was then shifted farther west to a spot nearer the foot of Kibo, at a height of 14,450 feet. Early next morning Abbott and Ehlers started together to ascend the peak on its northern side, and by seven o'clock had reached an altitude of 17,000 feet, when Abbott was suddenly seized with illness and could go no farther. Ehlers kept on by himself, and, to quote his article in *Petermann's Mitteilungen*, had "to make his way partly over sheets of sand and ashes, partly over beds

B

of volcanic debris, the difficulty of climbing being greatly enhanced by the newly-fallen snow, among which he frequently slid backwards several feet at a time." At a height of 18,000 feet he let his alpenstock fall into a chasm, and lost half an hour " sliding and crawling after it on all fours to a depth of 200 feet." Nevertheless, " after frequent pauses," he reached " the wall of ice which encircles the entire summit" shortly before ten o'clock. Here he spent some time in a vain search for a possible way of access to the highest point, but was eventually forced to retrace his steps and seek an opening farther to the west. At last, " after a painful climb," he " succeeded in reaching the north-western side of the ' summit' (*sic*), and gained a tolerably extensive view of the surroundings. There was no trace of a crater, and the ice formed a series of gentle undulations covered with a layer of newly-fallen snow." The altitude attained " could not have been less than 19,680 feet."

Ehlers' preposterous narrative was severely criticised by Dr. Baumann in the *Mitteilungen* of the German and Austrian Alpine Club. The paper called forth a reply from Ehlers, in the course of which he expressed himself more clearly, to the effect that, when he used the words " there was no trace of a crater," he ought to have said " of an *open* crater," believing, as he did, that the mouth of the crater was concealed and closed by the superimposed masses of ice and snow.

Ehlers then went on to explain that on the southern rim, at a distance of about a mile and a half, he observed a point which he took to be about 200 feet higher than that at which he stood, but was prevented from trying to reach it by the approach of clouds.

But the controversy was not permitted to end here. In the following year, fresh from a series of observations on the northern flank of Kibo, Herr Ludwig Purtscheller, afterwards my companion in 1889, felt constrained to add his protest to that of Baumann. "According to Dr. Abbott's account," says Purtscheller, "he and Ehlers left their camp on the plateau shortly before seven o'clock. By this hour, according to Ehlers, they had already reached an altitude of 17,000 feet. How these statements are to be reconciled with the fact that the camp lay at an altitude of only 14,430 feet, is a problem impossible to solve. Towards eight o'clock Dr. Abbott was compelled to give in on account of illness, and Ehlers went on alone, but, strange to say, both travellers were back in camp by two in the afternoon. Now, the height of Kibo on the north and north-west side is about 19,350 feet; and even had there been no newly-fallen snow to make the ascent more laborious, it would be impossible for Ehlers or any one else to reach the summit in seven hours. On the other hand, if Ehlers mistook the eastern for the northern aspect of the peak, in view of the difficulties presented by the rents and cracks in the ice-sheet at this point, the climb must have occupied him at least twelve hours. . . . Bearing these facts in mind, we can very well believe that Herr Ehlers saw no trace of a crater."

But before this article came under Ehlers' notice, he had written from East Africa to the *Kölnische Zeitung*, admitting that his first report had been misleading, and that in fact he had been mistaken in supposing he had reached the summit.

Ehlers has done next to nothing to augment our scientific knowledge of the Kilimanjaro region, but his humorous sketches of Jagga life and manners are very readable, and he has helped to foster the colonial spirit by bringing home with him several natives of Jagga for exhibition in Germany. Since Ehlers returned the Kilimanjaro states have been visited by a number of missionaries and sportsmen, of whom perhaps the most noteworthy is the young American, Mr. Chanler, who, proceeding to the region merely for the purpose of sport, has, nevertheless, distinguished himself by a thorough exploration of the lower slopes of the mountain.

During the last decade Kilimanjaro has been visited for various objects by no fewer than forty-nine Europeans. My own expedition of 1889 is the most recent, and what was accomplished in the course of it may be gathered from the following pages.

CHAPTER I.

TO THE SWAHILI COAST.

THE art of travel, like every other art, is only to be acquired by practice. In the choice of equipments especially—on the suitability of which so much depends—experience is the best, if not the only teacher. Nowadays, when all the world is on the move, and all sorts of travelling requisites are at the traveller's command, the difficulty is not so much to know what to take as what to omit, and beginners are far more likely to err in taking too much than in taking too little. For my own part, after three different trips to the interior of Africa, I should lay it down as a general rule that the various patent travelling effects so temptingly displayed and be-praised in our European warehouses, are one and all to be avoided. The collapsible tent furniture, lamps, and lanterns, the india-rubber air-beds and pillows of the advertisements, however convenient and useful in

A BORASSUS PALM.

countries where they can easily be repaired when necessary, are worse than useless in regions remote from civilisation.

The simplest mechanism, the most careful workmanship, the best materials,—these are the great considerations in the selection of an explorer's outfit, and accordingly, in most cases, the dearest proves the cheapest in the end.

Unfortunately, if we keep these three considerations always in view, it is not possible to "furnish throughout" in Germany. In certain articles—scientific instruments and arms, for instance—the preference is to be given to those of German make; but in others the foreigner excels us, and more especially the English, whose large colonial experience, and intimate acquaintance with everything that may be included under the term "sport," best enable them to meet the traveller's peculiar wants.

It may not be amiss if I here devote one or two pages to a few hints on the above subject. And first, as regards clothing. It is a vexed question, which it seems to me every one must decide for himself, whether woollen, silk, or cotton underclothing is the best for warm climates. For my own part, after trying all, I declare in favour of cotton, and particularly of knitted cotton, which has these advantages over the others:—it does not shrink in consequence either of perspiration or frequent washing; it absorbs the moisture from the skin and allows it to evaporate with equal ease; it may be thoroughly cleansed either with cold or warm water; and it is of all the most durable.

For the march, I should recommend, in addition, an ordinary pair of trousers, such as are made in Zanzibar at a very moderate figure, of a strong tan-coloured cotton material. A jacket of the same is useful for wearing in camp or in cool weather.

Thick woollen socks are the most comfortable for walking, and strong hob-nailed lacing boots, that come up well over the ankle. A pair of strong leather slippers, cut not too low in front, is indispensable for camp wear, or in case of accident to the foot.

The best head-gear for all weathers is an English sun-helmet, such as are supplied by Messrs. Silver & Co., London ; while a soft fez or smoking-cap should be kept for wearing in the shade—one with flaps for drawing down over the ears on a cold night to be preferred.

The tent and camp bedstead come next. These are to be had of such excellent quality from Mr. Benjamin Edgington, London, that nothing better can be desired. Edgington's double-roof ridge tent of specially prepared green rot-proof canvas, with ash poles and an outer fly, and Edgington's portable camp bedstead with ash supports and a thin cork mattress, have been used by Stanley, Wissmann, François, Kund, Johnston, and others with as much satisfaction as by myself. With a horsehair pillow, a Como rug for warm nights, and thick camel's-hair blankets for cold ones, the bedstead is complete.

Excellent folding tables and chairs, of simple construction, are furnished by Messrs. Silver & Co. Strong tin boxes, of a size and shape suitable for transport by porters, can best be obtained from F. A. Schulze, Fehrbelliner Strasse, Berlin, who has recently produced a most satisfactory article from my own design. At the same place may be had strong square lamps for tent use, and galvanised iron oil-cans and water-buckets. The bucket should be large enough to contain all the table and cooking utensils—which, of course, are best made of enamelled iron—the whole being enclosed by a strong lid. It is important that the canteen should be thus capable of being packed in the water-bucket, otherwise, in the hurry of striking camp in the early morning, things have a mysterious way of getting "lost," through the carelessness of the cook or the wilful oversight of the lazy porter.

The most satisfactory medicine-chest is that supplied at the Berlin Simons-Apotheke, prepared according to Dr. Falkenstein's directions for travellers in the tropics. The best plan is to have the medicines put up in doses in the form of lozenges, and the whole enclosed in a strong tin box, as a protection against breakage and damp.

Arms for the soldiers, and indeed for Europeans in general, have repeatedly been supplied by Immanuel Messert of Suhl. In this department the traveller may be left pretty much to indulge his own fancy; it is much more important that he should be a good shot, and that his rifle should be good of its kind, than that he should confine himself to a weapon of a particular calibre. There are, however, certain limitations imposed by the conditions of African sport, the size and shyness of the game, the distance at which one is sometimes compelled to take aim, and so forth. In common with other travellers, I have arrived at the conclusion that two guns only are necessary to meet every emergency—a .450 or .500 Express (a double-barrelled Lancaster or single-barrelled Mauser *), which may be used for all game, from a rhinoceros to an antelope; and a double-barrelled 12-bore fowling-piece, which with small shot, No. 5 (swan-shot), will bring down wild-fowl; with buckshot, gazelles and leopards. In case of attack by natives, large shot is always the best; and it is also advisable to carry a revolver to use at close quarters. Any one intending to visit the remote districts in which elephants are still to be met with, may take in addition a short double-barrelled 8-bore; but this heavy weapon is not necessary, as the .500 Express serves the

* The Austrian regulation weapon, so-called from its inventor.—*Tr.*

purpose almost equally well. For my own part, I never found it necessary to use my elephant-gun.

For ornithological collectors a small fowling-piece is indispensable.

Contrary to my custom on former expeditions, instead of taking empty cartridges, I this time carried a large quantity ready filled. The objection urged against carrying loaded cartridges is that they are apt to explode in transit. This danger, however, is entirely obviated by the present method of packing. On the other hand, the labour of filling the cartridges is so irksome to the sportsman, that a very little of it almost suffices to give him a distaste to sport altogether, not to speak of the risk he constantly runs of being taken completely at a disadvantage. I therefore strongly recommend that loaded cartridges only should be taken, those with brass cases being most suitable, as the paper ones are liable to be spoiled by damp and constant handling.

When the expedition has been organised with a view to scientific purposes, the following instruments may be taken in addition to the articles already named—

For determining latitudes, the small compendious, portable theodolite of Hildebrand & Schramm of Freiburg, in Saxony, is quite sufficient. Its vertical circle is graduated for direct readings of thirty seconds, and for calculated readings of fifteen seconds, and the instrument is perfectly adapted to the high meridian altitude of a tropical sun. The pocket chronometers of Lange & Sons of Glashütte, near Dresden, are sufficient for making fairly approximate determinations of longitudes, while one of Reis's collapsible measuring rods affords perhaps the most reliable means for the measurement of a base, and the determination of relative heights and distances.

Heights may be absolutely determined by means of the

barometer; but, as no convenient portable form of the mercurial barometer has yet been invented, the traveller is forced to fall back on the aneroid, controlled by the boiling-point thermometer. On my expedition to the mountains of Usambara in 1888, I managed to carry a mercurial barometer with me all the way, but it was more a source of worry than anything else, and in the end it got hopelessly out of order. Instruments that require delicate manipulation are quite unsuitable for roughing it in the wilds of Africa, and the aneroid and boiling-point thermometer answer very well for all practical purposes. My aneroid I got from Bohne of Berlin, and my thermometer from Fuess in the same city.

Fuess also supplied me with the indispensable sling thermometer, my psychrometer, and my self-registering thermometer. From Messrs. Cassella of London I obtained my large compasses, which fitted into the top of a pole that served as a stand; and E. Schneider of Vienna furnished me with smaller compasses, attached to square metal plates. These latter I used on the march. From Stegemann of Berlin I obtained a capital photographic apparatus, which did me good service. It was fitted with all the appliances for photographing groups and scenery, and with Monkhoven's dry plates, which are the best for tropical climates.

My scientific equipments were completed by the special appliances necessary for making zoological, botanical, and geological collections, with the needful maps and books. In addition, there were all the requirements for our prospective sojourn among the equatorial snows—thick warm clothing, Alpine boots, knapsacks, glacier ropes, ice-axes, snow-spectacles, &c., all of which were obtained in Münich, except a small tent from Edgington's, and two sheepskin sleeping-sacks from Leipzig.

Our preparations, which of course included a thousand

details it is impossible to enumerate here, occupied three months. Meanwhile, armed with letters of introduction from the Foreign Office, I put myself in communication with the British East African Company with a view to obtaining their permission to use the shortest road to Kilimanjaro, namely, that from Mombaza through the British sphere of interest. In London I was most kindly received. On being assured that the objects of the expedition were scientific, not political, and that I would do nothing prejudicial to British interests within the British sphere of influence, the Imperial British East African Company furnished me with letters of introduction to their agents, instructing them to further my interests by every means in their power.

One point, and that perhaps the most important, still remained to be settled—the choice of a travelling companion. From former experience I had learned that it was useless to dream of the ascent of Kilimanjaro, and a prolonged stay above the snow-line, without the aid of a companion familiar with mountaineering. Volunteers in abundance had come forward to offer their services, but none so far had seemed to meet all the requirements of the case. The choice of a travelling companion for the interior of Africa is a weighty matter at any time. The relationship is so intimate and so constant, there is such close community of interests and experiences, that either there must be the most perfect agreement in tastes and habits of mind between the two comrades, or the one must be in complete subordination to the other. In the present instance, the difficulty was enhanced by the fact that a thorough knowledge of Alpine climbing was an indispensable requisite. I had communicated with several Tyrolese and Swiss guides, but without being able to come to a decision, and was just on the point of making inquiries in other directions, when I unexpectedly received a letter which at once settled the question. Herr Ludwig Purtscheller of Salzburg, a teacher of gymnastics, and the associate during many expeditions of the two Zigmondys, wrote saying that there was nothing he would like better than to be permitted to join me in my enterprise. He was the very man I wanted, and I agreed to his proposal with an alacrity I never had cause to regret.

Meanwhile my goods had been packed and shipped at Bremen for Zanzibar, and the end of June saw Herr Purtscheller and myself in the train for Genoa *via* the St. Gothard. In Genoa, for the fifth time, I took up my quarters in that most charming of hotels, the Hôtel du Parc, pending the departure of our steamer.

But we were not permitted to quit the peaceful soil of Europe without an unpleasant reminder of the war then raging in our promised land. The East African blockade still continued, and the importation of arms and ammunition was strictly forbidden. I received a telegram from Bremen saying that the Lloyd had been obliged to leave my boxes of ammunition behind, as they could not take through packages for Zanzibar. I at once gave orders that the boxes should be sent on to Aden by the next steamer, which left a fortnight later, though I was much concerned to think I should not be able personally to see them stowed on board some French or English vessel, my engagements making it impossible for me to delay at Aden so long. An easy way out of the difficulty would have been to get the Government to take my arms on board a man-of-war; but such an exceptional favour seemed too great for a simple traveller to expect, who was not going out in any official capacity, but merely to explore the German Protectorate on his own account and at his own expense.

But our spirits were not to be damped by the thought of

difficulties, and our surroundings on board the North German Lloyd Company's steamer *Preussen* were too pleasant to allow us to dwell very long on the darker side of things. I had already made the voyage from Genoa to Aden on board the *Preussen* in the spring of 1888, and the year that had since elapsed had certainly not in any way detracted from the beauty and comfort of her arrangements. Some little inconvenience was caused by the presence on board of a large body of sailors and marines going out to relieve our troops on the German corvette *Carola*. But a set of better-behaved young fellows could not have been met with anywhere, and I experienced quite a thrill of patriotic pride when I saw how, in the Red Sea, with the thermometer at 94° F. in the shade, drill was gone through every day as usual, as if they were still in the cool climate of Kiel or Wilhelmshaven.

In the second-class and steerage was a strange mixture of odd characters, including a number of young men going out to try their luck in East Africa from mere love of adventure, and with the most incredibly absurd notions of the country and its inhabitants. For the most part, they were not long in finding their way home again.

In the hold were thousands of rounds of shell and shrapnel, but alas! not my ammunition.

We reached the barren, rocky coast of Aden within the specified time—five days. Three days later we were to catch the steamer of the *Messageries Maritimes*, which would convey us direct to Zanzibar. I always dislike Aden, that broiling, waterless eyrie among the rocks, with its atmosphere of coal-dust and English ennui; and this time nothing occurred to give me a better impression of it. Quite the contrary. The *Preussen* had just steamed off in the direction of Colombo, when Lloyd's agent came to inform me that a quantity of Zanzibar cargo had by accident been left in the hold, and among the rest our tents and bedsteads—in fact, nearly all our furniture. I telegraphed for them to be sent back ; but five weeks was the shortest period in which they could reach Zanzibar.

No arms and no tents! It was a bad beginning; but I knew that in case of necessity I should be able to replace a good many things in Zanzibar, and I therefore set about the main business of my stay in Aden, the procuring of eight Somál soldiers to accompany me. In this I met with better success. On my way to Europe in the winter of 1888, I had commissioned my two faithful Somál, Ali and Ahmed, to hold themselves in readiness with six trustworthy comrades, for a new expedition in the following summer. I had no sooner begun to make inquiries than I found Ahmed with half a dozen of his fellow-countrymen all ready to start. Ali meanwhile, grown weary of waiting for me, had joined another party only a week or two before.

It is advisable to have a number of Somál in every caravan, a judicious admixture of the foreign element being necessary to maintain discipline. The Somál, in their isolated position as foreigners, do not as a rule make common cause with the main body of the Swahili porters, but, recognising that their welfare depends on that of their leader, they make his interests their own. In other respects also they best fulfil the requirements of the situation, for they are distinguished by high courage, and their long and continued intercourse with the English has given them a certain familiarity with European ways, not to be found among other East African races. In spite of many predictions to the contrary, I have found the Somál the best personal servants, the best soldiers, and the best headmen of any. They must, of course, be treated with due consideration; allowance must be made for their peculiarities of race, custom, and education; and this is an art of which every one has not the knack. In one respect, the Bantu negroes have the advantage of the Somál: they stand the tropical climate better; but what the latter lack in physique they make up for a hundred times by their superior characteristics in other respects.

The agreement with my men having been signed at the German Consulate, we rowed out to the French steamer, and were soon tossing on the Indian Ocean before the July monsoon. The aspect of things on board the *Mendoza* was highly remarkable. The prevailing German colonial character of the company was even more marked than on board the *Preussen.* Among the passengers Germans were largely in the majority. There were young clerks and merchants returning from sick-leave in Europe; officers of the native regiments, some going out for the first time, others returning from furlough; officials of the East African and other Companies; red-cross volunteers for the troops, conspicuous everywhere with their badges on their arms; a small number of mechanics anxious to try their fortune in Zanzibar; and last, but not least, two Sisters of Mercy for the Zanzibar hospital. What interchanges of good feeling and good-fellowship there were! What endless fine sentiments and fine speeches; and —what boundless ignorance of all things African!

The wrong which has been committed in the best interests of the colony by our early East African colonising agents is no small one. Partly carried away by their tendency to idealise, partly for the deliberate purpose of gaining a following and raising funds for colonial enterprise, many of them have published the grossest misrepresentations of the new colony; and it will take much earnest work and cost many bitter experiences before men can be brought to their senses again, not only in East Africa, but in Europe. We have yet to learn the golden mean between extreme optimism on the one hand and extreme pessimism on the other. We must teach ourselves to view our new possessions without the aid of coloured spectacles, to see the country as it really is, to distinguish between what is good and what is bad, and, putting the imaginary and the impossible on one side, set ourselves steadily to utilise and turn to good account what there is of real, sterling value.

After a six days' run we found ourselves off the palm-fringed coast of the island of Pemba. Early next morning we came in sight of what looked like a gigantic dash followed by a point of exclamation—the island of Zanzibar with its lighthouse at the north-west point. In a few seconds the mail-flag fluttered gaily at the masthead, the signal, as we could see through our glasses, being passed on from the lighthouse to the still unseen town, where the hoisting of a flag on the Sultan's tower intimates to the inhabitants the approach of the eagerly expected European mail. For three hours we steam along the low-lying coast, only a few hundred yards from the dark palm-groves, among which nestle count-less native huts and villages, with here and there the more imposing front of a square Arab house.

The current in the Straits is against us, but the sea is smooth as glass. During the last few days, as we have gradually approached the equator, the mighty monsoon waves of the Indian Ocean have sunk and dwindled, and the fresh, free sea-breeze has fallen away. Yesterday it scarcely crisped the surface of the water, and to-day all is smooth and flat and grey, sea and sky alike, in the hot sweltering stillness of the atmosphere of the tropics. Far to the east, faintly shimmer-ing through the haze, may be descried the dim outline of a lofty range of mountains—Africa, the mountains of Usam-bara, scene of my last year's explorations and misfortunes!

On board the steamer all has been bustle and confusion since daybreak. The steam-crane rattles unceasingly as boxes and bales emerge from the hold. The ropes are loosened and the boats cleared; and, arrayed in the snowy whiteness of full tropical garb, the passengers take up their position on deck, scanning the horizon with their glasses, noting what is familiar with satisfaction, what is new with interest.

By and by the masts and hulls of a variety of craft, large and small, begin to dot the surface of the water, and at last, to the left of these, appear points and streaks of dazzling whiteness : it is the town of Zanzibar. High above the surrounding houses rises the quaint tower of the Sultan's palace, while beneath, the roads are crowded with shipping —merchant-vessels and the Sultan's fleet, German, English, Italian, and Portuguese men-of-war, the ungainly telegraph-ship, and a host of smaller craft, conspicuous among which are the curiously-rigged Arab dhows. Everything seems to indicate that we are approaching the most important town in equatorial East Africa.

Slowly we make our way towards a large red buoy, to which we are soon made fast by ropes. Immediately we are surrounded by a swarm of small boats, containing an odd medley of nationalities, negro, Indian, and European, the last representing a number of commercial firms and the various consuls. A constant interchange of friendly greetings is kept up, and the ladder has no sooner been let down with a rattle than there is an impatient scramble up the ship's side, and then ensue a hand-shaking and confusion of tongues which beggar all description.

My good friend Steifensand, the German Vice-Consul, is one of the first on board, and I am only too glad to accept his invitation to stay with him at the Consulate,

c

whither he has removed, and is conducting business in the absence of the Consul-General. Half an hour later I am exchanging news with my host in a cool airy room in the commodious Arab building which is his home for the time being.

In the evening a pleasant surprise awaited us. While we sat talking, two blacks came to offer their services in my new undertaking. These proved to be the Somâl, Ali, and the Pangani, Mwini Amani, both of whom had been members of my former caravan, and had remained faithful through all the mischances of the disastrous expedition of the year before. I shall have much to say of them hereafter.

Nine months had elapsed since my last visit to Zanzibar. As a rule, that is an interval scarcely long enough to produce a marked change in the aspect of any town, and more especially of an Oriental town. But within the last few months Zanzibar had experiencd no ordinary vicissitudes. The square whitewashed houses, with their smooth walls, flat roofs, and unglazed windows, were still the same. So, too, were the narrow, shady lanes, full of villainous sights and smells, the piles of ruins, the gigantic rubbish-heaps, and the confusion of mud-built huts constituting the dwellings of the Indian and negro portion of the community.

The life in the streets had likewise much the same aspect as of old. The Arab still stalked along with the pride and dignity of one who considers himself the undoubted lord of Africa; East Indians, their garb proclaiming their several religious persuasions, Mohammedan, Buddhist, or Brahmin, still formed the great proportion of the population after the negroes; and no change marked the bearing of the portly Parsi, the long-haired Baluchi, or the pale Goanese, with his downcast shifty eyes.

It was among the great mass of the people, among the Swahili themselves—the men in their long white garments, and the women with their flaunting attire and pert, forward manners—that, within this brief period of less than a year, a change, amounting almost to a revolution, had taken place. In the streets they seemed intentionally bent on making as much noise as possible. They no longer thought of making way for the passing European, or of saluting him with a respectful "Yambo;" or, if they did, it was in a jeering tone, and, in the case of a German, with some insulting remark superadded. "Bagamoyo boom, boom," was a cry in great vogue, the accent with which the imitative phrase was pronounced containing a whole volume of native criticism on the bombardment of Bagamoyo. The old negro air of humility and respect was gone, and had given place to impudence and swagger.

The cause of all this was not far to seek. At the beginning of the war Zanzibar was overrun with all sorts of bad characters from Europe and elsewhere, whose presence gave rise to continual disturbances, and even fighting. Drunken sailors from the war-ships of the different nations lying off the coast, a host of adventurers desirous of joining the troops under Wissmann, all the rag-tag and bobtail to be found wherever chance seems to promise a short cut to fortune, constantly made night hideous with their shouts of revelry and thoughtless firing of guns. All these had now disappeared, but the effects of their evil example were not so easily effaced, and they were cleverly made capital of by the anti-German faction, to foster among the populace the spirit of ill-will to our countrymen. Serious disturbances were of daily occurrence in one part or other of the town, and every night we expected an organised outbreak under the then Prince and present Sultan, Seyyid Ali, against us and our supposed ally, the late Sultan, Seyyid Khalifa. It was an anxious time.

In pleasing contrast to all this riot and disorder were the evidences of German military discipline and the results of the more kindly hand of charity. The crowd of officials had disappeared, leaving only three or four representatives of the East African Company for the collection of the customs. In the same street as the German Consulate two large houses were occupied by the Government officials and by the officers commanding our native troops, while a third was set apart as a military hospital under the management of the Sisters of Mercy. The old hospital had been considerably enlarged and improved, and was reserved for our sailors and the members of the German colony. In both institutions courage, patience, and good-will were the order of the day—virtues which, it is devoutly to be wished, will one day be extended more widely through the town and neighbourhood.

We had arrived in Zanzibar without arms and without tents. Accordingly my first care was to set about trying to supply our wants; and as, under the conditions of the blockade, all traffic in firearms was strictly prohibited, I was obliged to make application to the commander of the combined squadron, Rear-Admiral Fremantle. And here again my letters of introduction from the British Government stood me in good stead. The Admiral, who had thrown considerable difficulties in the way of Dr. Peters, because of the suspected political nature of his expedition, not only authorised me to buy what arms and ammunition I required, and granted me permission to take my caravan through the British Protectorate, but also offered the use of the British gunboat *Somali* for the conveyance of my men and goods to Mombaza.

I went to work with a will, and speedily purchased fifty

muzzle-loaders for my men, eight light breechloaders for the Somál, and a couple of double-barrelled rifles for ourselves, along with the necessary ammunition. To my great delight and astonishment, I managed to recover a repeating rifle which I had carried with me to Kilimanjaro in 1887, and again into the interior in 1888. There it was stolen from me when I was made prisoner by Bushiri. Throughout the insurrection, Bushiri, according to trustworthy accounts, continued to use it himself; but when the Germans stormed his camp at Bagamoyo, the rifle again fell into their hands, and being recognised as mine, was restored to me on my arrival in Zanzibar. I took it with me on this my third expedition, and again it rendered me excellent service.

Having ordered a number of tents from a Goanese sail-maker, and concluded an agreement with my old caravan contractor, the well-known Indian, Siwa Haji, for sixty Swahili porters, headmen, &c., I crossed over to Bagamoyo in the small steamer *Harmonie*, to consult the German Imperial Commissioner on certain important points.

On board were a hundred Sudanese troops who had fought for us at Tanga, and were now on their way back to their quarters in Bagamoyo. They belonged to the regiments which had been first levied, and were so badly provided in the matter of uniforms, that, now they had seen some service, they looked decidedly ragged. Their female belongings—short of stature and with faces like the Eskimo—accompanied them, carrying the camp utensils and their share of the plunder tied up in large bundles. All were remarkably quiet and orderly.

A four hours' passage beneath the blazing sun brought us to the flat sandy shore of Bagamoyo, where I was

received by my friends Herr von Wissmann and Herr von
Zelewski, and later on, in the fort, had the pleasure of
shaking hands with Herr von Gravenreuth and Herr Bohn-
dorff, the whilom companion of Dr. Junker. Most of the
others were strangers to me, but all looked in remarkably
good health.

When I visited Bagamoyo two years before, it was the
most important and populous town on the whole Swahili
coast. The roads were crowded with shipping, and the
streets thronged with busy wayfarers. Now, a solitary
dhow lay at anchor off the shore, and on taking a walk
through the town, I saw nothing but the ruins of houses
recently shelled, and a few Indians plying their trades in
tumbledown booths. The native population had disappeared,
their place being taken by a few Wanyamwezi, who, at
the beginning of the war, had come to Bagamoyo from
the interior with ivory. They thereupon placed themselves under the protection of our troops, and by and by
became such warm admirers of military discipline, that
whenever they met a European they drew themselves up
and saluted.

In many places Arab and Wazeguha prisoners worked
together in irons. The town had been fortified with
trenches and a strong fence of barbed wire, the four openings in which were guarded by the so-called "Zulus."
The Zulus are Watuta from the regions to the west of
Quilimane and Inhambane; they constitute by far the best
portion of our native regiments. On every occasion they
have conducted themselves in the field with great bravery;
and though the condition in which they keep their uniform
leaves much to be desired, that of their weapons is absolutely
faultless. They are paid at the rate of twenty rupees per
head per month.

A further detachment of Watuta were stationed as a guard on the road leading to the Kingani ferry, their quarters consisting of a hastily constructed shed of corrugated iron, of somewhat novel design. By means of walls and ramparts the old palaver house had been transformed into a fort, in which the Imperial Commissioner and his officers had taken up their abode, along with a large contingent of Sudanese with their women and children. The Watuta do not, like the Sudanese, consider it necessary to take their women and children with them in their undertakings—a circumstance which, from a military standpoint, establishes a decided preference in their favour.

The position of the fort had been further strengthened by cutting down all the coco-palms in the vicinity to a distance of three or four hundred yards, while four bastions defended with field-artillery commanded the surrounding country in all directions.

The French mission station, on the north side of the town, showed no signs of having been fortified. Here I had the pleasure of once more meeting my old friends Father Etienne and Brother Oscar. Throughout the war these missionaries had remained at their post unmolested, and they now pointed with pride to the remains of huts and the fragments of discarded household goods which lay scattered all around, as evidences that over six thousand people had received shelter and succour at their hands. It is greatly to Bushiri's credit that, while he treated as enemies the missionary representatives of the two European powers concerned in the blockade, he exempted the neutral French missionaries from all attack or annoyance.

The Imperial Commissioner having kindly supplied me with a spare military tent and a quantity of camp utensils, I continued my way to Dar-es-Salaam. Here the streets were laid in ruins, and only a scanty sprinkling of Indians and Greeks were to be seen in the vicinity of the strongly fortified citadel. Having visited the German mission station, which I found completely riddled with shot, I laid a few twigs of laurel at the foot of the tall mango trees which mark the graves of our brave naval officers, Wolf and Landfermann. The next day I returned to Zanzibar.

Of Bushiri I could learn nothing, except that after the defeat at Mpwapwa he had withdrawn towards the north, presumably with the intention of uniting with the Usambara chief, Simboja, in Mazindi. I could not help thinking he had designs on me a second time, for Mazindi lies directly on the Pangani route to Kilimanjaro. My ransom of the year 1888 must have been of considerable service to him.

Meanwhile I did not allow the thought of possibilities of evil to disturb me. All the preliminary difficulties which had threatened to swamp the expedition at the very outset had now been successfully overcome, and I proceeded to lay in a supply of the necessary articles of barter. In this respect every district in East Africa has its own particular "currency." Thus, to pay one's way to Kilimanjaro, the chief requisite is a good supply of fairly strong cotton cloth, white, crimson, and dark blue in colour, with beads for small change. Of the latter, different kinds are required for different places. Thus, in Taita and Taveta, they must be of medium size, and either crimson, or dark blue, or white; in Jagga, they must be extremely small, and pink or light blue; while in Ugweno, Kahé, and the Masai country, all beads must be dark blue and in strings. Iron and brass wire, of the thickness of telegraph wire, is also in demand, but it is not absolutely necessary, and all other articles of merchandise are almost worthless. You might just as well try to palm off Portuguese money on a German shopkeeper as hope to effect a purchase in Taveta with yellow beads or green woollen cloth. The coinage current at the coast—dollars, rupees, and copper small coins—ceases to be of use three days inland from Mombaza, though on the Pangani caravan route it is valid as far as Mazindi.

It goes without saying that in addition to the currency above described all sorts of showy and useful articles are eagerly accepted as presents, though their exchange value is *nil*. I therefore took with me a miscellaneous collection of watches, musical-boxes, small telephones, model steam-engines, many-bladed knives, masks, uniforms, and so forth. These I distributed among the various chiefs and headmen along my route, and seldom found them fail to have the desired effect.

It was not long before I had the satisfaction of seeing all my goods made up into the customary loads—each sixty pounds weight—and packed in matting or tin cases. Our stores included a dozen loads of rice for the men, for, as hardly any crops can be raised throughout the whole region between the coast and Taita, sufficient food is not to be obtained on the road. Siwa Haji being likewise ready with the stipulated number of porters, the contract, with the names of all the members of the expedition appended, was registered at the Sultan's—a precaution demanded by law, to ensure that no slave had enrolled himself without the consent of his master. Two days later the expedition went on board H.B.M.'s gunboat *Somali*, the use of which, as already stated, had been kindly promised to me by Admiral Fremantle, and in the afternoon of September 3rd we set sail from Zanzibar amid a chorus of friendly farewells and cheers.

Early next morning we delivered a bag of letters to a

British man-of-war lying off the coast of Pemba on the look-out for Arab slave-dhows, and at sunset of the same day we ran into the creek, the steep palm-clad shores of which surround the island and town of Mombaza. The same evening I received a visit from Mr. Buchanan, the representative of the British East African Company, who had been made aware beforehand of my coming. He kindly came to inform me that a sufficient number of boats would be ready at sunrise to convey my whole caravan without loss of time up the creek to Bandarini, the landing-place for our mission station of Rabai. He was as good as his word, and under the convoy of the *Somali* I saw my men pull off in four large boats. I myself followed them some hours later, after having breakfasted with Mr. Buchanan, in conversation with whom I became very strongly impressed with the idea that in the exploiting of British East Africa there would be no lack of intelligence, energy, or—capital.

In the afternoon we reached the lonely landing-place of Bandarin, now, as two years ago, our first camping-ground on African soil. The tents having been pitched, the men broke up into small "messes" of five or six, and disposed themselves around the fires to await the cooking of the evening meal. The aristocrats of the caravan, the Somál, gathered into a little knot by themselves beside the piled up baggage, and busied themselves with the burnishing of their weapons. It was Africa once more—the red arid soil, the dry thorny bush, the parched grey-green grass, the pure dry air, the cooing doves and chirping cycadæ of our promised land of travel and adventure. Once more I was in the midst of the familiar hum and bustle of the free caravan life ; once more I breathed the old " *bouquet d'Afrique,*" compounded of heaven knows what subtle odours gleaned from earth and air and flower, from the curling smoke of the wood-fire, from the very people even—and never to be forgotten by one who has once lived in it, laboured in it, and so at last grown to love it.

Success to the new venture!

STREET SCENE AT MOMBAZA.

CHAPTER II.

MOMBAZA TO TAVETA.

THE first few days of a journey into the interior of East Africa are as a rule the most trying period of the whole expedition. The traveller's natural delight in the new and grander aspects of Nature, in the free unconventional life, and the deeply interesting scientific facts that meet his eye on all sides, is spoilt at every turn, and his impressions weakened and be-littled, by the constant worry arising from the want of discipline among the as yet unruly porters, and by their unceasing attempts to desert. Their superfluous energy finds vent in wild shoutings and dancings, which they keep up as long as lungs and limbs hold out. By degrees, the continuous marching, frequently accompanied as it is by want of water, begins to tell, and their exuberant spirits tone down of themselves; but at first, while the traveller is still ignorant of the characters with which he has to deal, he neither knows which is the best way

SWAHILI PORTERS.

44

Members of the Caravan.

to quell the unruly or how to foster the influence of the better disposed. To begin by drawing the rein tightly engenders forebodings for the future, which find a present and practical outcome in incessant attempts at desertion so long as there is time and opportunity ; and in this instance, owing to the war, circumstances were only too favourable to misdemeanours of this kind. On the other hand, too great a display of leniency is sure to result in eventual loss of authority, and the porters are apt to take French leave soon after they have received the usual advance-money.

The preservation of the golden mean is accordingly very difficult, if not indeed impossible, and many a time I have been compelled at first to let things pass which later on would have met with summary punishment, consoling myself meanwhile with the thought of a future day of reckoning. This policy early gained for me among the men the reputation of being *mema sana* (very nice), a flattering estimate of my character which gradually changed, as I tightened my hand, to the opinion that I was very *mkali* (strict). I may, however, congratulate myself on having been fairly successful, for while deserters were leaving other caravans in dozens, I arrived at Taveta having lost only three, and these doubtful characters, of whose evil propensities I had already been warned at Mombaza. Before we were half-way to Kilimanjaro, the discipline of the caravan was as perfect as could be desired, the soldiers and porters obedient, the marching order exemplary, and the success of the expedition in this respect assured.

As the caravan leaves camp, let us hold a review and march-past of its various members, on whose qualities and capabilities so much depends.

After us Europeans, the two Swahili headmen and the Somál bodyguard rank first ; the latter claiming our foremost consideration on account of their superior characteristics. Their leader is the before-mentioned Ali, aged twenty-six, one of the members of my Mombaza expedition in 1888. In the affair at Pangani he was stripped of everything by Bushiri's slaves and turned adrift to find his way to the coast as best he might. He has great influence with his comrades, is intelligent and energetic in no common degree, and on various occasions has shown himself so trustworthy that I have appointed him to the general superintendence of the treasury and commissariat, subject, of course, to my own control. Of frank, prepossessing countenance and genial temperament, he is perhaps a little too much addicted to gossip; but he is staunch as a bulldog to his master's interests, and is respected accordingly by the rest of the caravan, to whom he is known as *Bwana* Ali. He has a remarkable talent for languages, speaking English, Arabic, Hindustani, and Ki-Swahili in addition to his native tongue.

After Ali comes Ahmed, the brave. He, too, is between twenty and thirty, was with me at the Pangani affair, and is my special favourite on account of his many exceptional qualities. The very embodiment of obligingness and readiness, whatever Ahmed does he does well, and—a remarkable thing for a negro—whenever he sees anything that ought to be done, he does it conscientiously without requiring to be told. He was the only man in the whole caravan with whom I never once had to find fault. Ahmed was my right hand in everything (and I had need of an extra one), and as, unfortunately for himself, he knew a little of both English and Ki-Swahili, he was constantly in demand. "Ahmed, where is this?" "Ahmed, what did you do with that?" was the cry from morning till night. On the march he was my aide-de-camp and gun-bearer, and walked immediately behind me; in camp he was my chamberlain, my valet, my butler, and general factotum. The men praised Ali with the lips, Ahmed with the heart. He was beloved by all.

Third on the list comes Mohammed Ali, better known as Arali, an insignificant-looking little fellow of thirty or thereabouts, shy and retiring as a rule, but brave and pertinacious enough on occasion. He had been Count Teleki's "boy" for two years on the Samburu expedition, and had a wide experience of the natives. To him therefore is intrusted the arduous task of doling out to the porters their weekly supply of goods for the purchase of provisions, as well as of catering for the Europeans and Somál. He did his duty admirably.

Of the remaining Somál, Mohammed, the lean and active, is the best; Bulhan, the slow and taciturn, the worst. Jama Seif, the cook, has seen service with the redcoats at Aden, and is a great worthy, though not exactly a Soyer in the exercise of his calling.

Close in the wake of the Somál, with whom he claims equality of birth, comes Mwini Amani, aged twenty-eight, a native of Pangani. He, too, shared the joys and sorrows of my former expedition, of which he was a most useful member, and along with Dr. Fischer and in various Arab caravans has traversed the whole of East Africa as far as Uganda, familiarising himself with the dialects and making friends everywhere. He acts as our guide, and always marches at the head of the caravan carrying the flag. Thanks to his iron constitution and great powers of endurance, he alone of all his companions was able to bear the hardships of our three weeks' sojourn on Kilimanjaro, at a height of over 13,000 feet. But perhaps his best quality is the imperturbable good-humour with which he accepts everything as it comes and makes the best of it. The one point on which he is touchy is the subject of his birth, a somewhat

unusual weakness for a Swahili. He is inordinately proud
of being a freeman like the Somál—a "black gentleman,"
he calls himself—and always insists on being treated as such
by his comrades.

Far above him in rank, but a long way behind him in
worth, is the Swahili leader or headman, Abedi, a native of
Zanzibar. As a slave of the influential Wadi Nasibu, himself
a slave of the Sultan, he has great influence with the Zanzibar
men, but is otherwise unpopular. Ugly, lazy, insolent, cowardly,
weak, dishonest, untruthful, he is a typical Zanzibari. Nevertheless I tolerate him, for he is personally responsible to Siwa
Haji for the behaviour of the rest of the caravan.

Better, but not much better, is the second headman,
Hailallah, an Arab slave, also from Zanzibar, and the greatest
tattler, mischief-maker, toad-eater, and toper going. Both he
and Abedi owe their position solely to the fact that from
among their large circle of acquaintances in their native town
they could easily and quickly get together a sufficient number
of porters for the undertaking. On the journey they generally
sided with the men against me, and had it not been for my
faithful Somál, I should sometimes have been hard put
to it.

Of the rank and file of the caravan, the Askari and
Wapagazi, or soldiers and porters, it remains only to mention
Ben Juma, our untiring choir-leader; Mbassa, the wit of the
party; and the easy-going, contented Wanyamwezi. As for the
rest, they were a very indifferent lot, constantly in need of the
whip to bring them to their senses. Their physical perform-
ances were something wonderful, however, and would do credit
to any respectable beast of burden, to which indeed, in many
respects, they bear a striking resemblance. "Pagazi like
donkey; much food, much go," says Ahmed in his pigeon
English, and it is true; for if your porter can but once a day

have his fill of rice, beans, or millet, he is fully equal to a tramp of five or six hours in the blazing sun, carrying, in addition to his load of sixty or sixty-five pounds, his gun and ammunition, a cooking-pot, a sleeping-mat, a water-calabash, and a number of other "unconsidered trifles." In order to get along with him it is above all things necessary to be able to talk to him in Ki-Swahili, and the language, fortunately, is so simple, that with a little trouble one may pick up in a couple of months quite as much as is required for the ordinary and somewhat limited topics of caravan life. After the trying experiences incident to my first journey, I thank the Lord that I was now no more exposed to the misunderstandings and misrepresentations of an interpreter.

On the march the same routine is gone through day after day and week after week. At the first streak of dawn I awake and call Ali, the captain of my Somál. Immediately the camp begins to show signs of animation. "*Ondoka, funga mkeka*" (Get up, fold up your mats!) cry the headmen. Yawning, and still half asleep, the men bestir themselves, crawl out of their cosy rugs, in which they have passed the night on the ground, gird up their loin-cloths, and begin to drag their loads from the stack in which they have been piled overnight. The Somál and Askari set to work to strike the tents and pack the beds and other furniture, keeping time to a rhythmic chant the while. Meantime our cook brings us a cup of steaming cocoa, which we drink standing, and snatch a morsel of cold meat. "*Tayari?*" (ready?) I inquire of the headman. "*Tayari*" (ready) is the reply. Having noted the time and the readings of my thermometer and barometer, I give the word to start, "*Haya!*" and the caravan falls into marching order.

At the head marches Mwini Amani, carrying the German flag, and with him the native leader of the caravan, if such

D

there be. With the very first step begins the troublesome task of plotting the route. At every slight change of direction I consult my watch and my compass, and carefully make a note of the readings. At every perceptible change of level I do the same by the aneroid. If any considerable hill or mountain comes in sight I take its bearings by the prismatic compass, and the result is likewise recorded in my field-book. Thus every two or three minutes some observation has to be made, not to speak of the bearings that are taken without making a halt. I never have my instruments out of my hand until we are in camp again.

Immediately behind me marches Ahmed, carrying my rifle, for the van of the procession is the best place for a stray shot at guinea-fowl or antelopes, and fresh meat is always a welcome addition to our bill of fare. Hunting, in the proper sense of the term, is of course out of the question while we are on the march.

Behind Ahmed, and headed by the circumspect Wanyamwezi, come the main body of the porters, as close as may be on each other's heels. The Somál follow, and after them their headmen, Herr Purtscheller bringing up the rear. All march in single file, for the so-called great caravan route is only a narrow pathway after all, in which two cannot walk abreast. On my former expeditions I took with me one or two Muscat donkeys in case of serious illness; but I never myself made any use of them, and this time I dispensed with them altogether. I ascribe the almost perfect health I have always enjoyed in Africa to the fact that I have made every step of my journeys on foot, the constant exercise keeping my bodily organs in good order.

For two hours we hold steadily on amid a running fire of laughter, jokes, and shouts. Then the gradual lengthening of the file shows it is time to call a halt. I pause under the shade of a tree, and while the stragglers close up, and loads are shifted and fastenings seen to, I take the bearings of conspicuous points in the neighbourhood, and if the occasion be opportune, perhaps one or two photographs. In twenty minutes or half-an-hour we are once more on the march, the stillness now unbroken save for an occasional shout—" Shimo ! " " Mawe ! " " Miti ! " " Mwiba ! " " Nyoka ! " " Siafu ! " whereby the unwary porter is warned that a hole, a stone, a stump, a thorn, a snake, or a colony of ants threatens his shoeless feet. In an hour and a half we stop to rest a second time, after which, as the porters gradually get more and more exhausted, it becomes necessary to halt at least once every hour.

As a rule, we reach camp before midday, availing our-selves of one of the spots habitually frequented by the caravans which have trodden this route from time imme-morial, and which have invariably been selected on account of their proximity to one of the rock-reservoirs peculiar to the region. Tents are pitched, and the Somál proceed to stack the baggage, keeping it off the ground by means of a layer of branches or stones, and covering it with a tarpaulin. The men gather grass and branches to make sleeping-sheds, while I, in the sweltering heat, set about taking the midday observation with my theodolite, Herr Purtscheller assisting by reading off the time. Before I have finished, the cook has made ready a light luncheon, which we partake of with due relish, in the consciousness of " something accom-plished, something done." My inner man thus fortified, I light my pipe and proceed to make a rough map of the road we have traversed, while Herr Purtscheller scours the neighbourhood in search of botanical and geological specimens. The men prepare their food, mend their torn clothing, eat, laugh. and sleep. A few, and notably a squint-eyed individual, by name Hassani, make a parade of their piety, and hasten to repeat their prayers in the eyes of all men, in season and out of season.

My map finished, I set out, accompanied by a Somali carrying my camera, in search of prey or pictures, whichever may come handiest. I am not at all afraid of losing myself, or of being carried away by the excitement of the chase ; for, to my shame as a Nimrod be it said, I have no enthusiasm for sport for its own sake, but only as a means towards gaining a more intimate knowledge of nature and nature's ways. I take no pleasure in the mere stalking or hunting of any creature, with the hope of getting a shot at it in the end ; and were it not for the necessity of supplying the pot, I should at all times be willing to lay aside my rifle and give myself up to the observation of the animal's habits as it disports itself in its native haunts.

On my return to camp it behoves me to mount the judge's chair, and to mete out condign punishment to evil-doers at the hands of the Somál, ten to twenty lashes being the quantum for ordinary offences. Herr Purtscheller performs the duties of doctor, and dispenses to his numerous patients suitable medicaments for the blisters, ulcers, thorn-pricks, and abrasions to which the flesh of the Swahili porter is heir.

Meantime the sun approaches the western horizon, and Ahmed and Mohammed have brought out the dinner-table and covered it with a snowy white cloth. Our indiarubber bath stands ready inside the tent, and after a refreshing plunge we sit down to dinner, prepared to do justice to the meal with the true explorer's appetite.

In conversing with friends in Europe, I usually find that they have the most absurd ideas on the subject of a traveller's ordinary fare, the tendency, as a rule, being to make it as scanty and unpalatable as possible. It does sometimes happen, in exceptional circumstances, that one is obliged to substitute for supper a tightening of the belt, but on the whole the traveller is himself to blame if his supplies run low and he is reduced to starvation. The native foods do not offer much variety, though they differ widely in different districts; but if the traveller is not too dainty and is prepared to make the best of what is to be had, it is wonderful what can be done. A great deal depends on how far he is willing and able to give directions to the cook for preparing native products in European ways—if he can occasionally lend a helping hand, so much the better. I made a point of taking with me from Europe or Zanzibar, in large quantities, only cbcoa, tea, salt, and rice, with a small supply of acetic acid, pepper, and saccharine, which last I used instead of sugar. I had no tinned meats of any kind, with the exception of three cases of corned beef, to be reserved for an emergency. Our wine-cellar consisted of two bottles of claret, two of brandy, and two of port. The claret we disposed of at an early date, the brandy among the snows of Kilimanjaro. One of the bottles of port, to the intense astonishment of our friends, we brought back with us to Zanzibar. Our daily drink was water, with a few drops of citric or acetic acid, and on the march very weak cold tea. That our bill of fare did not lack variety, let the following examples bear witness. Game-soup and guinea-fowl with rice, or rice-soup and antelope steak with wild spinage, or wild tomato-soup and roast zebra—all these, washed down with the unfailing cup of tea, were among the items included in the ordinary *carte* in uninhabited regions. In populous districts we had a yet more tempting selection. Broth and ox-tongue, roast beef with fresh vegetables, banana fritters and honey; or milk-soup, mutton cutlets and tomatoes, rice, bananas, and roast millet; or egg-soup, stewed fowl and sweet potatoes, with melons and other fruit by way of dessert—all these from time to time rejoiced the palate and made glad the heart at the close of a hard day's work.

After dinner the pipe is produced again, and we sit down to write up our diaries by the light of the lamp. Then we relax, and for an hour or so give ourselves up to idleness and the enjoyment of one another's society. By eight o'clock the camp is still and silent, and, cosily wrapped in our woollen blankets, we too stretch ourselves on our cork mattresses, to sleep soundly through the cool hours of the night. Borne from the distant plains, the deep roar of the lion, the hoarse bark of the leopard, and the eerie laugh of the hyena, is our weird but unheeded lullaby, until once more we are awakened at the first streak of dawn by the twittering of early song-birds, and rise refreshed and ready for whatever the day may have in store for us.

We left the coast on the morning of September 6th. Each man having been furnished with a gun, the long column began to wind over the undulating ground, which, gradually rising, culminates at last in the plateau on whose edge stands the Rabai Mission. Here the vegetation still feels the influence of the moist sea-breeze, and ridges and hollows alike are covered with verdant forest. A little way below Rabai we pass a plantation of coco-palms; beside it is a small station of the Imperial British East Africa Company, the first of the long line planned to extend to the Victoria Nyanza, by way of Taita, Ukamba, Lake Baringo, and Kavirondo.

At Rabai we were most kindly received by Mr. and Mrs. Burness, of the Church Missionary Society, and with them we spent a very pleasant hour. Having secured the services of a couple of mission boys and ten porters to carry rice,

we here bade farewell to things European and civilised, and commenced our journey towards the tree-studded plateau inland. The heavy showers of the past few days, which proclaimed the approach of the rainy season, had been general all over the region, and had already filled the rock-reservoirs on which we had to depend for our supply of water. Under their fostering influence the vegetation had begun to awake from its long sleep, and already showed signs of returning life and vigour.

The whole of the plateau country has the appearance of an arid, wooded wilderness, in which evergreens mingle with deciduous forms. The stiff clay soil is overgrown with coarse grasses, or with low perennial herbs. Towards the coast the trees grow tolerably close together, though they do not attain any considerable height, as they do among the mountains or along the banks of rivers. The trunks are short, the bark cracked, the branches gnarled, and in many instances withered. Impenetrable thickets of succulent shrubs form islands and belts everywhere in the open woods. As the coast zone is left behind and the inland regions approached, the vegetation assumes more and more such forms as, by their scanty array of leaves, present the smallest surface for the evaporation of moisture. In the vicinity of Taro, only three days' march from the sea, the evergreen forms begin to disappear, and thorny species become the most prominent. Towards the Maungu Mountains the open woods give place to a dense "hawthorn scrub," and on the farther side of the range the traveller suddenly enters the steppe-land. At first the uniformity is varied by occasional patches of thorn and bush; but beyond the mountains of Taita the boundless wilderness stretches away in dreary monotony.

The tract of country here briefly described is botanically divided into four regions corresponding to the climatic and geological conditions, and to the prevailing abundance or scarcity of water. As far as Taro, water is to be found in pools and in the natural rock-reservoirs even in the dry season ; between Taro and Maungu, Maungu and Ndara, and again between Taita and Taveta, there is absolutely none ; while on the heights of Maungu and on the western slopes of Ndara rain-water again occurs in natural reservoirs, and in Taita itself there are two running streams. In the rainy season water is also to be had in small pools close to Maungu and between Taita and Taveta.

In countries like east Central Africa, where the plains stretch for miles and miles unbroken by hills or ridges, the physiognomy of the landscape is determined almost entirely by the character of the vegetation. But the character of the vegetation itself depends less on the forms assumed by the organs of reproduction—the flowers and fruit—than on the appearance and arrangement of the organs of nutrition—the branches and leaves. This fact was strikingly illustrated in the present instance, when the period of growth and blossom had just begun. It mattered little whether the flowers were large or small, white or coloured, glowing in tropical abundance or altogether absent—the character of the landscape was but little affected. Leafless trees and bushes prevailed everywhere, their generally forbidding aspect plainly telling of a fierce struggle for existence under the greatest extremes of climate, and giving the impression that only a few species are represented as in the oak and beech forests of more temperate regions.

But the stem and branches are the mere vegetable skeleton, the leaves are the body. And here, in this desert region, either the leaves are all bipinnate, so as to present the smallest possible surface for evaporation, or they develop a tough, glossy cuticle, to prevent injury through excessive

transpiration. The woods are composed chiefly of tall evergreens—mimosæ, tamarinds, and olives—and of deciduous
trees, such as banyans, sycamores, and willows. Dwarf palms
and low oshur and sodada shrubs, epiphytic orchids, cane
and prairie grasses, with numerous tuberous and bulbous
species, find their place nearer the ground. Where there are
no trees these lower members of the vegetable kingdom
mingle inextricably with euphorbias, cucurbitaceæ, bulbous-
stemmed testudinariæ and aloes, and form impenetrable
thickets.

Protection against evaporation has been Nature's primary
consideration in the organisation of each and all of these
plants, for the drought to which they are subjected lasts for
months at a time. In the attainment of this object she
displays a wonderful fertility of resource. Certain species,
like the mimosæ, the banyans, and the sycamores, she has,
as already said, provided with pinnate or thick glossy leaves,
which at the commencement of the dry season drop away,
having duly fulfilled their nutritive function ; in others the
leaves are evergreen, but abnormally tough ; and most are
covered with an armour of thorns over stem and branch and
twig alike. In some cases the thorns take the place of leaves
altogether. The succulent plants are clothed as it were in
mail, which prevents the evaporation of the sap, and in plants
of the grass and onion tribe a store of moisture is laid up
in the underground tubers and bulbs.

When I passed through this region two years ago in the
month of July—that is to say, in the height of the dry season
—the landscape was painted in a dull grey monotone. On
the present journey the colouring was not much more lively,
for the young leaves had a grey or bluish sheen, and dead
grasses, branches, and tree-trunks were visible everywhere,
except in places where they had been destroyed by fire or

consumed by white ants. Nevertheless the breath of spring
had passed over the land. Many of the plants were pushing
out their young leaves, while others, and those the majority,
like our own alders, hazels, willows, and fruit-trees, were
crowned with a wealth of blossom while as yet their leaves
were still in bud. This phenomenon is not so much to be
wondered at among the trees of temperate climates, where the
rays of the spring sun affect the more delicate outer envelopes
of the flowers more quickly than those of the leaves; but
it is difficult to account for in equatorial climes, where the
stimulus derived from light and heat remains tolerably equal
throughout the year. The explanation seems to be in some
way connected with the necessity which exists that fertilisation
should have taken place before the pollen is spoiled by the
heavy rains.

The various lilies and orchids follow the example of the
plants we have just been describing; but the grasses first
produce leaves, and the succulent species new shoots. In
these last, the tubers have supplied a continuous store
of moisture throughout the whole of the dry season, and
thus, the plants are in a position to utilise at once, for the
purposes of growth, the surplus nourishment supplied by
the rains.

On the edge of the coast terrace the lofty borassus palm
is still to be met with, the last representative of a richer
and more prodigal flora. After that the palm disappears
altogether, and does not occur again until it is represented
among the mountains of Taita and on Kilimanjaro, by new
species.

Our first day's march was brought to a close at midday
by the side of the Moaje stream, at a spot where, two
years before, I had pitched my first camp when travelling

with Herr von Eberstein. The little stream had dwindled to
a few puddles, but our tents were beautifully shaded by two
large leafy mango-trees, in all probability sprung from chance
kernels thrown away by some passing coast porter, which had
found a congenial habitat close to the water's edge. As a
matter of course I had to listen to a good deal of grumbling
on the part of the men; the first day usually ends in numerous
little alterations and redistributions of loads. I soon put a
stop to all rebellious tendencies, however, by taking possession of the guns—a precaution nearly always necessary to
prevent desertion—and for the most part the men spent
the evening dancing and singing in the moonlight as if
possessed.

On stepping out of my tent in the early dewy morning,
the first thing I saw was two of the Rabai Mission boys
stealing quietly out of camp. Although the rice they had
carried had already been used up, as a matter of principle I
just as quietly sent three Somál after them and had them
brought back. As a punishment they were condemned to
carry the water for the whole caravan in the old petroleum-
tins I had bought for that purpose in Mombaza.

The guinea-fowl in the bushes on the margin of the
stream were clucking lustily as we prepared to strike camp,
and soon Ali appeared carrying two plump specimens for the
pot. Once more we plunged into the dull grey-green wilderness of bush and trees which hemmed us in on both sides,
making any view of the surrounding country wholly impossible.
Except the path, and an occasional scrap of cloth fluttering
from the prickles of a wait-a-bit thorn, nothing remained to
tell of travellers who had preceded us. Small game, such as
we usually come across in our own forests, there is here
apparently none, and the larger kinds shun the thickets,
where unknown dangers await them, and seek the more open

steppe-land. The birds, too, are inaudible and invisible, for it is only in pairing-time, which occurs during the rainy season, that they are to be heard calling to their mates. Then, also, the insects awake to life, but at present they are represented solely by huge millepeds. As yet we have only reached the period of the preliminary or early rains. These are very irregular. Yesterday there was a heavy fall at four in the morning, and to-day there was a succession of sharp showers between eleven and twelve.

Drenched to the skin, we reached the Magunga rivulet, and camped beneath a sycamore-tree. Like the Moaje, this stream consisted of a series of pools, and the water had a strong taste of alum. The spot was made memorable to me by the fact that here two years ago five porters managed to make good their escape with a quantity of our most valuable effects—maps, field-glasses, woollen clothing, and the like. This time too it looked as if things were coming to a crisis, and when I again took possession of the guns I was greeted with very black looks from certain members of the caravan, who, I could see, had evidently been meditating flight. A deputation waited on me to request that I would restore the arms and ammunition forthwith, and not expose my men to personal risk in "this hostile neighbourhood." In a well-directed speech I turned their pretended fears to ridicule, and succeeded in getting the laughter on my side. All night I made the Somál keep a sharp look-out, however, and several times before morning I took a turn round the camp myself.

With every step of our march inland the landscape grows more and more dreary. The early rains have as yet failed to make any impression on the district we have now reached, and the frequent patches of burned-up grass add to the general air of desolation. Here and there an ant-hill reveals the true red or yellowish-brown colour of the porous laterite.

Elsewhere the soil consists of a yellowish sand, overlying breccia-like reddish-grey sandstones, which show that we have left behind us the clay slate formations, and entered upon the narrow belt of carboniferous sandstones.

The day was terribly hot, and the men groaned audibly, but took heart again and went on right gallantly as they joined in the succession of spirited songs kept up by the Wanyamwezi in the van. At Goré the water-holes proved to be dried up, but in Samburu the reservoirs contained an abundant supply of what by courtesy was termed water, though in reality it was not much better than liquid mud. On our getting into camp some Wa-Duruma—as the natives from the villages hidden away in the surrounding jungle are called— came to offer goats and cattle for sale. I was only too delighted to seize the opportunity, and by way of magnet to draw my men onward purchased a fine ox to take with us to our next halting-place.

Although, that night, we Europeans shared the watch with the Somál, three porters managed to desert, but without goods or arms. They were the three of whom I had all along been suspicious, and I did not trouble myself much about them, feeling now secure of all the others. Moreover, we had reached the last inhabited spot before entering on the Taita wilderness, and those who had not hitherto attempted to escape might well be looked upon as willing followers. Then, too, had they not the immediate prospect of a plentiful banquet of ox-flesh?

Meanwhile, to drive the obstinate brute along the narrow path, scarcely wide enough for a loaded porter, was no easy matter. It was taken in hand by Mwini Amani and Arali, but the two fell out over something, and ended by coming to blows.

An hour's march brought us to the last of the Samburu

villages, around which the natives were busy clearing the ground, preparatory to sowing the grain in the coming rainy season. Rain-water was abundant in the numerous rock-reservoirs, here called *ngurungas.* The surface at this point begins to rise considerably, and culminates at last in the rounded hill of Taro, the last watering-place on the route until we reach Maungu. Here we camped at midday, and I was able to determine our position astronomically.

In the afternoon I left the porters to quarrel over the division of the ox, and set off to prospect the neighbourhood and have a closer look at the numerous *ngurungas.* These natural reservoirs, on which throughout the whole of east Central Africa man and beast alike mainly depend for the supply of water, are accounted for by other travellers on the theory that they have been gradually formed by the hand of man scooping out the water and mud contained in what were at first slight natural depressions in the rock. My investigations at Taro have led me to quite another conclusion. The sandstone here lies exposed in rounded blocks and ridges, which split superficially into foliated layers. In these, in the course of weathering, numerous round holes are worn, both in the upper surface and in the sides, so that the rock looks as if it were pock-pitted. Holes of all sizes occur together in the same block, but small holes predominate. The fact that the holes are to be found in the face of the blocks—that is to say, in a horizontal direction—sufficiently controverts the idea of the artificial origin of the *ngurungas,* for in these latter no water could collect to attract the attention of passing travellers. With the vertical holes it is different. If you put your finger into one of the smaller of these, you will find that it expands below like an inverted funnel, and contains a quantity of water. From this I am led to believe that the hole having originally arisen from the laminated structure of the rock, which seems peculiarly to favour the formation of these holes, the process of deepening and widening has been carried on by the chemical action of the water which lodges in it. Owing to the peculiar shape of the tiny reservoir the water is not so liable to evaporate, and its solvent properties are able to act upon the material of which the rock is built up, until, with the lapse of time, a cavity is formed capable of containing a quantity that will last through longer and longer periods of drought. By-and-by small plants and animals make their appearance, and the corrosive agency of the water is assisted by the acids set free in the decomposition of organic substances. Finally the cavity attracts the notice of man, who finds its contents repay the trouble of scooping them out, and thus he, too, mechanically assists in its enlargement. Thus year after year the process goes on, until at length we have the spacious *ngurunga*, large enough to contain a supply of water to serve whole caravans.

Ngurungas are of all sizes up to eight feet in diameter and six or seven feet deep. Unless immediately after the rains, the green slimy liquid they contain, if poured into a glass, would hardly be dignified by the name of water. Fortunately, in these regions we have no glasses to drink out of, and the addition of a few drops of acetic or citric acid makes it quite palatable. I may add that I have never known it to produce any evil effects, either on myself or among my men.

Next morning, each man having taken as much water as his calabash would hold, and with a reserve supply of five loads carried in the old petroleum-tins, we commenced our forced march of two days through the thorn wilderness towards Maungu. Half-an-hour beyond Taro, we reached the *ngurungas* of Makanga among the sandstone slabs of the level plain. Here we were met by a dozen Wa-Taita, desirous of accompanying the caravan as far as their native district, in the capacity of assistants to the porters. Of course, the porters pay for the hire of these assistants themselves, and so long as he has a rag of cloth or a handful of beads to spare, nothing seems to please the lazy Swahili better than to get a native to carry his load for him, while he plays the fine gentleman and walks behind at his ease. I have known men so well able to husband their weekly *posho* (allowance of goods for the purchase of provisions) that, with a little friendly assistance from a comrade in the way of a handful of grain, they have contrived to afford the luxury of a native substitute throughout nearly the whole of the journey.

On this march we only paused to rest every two or three hours, and did not pitch camp till evening. All day long we pushed doggedly on through the never-ending scrub and thickets. At midday we halted for an hour at a small dried-up marsh called Ziwa la Majumé. Just as we were on the point of starting there appeared from the other side of the trees a party consisting of between thirty and forty native porters of some unfamiliar tribe. The customary salutations having been exchanged, they volunteered the information that they came from Kilimanjaro, and were now on their way home to the coast, having been discharged by the American naturalist Dr. Abbott, who had no further use for their services. The story was plausible enough, but they seemed to me a suspicious-looking lot, and I was at a loss how to account for the presence of two donkeys and a couple of Arab half-breeds who formed part of the motley crew. Afterwards, in Taita, we learned that the spokesmen were slave-dealers, on their way to the coast with twenty Wa-Jagga slaves. We gathered from them, however, sundry important pieces of information as to the state of the road ahead, where water was to be had, the latest stories of Masai on the war-path, and more of a like kind, taking leave of them at last with a civil interchange of *kwaheris* (good-bye).

As we proceed westward a remarkable change takes place in the character of the soil and of the vegetation. The sandstones are replaced by crystalline slates, gneisses, and metamorphic rocks, all converted by the powerful atmospheric agencies into red laterite. At the same time the trees become more stunted, the bush more open and scrubby, the grass degenerates into miserable isolated tufts; everywhere the staring red soil is visible among the prevailing greys of this forbidding vegetation. It is not exactly an inviting prospect, yet this mingling of red with the greys of the lichen-clad trunks and branches and the bluish-greens of the opening leaves is not without a certain charm of colour peculiarly its own.

Owing to the absence of prominent features in the landscape from which to take bearings, the task of plotting the route had to be performed with unusual care, and I was soon thoroughly sick of it. Accordingly, I hailed with joy the rugged pyramidal mass of Kisigao, which became visible in the south-west for a few moments late in the afternoon. The porters, however, grumbled at the short halt.

I had already sent on the reserve supply of water to our appointed camping-ground, so that the main body of the caravan might feel they had some object in pushing on; and in the evening, after sunset, the weary and thirsty porters might have been seen staggering onwards beneath their heavy loads, urged now by threats, now by words of encouragement, until in the fast-gathering darkness the fires of the water-carriers became distinguishable among the trees, and with one more spurt we were in camp. Greedily each man swallowed the portion of water carefully doled out to him by Ali, for the calabashes were empty long ago. Then, after a hasty supper

E

of rice or maize left over from the last meal, they flung themselves down to sleep among the carelessly scattered loads, an
example we ourselves were glad to follow after a cupful of
pea-soup, which had been heated up for us over the blazing
camp-fire.　To the conservative instincts of the Swahili
porter a night thus spent in the open, and not at any of the
accustomed camping-grounds, is a veritable horror, especially
if it be in a spot destitute of trees or bush.　He has nothing
to lean against, nothing to shelter under, nowhere to hang his
various belongings.　In the present instance, however, we
were not so badly off.　There were plenty of bushes, and in
the men's exhausted condition, everything else was forgotten
in the overwhelming desire to rest.

At two in the morning I awoke shivering with cold and
soaked to the skin with the heavy dew.　The full-moon shone
in the zenith, and without delay I roused the snoring sleepers
to continue the march in the clear, cool night.　Soon all were
in motion, but first I committed our two remaining loads of
water to a couple of the most trustworthy, and sent them
ahead to await us half-way to Maungu.　Then, taking my
place at the head of the file, I continue to note the readings
of compass and barometer by the aid of a dark-lantern.　Not
a sound is heard as we steadily hold on our way between the
grey, thorny trees, looking weird and ghost-like in the moonlight.　Owing to the nature of the bush, the path curves about
in sinuous windings, more than doubling the distance we
have to traverse.　Slowly the moon sinks below the horizon,
all too swiftly the dawn steals across the east, chased into day
by the all-conquering sun, which once more starts triumphant
to run his course in the heavens, to the painful cost of weary
wanderers such as we.

In the course of the last hour we have left the arid forest
region behind, and are now in the midst of the wilderness of

thorn scrub. For miles the landscape has the appearance
of an immense flat plain, planted at almost regular intervals
with shrubs or low trees about the height of our ordinary
fruit-trees. This regularity is the result of the struggle for
air and moisture in this repellent waste. The trees vary
in height from six to twelve or thirteen feet, and occur
at intervals of from nine to twelve feet apart. They are
roughly pyramidal in form, and begin to branch not far from
the ground. With their grey trunks and branches festooned
with trailing lichens, their stiff twigs and large and numerous
thorns, they bear a striking resemblance to wild pear-trees in
winter.

It is only at rare intervals that a tuft of grass relieves
the glaring red of the otherwise naked earth; shrubs in the
proper sense of the term there are none. A slender creeping
plant, with a saccate tuberous stem, eighteen inches to three
feet long, is the one constant associate of the thorn-trees
throughout the whole area.

The trees at this season were for the most part in bud;
and some also displayed clusters of white or yellowish flowers.
Notwithstanding the external similarity of all forms, it was
easy to perceive that there were three prevailing species. Of
these, one with tri-lobate leaves and another with leaves finely
pinnate we recognised as having occurred on the other side
of Taro ; the third, which was still leafless, was new.

The most remarkable effect of the extremes of climate
on the flora of this region is, as we have elsewhere remarked,
the enormous development of thorns. These thorns are to
be regarded not so much as a defence against animals—for
there is nothing here to attract the plant-loving denizens of
the open steppes—as a protection against the drought of the
dry season, which here seems of extraordinary intensity. As
Grisebach points out in his classical work, *Vegetation der*

Erde, nature, throughout the organic world, is constantly utilising the same means for the attainment of the most varied ends, determining the organs according to the environment with the utmost exactitude and through the most minute modifications. In the case we are considering the plants are protected, on the one hand against drought and on the other against animals, by a partial suppression of the leaves, of which in a certain number the fibro-vascular bundles become indurated and form thorns from an inch and a half to two inches long. These later on develop into branches, and themselves give rise to other thorns. The thorns shoot out from the stem alternately with the true leaves and form a spiral, the extremity of each twig developing likewise into a sharp thorn. It is self-evident that with such a suppression of the foliage there must be a corresponding diminution of transpiration, and the tree is enabled to preserve its sap when, during the dry season, its roots cannot any longer obtain a supply of moisture. The thorns spring from the twigs, the twigs from the branches, and the branches from the trunk almost at right angles, the result being a form of vegetation of most angular outlines and forbidding aspect.

At last, on our left toward the north-west, appeared the cloud-capped mountains of Maungu. The porters, exhausted with their twenty hours' march almost without water, food, or sleep, and carrying loads of from seventy to eighty pounds, began to pluck up heart again, and, by dint of continuous coaxing and other arguments yet more persuasive, were induced to push on to the point where the water-carriers awaited us. With what eagerness they gulped down the dirty uninviting liquid, almost lukewarm after its long exposure to the sun in the tin petroleum-cans! Not a drop was lost. Then it was on again towards the camping-ground on the mountain, from which we were still separated by a long ridge of gneiss. It was impossible to maintain the usual compact line of march; but by midday every man was assembled under the sycamores of Maungu, enjoying the luxury of a wash in rain-water, which had to be fetched from a *ngurunga* half-way up the mountain-side.

From our coign of vantage on the slope we had a magnificent view of the surrounding country far and near, a pleasure which had been denied us in the plain below. Behind, the mountain rises steeply to a height of over 600 feet, clothed with tree-euphorbias almost to its summit. To the east, in boundless monotony, extends the dreary thorn wilderness we have just quitted; west of it, and sharply divided from it and its characteristic vegetation by the ridge of mountains, stretch the "bush and tree steppes" to the far horizon, where Ndara and the mountains of Taita loom up as a hazy wall, running towards the north. The picture does not present much variety, but one is thankful for small mercies in this part of East Africa.

The lonely camp at Maungu possessed no very great charms with which to tempt a caravan to a prolonged stay. Accordingly, their loads being exhausted, I that evening dismissed the porters I had brought from Rabai to carry rice, and sent them back to the coast with letters for Zanzibar and Europe. There was no fear of any of the others trying to run away along with them, now that they had the terrors of the road from Taro to Maungu behind them, though after the hardships already endured the next day's march of eight hours to Ndara was excessively trying.

We had barely entered the tree-steppes to the west of Maungu when we started a herd of hartebeeste (*Alcelaphus caama*), the first big game we had seen so far. Nor did we come upon any more, for the trees gradually gave place to thick bush, which is always avoided by game of this kind.

The soil to the west of Maungu is of the same red colour, but instead of being stiff and clayey, as on the eastern side, it is porous and sandy. Grass begins to show itself again among the clumps of mimosæ, where also appears a thorny shrub almost smothered with yellow blossoms, which give off a delicious odour of violets that attracts thousands of wild bees. In this case also the flowers come before the leaves. Wherever the ground rises a little there are thickets of euphorbias and liliaceæ linked together with creepers. Here, as elsewhere, the grass has largely been burnt away for clearings, leaving the black charred patches so familiar to the traveller in Africa at this season. The pungent smell of burning mingles with the flower-scented air, whilst here and there tongues of flame may be seen creeping along among the dry withered blades with an African deliberateness well calculated to upset our preconceived notions of sensational prairie fires,—stampeding cattle and terrified fugitives.

Throughout the march the rugged southern extremity of the Ndara chain was visible as an outstanding landmark, and we had to pass to the south of it in order to reach water, on the western side of the mountains. Slowly we approached the outlying hills of Manyani, where, in the depression which forms the approach, the prevailing laterites exchange their customary red colour for a dark-brown humus tint, always associated with that stern vegetation of which thorny mimosæ and aloes are the type. The ground is full of cracks, telling plainly of an insufficient rainfall, even in the wet season, and of heavy floods which wash away the surface soil before they have time to penetrate the layers beneath.

As we ascend the hills we note a number of dry watercourses, and pass the camping-ground of Marago ya Kanga, where I spent a night in July 1888. On the tree-crowned heights above a thunderstorm is raging, but we witness it from afar, as we wend our way in the broiling heat round the southern spur of the range, with its wealth of giant leafless baobabs. The western face of Ndara has the appearance of an immense wall of gneiss, along the foot of which we plod in a straggling column, until at length, far up the mountain-side, we descry the huts of the Sagala Mission station, and reach our camping-ground under a group of shady sycamore-trees by the side of a small pool.

Pitching our tents and announcing our arrival by the customary firing of guns, we were answered from above by a corresponding number of shots, and soon afterwards, by the aid of a glass, I was able to distinguish a European in tropical dress making his way downwards, accompanied by a party of natives. An hour later Mr. Wray of the Church Missionary Society was in my tent, having brought with him for the benefit of the new arrival, whosoever he might prove to be, a quantity of milk, fresh butter, and vegetables. Needless to say these unwonted dainties were duly appreciated.

All too quickly the time passed in a pleasant interchange of news, until at length the sinking sun warned my visitor that he must take his leave. When I bade him good-bye, I promised to pay him a visit at his own house on the following day.

As the inhabitants of Ndara have rather a bad name, my men were allowed for this night to retain possession of their guns and ammunition. In spite of strict injunctions to the contrary, the foolish fellows took advantage of the darkness to amuse themselves by firing off blank-cartridge, with the result that one of them received the contents of a gun in the middle of his back. There was peace after that. The influence of the night stole over me. Under the serene splendour of the zodiacal light I sat listening to the homely croaking of a frog in a neighbouring pool, mentally recalling scenes in the journey thus far, until at length my head drooped and my eyelids closed, and I fell fast asleep.

After the trying marches of the last few days it was necessary to allow the men some time to recruit. Most of them were suffering from sore feet, and many were quite lame. The prolonged halt likewise afforded me an opportunity of taking more extensive astronomical observations for the determination of time and latitude.

The morning of the day after our arrival at Ndara was pleasantly spent in a visit to the mission station, which I reached after an hour's stiff climbing. I found Mr. Wray in front of his corrugated iron dwelling, busily engaged in the construction of a primitive sugar-press, the sugar-cane growing remarkably well at this elevation. Close by, the skin of a lioness was spread out to dry, the animal having been shot by this "sporting parson" a fortnight before, at the spot where we were for the present encamped. Indoors there was a motley assortment of miscellaneous odds and ends, such as could only have been met with in the snuggery of a lonely bachelor in Central Africa, who had not left his station for over eight years. I was particularly struck with an iron stove which stood in one corner, and which must of course be a most useful acquisition in the cold nights of June and July, although the altitude is only some 600 feet above the plain below.

There was nothing remarkable in the surrounding groups of bee-hive-shaped huts,—the dwellings of the natives,—nor in the natives themselves, about whom sufficient has been said and written by other travellers. Beyond the mission-house the ground dips down into a charming valley, through which flows a babbling brook, its banks covered with a luxuriant profusion of sugar-canes and bananas, growing side by side with European vegetables, while sleek cattle graze upon the grassy slopes. The rock here, as on the outlying spurs of the mountain, is a hard quartzose gneiss, which from below has almost the appearance of granite.

The manifold shapes and shiftings of the clouds in this neighbourhood are among its most interesting features. The mountains of Ndara are the first barrier that the moisture-laden monsoons from the ocean encounter after their passage across the eastern plains. Here, accordingly, the moisture condenses into vapour, which partly falls as rain, and partly is wafted farther in the form of clouds until it reaches Taita, where it is again met and cooled by intervening mountain-tops. On the eastern side of the mountains of Taita the moisture is finally exhausted; beyond lie the barren steppes. But all day long from the surrounding plains the heated air rises continuously, forming upward currents sufficiently powerful to overcome the steady westward movement of the monsoons, and by these the clouds are tumbled and tossed about in all directions. As the plains cool towards evening, the upward currents are transformed into downward currents, and such clouds as still remain overhead again come under the influence of the monsoon and resume their journey westward.

The view from the summit of Ndara ranges southward as far as the isolated peak of Kisigao and the more distant mountains of Usambara. To the south-west it is bounded by the Paré mountains, and to the west by the mountains of Taita, which run north and south parallel with Ndara. Round the bases of these mountains sweep the boundless steppes, the whole looking like a calm, grey ocean studded with rocky islands. But while the ocean, with its rippling waves, is a type of life and its ceaseless unrest, the steppes, in their

death-like stillness, suggest rather the idea of Infinity, and
far more than ocean lead the mind to the contemplation of
things sublime.

After taking a hearty leave of my kind host at Sagala, I
returned to camp at midday. In the course of the afternoon
one of our best porters fell ill, and showed such marked
symptoms of small-pox that on resuming our march next
day we were forced to leave him behind, under the kindly
care of Mr. Wray. To no other disease is the negro so subject
as to small-pox, and cases are not unknown in which whole
caravans have been swept off by the fell scourge. Accordingly, I had provided myself plentifully with lymph, so that
in case of an outbreak I should be able to vaccinate all the
men. This, however, turned out to be the only case we had,
and on my return journey two months later I had the satisfaction of finding the invalid quite better, and took him back
with me to the coast.

On leaving the camp at Ndara we resumed our march
across the steppes, which, lying on the rainless side of the
mountain, have an even more grimly desolate aspect than on
the other side. An ashen grey is here the prevailing tone,
unmodified by the former brownish tint. Yet in spite of the
prevailing barrenness antelopes and lions abound, judging by
the numerous tracks we saw. After a march of two hours
we crossed the rising ground of Gogoloni, which runs as a
ridge of rocky quartz boulders across the plain between Ndara
and Taita, and kept on towards the rugged rocks of Javia,
the southern spur of the Taita range, and, like the southern
buttress of Ndara, a conspicuous feature in the landscape.
Towards midday we saw the broad, deep valley of the Mataté
river opening up beneath us, and half an hour later, after
wading across the muddy ford, we reached my old camping ground of 1887, and its verdant surroundings had

now, as then, an electrical effect on the spirits of my followers.

In response to the summons of our guns, a bustling crowd of natives soon surrounded us, and were speedily driving a trade in sugar-cane and fruits of various kinds. Unfortunately, it was not long before things began to get rather lively, for the Wa-Taita of this district richly deserve the unenviable reputation they have gained of being the greatest thieves and cheats in the region. As for the women, the worst has not been told of them. Many of my men had reason to remember for months the hours spent among the Arcadians of Mataté.

As might be expected, the Swahili found this land of plenty only too inviting, and loudly clamoured for a second day's halt. I had my work on Kilimanjaro to consider, however, and as the rainy season was approaching, when no mountaineering is possible, I could not look on any dallying by the way, however pleasant, as anything but waste of precious time.

I awoke next morning at the usual hour, but when I went out not a soul took the trouble to move, with the exception of the Somál. One or two looked up and smiled mockingly; it was a preconcerted mutiny. Four of the Zanzibaris were preparing their breakfast at one of the camp-fires. Restraining my wrath, I walked up to them and repeated my order, "*Haya, funga mkeka!*" For answer they stared at me stupidly, as if they had not understood. Then I laid hold of Ali's rhinoceros-hide whip, and began deliberately to lay it about the shoulders of the tallest of the four, till he yelled for mercy. The effect was magical. Before he had received his dozen, every man was on his feet scrambling for his load, and by sunrise the caravan was once more on the march, the crestfallen culprit coming in for a running fire of " chaff" from his more fortunate comrades.

A steep path leads upward through the bush along the rugged southern slopes of Javia. About half-way up it ceases to ascend, and at a height of some three or four hundred feet above the plain keeps on along the mountain-side, till once more it bends downwards towards the Bura stream. On the right it is overhung by precipitous cliffs of gneiss, while to the left it affords an uninterrupted view southward across the plains. The rocks are intercalated with thick strata of snowy crystalline limestone, dipping gently towards the north.

After three hours we began to descend into the valley of the Bura, which, like the Mataté, rises in the Taita mountains and flows southward. Here we pitched our tents on a grassy bank, at the edge of the wooded strip which borders the stream, and which, though scarcely twenty yards broad, includes trees of considerable height. This being the last point before Taveta at which water is to be obtained, I was fain to content myself with the short day's march.

Unfortunately, next morning circumstances compelled us to be rather later in starting than I could have wished. Another man had fallen sick and had to be sent back, and as there were several other things to be seen to, the sun was already well up before we got under weigh. In the stifling noonday heat we made our way down along the grassy bank of the stream. The belt of wood running along the watercourse is as sharply defined from the grass of the hill-side as any European forest from the surrounding fields and meadows. Here nature and not man is the restricting force, the limit of the trees exactly corresponding with the limit to which the fertilising influence of the stream has power to penetrate the soil.

Continuing our way across the southern bush-covered spurs of Taita, we rounded the rocky dome of Muria and resumed the tedious march across the widest stretch of tree-steppe throughout east Central Africa. The steppes here assume the characteristics which they maintain almost all the way to Kilimanjaro—the typical characteristics with which we have been familiarised through various works of African travel. The vegetation consists mainly of grass and low shrubs, with a sprinkling of thorny species, and every hundred or two hundred paces a tree or bush of the mimosa type; but there are no sycamores, no euphorbias or other succulent forms, and no creepers such as are met with in the more easterly districts. If the grass were not so poor and scanty these western plains might almost be compared to savannahs; but, as it is a small-bladed variety, and grows in isolated tufts, between which the red laterite soil is plainly visible, they may more fittingly be likened to steppes. For the most part the trees stand very wide apart, but occasionally they occur in clumps and associated with shrubs, imparting to the landscape the so-called park-like aspect, which is always a bad sign for the fertility of the soil.

All the trees, no matter of what type, grow vertically upwards for some distance before giving off branches, and then they throw them out all together in a horizontal direction, so that the general outline resembles as nearly as possible an umbrella or mushroom. They are all flat-topped, as if the upper branches had been cut away. Thousands upon thousands of these singular-looking trees, all of the same shape and the same brownish-grey colour, are scattered over the mottled surface of the waste, with its alternating patches of red soil and faded grass, imparting to the landscape a dreary monotony that can be better imagined than described.

The traveller, seeking shelter from the sun as he journeys on, is surprised to find that it is the branches and not the leaves he has to thank for whatever shade the trees afford.

On examination the reason proves to be that the pinnæ of the leaves are all folded together along the stems. They thus avoid the direct rays of the sun and so are protected from excessive evaporation. At night, on the other hand, when there are extremely heavy dews, the pinnæ spread themselves out so as to absorb as much of the moisture as possible, work in which they are specially assisted by the peculiar arrangement of the branches. They are all protected against animals by an effectual armour of thorns.

Once or twice we came upon one of the shapeless baobabs or monkey-bread trees, looking, among the trim mimosæ, like a roofless ruin among a group of well-kept cottages. Yet the baobab possesses a certain fitness to its surroundings, and especially harmonises with the larger representatives of the East African fauna—the elephant, the rhinoceros, and the giraffe. It is a relic of those early periods of time in which nature delighted in more colossal forms of life than now, and since that epoch no part of Central Africa has been submerged by the ocean. Not the geological features only, but also the fauna and flora continually remind us that we are on a continent of the highest antiquity, considered relatively to other parts of the earth's surface.

Wonderful in the extreme is the manner in which nature has adjusted the balance between the animal and its environment in these vast plains. The boundless reaches of wooded grass land, over which, owing to the open distribution of the trees, the eye roams unhindered for miles, seem the fitting habitat of the large herbivorous species which there find food and shelter. At night the heavy dews afford them a plentiful supply of water, and they probably know of *ngurungas* as yet undiscovered by man. With the exception of vultures, no birds are to be met with on the steppes, and insects are only to be seen in the rainy season.

Among the big game, the rhinoceros and the giraffe
are of somewhat exclusive habits ; they graze singly or in
small groups of two or three of their own species. The
ostrich is frequently seen mingling with other animals, but
only the antelope and the zebra can be said to be truly
gregarious. I have sometimes counted as many as two hundred and thirty head in a single herd, but each herd is broken
up into small troops, and comprises different species. From
afar the animals eye the approaching caravan with heads
upraised in suspicion. As we draw nearer, the smaller species
are the first to take to flight, and are followed shortly after
by the lumbering Taro antelope and hartebeest, whose young
ones look extremely comical as they bound away at the heels
of their elders, taking apparently aimless leaps into the air.
The graceful eland and other large antelopes are the next to
make off, and last of all the zebra, which does not seem to
realise the situation until it looks up to find its companions
in full flight; then after pausing a moment as if to measure
the distance, it runs forward a few steps and stops once or
twice, until, hesitating no longer, it dashes off at full gallop
to join the rest, the males as they go giving tongue like a
pack of hounds in full cry. Of course, the animals always
run with the wind. If the spectator remains motionless
they will go on quietly feeding, so that it is not the sense of
danger from the presence of man that drives them away, but
merely his movements—the signs of the presence of some
unfamiliar living thing.

Every observer must be struck with the general similarity
in colour, and partly also in form, of the larger African
mammals to the prevailing colours and features of the
regions they frequent. At a distance it is scarcely possible to tell a hartebeest at rest from one of the reddish
ant-heaps which everywhere abound ; the long-legged, long-

necked giraffe might easily pass for a dead mimosa, the
rhinoceros for a fallen trunk, the grey-brown zebra for a
clump of grass or thorn-scrub. It is only their movements
that betray their real character. The insects too have their
"magic mantle" of invisibility. No wonder it is difficult
to make a collection when the butterflies and crickets look
like leaves and dry blades, the cicadæ like leaf-stems, the
spiders like thorns, the phasmodeæ like bare twigs, the beetles
like stones and bits of earth, the moths like mosses and
lichens.

But this mimicry is carried deeper than mere external
form. By appropriate movements or apparent lifelessness,
or by the selection of a suitable haunt, each animal strives
to act the part, or find the setting, appropriate to its disguise.
Everywhere there is protection, and against all manner of
foes, nature displaying a vast fertility of resource in imitative
devices, such as could only have been developed in a primeval
continent like Africa.

The country between Taita and Kilimanjaro consists of a
series of low undulations running generally N.E. and S.W.
Each of these took from an hour to an hour and a half to
cross, and no sooner had we reached the summit of one than
another swelled up before us, with its grey-brown grass, its
grey-brown mimosæ, and reddish laterite soil. At sunset a
strong, cold wind set in from the south-west, and we were
glad to camp by the wayside and seek the comfort of a
roaring fire.

The moon was in its third quarter, and did not rise till
midnight. By its light the march was continued, to the
accompaniment of the distant roaring of a couple of lions.
Gradually we found ourselves enveloped in a thick, cold fog,
through which the branches of the acacias loomed ghost-like

and weird. The silence was unbroken save when some stray animal, alarmed by our approach, rushed wildly past us and vanished in the mist. Towards morning we made a short halt in order to warm ourselves, and found that the thermometer registered 47° F. Almost immediately we pushed on again.

With the first rays of the morning sun a magnificent spectacle burst upon us. All of a sudden the veil of mist was rent apart, and to our admiring gaze was revealed the snowy peak of Kilimanjaro, grand, majestic, more than earthly in the silver light of the morning. It was from this same spot that in June 1887 I had my first view of the mountain. For weeks I had thought of almost nothing else—for many weary days I had been journeying to see it. Day after day I had vainly scanned the boundless steppes, impatiently longing for the moment when the courtier clouds would sweep aside and reveal the monarch they so jealously guarded. After all, the spectacle burst upon me almost as a revelation. A streak of silver in the south showed where Lake Jipé glittered in the sunlight beneath the frowning heights of cloud-capped Ugweno; to the right a belt of trees marked the course of the crystal Lumi and the forest fastness of Taveta. Behind the woods lay a stretch of gently rising plain, and on the further side of it, towering up to a height of nearly 20,000 feet, the mighty mountain mass of Kilimanjaro. Through the light mists and vapours that clung about its lower slopes the wooded hills of Jagga showed darkly here and there, and above the clouds—apparently suspended in mid-air—hung the snowy dome of Kibo, the mountain's highest peak. Its sister-peak, the Mawenzi, was hidden behind a mass of heavy cumulus cloud—all except the magnificent unbroken sweep of its north-eastern slope. It was a picture full of contrasts—here the swelling heat of the

F

Equator, the naked negro, and the palm-trees of Taveta—
yonder, arctic snow and ice, and an atmosphere of god-like
repose, where once was the angry turmoil of a fiery volcano.

After our present arduous journey across the steppes, the
sublime spectacle once more burst upon us with all the overwhelming charm of novelty. For the moment all our weari-
ness was forgotten. We could only stand and gaze, while
the caravan rolled past unheeded and unheeding.

At length, having recovered from our first feelings of awe
and wonder, we commenced there and then to discuss the
possibility of an ascent, and even at that distance to look out
for possible points of access. I was almost sure that, over
the snow-clad eastern rim of the Kibo crater, I could catch
a glimpse of the dark interior of its western wall, and my
thoughts turned longingly to the time when I should be able
to reach it, and see for myself what the old Kibo crater was
really like.

But this was no time for prolonged observations and
speculations, and we hurried on to overtake the caravan.
The last few miles were the worst of the whole journey,
and we had not a single drop of water. As we gradually
approached the depression in which lie the Lumi and Lake
Jipé the heat grew more and more unbearable. At one
point we obtained a brief but inspiring glimpse of the silvery
sheet of water as it glittered in the morning sun, but after
passing another of my old camping-grounds at the empty
ngurungas of Lanjora-mdogo, there lay an arduous march of
four hours between us and the forest of Taveta. Every man
did his weary best, but in the end I had to push ahead alone
with Herr Purtscheller and six porters carrying what was
simply indispensable. All the rest had sunk down exhausted
by the way, and did not reach camp till next day, after a
supply of water had been sent back to them. Threading

our way through the maze of winding paths, we entered at last the shady paradise of Taveta, and climbed the numerous fences erected by the inhabitants as a protection against the marauding Masai. Creeping under the low gateway at sunset, on September 17, we found ourselves installed beside the cool swift-flowing Lumi, in the cosy little thatched house of the old English camp, now in a much more ruinous condition than when I last saw it in 1887.

CAMP-SCENE—WA-TAITA SELLING FOOD.

CHAPTER III.

AT MANDARA'S AND MAREALE'S.

JAGGA WARRIORS.

GRATEFUL as the cool wells of Damascus to the Bedouin of the desert is the shady paradise of Taveta to the thirsty soul of the coast porter. And indeed a greater contrast than that between the open scorching plains and the bosky bowers of this dim forest retreat can scarcely be conceived. If it be true, as has been said, that Egypt is the gift of the Nile, then Taveta is the gift of the Lumi, which, rising on the eastern slopes of Mawenzi, flows southward towards Lake Jipé in a deep channel, and, spreading underground, serves to nourish a tropical forest of unsurpassed luxuriance. The forest proper occupies the middle course of the river, and covers an area about a mile and a quarter long by scarcely a mile broad. Higher up, owing

to the unfavourable conformation of the ground, it dwindles
to a mere strip; while below, where the river broadens out
into a marsh ere it is finally lost in Lake Jipé, the vegetation
degenerates into a tangled thicket. But what the forest
lacks in extent it makes up in luxuriance of growth, richness of species, and the great size attained by the trees.

The line of demarcation between the forest and the arid
plains outside is sharply defined by a remarkable concourse
of the larger representatives of the typical steppe flora,
mimosæ, sycamores, tamarinds, adansonias, and kigelias, which
here combine to form an open wood. Although, to all appearance, these trees stand beyond the limit of the subterranean
water-level, they are sufficiently within range of the river to
benefit by its fertilising influence. Of extraordinary forms
there is no lack. The kigelias especially, with their gigantic
ashen-coloured, sausage-like fruits, look as if they had come
straight from some fabled land of Cocagne.

Immediately within the charmed circle stands the forest
proper, with its wealth of cotton-trees, banyans, palms, lianas,
and various *Ficus* species. Tall straight stems, springing
up to a height of perhaps one hundred feet before they begin
to branch, are everywhere predominant, and between them
the graceful raphia palm finds room to spread its glossy
leaves, many of them as much as forty or fifty feet long. In
the immediate proximity of the snow-fed stream, which glides
peacefully along its almost level course between banks never
more than twenty-five feet apart, nature simply revels in
wanton profusion and luxuriance. A single banana stem
amply suffices as a bridge across the river.

Two species of monkeys and a lemur, with large and small
hornbills and pigeons, are the commonest representatives
of the animal world. During the day silence reigns, but
at night the bark of the monkey, the chirp of the cicadæ,

and the ghoulish howl of the hyena resound through the
pillared halls of the forest, and mingle with the dull thud
of drums, beaten by the natives to scare away the wild
swine from their plantations.

The forest is the home of the Wa-kwafi branch of the
Wa-taveta tribe. In appearance, customs, and language
the Wa-kwafi are more akin to the Masai than to the
Bantu races of the coast-region. Nor are they more closely
allied to their neighbours of Jagga, whom, however, they
resemble in the possession of land and the cultivation of
the soil, whereas the Masai are purely nomadic. The men
follow the Masai fashion in their manner of twisting the
hair into strings, and carry a long-bladed spear and sword
of Masai pattern. Like that of the Masai warrior, also, their
clothing consists mainly of a layer of grease mixed with red
clay. The women are not behind-hand. Like their Masai
sisters, they shave the head, and wear coils of iron wire as
ear, neck, arm, and leg ornaments, while their clothing is an
apron-like garment of bullock's hide.

Their beehive-shaped grass huts are not clustered together
to form villages, but, as in Jagga, are scattered in small groups
throughout the forest. Three or four stand together within
a common palisade, the opening through which is so small
that their domestic animals (goats, fat-tailed sheep, and
humped cows) cannot get outside. The fowls alone enjoy
unlimited freedom.

Two years previously we had not been able to procure
a single head of cattle for food throughout the whole
of Taveta. Through fear of the Masai, who are notorious
cattle-stealers, the natives had reduced their stock to
the smallest possible limits. Two or three times since then
they had been successful in repelling Masai attacks, and,
taking courage again, had allowed their flocks to multiply

Camp at Taveta.   A Market Scene.

to a considerable extent. Like their neighbours of Jagga, however, they dared not venture to drive their cattle to the open fields, but were content to feed them in their enclosures. Oxen were to be had for about thirty rupees a head, goats for about one-third that sum—in fact, prices were much the same as at the coast. The danger by which the natives are constantly threatened, of being robbed of the hard-won fruits of their toil, is the great check to production throughout the whole of East Africa; the stock-rearing of the Wa-kwafi is an illustration.

As will readily be understood, Taveta—this oasis in the desert, lying on the borders of the dreaded Masai country— is the point upon which converge all the caravan-routes from the coast between Rufu and Sabaki. Of these, the most important are the routes from Mombaza and Pangani, which at Taveta meet those running southwards by Kilimanjaro to the Victoria Nyanza, and eastwards along the foot of the same mountain to Ukamba, the Kenia region, and Samburu. No caravan passes through Taveta without a halt of at least several days.

Taveta has also recently become the headquarters of the various English and American sportsmen, who seem bent on the systematic destruction of all the big game in the rich preserves of the Kilimanjaro district. Like the Englishman Johnston in 1886, a young American has now located himself here, in a charming little camp, comprising a dwelling-house, several huts, and a garden; in the absence of the master, we were received by a couple of servants, who had been left behind on account of illness.

Every caravan arriving in Taveta from the coast has to pay a tribute (*hongo*) in cloth and beads before any business can be transacted. It was formerly the custom to levy this blackmail with a great show of force, the warriors appearing in a body and executing a wild war-dance, accompanied by demoniacal whoops and yells. This time, however, we were met only by some representative elders, and matters were arranged in a quiet, business-like fashion.

After their recent compulsory mortification of the flesh, my men now abandoned themselves to the unstinted enjoyment of the good things of life, and spent their time in eating, drinking, sleeping, dancing, and flirting with the native damsels. Their only work was making up the beads into strings of the regulation length current in the district, the fibres of the raphia palm being used for this purpose as a substitute for thread. The occupation is one which affords abundant opportunity for pilfering, and a strict watch had to be kept while the loads were unpacked and made up again.

With the new milk daily brought to us as a present by a fantastically dressed warrior—a regular Taveta " masher "— Herr Purtscheller every evening concocted a delicious soup, the like of which I have never tasted before or since. Other delicacies were the perch-like fish from the Lumi, and the *pombé*, a sort of beer made from the fermented juice of the raphia palm. Unfortunately, *pombé* is a drink of a highly intoxicating nature, and I am afraid my porters owed a good many floggings to their over-indulgence in it. Even Ali, the Mohammedan Somali, was apparently unable to resist the temptation, and one evening, with maudlin tears in his eyes, gave himself up to many wise reflections on the frailty of the flesh in general, and of his own in particular. Before quitting this subject I must not omit to mention that we found young maize cobs roasted an excellent substitute for bread.

But in spite of, or rather on account of, the many dainties it affords, Taveta is by no means a healthy place to live in, and it was not long before we ourselves, as well as a number of the porters, began to suffer from fever and pains in the abdomen, a circumstance which reminded me that in 1887 I lost a man here from malaria.

On the day after our arrival I had sent messengers to the Jagga state of Moji, the so-called "kingdom" of the notorious chief Mandara. In his domain the English Church Missionary Society and the German East African Company have established stations. The year before, Mandara had sent a fine tusk of ivory to the German Emperor in Berlin, and now lived in the expectation of receiving large presents in return, a hope which was likely soon to be realised, as they had arrived in Zanzibar before I left. Knowing I should be the first German to visit him since his token of goodwill had been despatched, I bade my messengers ask if he was prepared to give me a good reception, notwithstanding the fact that I could only afford a comparatively small offering. His answer was short and to the point. I should be welcome " provided only I brought *something.*"

Meantime my men had recovered from the blistered feet from which most of them had been suffering after their trying march across the burning steppes, and on the morning of September 21st we resumed our tramp. Crossing the placid Mfurro (Lumi is the Swahili, not the native name) by a bridge of banana-stems, we again entered the primeval forest. In a thousand tiny channels and rivulets the river meanders through the shady thicket, beneath leafy tunnels of creepers festooned from tree to tree. An hour and a half's pushing and squeezing through this labyrinth of green brought us out on the western steppes, which differ from those to the east of Taveta only in displaying volcanic instead of laterite rock-formations.

To the north and north-west spreads the broad base of Kilimanjaro, its towering crest for the time being concealed by huge masses of heavy cumulus clouds. Of the green belt of Jagga nothing is to be seen. The lower part of the mountain, like the plains, is on this side covered only with grey-brown grass. In the south-east of the mountain we see the parasitic cones of the Wajimba group, and farther to the west and south the mountains of Ugweno rise from the plains like massive walls enshrouded in floating mists. Their rugged outlines contrast strikingly with the more gentle slopes of Kilimanjaro, and point to gneiss as the prevailing rock.

Our path lies straight towards the southern termination of the Wajimba Hills, on the south-east side of Kilimanjaro, the ground rising almost imperceptibly after we leave the Lumi. As we approach the hills, low deciduous trees with glossy leaves encroach more and more on the mimosæ of the grass-lands, the grass becomes richer and closer, the vegetation fresher and more luxuriant. The prevailing tint is no longer a dull grey or brown, but a light greenish-yellow, the whole landscape somewhat resembling a gigantic orchard in autumn. The young green leaves are beginning to push out in all directions, and the grass is shooting rapidly under the influence of the tropical spring. In the dry beds of the water-courses the ground is seen to consist of layers of grey volcanic ashes mixed with fragments of basalt. No game is visible anywhere; before the guns of English and American hunters it has all withdrawn to more secluded haunts.

A march of three hours brought us to the end of the bare Makessa Hills, and to the north, on the slopes above us, stretched the dark-green girdle of Jagga, with its woods and fertile plantations. The summit of the mountain was still concealed by clouds. Almost without being conscious of it, we had gradually ascended to a considerable height, and below us, on our left, the plains rolled away southward, one illimitable expanse of brown, until they mingled with the distant blue of the mountains of Ugweno.

Towards midday we hailed with delight the appearance of a long narrow belt of trees winding downwards along the mountain-side, and proclaiming to the thirsty traveller the presence of a running stream. Soon we were cooling our parched throats with the deliciously cold water of the Habari. After continuing our way westward across the steppe for another hour, we camped by the side of a second tree-shaded water-course, the Himo. This river flows down from the mountain in a channel some thirty feet deep, and it was at the bottom of this gully that our tents were pitched. The temperature of the water was 65° F., that of the atmosphere 85°. It may easily be imagined, therefore, how deliciously refreshing it was to bathe in the stream, and what a delightful beverage seemed its pure, cool water after the tepid liquid mud of the *ngurungas* of the steppes.

As we sauntered along the narrow stony strip at the bottom of the ravine, noting the volcanic ashes and agglomerates in the steep banks above, or adding to our collection by catching some of the splendid butterflies which were hovering about, we were suddenly hailed from the opposite side, and, looking up, were profoundly astonished to see a European, accompanied by several natives carrying a quantity of baggage. In a few seconds we were shaking hands with each other, the stranger having crossed the stream on the back of one of his servants. He proved to be one of the English missionaries from Moji, on his way to Taveta to fetch a fresh convert. Over the tea-table we had a pleasant chat, in the course of which I learned that in Moji, besides his colleague and the American naturalist Dr. Abbott, I might expect to meet Mr. Chanler, the owner of the charming camp at Taveta. After tea, the missionary proceeded on his way towards the Habari, where he intended to spend the night. The fact that he was going to bring his convert from Taveta is significant, since it shows that in Jagga, as at other mission stations in East Africa, Christianity is not generally in favour among the natives. In the large coast station at Frere-town, where the Gospel has been preached since the days of Rebmann in 1847, the converts are all either freed or bought slaves and their descendants, and in Moji they are the same, or else some of the more speculative youths from Taveta.

Our next day's march, through the grass and bush tracts along the southern base of the mountain, proved exceedingly monotonous and tiresome. The summit was enveloped in mist and clouds, as on the day before; but the plains of Kahé to the south, bounded ·by a ring of mountains—the Arusha range to the west, that of Ugweno to the east—looked all the clearer by contrast. A host of streams, their courses marked by long, winding belts of trees, flow south-wards. From time to time great clouds of dust are seen to rise in the distance, showing where herds of game are frisking together or have taken to flight on the approach of danger, real or imaginary. Sometimes the dust is caught up in a whirlwind and carried along for some distance, to vanish at last into nothingness on the flat brown plains. Always changing and always beautiful are the wonderful cloud-shadows, as they flit unceasingly across the landscape, imparting to it that magical charm of motion so painfully absent on the cloudless eastern steppes.

The ground we traverse rises and falls with the ridges lying between the ravines which furrow the flanks of the mountain. We are still in the region of parasitic cones; I counted as many as fourteen before beginning the ascent towards Moji. Their sides are seamed by numerous dry rivulets, which we have to cross, as our path keeps on almost due west.

The men walked with a will, having the prospect of Moji ahead, with its promise of rest and plenty. Early in the afternoon we reached, on the south side of the mountain, the foot of the great rib, on whose upper portion the little state of Moji is situated. Here we quitted the path, which continues westward along th● base of Kilimanjaro, and struck north by a road leading upwards towards the cultivated terrace of Jagga. Mountain-climbing is not much in the way of the Zanzibari porter, accustomed as he is to level ground, and accordingly our rate of progress was slow.

As we continue to rise, the bush gradually grows more and more dense, according as the trees of the steppes disappear, and the leafy shrubs and bushes increase. Characteristic mountain trees begin to appear along with tall reeds and grasses. The ground is full of holes, caused by Cape ant-eaters burrowing for the termites or white-ants. Soon the channels of the brooks on either side become deeper, and isolated huts and banana plantations dot the slopes, while the heat is tempered by a refreshing breeze from the plains. Here we are in the region of the mountain rains, and the vegetation suffers from no prolonged periods of drought, as its character and appearance plainly show. Everywhere the ground is clad with verdure, and the young shoots are springing rapidly.

Suddenly we found ourselves before a barricaded gateway, which barred our further progress. On the barricades being withdrawn we squeezed ourselves through, and found ourselves on one side of a steep ravine, while on the other we beheld a collection of conical huts—the residence of Mandara. My goal for the present, however, lay farther up the mountain, where on the heights waved a solitary Union Jack, and beyond it the flags of Germany and America.

With the usual salute of a volley from our guns, we made our entry into Moji. An immediate response re-echoed on all sides, and within five minutes the whole "kingdom" knew that a white man's caravan, including sixty-five porters, had arrived. After a stiff climb upwards, through a series of tiny valleys, carefully tilled and planted, we reached the English Mission station, where we were most hospitably entertained by Mr. Morris, who received us with open arms. Positively, there was bread on the table, an unwonted luxury which quite took our breath away!

Meanwhile my men climbed upwards another five hundred feet to the station of the German East African Company. When we ourselves followed some time later, we came upon a scene of the greatest bustle and animation. The American sportsman, Mr. Chanler, had arrived shortly before us with his followers, so that there were now about two hundred men encamped at this spot. Boisterous greetings were exchanged between many of the porters of the two caravans, who recognised old acquaintances. Among Mr. Chanler's people I myself observed two who had been with me on the expedition of 1887.

The tiny wooden building which forms the station has been kept in good repair by Dr. Abbott, who entered into possession on the removal of the German East African Company. The decoration of the interior has been carried out in the national colours, black, white, and red, and the earnest face of the Emperor Wilhelm II. looks down from the place of honour on the wall. In the evening there were no fewer than seven Europeans assembled round Dr. Abbott's hospitable board, a gathering as yet unprecedented, I fancy, in the annals of Kilimanjaro.

Early next morning I looked out the presents intended for Mandara, donned a spick and span new suit, and got my Somál smartened up for a state visit to the self-important chief. With the exception of carefully concealed revolvers, we carried no weapons, lest they should excite the old gentleman's insatiable cupidity. My two headmen, arrayed in spotless white tunics, were of course included in the party.

Passing the English Mission with a hasty greeting to Mr. Morris, whom I found busy in the exercise of the healing art among a number of natives, we descended the mountain by a path leading downwards along numerous steep slopes and rushing streams. At length we reached a fairly large quadrangular dwelling, one of the numerous country-seats of his swarthy Majesty. At a respectful distance from the closed door squatted a group of about a dozen " courtiers," conversing in whispers, lest they should disturb the sleeping monarch. The large numbers of Swahili who formerly used to hang about the court, and to whose skill in building Mandara owes several of the dwellings he has had erected in the coast style, have now almost entirely disappeared.

Our loud demands for admission were received with ex-pressions of horror on the part of the terrified guard. They had the desired effect, however, for presently a couple of pretty young women slipped out at the door, and we were invited by a voice from the interior to come in (*karibu*). In the windowless room, into which the daylight streamed through the open doorway, while a fire burning in the midst cast red reflections over walls and ceiling, Mandara was half lying, half sitting on his Swahili bedstead (*kitanda*). Near him squatted four of his older wives and a half-grown son, whose position, owing to the despotic jealousy of his father, is little better than that of a menial. The hut was divided

across the middle by a gaudy screen, against which ticked a
large clock. With the exception of an old chair, there was
no other furniture. This venerable relic I dragged towards
Mandara's bedside, after which we shook hands. He excused
himself for not rising on the ground that he was suffering
from severe pains in the legs. Spite of his fine Swahili shirt
the old warrior looked rather shabby, but his strongly-marked
swarthy face betrays an intelligence far superior to that of
the average negro, though from the curving nose and flashing
eye (Mandara has but one) it borrows something of a ferocious
expression. We eyed each other critically for some moments,
and I flattered myself he seemed even more favourably impressed with my appearance than I was with his.

After the usual formal salutations and inquiries we proceeded to business. I informed the chief of my intention to
try to ascend the mountain, and he promised me his assistance
with all apparent readiness. But while I spoke, his mind was
evidently far from the subject, and his eye wandered rest-
lessly towards the packages in the background. At last
his impatient curiosity quite got the better of him, and he
asked me bluntly what I had brought with me. The packages
were brought forward and unwrapped, and one after another
I produced pieces of red and blue cloth, silk coverlets, a
" golden diadem set with precious stones," a small telephone,
several masks with horrible grimaces, a suit of European
clothing, steel files and knives, a quantity of powder, some
medicines, and a number of other articles. In grandiloquent
language my first headman expatiated on the unexampled
virtues of the various gifts, and evoked from the recipient a
succession of gratified whistles. When my treasures were
exhausted Mandara asked me to give him a demonstration
with the telephone. Taking the one end in my hand I stepped
outside the door, and whispered along the wire that there

was nothing I appreciated so much as a good juicy piece of roast meat. "You have brought me a number of very fine things from Uleia (Europe)," returned the chief, "and are my honoured friend. But I still want some gin and a good double-barrelled rifle, and above all a few cannon." For these trifling extras I was obliged to refer him to the coming Imperial offering; upon which he seemed quite satisfied, and we parted the best of friends. Shortly after our return he sent us, as a mark of favour, a fine young cow, though it must be added that it was accompanied with a number of begging requests for whisky, cigars, revolver-cartridges, lead pencils, lacing shoes, a hat, and so forth.

I arrived at the station just in time to catch a splendid view of the grand volcanic cone of Mount Meru as it broke through the haze of the morning in the far west. Going on with my observations as usual, I was much hindered and annoyed by the incessant and shameless begging of a number of natives, who crowded about me, arrayed, to their extreme satisfaction, in nondescript garments of red flannel. Suddenly one of them extended his filthy paw, at the same time pronouncing the German words, "*Guten Tag.*" It turned out that they were the envoys Mandara had sent to Berlin, and who were now desirous of airing their European acquirements in the presence of the right man. Unfortunately their contact with civilisation has not improved them. Since their return to Jagga they do nothing but give themselves airs, and tyrannically lord it over those they are pleased to consider their inferiors. They absolutely refuse to work, and spend their time strutting about in their dirty flannels, worrying the life out of the missionaries and Dr. Abbott with their perpetual begging.

Not being very successful with me, one of them, with a broad grin, laid hands on a matchbox of Dr. Abbott's which

G

was lying on the table. Dr. Abbott did not seem to see the little joke, however, and seizing the offender by the arm soundly boxed his ears. Thereupon the whole pack fled howling and vowing vengeance to Mandara. The vengeance followed swift and sure. Mandara had not been on friendly terms with Dr. Abbott for some time, the latter having met the chief's continual demands for more plunder with a persistent negative. Accordingly, towards midday, a body of warriors appeared on the scene, drove away the women who had come to sell food, and, proceeding up the mountain, turned off our water-supply. At the same time Mandara sent me a special message to the effect that it was Dr. Abbott whom he wanted to punish, not me. It was very kind of him to say so, no doubt, but it wouldn't bring food and water to my men any more than to the other occupants of the station.

In the afternoon the men began to grumble loudly, and Dr. Abbott set off to see what he could do to mollify the offended chief. Meanwhile I passed the time pleasantly with Mr. Chanler, pacing the turf behind the house, and listening to his account of his recent hunting expedition on the plains to the north of Kilimanjaro. There the parasitic cones that stud the south side of the mountain are represented by a belt of marsh and small ponds, the neighbourhood of which perfectly swarms with game. No caravans visit it; only occasionally it is crossed by wandering hordes of Masai, to whom the narrow uninhabited forest zone on the mountain-side above affords a suitable site for their kraals, while their cattle find fresh pasture on the grassy slopes. Our own observations later on went to confirm Mr. Chanler's remarks.

Dr. Abbott returned towards evening. His tramp to Mandara's had proved of no avail, for the irate monarch had refused to see him. We had therefore to fall back on the

Doctor for stores, and the men had to fetch water from the nearest brook. Fortunately the Doctor was provisioned for several weeks ahead.

My troubles were all forgotten, however, when towards sunset the whole mountain for the first time unveiled itself from head to foot. The resemblance which Kilimanjaro bears to Etna, owing to its long, gradual slope upwards, and apart, of course, from its double peak, is not so apparent from Moji, because here Kibo occupies the foreground and rises more abruptly than it does from Marangu. Mawenzi is seen farther back to the north-east, while the foot of the Kibo peak lies in a straight line about thirteen miles from Moji. From Moji, which lies at a height of 4600 feet above the sea, to the base of Kibo at 14,400 feet, the ground rises at the rate of one foot in seven. From the base to the summit the ascent is very much more rapid.

A more sublime spectacle could not be imagined than that on which we gazed entranced, as, that evening, the clouds parted and the mountain stood revealed in all its proud serenity. The south-west side of the great ice-dome blushed red in the splendour of the setting sun, while farther to the east the snows of the summit lay in deep-blue shadow. Here and there the glistening, mysterious mantle was pierced by jagged points of dark-brown rock, as spots fleck the ermine of a king. And surely never monarch wore his royal robes more royally than this monarch of African mountains, Kilimanjaro. His foot rests on a carpet of velvety turf, and through the dark-green forest the steps of his throne reach downward to the earth, where man stands awestruck before the glory of his majesty. Art may have colours rich enough to fix one moment of this dazzling splendour, but neither brush nor pen can portray the unceasing play of colour—the wondrous purples of the summit deepening as in the Alpine afterglow;

the dull greens of the forest and the sepia shadows in the
ravines and hollows, growing ever darker as evening steals
on apace; and last, the gradual fading away of all, as the
sun sets, and over everything spreads the grey cloud-curtain
of the night. It is not a picture, but a pageant—a king
goes to his rest.

The unobstructed view of the mountain which we thus
obtained decided us not to attempt the ascent from this
more rugged and difficult side. We therefore resolved to
proceed as soon as possible to Marangu, whence in 1887 I
had ascended to the plateau at the saddle without encoun-
tering any obstacles worth mentioning.

Next morning, after a blowy night, during which the
minimum temperature was 43° F., I went down to Mandara's
accompanied by Herr Purtscheller and the Somâl, in order to
try to induce the chief to restore our water-supply and let
the women carry on the market as usual. I took with me
a bottle of whisky, as being the one thing he had all along
especially demanded. Inside his dusky dwelling we found
the irate sovereign on his couch with two of his youngest
wives. On my appearance one of them went away, but the
other remained where she was. I had no objections to make
to this breach of court etiquette; I thought, indeed, that
a good deal might be gained by a little wifely intercession.
Nor was I disappointed. I began by trying to soothe Mandara's injured feelings by a liberal application of flattery and
"soft sawder;" to this he grunted an unintelligible reply;
but when I went on to appeal to the lady of his heart for
confirmation of my extravagant compliments, I saw at once
that I was on the way to victory, and the production of the
whisky-bottle finally carried the day. From his bed he immediately gave orders that everything should be as I wished,
and only regretted that he could not leave the house to

see things put to rights himself. To his polite speeches I returned a grateful "*Inshallah*," which may just as easily be translated "Praise be to God" as "So God wills."

I was much struck during the conversation to find that when Mandara talks under the influence of strong excitement he has a pronounced lisp. His expression seemed even more fierce and cunning than on the day before. On the whole, I was far from favourably impressed by him, and the opinion I formed was shared by my companion, and by Dr. Abbott, Mr. Chanler, and the missionaries, who ought to know him best. If the earlier accounts of this native chief are true and not biassed, then all I can say is, that in these latter days he has altered very much for the worse. The arrogance of the petty tyrant is only surpassed by his greed and covetousness; and there is no doubt that these vices have been fostered and increased by the inordinate consideration he has always been accustomed to receive at the hands of Europeans. Mandara has for long been visited by Swahili caravans because he had always a supply of slaves at his disposal. As we saw later on, he has turned the whole of north-western Ugweno into a howling wilderness through his wars and slave-raids, and in all the Jagga outbreaks he was always the firebrand.

In the wake of the Swahili came the Europeans, and Mandara was clever enough to perceive what a mine of wealth the latter might prove to him, and did his best to keep them in his territory as long as possible; in this way it has come about that this paltry chief has played a somewhat important part in the history of the exploration of Kilimanjaro. Nevertheless, as when he robbed the unarmed missionary, New, his true nature from time to time became too strong for his customary politic amiability. Then the terms he made, on ceding his kingly rights, first with General

Matthews, and again a few weeks later with the representatives of the German East African Company, who paid him
better, show clearly enough his reasons for the conclusion of
a treaty granting to a European Power a protectorate over
his dominions. True, the majority of such treaties have not
been concluded without some ulterior motive on the part of
the natives, but on that very account it was mistaken policy to
bring a body of the marauding Mandara's relatives to Berlin,
and there present them to the Emperor as "envoys of the
Sultan of Jagga." These indiscriminating savages were turned
loose in the capital for a few days in order that they might feast
their eyes on all the wonders of European civilisation, and
become impressed with the idea of the greatness of Germany,
only to return to their native land not one whit the wiser
for all they had seen. How they behave themselves since
they have once more become established there has already
been described. The way to impress natives with our greatness and our power is not to take them out of Africa to show
them Germany, but to bring Germany to them in their native
land, as it were, and in some form intelligible to their crude
understanding. It is almost a certainty that the gifts sent
by the Emperor will only serve to increase Mandara's arrogant
pretensions. In the case of powerful native sovereigns, such
as those of Uganda, Lunda, and elsewhere, such favours may
have a good and far-reaching effect; but with a small potentate
like Mandara, whose dominions have an area of not more
than thirty square miles, and whose subjects number about
three thousand, they only do harm. Let us hope that the
career of the infirm and aged chief of Jagga is almost run.
In the western states he has been ousted by the brave and
energetic Sinna of Kiboso, and in the east he is threatened by
a second powerful rival, the young and honourable Mareale,
chief of Marangu.

I returned to the station by a roundabout way, in order to have a better opportunity of seeing the natives at work in the fields. Their methods are much the same as those in vogue at Marangu. On every ridge and hollow, and along the banks of every stream, men, women, and children alike were busy with hoe and mattock preparing the ground for the sowing of maize, millet, and beans, and the planting of tobacco, bananas, and sugar-cane, at the commencement of the approaching wet season. With the utmost care the plantations are cleared of all old roots and stumps, and the artificial irrigation channels thoroughly repaired where necessary. Outside the clearings the Mkindu palm (*Phœnix*) flourishes luxuriantly. It is the only species of palm indigenous to the region. As Kilimanjaro is plentifully supplied with water throughout the year, the tilling of the soil is not confined to the rainy season only. Moreover, any deficiency of moisture that may here and there exist is amply remedied by the irrigation channels, and plants such as the banana and sugar-cane, which ripen irrespective of the dry season, are cultivated all the year round. Tobacco, pulse, and cereals ripen only in the dry season, however, and they must therefore be sown out during the rains.

The art of constructing these irrigation channels, which keep the springing seed supplied with moisture during sowing-time, is among the most wonderful to be found among tribes like the Wa-jagga, in a comparatively backward stage of civilisation. As the channels of the streams grow deeper and deeper in their course downhill, it becomes more and more impossible for the fields that occupy the upper slopes of the valleys to derive any benefit from the flowing water. To remedy this evil, canals or trenches are dug along these uplying fields, and are connected with the upper course of the streams at points lying at the desired level, the water being thus more evenly distributed. The decision of quarrels arising out of the joint-proprietorship of these irrigation channels is one of the weightiest duties of the chief. Sometimes it happens in the dry season that the water is all carried off by the canals and the stream itself is exhausted before it reaches the plains, to be a fruitful source of disappointment to the weary traveller, who approaches it hoping to find the wherewithal to slake his thirst.

The fable that in tropical lands the natives have nothing to do but sit under the trees and let the ripe fruits drop into their mouths could not have originated in Jagga. The field-labourer in Europe wins his daily bread easily compared with the less fortunate Jagga negroes.

In the afternoon I bought some small capes made of hyrax skins, of a style formerly much in vogue, and two long spears of the most modern narrow-bladed pattern, which were quite works of art. Fashion varies even in Wa-jagga spears. When I was here in 1887, spears with long broad blades were all the rage; now they are all narrow and with blunt points. The long heavy spears generally spoken of as characteristic of Jagga only came in with the introduction of European iron wire. Up to that time the spears were universally small and short, like those still in use in the outlying districts of Kilimanjaro (Rombo, Useri, Majamé, &c.). The price of a large spear is a percussion-gun, and only in exceptional instances are other goods taken in exchange.

While I was haggling over my bargain, news was brought that once more our stream was in full flow. Hard upon the heels of the messenger came another from Mandara to ask whether we considered the water worth one bottle of brandy or two, brandy being the only remedy for the pains in his legs. We were of opinion that some glass beads would be equally efficacious, and sent a few accordingly. The

Berlin "envoys" had not ventured to put in an appearance again since Abbott's rough-and-ready lesson in discipline.

On the evening of the 24th September we made our preparations for the march to Marangu on the following morning, and at night we had a small adventure with a leopard which had been making tracks for the hen-house. Before the sun had risen over Mawenzi we were on the march once more, our faces towards the east, with a parting promise from Dr. Abbott that he would soon pay us a visit in Marangu.

The path from Moji to Marangu runs east through the Jagga states of Kirúa and Kilema at a height of about 4600 feet. Between Moji and Kirúa runs a deep ravine; between Kirúa and Kilema is the long ridge of Lasso, which extends from Mawenzi all the way to the plains; between Kilema and Marangu there is only the narrow Mué stream. On our left rise the cloudy heights of Kilimanjaro; on the right, below us, stretches the broad brown expanse of Kahé.

For the first two hours we traversed the undulating grounds of upper Moji, which are not so deeply furrowed by streams as the region below. Then, quitting the fields and plantations, we struck a narrow bridle-path, and began to descend the steep walls of the ravine between Moji and Kirúa, at the bottom of which foamed and tumbled the Nganga rivulet. The wreaths of rising mist, the clumps of bushes, the precipitous slopes of Kirúa, on which from time to time, as the mist for a moment lifted, we could distinguish broad patches of forest—these, with the noisy torrent and the temperature of 60° F., strongly recalled scenes in the Harz or Tyrol.

We had not proceeded far when we were met by a long procession of female slaves belonging to the chief of Kirúa, on their way to market in Moji with a quantity of beans. Our guide, a worthy representative of his chief, Mandara, profited by the delay occasioned by the meeting to make off with his advance-money (eight arm-lengths [*] of white cloth) under cover of the mist, leaving us to find our way to Mareale's as best we might. By this time the mist had become a fine drizzle, and the steep pathway was so slippery as to be positively dangerous. The porters, hampered with their heavy loads, were constantly slipping and sliding; scarcely one of them escaped a fall. At length we reached the stream, already much swollen with the rain, and wading across, began the breakneck ascent towards Kirúa. Here the state of the path was worse than ever, and the men had a terribly hard time of it. At one place I myself had a nasty fall, and broke a thermometer, which unfortunately could not be replaced.

Once at the top, we had to wait a considerable time before the whole caravan had straggled in. Among the surrounding vegetation I noticed wild mignonette, several species of ferns, and a number of small dracænas. Before us stretched the cultivated fields of Kirúa, bananas, as in Moji, occupying the higher ridges, yams and sweet potatoes the hollows and valleys. The same system of irrigation by means of artificial channels is also practised, and is greatly facilitated by the unusual number of streams which intersect the district. As a rule, the huts and gardens of the inhabitants are enclosed by well-kept hedges. As we passed along, the natives at work in the fields greeted us with polite and friendly salutations, contrasting strongly with the forward manners of the spoiled people of Moji.

Kidungadi, the chief of Kirúa, lives at some distance down the mountain. Leaving his dwelling on the right, we made our way slowly upwards along the cultivated slopes to the

---

[*] Arm-length = English cubit, or the length from the elbow to the forefinger, usually reckoned at 18 inches.—*Tr.*

ridge-like hill of Lasso, the crest of which was reached at midday. A charming prospect met our eyes. Before and beneath us, over an extent of many square miles, the whole country was one vast banana grove, sloping gently downwards from the forest zone to the plains, and bounded on the east by the hills of Msai and Rombo. It is divided into the states of Kilema, Marangu, Mamba, Mwika, and Msai, the boundaries of which are marked by various streams and rivulets. The only conspicuous break in all the soft expanse of green is a brick-red parasitic cone, near the summit of which Fumbo, chief of Kilema, has planted his snug little village. Farther east, in Marangu, the large new residence of Mareale is visible through the glass, its white flag fluttering in the breeze.

Having crossed the Mué, we continued our way for an hour under the shady bananas of Kilema and entered the domain of Mareale, after fording the river Ngona a short way above a point where it forms a fine waterfall, the sound of which was distinctly audible, though the fall itself was unseen.

In order to salute my old friend worthily, all the men were ordered to have their guns in readiness for a volley, and two of the Somál were sent ahead to announce our arrival. As I walked along my blood tingled with pleasurable excitement. For the first time I seemed to realise how much I had grown to love this little spot of earth in the pleasant days I had spent among its hospitable people two years before. I was familiar with its every hut—in every passer-by I recognised an old acquaintance. Soon we were met by messengers from Mareale, who in the name of their chief bade us heartily welcome. Then amid a volley from a hundred guns (the contents of one of which, unfortunately, was by accident lodged in my faithful Ahmed's shoulder), we took possession of a meadow surrounded by trees, and pitched our camp. My old camping-ground was already occupied by the huts of a Swahili caravan.

We had just had time to erect the tents, when the shouting of the natives announced the approach of Mareale and his small escort. His proud carriage and stately walk proclaim him at once the chief of the realm. With kindling eyes and a joyful smile of greeting he stepped forward to meet me. "*Yambo, yambo, Dakta Maya, yambo sana; umefika sasa, uhalli gani?*" ("Welcome, welcome, Dr. Meyer; you are most heartily welcome. So you have come at last! How are you?") was his friendly salutation. We shook hands long and heartily, after which I gave him a brief account of my journey thither and of my plans for the future. " I am so glad to hear what you tell me," he said. " You will have to be with us some time, and I hope we shall see a great deal of each other. But you must be tired; I shall leave you now to rest. To-morrow you must come and see my new house." I promised readily, and amid renewed hand-shakings and *Yambo sanas* he took his departure. It was a very different reception to that we had met with at Mandara's.

In the few minutes he had been in camp, Mareale had quite won the hearts of Herr Purtscheller and all my men, and, spite of the fatigues of the day, they entered heartily into the festivities consequent on the killing of the goat of welcome. And they had every need of a good feast, for they had to spend the night without shelter, and were thoroughly drenched by heavy torrents of rain. The first thing in the morning, therefore, they set to work to build huts, and soon our camping-ground was dotted with some fourteen little rustic habitations, one for each mess, made from the huge bundles of banana leaves that had been brought to the spot by the native women. A neat and

busy little village had sprung from the ground as if by magic. In the middle, a large space under a shady tree was reserved for the market-place, and across that side of the field occupied by the tents of the Europeans and Somál a fence was made, dividing their quarters from those of the men.

While all this was being done, Herr Purtscheller and I were busy selecting our presents for Mareale. It is almost ludicrous to think of the number of things a man must be able to do, be, and comprehend before he can be the successful lea⌐⌐r of an African scientific expedition; and it is not less wonderful what dormant faculties and qualities are awakened and developed by the exigencies of the explorer's life, the existence of which would never have been suspected under ordinary conditions. That he must be geologist, zoologist, botanist, ethnologist and meteorologist; astronomer, photographer and cartographer; artist, engineer, sportsman and physician; diplomatist, strategist and political economist; merchant, gunmaker, carpenter, tailor, shoemaker, blacksmith, cook, and a hundred other things, is, of course, understood; but I never dreamt I should have to fit together a sewing-machine, and give lessons in working it, until I found it out in making up that present for Mareale.

As soon as the machine was in working order we packed our miscellaneous assortment of cloth, beads, watches, revolvers, silk coverlets, bracelets, files, tea, concertinas, false-faces, bells, powder, shot and tobacco pipes, and set out to return Mareale's call. What formerly had been an open space in front of his very unpretending hut was now enclosed by a castellated stone wall about twelve feet high, with a single low and narrow opening. Within the court so formed stood the huts of Mareale's wives and children, and beside them a handsome house in the coast style, with a gable roof. The

interior was divided into several apartments, comfortably furnished as sitting and bed rooms, partly with Indian and partly
with European furniture. The only objection was that owing
to the entire absence of windows all the rooms were pitch dark,
what light there was being supplied by a smoky fire in the
middle of the floor. The house had been built for Mareale by
Swahili, whose labour was paid out of the slaves and cattle
taken by the chief in a recent war with Rombo, one of the
larger Jagga states.

With his usual amiability Mareale came out to receive us.
He was dressed in a beautiful Arab burnous, worn over a
Swahili tunic, and his head was covered with a crimson
turban. Banana beer was immediately produced, and after
pledging each other repeatedly out of the same gourd, we
displayed our presents. These were admired to our heart's
content; but the delight reached its climax when I showed
my skill with the sewing-machine. "I like this needle-
drum (*ngoma ma shindano*) better than my house and all its
belongings put together," exclaimed the chief. "Mandara
has a Swahili house as well as I have; but nobody has
anything like this in the whole of Jagga," and as a partial
proof of the sincerity of his gratification he at once ordered
a fine fat cow to be sent to our camp.

Like women everywhere, his wives and female slaves
(*surias*), who had been looking on with eager curiosity, were
mostly taken up with the ornaments. In 1887 Mareale's
chief wife was a daughter of Mandara's, whom he had bought
from her father for a hundred oxen, and who ruled the roost
more by reason of her birth than of her beauty. Now the
reigning favourite was a nice-looking young girl of sixteen.
But the former sultanas were all present, and were immensely
flattered to find that I recognised them again. I showed
them the photograph I had of them, and vainly endeavoured

to make them understand its meaning. Mareale alone recognised his likeness, and greeted it with a jubilant *mimi menyewe* ("me! me!"), another proof of his remarkable intelligence for a negro, he being the only one I ever met who seemed capable of even faintly grasping the true nature of a photograph.

Everything about the house and in the fields bore the stamp of the wise, personal superintendence of the master, and the loving respect with which he was universally looked up to by his subjects showed that as a ruler Mareale was both firm and just. There was nothing like this in Moji.

On the turf before the entrance to the court some twenty or more armed men lay, squatted, or stood, according to the whim of the moment. They were partly warriors on duty; partly Masai elders (*el morūa*) who had been exchanging cattle for iron wire; partly envoys from the neighbouring states of Rombo and Useri, with presents for the chief of Marangu. The warriors were not in full war array, the feather headdress, kidskin mantle, and leg ornaments being absent; but they were still the most conspicuous figures in the group, with their splendid spears and freshly-greased hair, which they wear in a mop of twisted tails falling both over the forehead and down the neck. The long wooden ear-stretcher, and the large round wooden plug pushed through the lobe of the ear, they wear in common with the people of Rombo and Useri, and, as is the custom throughout the whole of Jagga, the upper incisors are filed to a point, and the two middle lower ones broken out altogether. The conversation is loud rather than copious. Sometimes it takes the form of a harangue, the speaker standing up and emphasising his words with his short club, while his audience squat around at his feet, and never once interrupt the flowing periods. Sometimes it takes the form of an argument

between two, and again the audience is silently attentive.
The points are driven home with the exclamation, "*Somiriali!*" which, being interpreted, means, "By the chief
Mareale!"—*So* meaning *chief.* In language and gesture
they are nearly all born orators, and those who are not,
mostly acquire the art through constantly listening to so
much public speaking.

The group of idlers squatting round are not unworthy of
notice, if only for the peculiar attitude they assume. With
their knees drawn up to their chin, and their noses buried in
their garments, which they huddle about them for the sake of
greater warmth, they look like so many Peruvian mummies.
The arms and hands being wrapped up in the folds, cannot
be used for gesticulation; hence they endeavour to supply
its place by the most extraordinary facial contortions and
grimaces. The tongue, and not the forefinger, is used to
point with.

Upon the whole, the natives of Marangu are the most
lively in the group. The strangers from Rombo and Useri,
whose lives have not fallen in quite such pleasant places, are
the most taciturn.

As with Useri, Mareale also maintains friendly relations
with the larger western states of Jagga—Uru-Salika, Majamé,
and Moji—Mandara being at once his father-in-law and
brother-in-law. At the same time he has not joined the
league formed by the chiefs of these states and their depend-
encies against Sinna of Kiboso. In small semi-barbaric states,
peace and war alike depend purely on the will and self-
interest of the ruling despot. In Jagga, which includes the
whole of the inhabited and cultivated zone on the southern
and eastern flanks of Kilimanjaro, there are over twenty
such states, and the chiefs in one district are constantly
leaguing themselves together to make war upon those of

another. By war, of course, is not to be understood pitched battles and organised fighting. As a general rule the aim of the assailants is to make a surprise raid upon the enemy's territory, and take away the inhabitants as slaves. The huts are plundered and burned down, and the cattle driven off as the most valuable part of the spoil, but no deliberate injury is done to the plantations.

Surprises of this kind are not frequent, however. The system of placing guards is very well understood, and any vulnerable points along the boundary lines are fortified by deep trenches. On the first approach of danger the alarm is at once given, whereupon the defenders immediately muster, if they can, in superior numbers to the invaders; when this occurs the enemy discreetly withdraws. If the defenders are not strong enough to resist, they betake themselves to the woods and lie in hiding till the danger has passed over. There is very seldom any bloodshed.

After a successful fray, the victors return home rejoicing, and await the time when the vanquished shall seek revenge. If no revenge is attempted, then the conqueror returns to the attack again and again until there is nothing left worth carrying away, or until such time as the conquered are content to purchase peace by the payment of so much tribute. Rombo had come to terms with Mareale in the former way, Mamba in the latter.

When two adjoining states are at war with each other all communication with the states beyond is completely cut off. Neutral parties must either take the path running along the east and south sides of Kilimanjaro at the base of the mountain, or the more difficult track above the forest zone, with which every state in Jagga is connected by a separate by-path. I and my men have at different times been obliged to make use of both.

H

The total extent of Jagga is about five hundred square miles. Proceeding from east to west, the names of the various states and their approximate populations are as follows :—

Useri 6000	Kirúa 1000	Kombo. . . . 500
Rombo 5000	Moji 3000	Kindi and Moika 500
Mwika 500	Pokomo . . . 1000	Naruma . . . 500
Msai 500	Uru-Salika . . 3000	Majamé . . . 8000
Mamba 500	Uru-Salue . . . 2000	Shira 1000
Marangu . . . 3000	Kiboso (Lam-	Kibonoto . . . 1000
Kilema . . . 2000	bungu) . . . 6000	Wroni 1000

Total, 46,000.

The huts are of the familiar bee-hive shape. Every household has its own little group of two or three, which, together with a granary, occupy a small court surrounded by a stout palisade, the whole lying snugly ensconced in the midst of the owner's banana plantation. The only resemblance to a house, in the usual sense, is Mareale's own abode. After marriage, the sons as a rule continue to live in the same hut with their father, as long as there is room for the gradually increasing family. Allowing an average of ten persons, including slaves and grandparents, to each dwelling, the number of huts in Jagga may be reckoned at 4600.

According to the above calculation, the population is in the ratio of about ninety-two inhabitants to the square mile; but the fertility of the soil is so great that it could easily support double or triple that number, if the whole region were united under a capable ruler. If this condition is not realised, the probability is that the energetic and far-seeing Sinna of Kiboso will absorb the smaller states in the west; whereupon Mareale will be more than likely to follow his example in the east.

Judging from his previous history, Mareale is not a man likely to remain *in statu quo*. His father was chief of Marangu before him, but died when his son was only a year

Mormon— Native Homestead

and a half old. Thereupon the power was usurped by an uncle, and Mareale and his mother were banished. His childhood and early youth were spent partly in Moji with Mandara, partly in Kiboso with the father of Sinna. When barely twenty he headed a raid of the Wa-Kiboso against Marangu, and though he did not succeed in taking his uncle prisoner, he drove off all the cattle, and proved beyond a doubt that he was made of the right stuff.

But Mareale had "a friend at court" in the person of a younger brother, whom the uncle had not thought it worth while to send into exile. By secret machinations, this brother obtained for Mareale a numerous following in the state, and in the end the uncle was ousted and the rightful heir recalled. Immediately Mareale set about strengthening his position by a marriage with Mandara's daughter, and enriched his exchequer by successful raids upon Rombo and by trade with the Swahili caravans. After a while the brother who had so befriended him began to indulge his revolutionary tendencies by plotting against Mareale himself. He died mysteriously, having in all probability been stabbed by the chief's orders.

It is not at all impossible that some time in the future Mareale may have to take the field against his amiable father-in-law or a combination of rival states. It is "the custom of the country," Mandara himself having been repeatedly compelled to quit his domains and remain in hiding till the enemy had completed the work of plunder. Mareale, however, is not one to take a defeat quietly, or tamely brook any interference with his authority.

Our camp presents a lively scene every morning before the natives go to the fields, and again late in the afternoon, when the hard work of the day is over. With piled-up baskets and bulky loads the women and girls troop in with provisions for sale, and take up their position under the shady tree in the midst of the enclosure.   The women sit upon the ground with legs outstretched straight in front of them, or remain standing, perhaps the better to carry on their incessant chatter.   The girls, with bright, inquisitive eyes, get behind each other in twos and threes, giggling and laughing.   The foremost stands with her arms crossed over her naked breast, the rest come pressing close upon each other, each with an arm about the waist or the neck of the one immediately in front.   There is a varied assortment of edibles for sale : bananas, ripe for eating, and unripe for cooking, and also bananas in the form of flour ; three varieties of beans and green vegetables ; maize in grain and in the cob ; millet whole or ground ; sweet potatoes, large and small ; curdled milk and butter ; leaf tobacco, honey and fowls.   Sheep and cows are not included in the articles of merchandise, for, in virtue of his position, all the cattle belong to Mareale, who grants the nominal owners the right to use the milk and butter.   Meat is reserved solely for the chief's own table, and cannot be purchased except from him.   There is plenty to choose from in the way of vegetable food, however, and my men are as keen at a bargain as the native women. The transaction opens with the word " *mbuia* " (friend), the common Jagga salutation. The Swahili then names an absurdly low price for the article on sale, and is of course indignantly refused. He goes away, and comes back again, ten, twenty times, always offering a little more and a little more, and flourishing his tempting beads and bits of cloth. By degrees the two parties come within measurable distance of a mutual understanding, and then commences the process of sampling. The buyer tastes and tries, the seller handles and examines. Friends are called in to give their opinion and advice, and at length, every one being satisfied, the bargain is concluded.

For many years the favourite currency in Jagga, as else-where throughout Central Africa, has been the broad white cotton cloth known to the natives as *nguo*. This cloth is usually made up in *doti* of eight arm-lengths, but the Wa-Jagga reckon the *doti* at ten arm-lengths, or sufficient for a whole garment, which they throw around the person like a toga. When it comes to the question of measuring, the purchaser of course requests the good offices of the tallest of the bystanders, who invariably does his best to " cabbage " for his friend by drawing the cloth each time a little above the elbow. Bandera, the red cotton cloth, is only worn by the chiefs or their relatives on great occasions. As small coin, small blue and red beads are most in demand. These are sewn by the women on thick circular bands of leather, and worn as ornaments round the neck and wrists. The beads are all made in Venice, and are put up in bunches, each bunch containing ten twists, and each twist ten strings of a hundred each, the only form in which they are accepted in barter.

The following table shows the value of the more common native products, expressed in terms of cloth and beads :—

A cow . = 12 doti of 10 arm-lengths.
A goat . = 3 ,, ,, ,,
A sheep . = 4 ., ,, ,,
A small fowl = 2 doti = 3 twists of beads of 10 strings each.
20 bananas (unripe). ⎫
10 ,, (ripe) . ⎪
2 pints of millet . ⎬ = 1 arm-length = 1 twist of beads.
3 ,, beans . ⎪
4 ,, maize . ⎭

10 sweet potatoes (medium size) = 1 twist of beads.
2 pints of milk . . . = ,, ,,
2 lbs. of butter . . . = 5 arm-lengths.
1 load of firewood . . = 1 twist of beads.
1 packet of tobacco (6 lbs.) . = 8 arm-lengths.
2 pints of honey . . . = 1½ doti.

Blackberries, tomatoes, spinage, and the like are gathered in the woods by the children, and may be had at nominal prices. I had to make special terms for our milk and butter, in order to have the cows milked into our own vessels and the butter churned in our own churn. I had never been able to get over my prejudice in favour of calabashes cleansed with water instead of rinsed out with cow urine, as is the unsophisticated custom of Jagga.

Milk is obtained principally from the small, short-horned, humped cows; that of the goats and of the fat-tailed sheep, with their ram-like noses and heavy dewlaps (*vide* Illustration), being but seldom used. Neither the goat's milk nor the goat's flesh have the characteristic "high" European flavour. As in Taveta, for the sake of safety the cattle are all stall-fed.

One of the special delicacies we enjoyed in Jagga was a sort of thin pancake made of maize and millet flour mixed, and cooked in butter, the art of making which our cook had learned at Dr. Abbott's. They were so deliciously light and crisp that we had them at every meal.

Mareale came to see me every day, sometimes in the morning, sometimes in the afternoon. Comfortably installed in my arm-chair, he was never tired of talking to me about Jagga, Zanzibar, and Europe, though I am afraid that as yet the last is somewhat of a "dark continent" to him. If a new-comer arrived during the interview, before squatting with his comrades he first saluted the friend he had come to visit, then Mareale's followers, and lastly the chief himself. Rarely did Mareale leave me without taking away some small souvenir of the visit, such as a pencil, one or two needles, or some such trifle. It was quite a pleasure to see his child-like delight over these insignificant presents; and as soon as he received them, he hurried off home without stopping to say good-bye.

Usually in the evening some of the Swahili and Somál from the adjacent camp of the slave-dealers would come for an hour or two's gossip with my men, among whom they had a number of old acquaintances. As a rule, I went for a ramble in the neighbourhood, accompanied only by a single follower. To be alone with Nature, even for a little while, is a rare privilege amid the incessant hum and bustle of caravan-life; every day and all day long one has to be constantly answering questions and giving directions, or tolerating, with the best grace possible, the irritating curiosity of the natives, which is specially tiresome when one 'is absorbed in taking an observation or trying to work out a calculation. And early evening or late afternoon is the best time for the heights of Kilimanjaro. Then clear against the evening sky, above the grey layers of stratus which veil the mountain midway to the summit, rise the great white dome of Kibo and the dark jagged peak of Mawenzi, while backwards, against the sombre setting of the southern plains, the rugged outlines of Ugweno glow like gold in the setting sun.

The arrangements for a prolonged stay in camp were soon completed. Within the compound, and not far from the men's quarters, were erected two large huts, one as a store-house, the other for the man in charge of the goods. Near these was a smaller hut for the Somál, and a shed for cooking in, and behind these again a small garden, in which the seeds of lettuce, radish, cress, and spinage we had brought with us from Zanzibar soon began to sprout.

By the end of five days everything was so far in order that I proceeded to equip a small party for the ascent of the mountain. Selecting from among the porters a few of the hardiest and most willing, I set them to work to make warm

*

CHAPTER IV.

TO THE SUMMIT OF KIBO.

IN former attempts to ascend Kilimanjaro, the main difficulty was not so much the lack of suitable equipments as the impossibility of obtaining, at the higher altitudes, a supply of food sufficient to last during the prolonged stay necessary to a thorough survey of the more inaccessible heights.

Profiting by my experiences of 1887, I resolved to establish a station on the small plateau lying between the two peaks of Kibo and Mawenzi, at a height of 14,400 feet, from which I could accomplish the ascent and exploration of the mountain at my leisure. For this purpose I had provided myself in Zanzibar with a small, well-made tent, in place of the one lost at Aden. It was large enough to accommodate Herr Purtscheller and myself, with a black attendant if necessary, and was furnished with a waterproof indiarubber ground-sheet, a plentiful supply of camel's-hair blankets, and two large sheepskin sleeping sacks, which enveloped the entire person all but the face.

CLIMBING TACKLE.

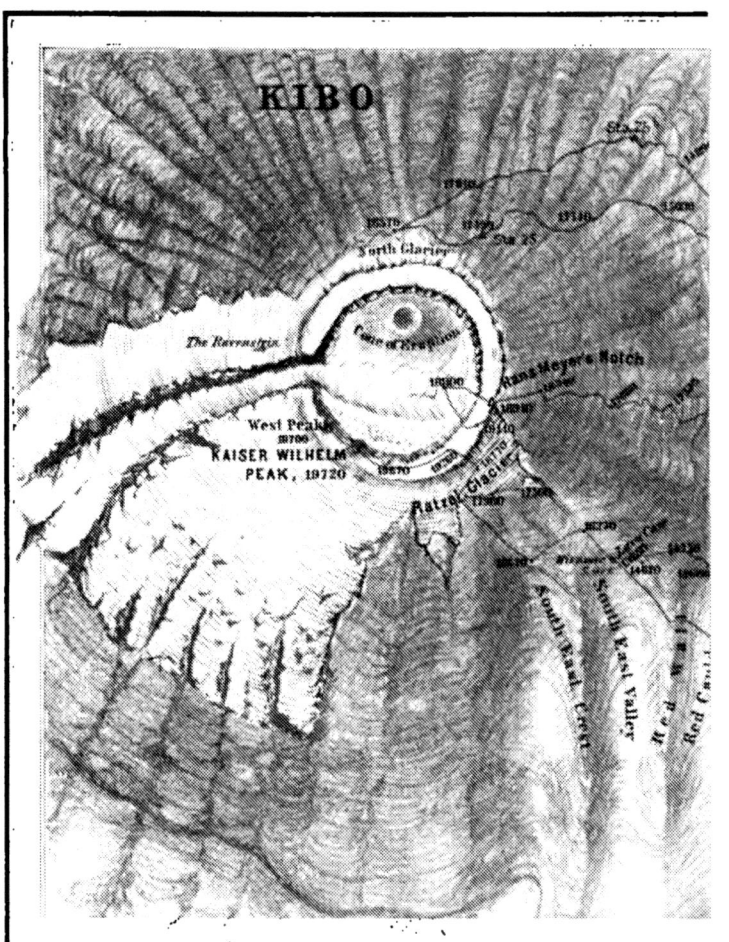

KIBO

The Ravenstein

North Glacier

West Peak

KAISER WILHELM
PEAK, 19720

Hans Meyer's Notch

Ratzel Glacier

South East Valley

Red Canal

A MAP OF THE
UPPER
KILIMANJARO.

Scale : 1 85000

Meters

Yards 1760   0   Engl. Miles.

Our outfit consisted of warm woollen clothing and gloves, strong Alpine boots, knapsacks, ice-axes, Manilla rope, snow-spectacles, and veils. Herr Purtscheller was also the happy possessor of a pair of climbing-irons, but mine had gone on to Ceylon with the tent. Our scientific instruments included a theodolite, a boiling-point thermometer, an aneroid, a maximum-minimum thermometer, compasses for taking bearings and making route-surveys, and the photographic apparatus, together with everything needful for preserving geological and botanical specimens.

In case of accidents, and also in order that we might be kept regularly and sufficiently provisioned, I deemed it advisable to erect, between the camp at Marangu's and that at the plateau, an intermediate station or half-way camp at the upper limit of the forest zone. Here we left the large tent and our picked body of attendants with the exception of one. Arrangements were made that every third day four of the Marangu men should proceed with meat, beans, bananas, butter and bread to the intermediate station, and that two of the men stationed there should thence convey our share to us in the upper camp, each relay returning immediately afterwards to its respective starting-point. My plans succeeded so well that in little more than three weeks we had achieved the ascent of the mountain, and completed our observations and explorations in the region of the summit.

The day of our departure for the higher zones (September 28) was preceded by a night of thunder and lightning accompanied by torrents of rain, which soaked through all the huts and tents with the exception of the large one, and obliged us to spend the morning in drying our clothes and provisions. Unfortunately, the meat which I had caused to be cut into strips and smoked shared the fate of our other stores, an accident which did not tend to improve its flavour. Nevertheless we had it dried again, and later on were very glad to get it.

The little expedition was not fairly under weigh until nearly midday. Besides ourselves, it included the two head-men, nine porters, Mwini Amani of Pangani, and the Somál Mohammed, Abdallah, and Ahmed, of whom the last was to act as cook. The large tent accompanied us, ready to be set up on reaching its destination. A code of rules had been drawn up for the benefit of those of the caravan who remained behind at Marangu under the command of Ali, the faithful Somál captain, and the guardianship of Mareale, who promised to keep a watchful eye upon them. Nevertheless I set out in anything but an easy frame of mind, for I had learned from former experience, on similar occasions, that my absence was likely to prove the beginning of all sorts of irregularities, such as might endanger the welfare of the whole expedition. Events showed that my fears had not been groundless.

Mareale had promised us two guides, but by the time we were ready to start only one had put in an appearance; the other was to follow in the evening.

At a steady pace we began to ascend the mountain, the path sloping gently upwards under cool, shady banana groves, or through patches of open grass-land, kept green and fresh by many a murmuring brook and gliding water-channel. Looking upwards towards the spot where the Monjo stream falls in a foaming cataract over a ledge of basalt, we had a passing peep of a group of huts where last year Dr. Abbott and his caravan made a stay of several months, but they were now deserted and left to the mercy of wind and weather. Beyond these, from one of a series of hillocks, we had a magnificent view of the whole surrounding country. There were no rugged outlines anywhere, only a succession of gentle undulations, stretching far away below us and to the right and left, in a sea of tender green, relieved by a wealth of flowers and bush and clustering masses of bananas. Far in the haze of distance Lake Jipé glittered like a silver shield beneath the dim blue outlines of the mountains of Ugweno and Paré, while towards the west the view across the steppes was intercepted by the long wooded line of the Lasso hills, from the summit of which we obtained the first glimpse of this favoured land as we crossed them on our way from Moji. Following the Lasso hills upward towards the higher slopes of Kilimanjaro, the eye lost itself in the mist-wreaths of the forest zone and the dark-grey cloud-cap so seldom lifted from the mountain's sombre brow.

As we ascended, the barometer continued to fall, and at length indicated an altitude of about 5570 feet as we left the last banana plantation behind us and entered the region of ferns and shrubs, which passes over into the belt of primeval forest.

As on a former occasion (1887), our guide tried hard to persuade us to camp in this very inviting neighbourhood, although it was still comparatively early; but now, as then, I turned a deaf ear to all his representations, and after a short rest pushed onward and upward to where the forest loomed ahead. The guide protested volubly and forcibly, and capered about like a madman; but we paid no heed to his frantic demonstrations, and left him to follow when he should have danced himself back to his ordinary senses.

The path was now almost lost in a tangle of vegetation, which proved a severe trial to the strength and patience of our somewhat weary porters. As we struggled on, we were met by a number of Marangu natives, in a state of absolute nudity. They were laden with huge bundles of firewood, and they told us, amid great excitement, that they had just seen four elephants close at hand. We ourselves saw nothing of them, however, perhaps because our attention was wholly absorbed in picking our steps, so as to avoid falling into one of the numerous elephant traps with which our way was beset, and which consist of a pit about twenty feet deep, concealed by a layer of ferns. In spite of the utmost care, I only escaped coming to grief in one by a hair's breadth.

The belt of bush and ferns through which we were now pressing is not so much the result of climatic conditions as of the periodical burning to which the vegetation is subjected by the Wa-Jagga, who in this way secure fresh ground for cultivation. This opinion is corroborated by the fact that in patches to which the blaze has not extended, the characteristic forms of the forest zone continue right down the mountain-side. As the moisture decreases, they gradually become less luxuriant and mingle more and more with representatives of the typical flora of the steppes, until at length the latter entirely predominate. Even within the fern zone examples of both types—primeval forest and steppe vegetation—are to be met with.

The limit of the fern zone also indicates the limit of possible cultivation, for the great and constant supply of moisture through which the forest has originated and is maintained, renders further clearing by fire impracticable. At this elevation, however, the climate alone would probably prove an insuperable barrier to the cultivation of tropical plants.

In 1887 we ascended by a path considerably to the west of our present route, but here too we reached the lower limit of the wooded region at a height of about 6430 feet. As we proceeded, the pathway became more open, the bush gradually thinned, the ferns disappeared, and solitary trees—hoary harbingers of the forest, grey with moss and lichen—stretched out their grizzled arms to us on all sides. Under the dripping boughs we journeyed on, and emerged at length upon an open plot of ground covered with tall grasses, by the side of a babbling brook—the Rua—half concealed beneath a wealth of herbs and shrubs. Here we pitched our first mountain-camp.

Any lingering doubts we may have entertained as to Ahmed's culinary skill were pleasantly dispelled over supper, and, spite of the mist and the raw damp atmosphere, we spent a very cosy evening and a no less comfortable night, though awakened once or twice by the trumpeting of elephants. On our arrival in camp, the guide had been sent back to Marangu, under the escort of Mwini Amani, with strict injunctions to return early next morning, and bring his defaulting comrade with him. Before they made their appearance, laden with a supply of food, we had ample time to procure specimens of the numerous orchids which graced our camping-ground. Then the march was resumed, and we began making our way upwards through the primeval forest.

Day after day, year in, year out, no matter what the season, this region of perpetual cloud is likewise the region of perpetual humidity. Wherever a constant supply of moisture is associated with uniform drainage, the natural forest universally attains the utmost luxuriance possible within the limits imposed by the prevailing temperature. In the forest region of Kilimanjaro both these conditions are fulfilled almost to perfection, for there is no interruption of the rainfall worth speaking of, and the gentle gradients characteristic of the volcanic form of mountain provide for the equal distribution of the surface water. Why the northern aspect of the mountain should in these respects be less favoured, is a question we shall endeavour to answer later on.

Thus, experiencing no marked change of season, no definite period of prolonged drought, the trees would be apt to suffer from excess of moisture were the leaves not specially organised with a view to free and incessant transpiration. Accordingly, evergreen forms preponderate, the only deciduous forms being the herbaceous plants and some of the smaller bushes. Here the conditions are the exact reverse of those that surround the flora of the steppes, and all the organs are arranged and modified so as to facilitate the process of evaporation. The pandanus, dracæna, and similar species have the upper surface of the leaf smooth and waxy, which serves to keep the stomata open, while in others, such as *Clavija* and *Rhus*, the same end is achieved by means of a coating of hairs. Along the course of the streams, where the struggle for light and air is keenest, the ferns and other plants exhibit a tendency towards an extraordinary development of leaves, as presenting the largest possible evaporating surface. Species which elsewhere are characterised by comparatively scanty foliage here produce leaves of astonishing size and number.

No sooner had we entered this conservatory of luxuriant greenery than we were soaked to the skin. The tall wet undergrowth met above our heads, and at every step the trees grew closer and closer together, festooned and bound stem to stem by endless and inextricable trails of creeper, and beneath this leafy canopy stretched a dainty carpet of rich green ferns, unbroken save by the brown band of our boggy pathway. Bough and trunk and creeper alike were covered with an endless variety of parasites true and false, of which by far the most common and conspicuous was a long yellowish-brown hanging moss. They were all as full of water as a sponge, and mercilessly added their quota to our dripping misery. The porters especially were in a pitiable condition, and had hard work as they followed the endless windings of the path, now bending to avoid a threatening branch, now forcibly pushing their way between the serried stems, or climbing with their heavy loads over some fallen trunk that blocked the way. Fortunately the ascent was nowhere steep.

From time to time we emerged from the prevailing twilight upon some open space, where we hailed with gladness the cheering light of heaven, and delightedly inhaled its fresh free air. It is singular how sharply these plots of greensward are separated from the dense forest around them. The transition from the grass by which they are overgrown to forms of giant girth and height is as abrupt as that from the barren steppes to the belt of wood that accompanies the course of some stream, and would seem to indicate that their origin is artificial rather than natural. Arborescent heaths and sumach trees form the enclosing hedge, and the grass of the clearings is sprinkled with three species of orchids, two green and one red. On the higher grounds a red iris and red and yellow everlasting flowers (*Helichrysum*) are also common.

Everywhere we came upon abundant traces of elephants. In the spongy ground each of their footprints had become a pool a foot deep, which we were obliged carefully to avoid, while the broken branches and uprooted stems with which they had strewed the way were a constant source of annoyance. In many places also the ground had been rucked up and befouled by buffaloes. From time to time the silence was broken by the hoarse bark of the monkey or the mournful cry of the hornbill, but on the whole the forest showed remarkably few signs of animal life. At no point did we obtain anything approaching to a view, either downward towards the plains or upward towards the mountain heights.

Slowly we plodded on in the stillness and the gloom, till at length, in the afternoon, we reached a narrow grassy strip, which here stretches down into the very heart of the forest from the open grass-lands beyond its upper limit. It has

I*

in all probability originated accidentally, the flames having gradually crept farther and farther downwards during successive burnings of the grass above. Along this strip the path led more steeply upwards, while the trees hemmed it in on either side, the heaths gradually gaining upon all other forms as the elevation increased. At a height of 8500 feet we reached a kind of terrace where the ascent was more gradual, and the grass strip widened into open pasture-land. Although clumps of trees still studded the foreground, we were now beyond the precincts of the dense primeval forest.

We stood on the south-eastern side of Mawenzi, of whose jagged rocks we now and then obtained a momentary glimpse between the rolling masses of cumulus cloud which enshrouded the summit. Downwards along its eastern flank stretched a series of parasitic cones of considerable size. Between these the path we had hitherto followed continued in a north-easterly direction, along the upper edge of the forest, towards the Jagga states of Rombo and Useri. We, however, struck westward across the grass-land towards the southern face of the peak, and just as the mist began to fall reached the foot of the westmost parasitic cone. There, at an elevation of 8710 feet, we camped for the night, close to the upper limit of the forest, by the side of a small, ice-cold stream—the Kifinika.

Through the surrounding mist the long grey lichens, hanging from the branches, waved weird and ghostly in the chilly evening breeze. Half frozen, the men huddled together over the sputtering camp-fire, which could scarcely be got to burn on account of the damp. The thermometer stood at 43° F., and my fingers being too benumbed either to write or work, I crept forthwith into my sleeping sack, and blessed the memory of the good old wether whose fleecy fell now stood me in such excellent stead.

With the thermometer at 36° Fahr., and hoarfrost on the ground, the men were hardly to be blamed if, next morning (Nov. 1st), they were some hours later than usual in leaving the warm shelter of their huts. About eight o'clock the mist began to clear, however, and all were ready to follow the guides into the forest, which here stretches somewhat farther up the mountain. We had to begin by trampling down a path for ourselves through the dense undergrowth—a sufficiently hard task, although in this uplying region the trees do not stand close together, nor are there any more of the tiresome creepers, which at all times make progress so difficult. Colossal rhododendrons, dracænas, and heaths are the prevailing forms, no longer covered with brownish moss, but draped with grey lichens, while the undergrowth largely consists of reeds and rushes mingled with tall Umbelliferæ. The soil, which in the lower forest region was brown and boggy, is here a blackish humus, and the rock no more exhibits a close basaltic structure, but is coarsely crystalline.

The men marched splendidly, without a word of urging; they were the pick of the caravan. As they got gradually warmed up with walking, their miserable plight of the evening before became a source of much fun and merriment, which reached a climax when one of the guides surprised an unsuspecting rodent, that had unduly prolonged its morning nap, and, in spite of its energetic struggles and terrified cries, carried it off in triumph tied fast to a forked stick.

Continuing westward and upward for about an hour, we reached a small stream—the Ngona mdogo—which has hollowed out a channel through one of the beds of lava. Here in 1887 we had our first view of Mawenzi, which, in its mantle of newly-fallen snow, looked wonderfully near. To-day, however, the peak was invisible, and we gazed blankly upon a grey expanse of mist. Crossing the deep ravine formed by another stream—the Ngona mkuba—which we had already crossed lower down, where it forms the boundary between Marangu and Kilema, we struck the neutral path that traverses the upper grass-lands, skirting the edge of the forest all the way from Useri to Majamé, at about the same distance up the mountain-side. This path we continued to follow for some hours, occasionally passing some offshoot from the forest running upwards into the grass-land wherever there was a watercourse, or other suitable conditions.

The average limit of the forest belt is about 9500 feet, the extreme limit imposed by the climatic conditions being some six or seven hundred feet higher. The region lying between these two altitudes is the special habitat of the heaths. Here they appear as trees, shattered and riven by the mountain-winds and hoary with trailing lichens, but still able to weather the storms. In the form of low shrubs they are scattered throughout the whole of the grassy uplands, reaching as far as the plateau at the saddle, at a height of over 13,000 feet. The extreme hardiness of these plants is mainly due to the peculiar formation of the leaves : the upper surface is smooth and destitute of pores, and the stomata all open on the under surface, over which the edges are closely curled. The free exhalation of the moisture and gases is thus guaranteed, no matter how dense and persistent the mist by which they are surrounded, and the evaporation so essential to the life of the plant goes on as long as the leaflets are exposed, for occasional brief intervals, to dry air and sunshine.

Several species of *Proteaceæ* and rue, with bracken, everlasting flowers, and bilberries, grow alongside the heaths in the higher regions. Many of these were now in full bloom, and offered a rich harvest to the wild bees ; and it was for their benefit that the Wa-Jagga had in several places

hung on the trees the hollow wooden cylinders which are in general use throughout East Africa for the collection of honey. Towards midday we had reason to know that the sun could shine here as well as in Jagga, but the cool mountain-breeze fanned our foreheads, and combined with the familiar forms of the vegetation to suggest pleasant thoughts and happy memories of home and fatherland.

Presently from the sea of clouds which rolled over the forest and hid the plains below, the mist stole up and round us again, enveloping us for the rest of the day. Leaping across the sparkling Mué, where as yet it is little more than a tiny rill, we left the path and struck upwards towards the spot where, following the example of Mr. H. H. Johnston, Von Eberstein and I had fixed our station from which to attempt the ascent of Kibo in 1887. Continuing along the upward course of the Mué, which I had formerly dubbed the Senecio, because on its banks we found our first example of *Senecio Johnstoni*, we left behind us the huts that marked the camping-ground of Dr. Abbott and Ehlers in 1889, and pitched our large tent in a sheltered hollow by the side of the stream, whose steep banks were still richly clad with heaths and sumach trees. On the heights above, the ice-fields of Kibo sparkled temptingly, as if to lure us onward and upward to try their gleaming slopes.

As latterly we had been proceeding in a horizontal direction westwards rather than upwards, we were still not far above the forest. Our height above the sea was 9480 feet.

Here, then, we fixed the site of our intermediate station, between Marangu and the saddle plateau, and here the large tent was to remain for the next few weeks. The men set about the necessary work without delay. Two water-tight huts of grass and brushwood were speedily run up; leaves were collected for bedding; a supply of firewood was cut and piled, and places were prepared for the fires. Before sunset the camp was completed.

In preparation for our ascent to the saddle the next day, I packed our most essential equipments in a tin box, made up the sleeping-sacks and blankets into a second load, the small tent forming a third, the camp-kettle and provisions a fourth, the photographic apparatus a fifth, and the theodolite a sixth, which as usual was intrusted to Mwini Amani.

In the glow of the early morning sunshine the little caravan of eight took its way up the mountain. For some distance we were accompanied by the rest of the men, until at length I bade them a cheery farewell, and sent them back to their lonely camp. All who went with me had been provided with woollen underclothing, and as far as possible with some sort of covering for the feet. Many of them had borrowed coats and trousers from the Somál, and, in expectation of severe cold, all were swathed to suffocation in warm wraps, which one by one they were glad to cast off immediately we began to climb in earnest.

From the ridge along which we went the grass-land stretched right and left for miles, sloping downwards like a roof from the edge of the saddle plateau to the dark line of the forest. The edge of the plateau runs in a fairly horizontal line from Mawenzi to Kibo; from where we stood it looked like the saddle between the two peaks, the higher plateau behind being concealed from view. All that was to be seen of the peaks themselves was the white ice-helmet of Kibo and the jagged crown of Mawenzi, and soon they too passed out of sight. We had seen enough, however, for the plotting of the route. I took the lead, and, as formerly in 1887, made towards the middle of the plateau, following the line of a lightly rounded ridge of lava, which ran almost straight towards the required point, between two deep ravines.

Among the dewy grass we repeatedly startled a small grey antelope of a species unknown to me, and numbers of gaily plumaged sunbirds flew from bush to bush sucking the honey from the pale yellow flowers of the smaller *Proteaceæ.* For two hours we continued upwards along the gently sloping sheet of lava, which at first was closely carpeted with grass, and higher up with blossoming heaths and everlastings. As soon as we had left the grass behind, we began to make way more rapidly, the rough detritus affording a better footing. On our left, towards the west, farther progress in that direction was now barred by one of the ravines. In the easily-eroded material of the broad lava sheets of this region, the stream has gradually carved out for itself a gorge varying from 150 to 200 feet deep, and from 80 to 100 feet wide. The edges are perfectly sharp and clean-cut, and the sides go sheer down like those of a crevasse in a glacier. It was at the source of this stream that we camped in July 1887, and there, in the depth of the tropical winter, we found the first snow on the mountain, whence we christened the spring the *Schneequelle,* or "spring in the snow." At that time the water came down in a merry babbling brook, but now, in the dry season, it lay in silent pools, apparently fed by underground springs. What struck us most on seeing the bed thus exposed was the remarkably small amount of force which has sufficed, in the course of ages, to wear away the soft volcanic rock to such an astounding depth. For the first time we began to have some faint conception of the vast ravages gradually wrought by wind and weather on the slopes of Mawenzi, now a mere relic of its former greatness.

At the bottom of the gorge, on the brink of some of the pools, we noticed several isolated and weather-beaten specimens of *Senecio Johnstoni,* an extraordinary arborescent plant, looking in the distance somewhat like a human being, but in reality consisting of a dark smooth trunk six or eight feet high, and surmounted by a huge crown of grey withered leaves. When seen through the mist, it is easy to understand how a kindred species of these curious trees, indigenous to the Tropical Andes, should have come to be called "*fraile-jones*" or monk's cowls. In the Andes, as on Kilimanjaro, they occur only in marshy places. The precipitous rocks on either side were almost entirely bare, and displayed in section a complete system of fantastically curved and crumpled layers of lava of varying colour and hardness.

Keeping along the edge of the ravine, we continued our way upwards, passed a small tributary stream, now almost dry like the other, and gradually approached the point we had been keeping in view, over increasingly coarse volcanic débris. Here the ravine widened into a glen, which we were able to cross; and having gained the other side, we scrambled painfully on over the loose detritus in the direction of the more gentle incline up the southern part of the plateau, which leads by a long slope towards the highest point of the saddle.

Soon Kibo came once more into view, and we pressed on towards it, until at length we were compelled by sheer exhaustion to camp on the edge of another ravine, scarcely so steep as the first. In the pools at the bottom there was a supply of water sufficient to last us for some weeks, and later on we were obliged to have recourse to it, Mwini Amani carrying it up daily to our camping-ground above. I had hoped on this day to be able to go on a good deal farther, and get somewhat nearer to Kibo; but the men were so thoroughly done up that, immediately on getting into camp, they flung themselves down among the boulders, and slept the whole afternoon, heedless alike of mist and cold. Towards evening they bestirred themselves a little, and having had their supper, crept into what sheltered crannies they could find, under ledges of rock or in the hollows of the lava beds, and there spent the night as best they could.

All the afternoon and evening Kibo and Mawenzi remained sullenly wrapt in mist. The landscape here is almost melancholy in its sombre monotony. As far as the eye can reach, nothing is to be seen save dark grey blocks of lava scattered over the gravelly or sandy ground. Neither grass nor bush relieves the dreary waste ; no sound of living creature greets the ear. The silence is unbroken save for the eerie sough of the wind as it whistles among the boulders or rustles the crisp leaves of some starveling shrub and wafts the misty wreaths across the drear expanse of grey. The scene contrasts strongly with that on the farther edge of the plateau, which lies only some 700 feet lower. There the beds of lava are covered with grassy turf, and lower down are studded with bushes and trees, whose growth is favoured by the character of the soil, the result of the equal weathering of the surface layers of rock. Here, on the other hand, owing to the absence of any gregarious form of vegetation, which the climatic conditions would render impossible, the extreme difference in the temperature of day and night causes the walls of lava to split into blocks averaging about ten or twelve cubic feet in size. In places where the process of splitting is still incomplete, or where the angle of inclination is not sufficient to cause the blocks to fall by their own weight, the rent and cracked masses of lava assume the characteristic tortoiseshell-like appearance which excited so much remark on the part of Mr. H. H. Johnston. In the fissures between the larger fragments, the small crumble to sand and dust, and are blown hither and thither unceasingly by the wind, so that it is only here and there in the more sheltered nooks that an isolated shrub or a solitary tuft of flowers manages to struggle into life.

Amid these depressing surroundings rather an amusing incident occurred. As I was scrambling about in search of botanical specimens, my foot struck against something that gave out a sharp metallic sound, and looking down, I discovered a sadly battered empty preserved-meat tin bearing the pathetically homely inscription, " Irish Stew." A few steps farther on, I came upon a tattered sheet of the Salvation Army newspaper *En Avant*. Evidently we had chanced upon the same camping-ground that Dr. Abbott and Ehlers had used the year before, for in the station at Moji this same chronicle of Salvation Army doings had been one of the stock funds of amusement. All the same, I took the motto " *En Avant* " as a favourable augury for us under our present circumstances.

A bitterly cold wind set in after sundown from the direction of Kibo, and we were glad to take refuge in our tent and creep into our sleeping-sacks, feeling no desire to leave them again for the next twelve hours. Nevertheless, while the early morning sun still shone on the icy crown of the higher peak, and cast long shadows across the western side of its sister, Mawenzi, we had crossed the ravine which lies almost midway between the two, and were hastening towards the centre of the base of Kibo. The whole of the peak was now visible in one clear sweep from top to bottom. Its base rested on the plateau, unobscured by any intervening terrace, the ground sloping smoothly upwards to its feet. The series of parasitic hills along the saddle lay to the right, and even the jagged snowless wall of Mawenzi no longer intercepted the view.

In the dry, clear, highly-rarefied atmosphere the distant heights looked deceptively near. The men tramped on bravely, but the lava beds seemed as if they would never come to an end. For half-an-hour we rested in a hollow by a small patch of green grass, which we found to be nourished by an underground spring. Here the landscape began to show more variety of colour. The sheet of volcanic ashes over which we were now passing was of a warm brick-red intersected by bands of dull yellow ; the hills on the saddle, from which the ashes have originally proceeded, are of the same ruddy tint, while the volcanic débris at the foot of Kibo is brown, its cliffs and precipices a dark bluish-grey, its icy cap a dazzling white, faintly lined with palest blue, and the overarching firmament a deep ultramarine. But the effect is never glaring ; all the varying hues are blended and toned into each other in a magnificent symphony of colour which harmonises in every essential with the beauty and grandeur of the mountain forms.

On the farther side of the sheet of ashes, which we crossed as quickly and easily as if it had been a threshing-floor, I espied a spot which looked as if it had been expressly made for camping purposes. Immediately below a large and conspicuous mass of rock, which later on went by the name of the "*Viermän-nerstein*," or Four Men's Rock, was a pile of smaller blocks, forming a protecting wall against the icy winds blowing from the snow-fields of Kibo. At a bend in this wall we found a little plot of ground, on whose porous ashen soil our tiny tent rested as snugly and securely as on Abraham's bosom. Close by was a sheltered place for the fire, and in a crevice between the stones a sleeping place for Mwini Amani; lined with bundles of everlastings and rue, and covered with thick, woollen blankets, it was soon transformed into quite a cosy little nest. Other chinks and gaps afforded abundant accommodation for our various stores and equipments, and a supply of firewood was obtainable from a number of woody Euryops bushes with squamous leaves, two species of which still contrived to exist, even at this elevation, in the sheltered spot

we had now reached.   On the top of the "*Viermännerstein*" I
planted the German flag, propping it up with a pyramid of
stones.   Later on it served to indicate our whereabouts to
the relays of porters who brought us our supplies of provisions.   The five men who had thus far accompanied us were
sent back after a short rest, in order that they might reach
the camp at the Mué by sundown, and it was not without
a certain eerie feeling of solitude that we watched them
slowly disappear behind the ridge of lava, and found ourselves
alone on Kibo.

While Mwini busied himself with the fire and the cooking, it being exactly midday, I took an observation for
latitude, and thus obtained the first definite point to start
from for all future compass-bearings and the plotting of our
route.   After lunch I took a walk northwards in the direction
of the three cinder cones which rise at the base of Kibo, on
its eastern side.   Crossing a broad sheet of volcanic mud,
hardened to the consistency of asphalte, I reached our old
camping-ground of 1887 on the south side of the "Triplets,"
as we had been wont to call the group of cones in question.
Here I came upon the fragments of a boiling-point thermometer, which, to our great vexation, had then been broken
while taking an observation.

In the depression between the "Triplets" and the cone
which occupies the centre of the plateau, as in every sheltered situation where it was possible for vegetation to exist,
we observed numerous footprints of some large ruminant.
In 1887 I did not see the animal myself, but this time,
in the vicinity of the red central hill, I remarked three
small herds of eland, each comprising six or eight head,
leisurely cropping the scanty patches of grass and herbage.
Needless to say, the eland are not indigenous to the region, but
come up from below during the warmer part of the day.   A

Kibo from the S.E.   View from Camp on the Saddle Plateau (14,200 ft.)

species of stonechat does, however, make its home in these inhospitable wastes ; and so little do these tiny creature know of the shyness born of the fear of man, that they came to the tent-door and picked up the food we put down for them from among our very feet.

The latter part of the afternoon was taken up with our preparations for the ascent of Kibo, which we had resolved to attempt early next morning. We had reached a height of 14,200 feet, and were still about a mile and a half from the actual cone, which towers upward for another 5510 feet, its base measuring about four miles in breadth. On the right half of the cone, the ice-cap is quite narrow, and towards the edge assumes a deep blue tinge ; the precipices and ridges of lava below are here quite free of ice. On the left side, again, the ice descends almost to the base of the cone in long tongues full of great rents and chasms. In the middle, that is, on the side facing us, a broad sheet of ice comes downward, filling up the valley between two long, high ridges of rock. It too is full of rents and cracks, and looks by no means inviting. At a point about two-thirds of the way up, the left-hand ridge disappears beneath the great ice mantle which hides the summit, and here the slope seems to be somewhat less precipitous, and the ice scarcely so much fissured as elsewhere. The shortest road to the highest part of the crater rim, which lies on the southern side of the mountain, seemed to lie across the ice at this point.

Our plan was to follow the ridge aforesaid to where it met the snow-line, and thence begin the climb across the ice-cap. The way was long, and we knew we must make up our minds for some hard work, but the uncertainty of what the next day might bring forth kept us awake all night, and deprived us of the rest we so much needed.

Every quarter of an hour, from one o'clock onwards, we kept striking matches to see the time. At half-past two we crept out of the tent. The night was cold and pitch dark—not a trace of the moonlight we had hoped for. As quickly as might be, we strapped our knapsacks on our backs, took our ice-axes in our hands, and lighted our lanterns. "*Kwaheri*" (good-bye), I called out to Mwini as I passed his cleft in the rocks. "*Kwaheri bwana na rudi salama*" (good-bye, sir, and a safe return to you), was the answer. "*Inshallah*" (if it be the will of God), I replied, and we stepped forth into the night.

As long as we were crossing the level ground, we had only to keep a look-out for the débris and blocks of stone which were lying scattered about. Soon, however, we reached a deep recess or corrie that penetrates the base of the mountain ; down the side of this we slowly made our way until we reached the talus at the bottom, and again began to scramble upwards over a chaos of fallen boulders. In the utter darkness it was desperately hard work, and more than once we came to grief and were badly bruised and scratched. Fortunately our lanterns, which were of Muscovy glass, sustained no damage, though every time we fell they were extinguished, and the business of relighting them in the strong wind that was blowing tried our patience sadly. It seemed to me that Purtscheller, who was leading, kept somewhat too far northwards, to the right ; I held on in a more easterly direction, as far as possible in a straight line for the middle of the peak. Suddenly, when morning broke, we discovered right across our path and 500 feet below us, the ravine for the southern side of which we had all along supposed ourselves to be making. We had struck too far to the north, and there was nothing for it but to descend the dizzy cliffs, scramble across the mass of loose stones and rubbish at the bottom, and scale the beetling precipices opposite. By this unfortunate mistake we lost a whole precious hour of the best part of the day.

Having safely scrambled down, after a short rest, we for some time followed the upward course of the bed of detritus, leaving the last traces of flowering vegetation behind at a height of 15,420 feet. At half-past six we passed a transverse dyke of lava, which intersects the valley about half-way up, and towards seven, at a height of 16,400 feet, came upon the first flakes of snow, as we paused under the shelter of the rocks on the south side. On the north side, which is sheltered from the " upper trade winds," snow occurs in almost continuous patches from this point upwards to where the lower end of the ice-sheet enters the valley, at a height of 17,580 feet. There the melting ice forms two small streams, which are soon lost among the detritus below. The view across the rock-strewn talus in both directions is singularly impressive. Above towers the massive wall of ice, and beneath, the valley runs steeply downwards, and far below bends towards the south. Its jagged sides are cut and carved by the erosive force of time and weather,—here seamed with dykes of lava, there polished and scratched through the action of ice,—while from time to time the roar of the wind or the crash of falling rocks testifies to the unceasing activity of Nature.

It was not until twenty minutes past seven that we reached the comb of the ridge which we had yesterday selected as affording probably the best approach to the summit, and, panting for breath, began scrambling upwards along the crest over the firm rock and loose débris. Every ten minutes we had to pause a few seconds to give heart and lungs a rest, for we were now far above the height of Mont Blanc, and the increasing rarity of the atmosphere made itself more and more painfully felt. By a quarter-past eight we had climbed over crags and boulders to a height of 17,060 feet, and halted for half-an-hour. A mouthful of melted snow mixed with citric acid served to allay the painful dryness in our throats, but we did not feel in the least hungry. Looking backwards, we saw that we were already above the summit of Mawenzi, which showed a rich ruddy brown in the dazzling sunlight. The mist was creeping slowly up towards the saddle plateau, the cinder cones in the centre of which looked like so many molehills. Over the forest hung a thick veil of silver-grey cloud, and beyond it floating masses of cumulus clouds, their under-sides tinged with a roseate hue, the reflection of the brick-red soil of the steppes below. The steppes themselves were only dimly visible through the haze of evaporating moisture ascending from their surface. Above, the icy helmet of Kibo gleamed and glittered apparently close at hand.

Continuing the ascent, shortly before nine o'clock we reached a precipice, over the brink of which we gazed with awe into an abyss running sheer downwards to a depth of nearly 3000 feet. Along its edge we gradually worked our way upwards, until we reached the lower margin of the solid sheet of ice that crowns the summit of the mountain, at a height of 17,980 feet.

At this point the passage from rock to ice is not so abrupt as elsewhere. Instead of the usual bright blue wall seventy to a hundred feet high, a sloping platform some sixty feet in width connects the rock below with the compact dome of ice above. The latter, however, rises immediately at an angle of about 35°, so that without ice-axes it is absolutely impossible to scale it. There could no longer be any doubt that with the proper tackle the ascent of the summit was from this point perfectly practicable. Whether or not we might meet with some insuperable obstacle farther on, and whether our strength would hold out long enough, were matters which still remained to be tested. In such an undertaking, there is a vast difference between starting comfortably from some Alpine hotel, with a goodly supply of bread, ham, eggs, and wine, and setting out, as in this case, after a fortnight's forced march across the East African steppes, from a small tent, and with but scant provision of insipid dried meat, cold rice, and citric acid. More than once we made a feeble attempt to attack some of these uninviting viands, with but poor success, for our appetite was completely gone.

We now donned our veils and snow-spectacles, and bound ourselves together with the rope. Purtscheller also fastened on his climbing irons, while I, unfortunately, was obliged to trust solely to my strong hob-nailed boots.

At 10.30, with a cheery " Now then ! " we began the toilsome work of cutting steps in the ice, which was as hard as glass, and, when broken, proved to be as clear. The task was no easy one : each step cost some twenty strokes of the axe. Little by little we made our way upwards over the smooth slippery wall, compelled at first, owing to its frightful steepness, to take a slanting course to the right, but afterwards making straight towards the summit. By-and-by we came to the margin of a wide depression, the extension upwards of the ravine we had crossed in the morning. Here the ice presented such an alarming array of yawning cracks and crevasses, that we almost feared we should be compelled to turn back. At every step Purtscheller tested with his axe the fragile bridges of ice and snow that spanned the crevasses ; one after another they were found to hold, and one after another we left them behind us, till at length, at halfpast twelve, we reached the bottom of the last icy precipice, at an altitude of 18,700 feet. In memory of a friend, we

K

called this, our first glacier on Kilimanjaro, the "Ratzel glacier."[1]

We now sat down for another much-needed rest, and again tried to eat a little—this time with somewhat better success. What from the plateau had appeared the highest part of the ice-cap was now beneath us, and the lower zones of the mountain, with their sea of floating clouds, had disappeared from sight.

It may have caused some surprise that all along I have continued to speak of ice, and not of snow, as might have been expected. But, as a matter of fact, at this season of the year there was hardly any snow on Kibo worth mentioning. What from beneath appeared to be snow of the most dazzling whiteness, was in reality the weathered surface of the mantle of ice which covers the rugged shoulders of the old volcano in a compact mass, averaging 180 to 200 feet in thickness. On entering the valleys and hollows, the ice assumes the familiar glacier form, and penetrates, as we have seen, a considerable way down the mountain-side.

Although the temperature was little above freezing-point, the reflection of the sun's rays in the highly rarefied atmosphere was so dazzling and painful, that, in spite of veils and spectacles, the skin peeled from our faces and necks, and for days afterwards my eyes required the protection of blue glasses.

The appearance of one or two floating wreaths of mist caused us to start to our feet in alarm, and resume our climbing with all possible speed. Breathing now became so difficult that every fifty steps we had to stop, bending forward and gasping for air. It has been estimated that at a height of 19,000 feet the oxygen of the atmosphere amounts only to 48 per cent., and the humidity to 15 per cent., of

[1] F. Ratzel, Professor of Geography in the University of Leipzig.—*Tr.*

the average at the sea-level. Taking this into account, and remembering the tremendous physical and nervous strain to which we were subjected, it is little wonder that we felt so sorely put to it.

As we proceeded, the ice became increasingly corroded, and the surface assumed more and more the *nieve penitente* appearance described by Dr. Paul Güssfeldt in his account of Aconcagua, in Chili. Honeycombed in many places to a depth of over six feet, and weathered into countless grooves and ruts and pointed spikes, the ice-field formed a veritable series of natural *trous-de-loup*. Again and again the treacherous crust gave way beneath us, and we sank up to the armpits in one of these dangerous pitfalls. Our strength began to give way with alarming rapidity, and still above us towered the icy wall, and still our goal seemed as distant as ever. "Onwards," I said to myself with set teeth; "it must come to an end some time."

At last, towards two o'clock, we found ourselves close to the top. A few more steps in eager anticipation and the secret of Kibo lay unveiled before us—at our feet yawned a gigantic crater with precipitous walls, occupying the entire summit of the mountain.

The sight burst upon us with such unexpected suddenness that, for a moment, it quite took away our breath. We seated ourselves and looked around. The first glance told us that we had still more work ahead. The most lofty elevation of Kibo lay to our left, on the southern rim of the crater, where three jagged pinnacles of rock towered yet a few hundred feet above the southern slope of the ice-cap. We could not have reached them in less than another hour and a half, even had we been in a condition to attempt it. Moreover, we should then have been obliged to bivouac there for the night, which would have been simple madness, as we were destitute of protection against the cold. We had had eleven hours of exceptionally hard climbing over unknown ground, at an altitude, roughly speaking, of from 14,500 to 19,300 feet, and in making the descent it seemed likely we should also have to reckon with the mist, which now slowly began to draw towards us. Everything considered, therefore, we deemed it our wisest course to make the best of our way down with all possible speed, consoling ourselves, meanwhile, for the present partial disappointment with the resolve to return in three days to achieve the conquest of the highest point.

So far, we had every reason to be satisfied with the results of our first ascent. The existence of the long-suspected crater at the summit of the mountain had been demonstrated ; its extent, the appearance of the cone, and the general conformation of its rocks and of its ice had been ascertained, as well as the peculiar characteristics of the ice-sheet ; the way to the highest point had been determined, and the altitude of the point we had reached fixed at 19,260 feet.

Comforting ourselves with these considerations, at twenty minutes past two we commenced the descent. Among the trailing wreaths of mist, I without climbing-irons, and both of us so exhausted that at one time Herr Purtscheller became quite faint, we made but slow progress down the slippery wall. A little way from the summit we found that the action of the sun's rays had been so intense as almost to obliterate the steps we had hewn, and for the most part we were compelled to renew them. It was killing work for our wearied limbs, and was rendered ten times more trying by our dangerous situation : a single false move on the part of either of us would have precipitated both into the yawning depths below. But once more the will proved superior to the flesh, and, breathing more freely, towards four o'clock we again had the satisfaction of planting our feet on the solid rock. Here we allowed ourselves half-an-hour's rest, and during that time sat silently watching the tumbling masses of cloud, which alone gave life and motion to the stern majesty of the scene around us. Then, slipping and sliding, we made our way down the detritus heaps lining the side of the valley we had crossed in the morning, and still more swiftly continued downwards over the long sloping talus at the bottom. The precipitous wall of cliffs on the north side of the ravine still lay between us and our camp, and taxed our failing energies to the utmost as we struggled up it. It too was scaled at last, however, and then, in the fast gathering twilight, our feet winged with the prospect of a hot supper and a comfortable bed, we scrambled hastily over the blocks and scattered fragments of the plateau in the direction of our tent. It was quite dark when we reached it shortly before seven o'clock, the welcome glow of Mwini's roaring camp-fire having served as a beacon to guide our weary footsteps. The rice was cooking in the pot, and right good we thought it, as we ate it with our roast dried meat, and washed it down with a mouthful of hot tea and brandy. But we were too tired to sleep; our heads ached, our skin and eyes smarted painfully; every muscle quivered, and we were feverish and restless. At last, utterly worn out, we fell asleep towards morning, and remained buried in a profound slumber till nearly midday.

In the afternoon I took some necessary observations. The reading of the aneroid was noted, and corrected by the boiling-point thermometer, the temperature of the ground and of the atmosphere was taken, and also the humidity of the latter. Then we took a round of bearings, and added to our botanical, geological, and photographic collections, filling up the odd moments with other work of a like nature.

I know of no occupation more satisfactory and interesting to one who is moderately skilled in the use of his instruments than taking observations such as we have just alluded to. No extraordinary tax is made upon the mind; it is mechanical dexterity, the result of practice, that is required more than theoretical knowledge. The traveller has no time to work out all the details of his observations as he goes along, and accordingly he confines himself to collecting the greatest possible amount of material for use during future leisure. Recognising this as a guiding principle, he has the satisfactory assurance of knowing that, when his observations have afterwards been computed, he has added his quota to scientific knowledge in the shape of trustworthy numerical values, however small may have been the outcome of his journey in other respects. The same may be said in regard to the collection of geological, botanical, and zoological specimens; to ensure good results, it is only necessary to get together as varied an assemblage of specimens as may be, and afterwards proceed to the arrangement of them according to an adequate scheme.

With photographs it is somewhat different. That property of photography by which it brings out with equal fidelity all the features of an object, without regard to their relative importance, is as disadvantageous where only the leading characteristics are wanted, as under other circumstances it is invaluable. Precisely on account of this property, however, it is eminently suited for the scenery of the uplands of Kilimanjaro. The outlines are so grand and so simple, that an artist would find nothing to add and nothing to omit; and thus, with its correct perspective and faithful reproduction of every detail, photography becomes the best means of preserving the impression the scene conveys, and must materially help the traveller in painting a word-picture of what he saw, provided always he has an appreciative eye for its most striking effects. To endeavour rightly to know and understand these is a task replete with magic charm. Nature appears in such marvellous and varied guise in these equatorial volcanic mountain heights, that it is an education in itself to determine how much is borrowed from fire and how much from air; what is the relation of one feature to the other, and to the organic life found in connection with each; and finally, how all may be combined into an intelligent and intelligible picture.

In the evening, long after the sun had gone down in purple splendour behind the cone of Meru, which showed itself on the horizon to the west of Kibo, we sat by the fire among the all-enshrouding mist, meditating plans for the next day. Our distance from the ice, in regard to which we had been so cruelly deceived, owing to the extreme purity of the atmosphere and the unbroken simplicity of the volcanic outlines, seemed to make it indispensable that we should camp farther up the mountain, if we were to reach the summit in time for a prolonged survey. The following day we resolved to devote to the selection of a suitable site for this purpose.

A bright moonlight night, during which the thermometer registered a minimum temperature of 15° F., was followed by a lovely morning. As there was no particular reason to hurry, we allowed ourselves the luxury of a late start, and did not strike camp until nearly midday. Purtscheller and I carried the provisions, climbing tackle, water, and so forth, while our man struggled with the sleeping sacks and other bulky articles. A very comical figure Mwini cut in his nondescript alpine rig-out. Over his skinny shanks he had drawn a couple of pairs of ragged woollen drawers, which at fifty different points afforded interesting glimpses of a faded woollen shirt. The tattered remnants of an old red military jacket, which had once adorned the shoulders of some dashing Scotch sergeant, did duty as a coat, while his feet were covered—or revealed—by a pair of my cast-off socks and an old pair of yellow slippers. Of his face nothing was visible except the nose, his whole head and neck being swathed in the voluminous folds of a gigantic turban, which, girt around his loins, on ordinary occasions was his only dress.

Following our old route of October 3, we reached the valley of the great glacier about four o'clock, and continued to climb upwards along the bottom until nearly six. By this time the mist had come down upon us, and, stumbling across a convenient hollow in the rocks, we resolved to camp for the night. The altitude was 15,260 feet, or about the height of the summit of Monte Rosa. There was, of course, nothing with which to make a fire, but everlasting flowers still grew in abundance, and Mwini gathered great bunches of them wherewith to line our rocky eyrie. In our sleeping sacks and with plenty of blankets, we passed on the whole a tolerably comfortable night, in spite of a temperature of 10° Fahr. At three in the morning we awoke, in capital trim for our climb to the summit, and this time Njaro, the spirit of the mountain, was propitious—we succeeded in reaching our goal.

For the first hour it was bright moonlight, but by-and-by the moon went down, and we were forced to depend on our lanterns to aid us in picking our way up the slippery lava ridge. The higher we climbed the rarer grew the atmosphere and the more brilliant the light of the stars. Never in my life have I seen anything to equal the steady lustre of this tropical starlight. The planets seemed to glow with a still splendour which was more than earthly, and even the fiery brilliance of Sirius and Regulus was mellowed and softened. Towards

morning the chastened glory of the zodiacal light streamed
upwards from the horizon almost to the zenith, rivalling the
mild effulgence of the Milky Way and the Magellanic clouds,
till the whole firmament seemed luminous with light divine.
Assuredly, the nights of lower earth know nothing of this
celestial silver radiance.

Shortly after dawn we reached the lower end of the Ratzel
glacier (17,580 feet). Here, trembling with cold, we sat
down to await the sunrise, huddled close together for the
sake of the extra warmth. A little after six o'clock the sun
rose behind the rugged peak of Mawenzi, and before long
we reached the foot of the wall of ice we had climbed on
the 3rd October. To our intense delight, we found the steps
we had then cut not so very much the worse for the two
days' exposure, and, as we now knew the nature of the path
ahead, we made our way upwards with comparative rapidity.
By eight o'clock we had crossed the great crevasse at an
altitude of 18,770 feet, and, although the difficulty of breathing and the physical strain were as great as on the former
occasion, we felt far less exhausted, our minds being so much
more free of anxiety. We were both in the highest spirits,
and already began to congratulate ourselves on the success of
our enterprise.

At a quarter to nine we reached our old point on the
crater rim at an altitude of 19,260 feet, but almost immediately pushed on again, all eager to reach the little outstanding pinnacle on the southern side, on which our hearts were
set. The path sloped gently upwards, skirting the edge
of the crater in a south-westerly direction, and scarcely had
we started when we again came in sight of the dark mass of
rock on the southern side of the summit (see p. 82) which
first attracted our attention in September, from the steppes
before Taveta. It had almost passed from our mind, for since

that one brief glimpse it had been hidden from view by the bulging ice-cap.

Our further progress presented no particular difficulty apart from the weathered surface of the ice and snow, to which by this time we had become pretty well accustomed. Passing a curiously shaped detached wall of ice about twenty feet in height, after a gradual ascent of an hour and a half, we reached the foot of the three rocky pinnacles, which we found to consist solely of loose blocks. These we climbed, one after the other, in a leisurely and systematic fashion, and found by the aneroid that the central one of the three attained an altitude of 19,700 feet, overtopping the others by some forty or fifty feet. I was the first to set foot on the culminating peak, which we reached at half-past ten o'clock. Taking out a small German flag, which I had brought with me for the purpose in my knapsack, I planted it on the weather-beaten lava summit with three ringing cheers, and in virtue of my right as its first discoverer christened this hitherto unknown and unnamed mountain peak—the loftiest spot in Africa and in the German Empire—*Kaiser Wilhelm's Peak.* Then we gave three cheers more for the Emperor, and shook hands in mutual congratulation.

Njaro, the guardian spirit of the mountain, seemed to take his conquest with a good grace, for neither snow nor tempest marred our triumphal invasion of his sanctuary. The ice-fields flashed and glittered in the dazzling sunlight, the wind sighed whisperingly in the crannies and crevices, and in the depths of the yawning cauldron at our feet light wreaths of vapour curled softly and ceaselessly.

For a few minutes we gave ourselves up to the impressive charm of our surroundings, and then suddenly awoke to the prosaic fact that it was long past breakfast-time, and that our inner man was becoming significantly con-

scious of "a felt want." Having deposited the topmost stone of the pile in my knapsack, we made our way back to the edge of the crater. Here we sat down, and after a hearty meal, proceeded to make a closer inspection of our surroundings. The sun was broiling hot, but the light north-easterly wind considerably modified the temperature, which by the sling thermometer we ascertained to be 36° Fahr. The only traces of vegetation observable were a few scraggy lichens.

Having taken the bearings, I proceeded to make a rough sketch of the crater, of which we had a magnificent view from the position we occupied. The depth is between 600 and 700 feet, and the diameter something over 2000 yards. Its walls are composed of ashy-grey and reddish-brown lava; on the southern side they are entirely free from ice, and descend almost perpendicularly to the bottom of the cauldron, which is covered with a layer of mud and ashes. On the north side, the ice is particularly massive, and slopes down in a series of blue and white terraces, which at the bottom partially cover a flattened brown cone of eruption composed of lava and ashes, the height of which cannot be much under 500 feet. The western wall is divided by an enormous cleft, through which the ice that at this point covers the bottom of the crater issues in the form of a glacier. How strange to think of the contrast between this icy stream and the former fiery incandescence of its bed—between this scene of sublime repose and solemn silence and the far-off time when the glowing rock issued red and molten from the womb of the mountain, shaken to its very centre by its mighty birth-pangs. It is a spectacle of imposing majesty and unapproachable grandeur, and the effect in our case was enhanced by the consciousness that we of all men were the first to gaze upon it: it was a never-to-be-forgotten experience.

We were reminded of the ·flight of time and abruptly recalled from our rhapsodies by the appearance of numerous floating wreaths of mist. Profiting by this warning, we at once commenced the descent, but before we had well started the mist was round us like a winding-sheet. Hurry as we might, it was slow work making our way over the brittle and slippery ice, and the passage of the Ratzel glacier occupied us fully a couple of hours. Our hands were so benumbed with cold that we could scarcely hold our ice-axes. Once I missed my footing and remained suspended in mid-air, hanging on to the handle of my axe, the blade of which was embedded in the ice above. Fortunately it did not give way, else we should both inevitably have been precipitated into the abyss below; with a little effort I managed to recover my foothold, and on we went again.

At one o'clock we reached the lower limit of the ice without breaking our bones, though as much could scarce be said of the state of our skin. Here we divested ourselves of our veils and spectacles, and, to Purtscheller's intense astonishment, I drew from my pocket a handful of cigarettes and a couple of cakes of chocolate, which I had been hoarding up as a little surprise for him ever since we left the coast. We sat down and demolished our treasures on the spot, enjoying ourselves like schoolboys in a pastry-cook's.

Now that the work we had come to do was an accomplished fact, we felt as merry as crickets, and when we rose to resume our march, it was as much as we could do to refrain from letting off our exuberant spirits in a regular race downhill over the masses of débris that lay between us and our sleeping-place of the night before. With many an echoing shout we warned Mwini of our coming, so that by the time

we reached the little hollow among the rocks, our trusty
servant stood awaiting us with everything packed ready for
continuing the journey to the camp at the saddle. As we
went along, I gave Mwini an account of our doings since
we had quitted him. The story of our difficulties did not
seem to impress him much. "*Haithuru; umefika sasa
ju kabisa, bassi*" ("It's all right; you got to the top at
last") was his invariable comment whenever I stopped to
take breath.

By sunset we sat at our tent-door awaiting the cooking
of a large potful of rice. The last rays of the sun gilded the
distant summit of Meru, and in the rosy evening light Kibo
seemed to beam down on us in quite a friendly fashion, as
the only mortals who had ever ventured to penetrate his
snowy fastness. We were in a very amiable frame of mind
ourselves, and, notwithstanding all the toil and trouble my
self-appointed task had cost me, I don't think I would that
night have changed places with anybody in the world.

We sat on talking far into the night, and, when at length
we did go to bed, it was with the firm intention of making the
most of the morrow as a day of rest, preparatory to an attack
on Mawenzi the day following.

But

> "The best-laid schemes o' mice and men gang aft agley."

During the night Mawenzi was visited by a snowstorm, and
in the morning even the plateau was covered with a slight
coating of snow. After the sun rose the snow rapidly disappeared, and I spent the forenoon photographing the
mountain scenery, while Purtscheller visited the "Triplets"
in search of geological specimens. I had just succeeded
in obtaining what I thought to be some very satisfactory
views, when, towards midday, a relay of men came up from

the half-way camp with fresh supplies of provisions. They brought the alarming news that my presence was required in Marangu at once, a dispute having arisen between Mareale and my caravan over the flag we displayed at our quarters there. I at once suspected a plot on the part of some of the coast slave-dealers then in Marangu, one or two of whom I knew had reason to bear me a grudge, and I resolved to proceed to the scene of the quarrel without delay.

Arranging with Purtscheller to await me or a message from me at the half-way camp, shortly after noon I set out to accompany the messengers thither myself. After a rapid march of five hours we reached our destination for the time being, where I found the inmates apparently quite at home, and greatly overjoyed to see me. Mingled with their shouts of welcome, I was much astonished to hear the lowing of an ox, which, on inquiry, proved to have been sent up by Mareale, with a thoughtful consideration for our welfare which I thought augured well for the settlement of the dispute.

Refreshing myself with a much-needed bath in the Mué, I continued my way downwards, accompanied by four men. The air, the hills, the plains, were all beautifully clear—I could even take a bearing of the distant mountains of Ndara. What a splendid day we had lost for Mawenzi !

With all possible speed we hurried along. Since last we passed that way the tall dry grass had all been burned down, probably in consequence of our deserted camp-fire at the Kifinika having spread, and from the ashes which rose as we went along I was soon as black as any of my followers. Just before we entered the forest we met a band of Useri, armed with small-bladed spears and shields of hide. On account of the drought prevailing at the time in the state of Useri, they had been compelled to drive their herds of goats farther up the mountain, to the fresh pasture-land on its southern side. In the forest itself we met another band of the same tribe, who had been to Marangu to barter their cattle for millet and beans, and were now returning homewards by the neutral path, to avoid passing through Rombo.

With blistered feet and tired to death after the nine hours' march from the breezy uplands to the comparatively close atmosphere of Jagga, I limped at last into the little station at Marangu. My sudden arrival was hailed with a storm of delight of almost absurd extravagance, which even the frightful appearance of my face — peeled and swollen with the sun and wind of the glaciers — scarcely was able to modify.

Rumour, as usual, had made a mountain of a mole-hill. On inquiring the cause of the dispute between Mareale and my men, it turned out that, incited, as I had suspected, by the coast traders, the chief had required us either to lower the German flag or pay him an indemnity of a thousand dollars. If one or other of these alternatives was not complied with within five days, the station was to be stormed by Mareale's warriors. With proper spirit, the Somál had refused to lower the flag, and, not knowing what to do next, had thought the best thing was to communicate with me.

Mareale needed no invitation to come to see me. As soon as he heard of my arrival he came at once, and I could see at a glance he was beginning to be ashamed of himself. I explained to him that the hoisting of the national colours over my tent was a matter of no importance to either of us, since the possession of Kilimanjaro was a point which had been settled between the English and the Germans at head-quarters long ago. I further reminded him of what he knew already—that I had merely come to ascend and explore the mountain in the interests of science ; and the matter was

finally settled by my agreeing to fly, in addition to the
objectionable "*baruti-na-damu-flag*" (or "blood-and-powder-
flag," as he was pleased to style our national ensign, from its
red and black colours), a second flag showing a white star
on a red ground, and supposed to represent the colours of
Mareale's house.

In the evening, to show that there was no ill-feeling, I
treated the natives to a display of fireworks, in the course of
which a spark from a rocket set fire to one of the men's
huts. During the night the windows of heaven were opened,
and on my devoted countenance—thickly smeared with a
layer of zinc ointment to allay the smart of the blisters—it
rained, not water, alas! but white ants and bits of straw. Over
the spectacle I presented next morning to the eyes of my
affrighted porters it is as well to draw a veil.

The day was spent in writing, for the benefit of my friends
in Europe, an account of my experiences thus far, which was
duly transmitted to them by means of the post-runner of the
Moji mission, who happened to be leaving for the coast in the
course of a day or two. We had as yet received no letters
from home, but they were expected by the end of another
week, and I left orders that they should be forwarded to us
at the saddle plateau immediately they arrived. Thanks to
the presence of the English missionaries, matters have already
advanced so far in Jagga that the Europeans stationed there
get their letters and newspapers not more than a month old.
The most inveterate hermit could not object to this pleasant
feature in his exile; for, however much a European may
revel in the untrammelled freedom of African life—however
much he may rejoice to be rid of hollow forms and ceremonies,
he is still too much a social animal not to pine in solitude
for tidings of family and friends, and too much a civilised
animal to be able to forego without a pang all knowledge

of how the world wags in lands where the blessings of civilisation carry with them their accustomed curse.

Having dispatched two men to Moji with the bulky packet,
I was ready to return to the scene of my labours. Once more
it was "*Per aspera ad astra!*"

LOWER END OF THE RATZEL GLACIER.

CHAPTER V.

TEN DAYS ABOVE FIFTEEN THOUSAND FEET.

ONCE more "*per aspera ad astra!*" The "asperities" commenced from the very first, for we crammed into a single day what formerly had occupied two days and a half, climbing from Marangu to the half-way camp between sunrise and sunset. Up through the green banana plantations, over the murmuring mountain streams, on through the emerald twilight of the forest and across the breezy uplands —on and on we steadily tramped, reaching the Mué at eventide, in time to reassure my little band of attendants, who had spent the last three days in the greatest anxiety. I found Herr Purtscheller waiting for me, and, although considerably knocked up after my recent exertions, I at once made the necessary arrangements for moving up to the plateau next morning.

TYPICAL PLANTS FROM THE UPPER REGIONS OF KILIMANJARO.

During the night occurred what might have been a serious disaster. Notwithstanding the strictest injunctions to the contrary, some of the men had secretly kindled a fire inside their hut. All of a sudden the hut burst into a blaze, and almost before we were aware, the wind was carrying the flames in the direction of our tent. In less time than it takes to write it, we had the tent hauled down, while the men set to work to thrash out the flames with branches and bushes. In five minutes all was over. The culprits were sufficiently punished by the loss of all their belongings, and wore an exceedingly hang-dog look as they sneaked off with their comrades to the shelter of the two remaining huts, while we had our tent removed a good distance off, to be out of reach of such mischances in the future.

After a plentiful meal of rice and honey—a feast of the gods in Central Africa—we once more started on our way upwards. Accompanied by four men carrying the same equipments as formerly, we pursued our old route along the edge of the ravine, and at the end of three hours crossed the rivulet rising from the Schneequelle, with its lonely grey senecios. This time, instead of turning to the left in the direction of Kibo, we kept on along the bank of the stream, as in 1887. The stream here flows through a grassy hollow about 150 feet wide, the bottom of which is strewn with large boulders, while on either side rises a ridge of lava covered with loose stones and a scanty sprinkling of low herbs. The ascent was comparatively easy, but in the damp, raw mist it was bitterly cold, and the men were soon perfectly benumbed. "Ah Bwana," cried first one and then another, with chattering teeth,—"Ah Bwana, you have brought us here to die." There was little fear of that, of course, but nevertheless I thought it as well to halt as soon as we had reached the source of the stream where once before we had pitched our tents in July 1887. The circle of stones we had ranged around our camp was still standing, and the tent was set up in the old place. The men found a comfortable shelter in the caves in the adjoining wall of lava, and, under the influence of a roaring fire and a meal of hot bean-porridge, gradually thawed so far as to strike up some of their melancholy, monotonous Zanzibar songs. Only Mohammed still looked glum, and swore that on this accursed mountain "the —— beans would never grow soft though you cooked them for a century." His observation was as correct as it was forcible, for at our present elevation water boiled at 190° F., a point much too low for cooking purposes. After this we took the precaution to have the beans cooked at the half-way camp before they were brought up to us.

During the night the wind suddenly changed, and, blowing from the ice-fields of Kibo, brought the minimum temperature down to 15° F. In the morning everything was covered with a white rime, which speedily disappeared, however, under the rays of the rising sun. Soon we were once more on our way up the valley, the ridge on the left gradually sloping away as we ascended, that on the right becoming higher and more rugged. To the best of my recollection the latter ended in a rocky hill not far from the foot of Mawenzi, and we followed it the greater part of the way, the dust and ashes between the blocks affording a good foothold.

At every step we obtained a better view of Kibo, and were even able to distinguish the familiar "Viermännerstein." Reaching at last the hill I had in view, we established ourselves on its south-western slope, and pitched our tent in the shelter of two great masses of rock, which had apparently rolled down from the heights above (see Illustration). The altitude we ascertained to be 14,300 feet, but there were plenty of Euryops bushes for firewood, and otherwise the site

Mawenzi from the S.W.   View from Camp on the Saddle Plateau (14,200 ft.)

seemed very suitable for our purpose. The only drawback was the want of water—a want which entailed a great deal of extra work on Mwini Amani, who again was our only attendant. The nearest spring was the Schneequelle, where we had camped overnight, and every drop of water we used had to be fetched by Mwini all that distance.

The first thing we did after kindling a fire was to set about taking the midday observation for latitude. Afterwards we climbed the hill, which rose steeply behind the camp. At the summit were two flattened peaks connected by a narrow *col*, from which we concluded that here was the original source of the lava stream along which we had ascended in the morning. The hill had a precipitous face on all sides, especially towards the west, where it sank down directly into a deep ravine, on the farther side of which lay another cone and another lava stream. Almost straight behind these rose the red central hill on the saddle, and behind that again the "Triplets" at the foot of the cloud-piercing Kibo. Except along the lower limit of the ice-cap, which forms a bold zigzag, the eye in this direction rested only upon straight or gently-curving lines. A conspicuous feature was the descending streams of lava, which stretch downwards along the mountain-side in long regular ridges like railway embankments. Towards the north the view ranged uninterruptedly over the saddle plateau, but the plains beyond were still invisible. There was a marked contrast when we turned towards the east. Here there were no more straight lines and pleasant curves, but dark and threatening the shattered bulwarks of Mawenzi rose sternly into the upper air. Like some gigantic ruin, its rugged, weather-beaten summit stood out jagged and defiant against the sky-line, rising gradually from south to north in a series of fantastic peaks and pinnacles.

In the immediate foreground the south-western side of

Mawenzi was covered with loose volcanic débris, which formed a gigantic talus sloping steeply downwards from a rocky ridge, apparently connected with the series of pinnacles which lead toward the topmost peak. This ridge was accordingly selected as the point towards which to direct our steps on the morrow, though a single glance upward sufficed to show we had no easy climb before us.

Having completed our survey, we turned our footsteps "homeward," laden with chips of rock, some of them crusted with lichens, the only form of vegetation to be met with on the cone. The rest of the day was spent in making our preparations for a first assault on Mawenzi next morning (October 13th).

A bitter north-east wind was blowing when we awoke about 4 A.M., and set out in the moonlight, axe and rope in hand. Mwini heard us stirring, and as usual called his cheery "Safe return!" after us. There is a vein of inborn superstition in every one, and I had grown so used to Mwini's parting salutation by way of benediction to our more important undertakings, that I verily believe I should have thought it a presage of evil had he happened to omit it.

With the accustomed happy omen ringing in our ears, we set our faces eastward and upward, and followed the direction of the hollow between the lava sheets to the east of our hill. Crossing several transverse dykes and a series of "tortoise-shell" boulders, we reached the bottom of the talus at dawn. The dark walls and pinnacles of Mawenzi gradually became visible in the growing daylight, and the incomparable lustre of Venus slowly died away as the sun rose.

The ground at this point was moist and boggy, and was covered with green, springy turf, abundantly marked with the footprints and droppings of the eland. The altitude we ascertained to be 15,260 feet. Continuing our way upwards, we reached a tiny spring welling up from beneath a large slab of rock. The water was frozen over, for, although the sun was already up, its rays do not reach this side of the mountain until after 10 A.M. Vegetation appeared in patches among the débris up to a height of 15,420 feet, where we came upon a second spring and the highest flowering plants that we observed on Kilimanjaro.

The ascent now became excessively toilsome. At every step the loose stones gave way beneath our feet, and every few minutes we had to pause to take breath. Turning for a moment to look back, we could see beyond the sunny slopes of Kibo the level plain of Nyiri slumbering in the morning light, while to the left, from among the stratus clouds of the steppes, towered the magnificent cone of Meru, like some vast cyclopean pyramid.

And now began the most breakneck bit of climbing it has ever been my lot to experience. Turning to the left when about two-thirds of the way up the talus, we began the ascent of the lava cliffs that fence it in on one side. Tying ourselves together by the rope, we worked our way gradually upwards for another hundred feet, through the openings of vertical fissures, and along the narrow ledges and pinnacles of the lava beds, which here dip towards the north. Purtscheller went first, and, although he is so short-sighted that he is obliged to wear spectacles, he displayed the most surprising aptitude for finding a way round awkward corners and along the face of dizzy precipices where to proceed seemed impossible. Once he disappeared from view through a cleft, and I heard him call out that without wings it was impossible to go any further; but a few yards to the right we managed to find a footing. First the ice-axes (which were worse than useless to us on this occasion) were slung over by the rope, then I followed—always trying the ledges before I ventured upon them; for, although they had borne Purtscheller's weight, it did not follow that they would bear mine, as I am a man of heavier build than he is. As often as not they gave way, and much time and trouble was lost in seeking a firmer foothold. We had to work with our hands as much as with our feet, for the steepness and jaggedness of these lava cliffs is without parallel. A dozen of times I was left suspended in mid-air, clinging to the rope or jammed fast in the jaws of the cleft we were attempting to cross, while the crumbling rock gave way beneath me, and went crashing into the depths below. Sometimes we had to crawl on our stomachs along a ledge eighteen inches wide, and sometimes we had to wriggle ourselves upwards between two smooth faces of rock, by squeezing our knees and elbows against the sides. We had no time to think of anything but the work of the moment—every nerve and muscle was strained to reach the jagged zigzag above. In case we should have to return the same way, as we went along we marked our route with pieces of red paper weighted with stones, but it must be confessed we both fervently hoped the precaution would prove needless.

Three and a half hours of this desperate climbing on hands and knees brought us at length to the narrow *col* along which we hoped to make our way to the line of peaks above. When still a short distance from the foot, on looking up I suddenly caught a glimpse of the sky on the other side, not *above* the *col*, but through a rent which here split it in two. The crumbling wall of lava was barely more than a yard broad, and looked as if it were scarcely strong enough to bear our weight. There was no choice, however, and, come what might, we resolved to risk it.

Viewed from this point, the jaggedness of the mountain summit beggars all description. The rock is so brittle, and is cut and carved into such countless points and spikes and teeth, that I can only compare it to the edge of a saw. The wonder is how it has escaped being entirely weathered away. Although there was scarcely a breath of wind, the sound of falling fragments sounded continually in our ears, showing how utterly rotten is the material of which the rock is composed.

Partly along the top of the crazy parapet, partly close beneath it, we slowly made our way to its apparent point of junction with the central crest. Our prospects of success looked tolerably hopeful, and our spirits rose accordingly. Judge of our disappointment and chagrin when we suddenly saw a tremendous chasm yawning at our feet, and completely cutting us off from the loftier peaks beyond.

For a moment we felt completely checkmated; then, remembering our recent achievements on Kibo, we plucked up heart again, and, since nothing more was to be made of the summit for that day, resolved to see what it was like on the other side of the ridge along which we had ascended. To descend on that side of the mountain promised at least to be easier than to return by the way we had come, and, having ascertained that the altitude was 16,700 feet, we turned to commence the descent. After we had climbed downwards for a little way, we again reached a talus of débris, down which we slid at a rapid rate, until we were once more suddenly brought up short on the edge of a precipice running sheer downwards to a depth of 600 or 700 feet. Fate seemed to be against us, and it almost looked as if we were to be beaten here again; but at length, after an anxious search, I succeeded in discovering a narrow channel choked with ice—the only ice we saw on Mawenzi. We had to proceed with the utmost caution, letting ourselves down with the rope. It was by no means an easy matter, and every moment we were in danger of being crushed to death by the avalanches of stones which constantly kept falling from above. We had got about half-way down, when crash came a tremendous volley, and then another and another, following each other with alarming rapidity. Dodging this mountain artillery as best we might, we at last reached the bottom of the precipitous talus, and sat down under the shelter of the biggest boulder we could find, and had our first rest and the first morsel of food that day.

It was half-past two o'clock, and the clouds were sweeping and swirling in misty wreaths around the peaks overhead. On all sides the cliffs rose precipitously to a height of over 2000 feet, culminating in the mighty wall that is crowned by the topmost pinnacle of the mountain. The diversity of colour displayed in the superimposed layers of different kinds of lava was perfectly marvellous, ranging from dull yellow to light red through greyish blue, green, brown, and a variety of other shades. It was a veritable geologist's Paradise—the Promised Land of the mineralogist and the petrographer.

Rounding the lower end of a rugged ridge of red lava, which runs westward from this point, we continued our way downwards past a low circular crater some 120 paces in diameter, and after another two hours' scramble in the driving mist arrived at last in camp, where we found Mwini anxiously awaiting us.

In the evening, large numbers of rock-swallows came circling round our camp-fire, and, with our old friends the cheery little stonechats, helped to enliven our loneliness with their pleasant twitter. After dark we sat watching the grass-fires in the southern plains—here creeping along like some gigantic fiery serpent, there flickering and twinkling like the lights of a great city. But all the lights of earth grew pale and commonplace before the brighter effulgence of the lights

of heaven, wondrous among which was the silver cone of the
zodiacal light, its base resting on the far horizon, its apex
stretching upward to the Scorpion, with a radiance which
outshone the chastened glory of the Milky Way.

Before returning to make another attempt on Mawenzi on
October 15th, we were compelled to grant our throbbing limbs
the luxury of a day's rest. I spent the time taking a round
of angles with the theodolite, and at midday took a second
observation for latitude. Mwini, whilst on his way to the
spring for water, had been doing a little exploration on his
own account, and returned triumphantly carrying an empty
tin, which, judging from the brilliant legend still legible
thereon, had once contained mock-turtle soup. It had probably been left behind by the English hunting-party under
Jackson and Harvey, who were known to have spent some
time in this neighbourhood. On the principle of letting
nothing be lost, we turned the tin to account as a water-
pitcher.

Shortly after noon we were suddenly overtaken by a
tremendous storm of sleet and hail, which in less than
half-an-hour sent the thermometer down with a run from 79°
to 40° F. A thick mist settled round us for the rest of the
afternoon, but it cleared away towards sunset, and once
more the weather promised well for the morrow.

We had come to the conclusion that our best plan would be
to ascend the great western talus a second time ; but, instead
of turning aside to the lava wall on the left, we resolved to
make straight for the great notch in the central crest, from
which we hoped to find a way, if not to the loftiest pinnacle
of all, at least to one of its near neighbours. But our great
intentions very nearly came to grief for that day, at any rate,
through a too zealous adherence to the same excellent principle which had prompted the preservation of the empty soup

tin. We had both partaken too freely of some over-ripe bananas, which we thought it would be waste to throw away, and the result was a violent colic, which kept us awake the better part of the night. Nevertheless, at half-past five in the morning we decided to make a start, and left our tent just as dawn was beginning to break. The moon was still up, and Venus glowed in the heavens with remarkable brilliancy.

We were both still too much taken up with our inward sorrows to be very lively company, and scarcely a word was spoken as we tramped on one behind the other to the foot of the heap of detritus. We stopped a few seconds to recover breath on the little patch of turf half way up the talus (15,260 feet), and, although the temperature was six degrees below freezing-point, the water was trickling freely from its rocky source.

From this point we followed our old track for a considerable distance, then, turning to the right, kept on directly towards the central crest, the bottom of which we reached shortly after seven o'clock. The altitude we found to be 16,400 feet.

From ledge to ledge and ridge to ridge we now toiled slowly and painfully upwards on our hands and knees, till we reached a narrow neck of rock somewhat nearer the highest point than the notch we originally had in view. Half-an-hour later, with the aid of the rope, we managed to scramble to the summit of the towering mass of rock on our left, and then saw that between us and the goal of our desires, which was about four hundred yards distant, there yet lay two jagged peaks. The ridge on which we stood was so narrow and so broken that it was utterly impossible it could bear the weight of two men. To seek to pass round by the base of the peaks seemed an equally hopeless venture, and once more we had to acknowledge ourselves foiled.

A fresh breeze blew from the north-east, and the clear atmosphere favoured a view on almost every side. Only the eastern
plains were concealed by a bank of mist, but above this, on
the horizon, rose the mountains of Taita, Usambara, and Paré.
Our immediate surroundings presented a spectacle far more
wonderful and interesting. We stood on the brink of an
abysmal gulf, surrounded by an array of peaks, and spires, and
craggy pinnacles impossible to describe. On this, its eastern
side, from an altitude of about 16,830 feet, the mountain
sinks sheer downwards into a gigantic cauldron, the sides of
which are scarred with innumerable rugged ravines. As we
gazed from our dizzy height upon the hills and valleys, the
streams and bushes, the endless profusion of gullies and
gorges 6000 or 7000 feet below, it seemed as if we had
a bird's-eye view of earth from a balloon. I was at first
inclined to believe that here we had the original vent of
the ancient volcano, but I could not reconcile this supposition with the prevailing dip of the beds of lava—at
all events I could not be quite sure of it. Next to the
Kibo crater, this was the most wonderful sight we saw on
Kilimanjaro.

Nothing could be more marked than the contrast between the external appearance of these two extinct volcanoes
—Kibo with the unbroken, gradual slopes of the typical
volcanic cone — Mawenzi with its bewildering display of
many-coloured lavas and its fantastically carved outlines, the
result of long ages of exposure, combined with the tendency
of its component rocks to split vertically rather than horizon-
tally. The hand of time has left its impress upon Kibo
too, but the havoc it has wrought is not to be detected at
a distance. From where we were standing, the icy dome
stood out in clear relief against the azure background of the
sky. The Kaiser Wilhelm's Peak was plainly discernible,

and we could even make out the position of the cone of eruption within the crater.

Once more the midday mists began to draw towards the summit of the mountain, warning us that it was time to depart. In the excitement of climbing, the morning's indisposition had been long ago forgotten, and as soon as we had made the descent of the ridge of rocks we gladly laid aside the rope and commenced a headlong scramble down the talus. Meeting with no obstacle worth mentioning, we were soon at the bottom, and by noon were taking our ease, if not exactly in our inn, at least in what was nearly as good—the comfortable neighbourhood of our cheery camp-fire.

A pleasant surprise awaited us. Besides a fresh supply of provisions for the delectation of our souls, which seemed daily growing more material at the expense of our bodies, the men from below had brought a packet of letters and papers, forwarded to us from the mission station in Moji. A delightful hour was spent in the perusal of home and coast news, which we read between the whiffs of a fragrant cigar, one of a bundle of choice Havanas thoughtfully included in the post-packet by friend Steifensand of Zanzibar. Even a snowstorm, which came down on us in the course of the afternoon, failed to disturb the equanimity produced by these gifts of the gods, though our little tent afforded us but scanty shelter. By sunset there was an inch of snow on the ground as far as the lower edge of the plateau, and during the night the thermometer fell to 16° below freezing-point.

In order to tell the story of our three ascents of Mawenzi continuously, we must here anticipate the actual course of events by a few days, omitting in the meantime the account of two ascents of Kibo which we made in the interval.

This time we resolved to attack Mawenzi from the north, in the hope of meeting with better success than had

crowned our efforts hitherto. In the event of a third failure to reach the summit, we consoled ourselves beforehand with the thought that we should at least learn something of the character of the north side of Kilimanjaro, a region as yet totally unexplored.

On October 21st, at the usual hour—half-past five—we were up and on the way. The moon was in its last quarter; consequently, owing to the want of light, our progress was somewhat slow. The sun was already up when we reached the rocky ridge which here runs downward in a north-westerly direction as a continuation of the central crest.

It seemed that once again we were doomed to defeat, for even at this distance we could see that it would be a mere waste of time to attempt to approach the summit from this side. The morning was bitterly cold, the aneroid in my coat-pocket registering a temperature of only 11° Fahr., and, spite of thick woollen gloves, my fingers were soon quite benumbed. Hurrying on over the heaps of blocks and boulders, by degrees we got warmed up, and felt richly repaid for our toil and trouble when at length the northern plains became visible through the morning mists.

At last we found the way barred by a precipitous wall of lava, which seemed to forbid farther progress in a northerly direction. But Purtscheller's unerring instinct once more stood us in good stead, and with no worse accident than some slight scraping of shins and elbows, we managed to find a way to the top (15,190 feet). Here we had an unobstructed view of the northern slopes of the mountain and of the plains below. All was loneliness and desolation. No smiling fields, no cosy village met the eye; the boundless wilderness, the happy hunting-ground of the lion and the hyena, stretched on and on for miles into the dim grey haze of distance.

Beneath us, the forest zone was bounded by a belt of grass-land above and below, but there was nothing resembling the fertile terrace of Jagga on the southern side of the mountain. The forest itself is neither so dense nor so broad, and gradually tapers away towards the west. In the midst of the plains, at a distance of about twelve miles from the edge of the forest, there is a belt of lake-like marshes, fed by two rivulets rising on Mawenzi and by a stream from Kibo. Between the base of Kilimanjaro and the distant mountains of Kiulu in the north-east, the whole region is plentifully dotted with small parasitic cones. Everywhere there are marked traces of volcanic activity, and, if I am not mistaken, I saw clouds of steam issuing from a conical peak far to the north.

We had now reached our most northerly point, and turning in an easterly direction, we took our way across one of the huge tali of débris of such frequent occurrence on the sides of Mawenzi. It was bounded at its farther extremity by a line of cliffs, at the bottom of which (15,420 feet) we discovered a tiny lakelet, sparkling like a jewel in a setting of gladsome green. Sixteen hundred feet above towered the titanic rampart of the central crest, unapproachable here as elsewhere.

Where the north-eastern ridge starts from the massive barrier above, there is a deep notch, which we had kept in view as a point at which to aim. We reached it about half-past nine, and were once more confronted by the great abyss on whose western brink we had stood when we reached our highest point on the second ascent. More than ever I felt inclined to believe that this was the original crater of Mawenzi, but even yet I cannot quite make up my mind on the subject. Our altitude was 16,140 feet.

Beyond the yawning cauldron and the rocky spurs below, we had a magnificent view over the plains to the east and south-east, from the conical Julu mountains on the left to the mountains of Taita and the distant ranges of Paré and Ugweno on the extreme right. The most attractive features in the landscape are its three lakes, Jipé, Jala, and Tsavo— Jipé long and narrow, Jala round and rock-girdled, Tsavo many-branched and marshy. Narrowing the vision so as to take in the lower zones of Kilimanjaro, we once more caught a glimpse of the green banana plantations of Jagga, the eastern states of Rombo, Msai, Mwika, and Marangu lying close beneath the shaggy girdle of the forest.

We set our faces campwards shortly after midday. On the way back, Purtscheller never ceased to lament that again we had failed to achieve the primary object of the morning's enterprise—the final ascent of the summit. It was no doubt a deep disappointment to both of us, but I thought that on the whole we had great reason to be satisfied with the results of our day's work. The objects of my expedition were principally geographical, and in a geographical aspect the present excursion had proved most valuable, if only for the excellent opportunities it had afforded us of studying the topography of the region. In this respect we had omitted nothing essential, and although it is true that had we been successful in reaching the summit we should have felt our task to be more complete, still under the circumstances I did not feel justified in wasting further time on this difficult undertaking. I leave it to some aspiring explorer of the future, who may perhaps find a way to snatch his laurels from the rugged brow of the hoary Mawenzi.

We had still work to do on Kibo. I could not consider my survey of the peak complete until I had explored its northern aspect—as yet totally unknown—and approached the summit from a different point, in order to perfect my observations of the crater by viewing it from both sides.

M

With these objects in view, we left our camp on October 17th, shortly after 3 A.M., and set out in a north-westerly direction across the broad sheets of mud and ashes to the north of the hills on the saddle. A tramp of two hours and a quarter brought us, shortly before sunrise, to a wide hollow, which stretches from the north-eastern base of Kibo to the grass-lands below. The north and north-eastern sides of the peak are traversed by long lines of débris, a number of which converge at the head of the hollow and extend downwards as a broad talus. Above, the lower limit of the ice-cap lies evenly along the rim of the crater, without any of the tongue-like processes by which it is distinguished to the south.

Commencing the ascent, we were obliged to cut obliquely across a series of ravines choked with débris and separated by ridges of lava, the passage of which was excessively tiresome and difficult. Towards the east the shifting panorama of cloud and sky grew ever more wonderful as we ascended. On our ever-widening horizon the overarching vault of sunny blue seemed to rest on a broad band of rosy vapour, gradually melting into the veil of soft grey haze which hid the plains. The lower slopes of the mountain were clear, showing first a broad belt of sand and débris at a height of about 13,000 feet, then a stretch of pasture-land studded with bushes, and lower down an interrupted strip of forest, which gradually thinned and disappeared towards the west. Here and there among the trees a curling column of smoke told of the kraals of wandering Masai, or of their semi-serfs, the Wa-ndorobbo, who gain their livelihood solely by the chase. The forest being here so comparatively scanty, and there being absolutely no cultivated zone, it is easy to understand how the herds of eland come up from the plains to the saddle plateau, where from time to time we had seen them grazing.

On the north side of the mountain we had hoped to find a comparatively easy way to the ice-cap, for another traveller relates that he here succeeded in reaching it provided only with a stick. I am sorry to say we were sadly disappointed. After five hours' hard climbing in a north-westerly direction, over the ridges of lava and the hollows which separated them, we were forced to give in. At an average elevation of 18,700 feet the ice abruptly rose above us as a compact, continuous wall, 100 to 120 feet high, and we were soon convinced that it was impossible to scale it without the assistance of a number of men, and every facility which the science of Alpine climbing could supply.

At an altitude of 18,570 feet we sat down to rest by the side of a forked glacier, from whose lower end the melting ice issued in the form of two small streams. The glare of the sun was intense, and a mysterious rustling, crackling sound went on continuously in the rents and cracks of the icy wall above. Whilst I was occupied with taking bearings, Purtscheller propped himself against a block of lava, and gave proof of his enviable power of going to sleep at any moment and in any position. Just before midday, however, the mists began as usual to draw towards us; so putting away the instruments, we began to make the best of our way downwards.

Crossing the series of ridges and hollows—sixteen in number—at a lower level than in the course of the ascent in the morning, at a height of 15,910 feet we came upon a small glacier occupying the space between two ridges, which had evidently originated by a fall of ice from above. Here we refreshed ourselves with a draught of the beautifully clear water which issued from it, and resumed our way downwards along the bottom of the wide hollow we had crossed in the morning. Slipping and sliding among the loose débris, we by-and-by discovered that we had passed the level of the saddle plateau; and thereupon we had to retrace our steps and make our way upwards again, which prolonged our ten hours' climb by yet another hour of hard work. It was almost six o'clock when we came in sight of our little tent, looking very cosy and inviting in its sheltered nook beneath the shadow of the hill behind. From afar our ears were greeted by Mwini's jubilant shouts, informing us of the welcome arrival of cooked fowls and "soft" beans. It was "virtue rewarded" once more. We had never yet returned from any of our excursions without finding some pleasant surprise awaiting us in camp; and I must say I think we enjoyed our commonplace fare, more than many a sated Alpine tourist the Pommery and Greno of his luxurious hotel.

Rather than risk being beaten back from the summit of Kibó a second time, on preparing to make our last ascent, we resolved once more to bivouac some way up the peak. To this end we had selected, on our way back from the exploration of the north side, a spot to the north of the "Triplets," that promised excellent shelter in the caves between the boulders with which it was strewn. It was situated immediately beneath the great notch in the ice-cap towards which I had unsuccessfully aimed in 1887, and now I was determined to give it one more trial.

Mwini Amani did not seem greatly to relish the prospect of another night so near the stars, and pulled rather a wry face when our proposals were mooted to him. Nevertheless, when we set out for the heights at two o'clock in the afternoon of October 18th, he stood ready to follow us with the sleeping-sacks and blankets, while we, as before, did our best to grapple with the rest of our belongings. The day was clear and bright up here on the saddle, and it was strange to

watch the great masses of clouds sailing slowly towards us
from the south and north, and see them mount suddenly
upwards and melt into space as they reached the edge of
the plateau.

The caves (15,390 feet) were reached shortly before five
o'clock. They are simply caused by the manner in which
the blocks of lava have accidentally fallen together; and in
one of them—a large roomy chamber with a narrow opening
—we found everything that could be desired in the way of
a sleeping-place.

Imagine our astonishment, on entering into possession of
our eligible quarters, when we discovered that we were by no
means the first occupants. Close to the entrance were traces
of a recent fire, with a number of bones belonging to some
large animal, probably an eland, and some rags of banana
matting. The tell-tale footprint on the sand was not more of
a surprise to Crusoe on his desert island. Even Mwini forgot
his accustomed air of lofty indifference so far as to indulge in
a series of undignified "clicks."

From the nature of the remains, we saw at once that we
had not lighted on the scene of any former European encampment, and it was equally certain that none of the Wa-jagga
tribes would have ventured thus far up the mountain. We
came to the conclusion, therefore, that the former tenants of
our cave must have belonged to the Wa-ndorobbo, parties of
whom are known to follow the chase into remote districts of
the mountain, though we had not before suspected that they
penetrated thus far. Apparently, having succeeded in bringing down their game, they had stayed to "make a night
of it" on the spot. It was another discovery of "fossil
remains" to add to that of the empty soup tin and the Salvation Army newspaper.

During the night we experienced the hitherto unprecedented temperature of 7° Fahr., but slept comfortably enough till about a quarter to four, when we awoke to find the moon ready to light us on our upward way. For three hours we climbed over a talus so steep and so extensive as quite to put to shame anything of a similar kind to be met with in the Alps. The angle of the slope was at first comparatively slight, but afterwards increased abruptly to 30° or 35°. Leaving on the left the depression up which I had attempted the ascent in 1887, we crossed a number of transverse ridges, and, pressing steadily upwards, shortly before sunrise reached the upper end of the talus, at an altitude of 18,040 feet.

A bitterly cold wind was blowing from the north, and we availed ourselves of the friendly shelter of a neighbouring rock to snatch a much-needed rest of half-an-hour. Here we watched the sun as he leaped up triumphantly from behind the rocky pinnacles of Mawenzi. The plains below were hidden by a thick layer of heavy cumulus clouds, high above which, in the south, floated distinctly marked dark flecks of cirrus, moving slowly towards the south-west. Kibo above, the plateau beneath, and Mawenzi facing us, shone grey and brown and red in the rays of the morning sun.

We continued our way upwards along ridges of weathered lava and obsidian, displaying all the colours of the rainbow in marvellously beautiful combinations. Slowly but surely we approached the ice-cap, and at last, at half-past seven, arrived at its lower limit at an altitude of 18,910 feet. Immediately above us was the great notch on the eastern side of the crater; to the left, 600 or 700 feet below, was the wall of ice which had effectually barred my progress in my former attempt to reach the summit from this side. To the right the ice extended in an unbroken line towards the north,

Kibo from the E. View from the Mawenzi Camp (14,300 ft.)

presenting a slightly overhanging series of massive cliffs of nearly uniform height.

Pausing only to get our ice-tackle in order, we commenced the ascent of the ice-cap, which at first proved so slippery and so steep that once more we were obliged to have recourse to the tedious process of hewing steps. About ten minutes of this work brought us to the notch, whence, from a different standpoint, we again had a full view of the crater. Here projecting points and bosses of rock were visible through the ice, and everything seemed to promise such easy progress that Purtscheller gave it as his opinion we should reach the cone at the bottom in an hour, and be back in camp by mid-day. A little experience of the *nieve penitente* surface of the ice ahead soon caused us to modify our sanguine expectations, and presently we were beset by a series of obstacles which sufficiently proved the wisdom of the pithy adage which forbids the counting of chickens before they are hatched.

The ice-sheet stretched in a compact mass to the foot of the small central cone below, and its surface was tremendously weathered by sun and wind. Without wasting much time in reflection, we plunged into our difficulties forthwith, and soon became involved in a chaos of ruts and rents and jagged points, amid which it was next to impossible to find a footing. Often, when we thought we had succeeded in doing so, the brittle crust gave way beneath us, and we found ourselves up to the armpits, struggling to extricate ourselves from the jaws of a crevasse. Needless to say, our hands were soon bruised and bleeding, and, in spite of warm gloves, our fingers were perfectly benumbed.

We were about half-way through this terrific bit of work when we came upon what was perhaps as wonderful a discovery as any we made on Kilimanjaro. It almost savours of the fabulous, but here in this stern frost-bound region, at the very summit of a mountain 20,000 feet high, we lighted on the dead body of an antelope—one of the small species we had noticed on the pasture-lands below. How the animal came there it is impossible to say. In all probability it had made its way upward by the same path as ourselves at a time when the ice was covered with its winter coating of snow, and, overtaken in these lofty solitudes by the fury of a mountain-storm, had paid with its life the penalty of its adventurous curiosity.

At the end of three-quarters of an hour we stood on the stony ground at the bottom of the crater, and prepared to continue our way over the terribly fissured ice-sheets which still lay between us and the brown lavas and ashes of the central parasitic cone. Having ascertained that the altitude here was 18,930 feet, we pressed onwards with desperate energy, until at last Purtscheller drew up short, and declared that, if I insisted on going forward, he would not answer for the consequences. It did indeed seem a hopeless struggle ; so reluctantly I was compelled to relinquish the idea of reaching the cone, and content myself with a thorough survey of the bottom of the crater. We lingered until nine o'clock, spending the time in taking various observations, after which we made our way up the southern side of the notch to the ice on the rim of the crater above. The altitude at this point was 19,240 feet, and the temperature in the sun, as shown by the ordinary thermometer, was 54° F. The sling thermometer registered only 32° F. We remained here a quarter of an hour, during which I made a sketch of the crater, and took a number of bearings.

The view from our present standpoint embraced the whole of the southern, eastern, and northern aspects of the crater, and thus enabled us to complete our former survey, and to confirm the observations already made. The bottom consists of a layer of mud and ashes, partially covered with ice. It is deepest towards the west, in the immediate vicinity of the great cleft, and highest towards the north, where it is concealed by the vast ice-sheet that stretches downwards from the rim, and to a large extent overrides the central parasitic cone. The variety of colour and form displayed in the grand terrace-like galleries of the sides and in the tumbled sea of ice below is a spectacle of rare and exquisite beauty. We did not dare for long give ourselves up to the enjoyment of it, however, and, tearing ourselves reluctantly away, with one last, lingering look in the direction of "our" crater and "our" Kaiser Wilhelm's Peak, we bade farewell to the icy heights of Kibo, probably for ever.

The descent to the bottom of the notch was a stiffish bit of work, involving the cutting of a large number of steps; but by ten o'clock we were once more on the level of the outer ring of ice, and continued our way downwards with all possible speed, in order to escape the fast-gathering mist. We slid down the stony slopes between us and our cave in about a fourth of the time it had taken us to climb them, and, picking up Mwini, who, warned by our shouts, stood ready waiting for us, without halting to rest, we went briskly forward in the direction of our tent.

On the way we took time to ascend the red cinder cone on the saddle (14,830 feet), and utilised the opportunity to ascertain its height, and the main details of its geological structure. By three o'clock we were "at home," thankful once more to lay aside ice-axe and knapsack. Evidently we had not left the heights a moment too soon, for all the afternoon they were concealed by a brooding mass of cloud; and when at eventide the icy dome once more stood forth against the rosy background of the sky, it was white with a fresh coating of newly-fallen snow.

We bade farewell to our camp at the saddle plateau on the 22nd October. The day before we had been surprised by the sudden appearance of Ali, the soldier whom, it will be remembered, I had left in charge of the camp at Marangu. He was the bearer of evil tidings. The men were mutinous; several of them had been flogged; I must return at once. There seemed indeed to be nothing else for it, and thereupon we resolved to consider our work in the upper regions of Kilimanjaro at an end. Upon the whole, it had been satisfactory, and therefore pleasant. Excluding the four days we had lost whilst I was absent in Marangu at the time of the dispute with Mareale, we had spent altogether sixteen days between the altitudes of 15,000 and 20,000 feet. In that time we had made four ascents of Kibo and three of Mawenzi; we had reached the culminating peak of the mountain, ascertained the existence of a great crater at the summit, discovered the first African glaciers, and made a tolerably thorough survey of the higher altitudes, the results of our explorations being recorded in a fairly complete series of photographs, sketches, notes, and specimens.

In all our efforts we had been ably seconded by our faithful henchman, Mwini Amani, who relieved us altogether of the thousand and one trifling duties which form such an irritating yet inevitable part of camp-life. The time that is wasted in gathering firewood, carrying water, oiling boots, and doing similar necessary but irksome work, is incalculable; but Mwini was equal to it all, and our hands were left free for other duties. In one respect only he had failed us—he was an atrocious cook; and after one or two attempts to swallow some of the smoky, unsavoury messes he produced, we were obliged to fall back on our own resources, and cook our meals ourselves. This, and the want of a sufficient supply of water to wash in, seemed far greater hardships than the early start in snow and wind or a bed overnight in a hole among the rocks. Only those who have tried it can understand what it means to be obliged to forego one's customary ablutions. The only thing about which Purtscheller and I ever quarrelled was the washing of the dishes; not that we were so overwhelmingly anxious to save each other trouble, but because each hungered for the luxury of a pair of clean hands. Camp-life on Kilimanjaro is a capital school for the practice of self-denial.

But we had much to compensate us for all we had to give up. The charm of the mountain scenery, the clear, crisp atmosphere, the tonic of "a labour we delight in," and the consciousness now and again of success achieved, all went far to make of our fortnight's arduous toil a happy sequence of red-letter days.

The days by courtesy called days of rest were never by any means days of idleness. Early morning saw us up and doing — photographing, measuring, hunting up specimens for our various collections—while the plateau lay bathed in a flood of golden sunlight, and over the forest hung a veil of silvery cloud. Our geological work was especially delightful. Beneath the magic stroke of the hammer ordinary, everyday-looking fragments revealed the most varied and wonderful mineral treasures. Every rock seemed to differ from another, not only in form but in substance. In half-an-hour it was no uncommon thing for us to pick up specimens of as many as two-and-twenty different kinds.

Our movements in these lofty altitudes were very much regulated by the state of the clouds. As the sun rose higher and higher in the heavens, and soft white flecks and misty wreaths began to float across the heights above, we hastened to get back from our morning ramble, lest we should lose the noonday clearness before we had taken the customary observation. Shortly after noon, on each side of the plateau, distinct upward currents set in from below, bearing aloft the great grey masses of cloud, and ranging them opposite to each other in battle array. Just as they rise above the edge they are caught in the current of the plateau, and whirled suddenly upward like the smoke from two opposing batteries, to drift slowly away across the skies on the wings of a higher current still.

As soon as the sun becomes obscured by the clouds the temperature undergoes a sudden change. On one occasion, in the course of a single quarter of an hour, the thermometer fell from 83° to 33° Fahr.; and whenever the mist came as the herald of a snowstorm, the fall was even greater.

These sudden changes of temperature largely account for the tremendous extent to which the rocks of the region are shattered and splintered. The porous lavas that bulk so largely in the formations of Kilimanjaro offer but little resistance to the destructive influences of nature, and in many instances they are weathered to a considerable depth, and crumble into dust and fragments almost at a breath. Huge blocks of the more compact species lie scattered here and there, but they likewise are being slowly worn away, and the process is assisted by the lichens which cling to their weathered surface.

To a similar cause, acting in conjunction with equally sudden variations of moisture, and the fierce struggle for existence under the most adverse conditions of soil and climate, the flora of the region also owes many of its characteristic peculiarities. Anything like gregarious vegetation comprising numerous species and numerous individuals is only to be met with in especially favoured situations, as on the detritus heaps on the western side of Mawenzi, or in the hollows between the hills on the plateau, where there is an approach to something like turf; or again under the shelter of the hill behind our camp on Mawenzi, where the Euryops bushes occur in fairly large patches, and grow to a height of about eighteen inches.

All the representative genera, *Gnaphalia, Artemisia, Helio-chrysa,* and meadow-grasses, are provided with a coating of light grey hairs, which serves as a protection at once against extremes of temperature and extremes of moisture, and has the effect of producing a close external resemblance among all the different species. The leaves and flowers either grow close together in thick concave clumps, to protect themselves against frost and excessive transpiration, or they creep along the surface of the earth, for the sake of the extra warmth. Besides yellow and violet, the prevailing colour alike of leaf, and stem, and flower is the blue anthocyan tint, which possesses the remarkable property of absorbing the intense light of these upper regions, and transforming it into heat.

The animal kingdom is but sparsely represented by a few rock-swallows, stonechats, lizards, beetles, spiders, and bees, all of a uniform dark grey colour—a sombre tint which not only absorbs the rays of the sun, but also makes the animals invisible to their enemies against the dark background of the prevailing volcanic rocks.

Every evening as the hour of sunset draws near, the temperature falls, the wind dies away, the mists disappear, and once more Kibo and Mawenzi stand out in all their majesty. As the sun sinks in purple splendour between the peaks of Kibo and Meru, the plains below, with their rivers and mountains, are at their loveliest. But the glorious spectacle is of short duration. Darkness draws on apace, the stars come out one by one, and with the approach of nightfall an icy wind sets in from the mountain-top, and it becomes intensely cold, the thermometer, which some few hours before may have stood as high as 80° or 82° Fahr., falling to 6° or 8° Fahr.

When it was announced to the men at the half-way camp that their stay in the region of cold and mist was about to draw to a close, they displayed an altogether remarkable alacrity in hurrying on the necessary preparations. On the morning of our departure they made their appearance at the saddle by half-past nine, having left their quarters before sunrise so as to be able to join us in plenty of time. In ten minutes they had everything packed and ready for the road, and set out across the plateau at a good round pace. Half gladly, half regretfully, we bade farewell to the scene of our recent exploits and adventures, and prepared to follow our porters along the narrow path, now trodden hard with daily usage. The men were in high spirits, and laughed and chattered gleefully as they hurried along. Stopping only to snatch a refreshing draught of water at the "Schnee-quelle," we left behind the marshy ground and lonely senecios of the lower edge of the plateau, and, crossing the stream, entered the dewy grass-lands below. By two o'clock we were in camp, having accomplished in less than four hours a march which had formerly occupied two days.

Next morning, along with Mwini Amani, I started off ahead of the little caravan, in order to have time to take a few photos on the outskirts of the forest. I had my head under the cloth and was busy focussing, when I was suddenly startled by a cry of *tembo, tembo* (elephants), from Mwini. On looking up, sure enough there were two stately elephants leisurely making off in the direction of the trees, among which they finally disappeared.

Without further adventure we pursued our march downwards through the twilight stillness of the forest till we came

within sight of the confines of Kilema and Marangu. Here,
on the hill of Kilema, we were confronted with the unusual
spectacle of a long column of men slowly making its way
upward amid an uninterrupted firing of guns. Knowing that
Mareale and Fumba, the chief of Kilema, were by no means
on friendly terms, I jumped to the conclusion that war had at
length been declared between them. My fears on that score
were relieved, however, by a band of wood-cutters we met,
who told us that the men belonged to a large Swahili caravan
that had just arrived in Taveta on their way to Masai Land.
The detachment we had seen belonged to a foraging party
who had come to Jagga for the purpose of buying food.

But as I thought of my mutinous men this intelligence
suggested a new cause of uneasiness, and with all possible
speed I hastened on towards Marangu. I arrived in camp
shortly after midday, and a single glance served to show me
that my fears were groundless—everything was quiet. Even
Ali's reported mutiny turned out to be nothing more than a
quarrel between the porters and the over-zealous Somál, in
which the latter had got the worst of it, while trying to
enforce discipline by a too liberal application of the whip.

Our arrival was celebrated with endless feasting and firing
of guns, and the evening's rejoicings terminated in a grand
display of fireworks, in which, as a special favour, Mareale
was allowed to let off the rockets himself.

Before setting out on an excursion we now proposed to
make to the mountains of Ugweno, I had intended spending a few days in our comfortable quarters at Marangu, in
order to rest and put my affairs in order. But my hopes of
a holiday were doomed to disappointment, for the camp was
kept in a state of perpetual turmoil by detachments from the
large Swahili caravan, who came to buy food at the daily
market. Their appearance was the signal for endless quarrel-

lings and wranglings, and at last matters reached such a pitch, that one day I had to sally forth with my soldiers and clear the compound. Scarcely had we turned our backs, when a number of shots came dropping over the fence, and a bullet lodged in one of the posts of Purtscheller's hut. It was as much as I could do to keep the Somál from returning the fire, but, ordering the latter to their quarters, I sent a message to the offenders warning them that if they did not desist I should speedily find means to make them.

We had peace for one day after that, but on the next there was a repetition of the firing, and some of the kitchen utensils came to grief. Thereupon I sent my ultimatum to Mareale— either the Swahili caravan must be turned out of Marangu, bag and baggage, by noon, or I would at once set out for Moji, and return with reinforcements from Mandara, who, as Mareale knew, would be only too glad of an excuse to make war on him.

In answer to this threat, Mareale himself was promptly on the spot, apparently deeply hurt that I should have doubted his friendly intentions. He promised that the obnoxious Swahili should be sent away forthwith; and sure enough, in the course of an hour or two, I had the satisfaction of seeing them defiling past on their way out of the state. The Arab leader of the caravan came to make his apologies for his men's misconduct, and departed, beaming, with the customary present of cloth and beads. Nevertheless, as the caravan finally took its leave, one or two stray shots came pattering into the enclosure, one of them actually snapping a branch immediately over my tent.

The unpleasant impression left by this episode was presently forgotten in the advent of a visitor—Mr. Morris of the Moji mission. The next few days passed quickly in arranging our collections and writing letters for Europe, prior to setting out on the trip to Ugweno. This lovely mountainous district, lying to the south of Kilimanjaro, had never before been visited by any European, with the exception of Dr. Kersten, who travelled along its eastern margin, and made the interesting discovery of the iron furnaces of Usangi. The latter state is also occasionally visited by Arab and Swahili caravans trading in cattle and slaves; but, as a whole, the district may be said to be totally unexplored.

By the advice of Mareale, I resolved to approach Ugweno from the west by way of the Kahé plains, thereafter to cross the country eastwards to Usangi, descend thence into the basin of Lake Jipé and the river Rufu, and so back again in a northerly direction to Marangu. We calculated that a caravan of twenty men would be sufficient to carry all that was necessary for the expedition, on which we expected to be absent between two and three weeks. It turned out that in the course of his many wanderings Mwini Amani had once stayed some time in Usangi, and knew something of the language. He therefore accompanied us in the capacity of interpreter.

All our preparations were completed in the course of a day, and I was not sorry to have the prospect of being once more on the move, if only to escape from the offensive sights and smells of our camp, whose very imperfect sanitary arrangements made it anything but a desirable residence. My endeavours to get away as frequently as possible from my disagreeable surroundings nearly cost me dear. It was my custom every evening to take a stroll, which I generally prolonged as much as possible. Returning as usual on the day before our departure, I sat down to enjoy the evening cool and quiet, in the brilliant moonlight. Tempted by the beauty of the night, I sat on musing until quite late, when suddenly I was awakened by an angry snarl almost at my elbow, as it

N

seemed. Looking up with a swift sense of danger, I saw, not twenty paces distant, a leopard stealthily creeping towards me. Unarmed as I was, all I could do was to utter a loud shout, and incontinently take to my heels. I suppose I must still have looked rather alarmed when I got into camp, for immediately it went about among the men that the Bwana had seen a ghost. I did not take the trouble to undeceive them— in a Swahili caravan you cannot be too careful in preserving your prestige.

CAMP AT THE FOOT OF MAWENZI.

CHAPTER VI.

THROUGH THE UGWENO COUNTRY.

STAY-AT-HOME folks are often greatly exercised to know how the traveller in unexplored countries like Central Africa is able to find his way from place to place; and when you tell them, "Simply by means of the native paths and the native guides," they assume an air of aggrieved surprise, as if you had done them a mortal injury by mentioning such commonplaces in connection with a region where they have been taught to expect only the marvellous and unusual. Nevertheless, the fact remains, however unpalatable it may be to the sensation-loving devourer of modern books of African travel.

In East Africa there are paths everywhere, leading from one inhabited district to the next. These are not roads in the usual sense of the term, but mere footpaths, trodden

BABOONS AMONG THE
BRANCHES OF A DÛM PALM.

out by long usage, and only wide enough for a single person. The so-called "great caravan route" is nothing more than just such a footpath, along which the caravans must pass in Indian-file.

"For a consideration" in cloth or beads, guides are to be had almost everywhere; but there are, of course, guides *and* guides, and the really good guide is a *rara avis*. It is on your guide that you must depend for all information as to the country through which you are passing, the names of the mountains, rivers, and villages, and for other details that are essential for the construction of satisfactory route-surveys and maps. It is not enough, therefore, that he should merely be able to lead the way; he must also be thoroughly acquainted with the local topography, or, where his own knowledge fails, must be able to supplement it as he goes along. The latter is a task requiring the utmost tact; for the natives, unable to appreciate the motives which inspire the white man's manifold questionings, and, at the best, inclined to distrust him as a stranger, either pretend stupidity, or plead ignorance, or wilfully give misleading answers. The guides themselves are often guilty of similar malpractices, but by the exercise of a little tact the desired information is generally forthcoming. An adroit question now and then, or, better still, a timely present, is a wonderful stimulant to the native memory.

As a rule, the inhabitants are exceedingly well up in all the local surroundings, but in Africa, as elsewhere, they are occasionally so stupid that, though they may have spent all their lives in a district, they cannot tell the names even of its most prominent features. Nothing is more aggravating than a guide of this type, except perhaps his kinsman, the good-natured guide, who, rather than meet your look of disappointment when he cannot tell you what to call the river you are crossing or the mountain that is just visible on the horizon, confidently mentions the first name that occurs to him, to your endless confusion and mystification.

A guide—or more frequently two guides, for the sake of company on the way back—accompanies the caravan from its starting-point as far as the friendly relations of his tribe extend, when his place is taken by another, and so on until the final stopping-place is reached. Sometimes, among the members of the caravan, a man may be found who has been over the ground before, and so is capable of acting as guide, like Mwini Amani, for example, who acted throughout the whole expedition with the greatest tact and intelligence. In the Kilimanjaro district his knowledge of the language made me almost entirely dependent on him, and on the Ugweno expedition he was again our interpreter. No guides were to be found in Marangu who would accompany us farther than the Kahé plains, and so far I could afford to dispense with them, since several of my men already knew the road, and I had myself partly explored it on my way from Taveta in 1887.

We set out from Marangu on the last day of October. Besides ourselves, the caravan included seventeen porters, two soldiers, the headman Abed, four Somál, and the indispensable Mwini Amani—twenty-seven in all.

Mareale came to see us off, bringing with him a fine goat as a parting gift. We were accompanied as far as the "gate" of the state by the chief's son, a bright little fellow of five, who marched at the head of the line of laden porters, proudly carrying the flag. Leaving the banana plantations behind us, we passed rapidly down the gentle, shady slopes, with their wealth of bush and twining creeper, and crossed the deep ravine of the Mabongo at an elevation of 3770 feet. Along the winding pathway the men hied merrily on, the milk and butter of Marangu oozing out at every pore in rivers of perspiration, which seemed to afford the easily-tickled Swahili endless amusement. As we continued the descent, the wood gradually became more open—more and more intermingled with forms characteristic of the steppes. Soon we had left it behind altogether, and emerged upon a treeless tract covered with gigantic grasses, which the natives were busy cutting and binding into sheaves, to be utilised as fodder and bedding for the cattle, or as thatch for their beehive huts. A little farther down, and we were once more in sight of the great tree steppes, and beheld the massive mountains of Ugweno rising abruptly from their midst. To the left shimmered the silvery Lake Jipé, to the right the sombre green of the Kahé forest showed darkly against the red of the surrounding plains, and behind,—back in the direction of Kilimanjaro,—two great white masses of cumulus cloud hung peacefully in the azure sky, showing where Kibo and Mawenzi lay wrapped in noonday slumber.

At our old camp by the Himo, which we reached towards noon, a sad disappointment awaited us. We had been looking forward with pleasure to spending another night in this charming little nook; but the large Swahili caravan, which had already proved such a fruitful source of annoyance to us in Marangu, had left it little better than a stinking dunghill, and we were obliged to seek out another camping-ground some distance off, on the other side of the stream. One consolation, however, we had in the rich addition we were able to make to our collection of butterflies from among the large and varied assortment now attracted to the spot.

Leaving the Himo on our left, the road to Mandara's on our right, we next morning struck a stony path leading across the tract of arid steppe, which here slopes gently downward in the direction of Kahé. The mountains of Ugweno were shrouded in heavy rain-clouds, but a swelling hill in the

Kahé district still served as a conspicuous landmark. As we marched along in the direction of the plains, the game every moment grew more numerous. Herds of antelope, zebra, and hartebeeste gambolled in the distance ; a male ostrich strutted solemnly along well out of range ; and a couple of rhinoceroses, with waving tail and uplifted nostril, stood suspiciously sniffing the caravan as it wound rapidly past.

We were so much absorbed in watching the movements of the various animals that we lost the path, and in the maze of intersecting game-paths, which crossed each other in all directions, we were unable to strike it again. There was nothing for it but to make straight across country in the direction of the hill. For an hour we kept on among the long, coarse grass, and through a small grove of leafless baobabs, which might almost have been mistaken for oak trees in winter, had the broiling sunshine not proclaimed East Central Africa with such convincing power. Leaving the grove, we reached the Nassai rivulet, with its overarching tunnel of leafy raphia palms. Undeterred by the numerous traces of crocodiles in the soft mud, we waded across, and entered a grove of dûm palms, apparently of boundless extent. The fruit of this species of palm is about the size of an apple, and has a fibrous, woody rind, which tastes not unlike St. John's bread—the "locusts" of our childhood. It seemed to find much acceptance with the troops of baboons which swarmed in the branches, and greedily stuffed their cheeks with the toothsome fare.

Crossing the Nassai a second time by an impromptu bridge made of a fallen tree, we came in sight of the forest of Kahé, and by-and-by reached the sluggish river Dehu, on whose farther bank the cosy beehive-shaped huts and green banana plantations held out an inviting promise of peace and plenty. It was high time to call a halt, for during the long holiday in Marangu the men had become unaccustomed to tramping along burning pathways, and in many cases their feet were now in a dreadful condition. My supply of zinc ointment was nearly exhausted before we got them all doctored that afternoon.

On my journey in 1887, we entered the Kahé district and pitched our camp in the forest, and so had a splendid opportunity of observing its most interesting denizens, the beautiful Guereza monkeys (*Colobus Guereza*, var. *caudatus*). According to the natives, these monkeys never approach the fields and plantations; but in the tall "gallery" forest they are to be seen in little bands of from four to eight, each troop embracing the members of a single family. Their presence is first proclaimed by the peculiar humming noise they keep up incessantly while at rest, and which, when they are alarmed, ceases abruptly. On the approach of man, the monkeys do not take to flight, but quietly slip behind some leafy branch or massive bole, and peer at the intruder with a curiosity apparently equal to his own. By-and-by the leading male cautiously ventures out again, gradually drawing nearer, and stopping from time to time to utter his strange inquiring cry, which is not unlike the gobbling of a turkey, followed by a more or less prolonged *oâ*. At the sound of a shot, every head is once more quickly withdrawn, but the creatures do not take to flight in the usual sense of the phrase. They bound away in long swift leaps, but there is no undignified hurrying or scuttling, and it is a beautiful sight to see them as they spring from bough to bough, their long white tails and the white fringe along either side of the body streaming behind them as they go. As the Guereza is difficult to kill, it is seldom attacked by the natives, though the skins are much in demand among the Masai, by whom they are greatly prized as war-mantles.

This time, in order to avoid the *hongo* (toll for right of way), we did not cross the boundary-line of Kahé, but with a volley summoned the natives to bring their bananas, millet, and honey across the stream to our camp, where we secured them on the usual terms. Like the Wa-taveta, a tribe they closely resemble in appearance, manners, and speech, the people of Kahé are vegetarians by compulsion rather than by choice, fear of the Masai and of Mandara having induced them to give up entirely the rearing of cattle.

In the course of conversation with several old gentlemen whose confidence I won by a present of snuff and some packets of percussion-caps, I gathered that the Dehu is the name here given to our old acquaintance the Mué, to whose cradle-song we had listened on the slopes of Mawenzi. Uniting with the Kirerema on the right and the Nassai on the left, the Mué or Dehu finally joins the Rufu, the most important river to the south of Kilimanjaro. The Kahé forest occupies the fork between the Dehu and the Kirerema.

A close, oppressive night, during which the mosquitoes swarmed in myriads, was brought to a close by a tremendous thunderstorm. The flashes of lightning followed each other at the rate of forty to the minute, with an effect which was literally blinding. The sky seemed to be one vast sheet·of flame ; but I noticed that the electrical discharges mostly occurred among the clouds, and did not strike the earth. This fact goes far to explain why the negro, who, as a rule, stands in such awe of the forces of Nature, has no fear of a thunderstorm. The storm had come down upon us from Kilimanjaro, and gradually passed away in the direction of Ugweno. While it lasted the temperature fell rapidly from 83° to 67° F.

Next morning we had a long palaver with the natives, who seemed peculiarly unwilling to offer themselves as guides, for the very good reason that all former attempts made by Europeans to penetrate the country of Ugweno had been frustrated by the inhabitants at the point of the spear.   At length two young men yielded to the inducements I held out so far as to pledge themselves to accompany us to the boundary, distant a march of about a day and a half.

This important matter arranged, we set out at once.   For about two hours the path led along the left bank of the Dehu, across one of the dazzling salt reaches common to the region, which was much ploughed up by the hoofs of the numerous wild animals that are in the habit of coming to lick the salt or drink the water from the river.   Crossing the Nassai for the third time, close to its confluence with the Dehu, we continued our way among scattered groves of palm-trees till we reached the gallery forest of the river Rufu, here a stream some forty feet wide, spanned by a gigantic tree which forms a rough and ready, and rather slippery bridge.

Here the pathway came to an end, for, although the Wa-kahé and the Wa-gweno are on friendly terms, they both live in such terror of the marauding hordes of Masai, who from time to time scour the plains in this direction, that they prefer to limit the communication between the two districts rather than give the common enemy a clue to their where-abouts, such as would be afforded by fresh footprints on a beaten track.   Accordingly, we were once more compelled to follow the game-paths, so far as they went in the required direction.   Every now and then we startled some solitary rhinoceros on the way to his accustomed drinking-place. For a moment the lumbering animal would pause to sniff and stare, then trot slowly off down some convenient by-path.

At every sound the two guides stopped uneasily to listen, then plodded on again bent nearly double in their anxiety that no recent trace of the dreaded Masai should escape their notice. For my part, judging from what I had already seen of these redoubtable warriors, I stood much less in fear of them than of the dense tract of thorny undergrowth through which we were now passing; and it was with feelings of no small admiration that I watched my heavily-laden porters, with their shoeless feet and scanty clothing, as they plunged doggedly on through the pathless wilderness, under the pitiless glare of the tropical sun.

We were now visibly approaching the south-western extremity of the mountains of Ugweno, which here form a somewhat acute angle as they rise abruptly from the plains. The great bay formed by the two projecting spurs at the northern termination of the range was no longer to be seen, but to the south the mountains stretched away in an unbroken line as straight and almost as smooth as a wall, and unrelieved by any form of vegetation, with the exception of an occasional baobab, mimosa, or tree-euphorbia.

As we crossed the boundary-line between the volcanic formations of the Kilimanjaro region and the archaic rocks of Ugweno, the ground gradually began to rise. The rounded fragments of basalt and lava, probably carried down by the Rufu, now gave place to beds of crumbling gneiss, in some places so far decomposed as to form a layer of bright red laterite soil. Across the wide grey plains of the Rufu the eye ranged unhindered for miles to where, on the far horizon, loomed the distant mountains of Sogonoi. Here and there, from a Masai encampment, a curling smoke-wreath rose lazily skyward; but the thought of the Masai no longer troubled us —we were out of their " beat."

The clouds, which for some time had been gathering threateningly overhead, now burst in another terrific thunderstorm, followed by a steady downpour of rain, which lasted the whole afternoon, and reduced my shivering porters to a state of indescribable misery. Every drop of water was absorbed as it fell by the thirsty earth, and as there was here neither stream nor ngurunga, to camp was out of the question.

At last, towards sunset, we reached the dry bed of what in the wet season is a mountain rivulet, the Mrushunga. At a spot about half-way up the precipitous slope, a belt of vivid green proclaimed the presence of water, and thither we now directed our steps along one of a series of converging game-paths, some of them so broad and regular that they might have been constructed under the supervision of a Roads' Committee. In the midst of a shady thicket we pitched our tent, beside a group of rocky pools, which the recent rain had filled to the brim with a dark brownish liquid, not very inviting to look at, but still wholesome enough for drinking purposes.

The men set to work to make themselves comfortable for the night, and soon a blazing fire and a warm supper had restored their customary light-heartedness and good-humour. As we sat down at our little table in the lamp-light, the full charm of camp-life in Africa once more stole over me—a charm which none can know save those who have experienced it. There is something peculiarly attractive in its very incongruities—in camp, the cosy little tent, the convenient furniture, and the numerous excellent substitutes for home-comforts ; without, the boundless wilderness, the gleaming watch-fires of the Masai, the howling of the wild beasts we had scared from their accustomed drinking-place. You have Africa and Europe, savagery and refinement, hardship and ease, brought together in sharpest contrast; but each only serves to enhance the other, and without experience of both it is impossible justly to estimate the value of either.

We had as yet seen no signs of human habitation, but next morning, on a pathway at the foot of the hill, we came upon some chewed fragments of sugar-cane, from which we inferred the recent presence of some one belonging to an agricultural tribe, although all traces of footprints had been washed away by the rain. Concluding from this that the path must lead to an inhabited region, we followed it up the mountain-side, which was here exceedingly steep. At one place, the ground for a considerable distance was thickly strewn with fragments of iron ore, which appears to have been exposed as the result of sub-aërial denudation acting on the numerous quartz veins by which the gneiss is here intersected. It is possible also that the ore may have come from the volcanic cones in the plain below; but this I do not think probable, as the ore occurs in lodes, and is also met with in the interior and on the eastern side of Ugweno, where there is no trace of recent volcanic activity.

The Zanzibaris seemed to have no idea of the nature of the discovery, and were very much astonished to hear that the stone was the *chuma,* of which their knives and chains were made. One and all they thereupon began to stow away as many chips as they could conveniently carry, hoping at some future time to be able to turn them to good account.

Continuing our way upwards, we entered a narrow ravine, at the bottom of which was a tiny, thread-like watercourse, and farther up a small banana plantation—the first we had seen in Ugweno. Suddenly, on the slopes above, we caught sight of a group of natives; but no sooner were they aware of our presence than they turned and fled precipitately. Our guides called to them to stop, but they paid no attention, and in a few minutes the heights above bristled with armed warriors, who with loud cries and fierce gesticulations dared us to advance farther. Calling a halt, we sent up Mwini, Abed,

and the two guides to hold a parley. The warriors immediately squatted themselves in an expectant semicircle, and
the proceedings commenced as usual with a long oration
on the part of the Wa-gweno leader. This was followed by
another and another from different speakers, occasionally interrupted by grunts of assent or disapproval from one or other of
the surrounding audience. This sort of thing went on for two
hours; then I grew tired of it, and brought the palaver to
an abrupt close by ordering my men to march on. We were
met by Mwini Amani and a deputation of the natives, who
in appearance, manners, and speech resemble the Wa-shamba,
a tribe whose acquaintance I made when in Usambara in
1888. They received us with a mixture of timidity and suspicion; but when I assured them that I was neither a friend
of the Masai nor of Mandara, they became more cordial, and
the spokesman, who was the leader of the band, wanted
to "make brothers" with me. I referred him to Mwini.
"The Mzungu," I said, "makes brothers with none but kings."
Duly impressed by my haughty manner, the warrior offered
no objection, and Mwini stepped forward. With a thorn,
each of the high contracting parties scratched the skin on
his breast till the blood came, the bystanders watching the
operation with intense interest, and accompanying it by a
measured chant. Each next licked a few drops of the other's
blood, and pledged themselves to eternal friendship, the most
frightful curses being invoked on whoever should first violate
the bond.

The ceremony over, we resumed our way upward through
the creeper-bound thicket, preceded by the entire company.
Reaching a valley rich in maize and banana plantations, we
were met by the main body of the tribe, who treated us to a wild
war-chant, not unlike that of the Masai. The singing ended,
we were conducted to a spot under a group of trees, where

we pitched our camp, and proceeded to make ourselves as comfortable as circumstances would permit, though we did not dare to lay down our arms. I did not much like the look of our new "brothers." They had never seen even a Swahili caravan before, and we, of course, were the first Europeans who had ever visited the district. Nor did they seem inclined to improve their opportunities by cultivating our acquaintance, but stood shyly and suspiciously aloof, refusing even to sell us food until the "*Fuma*" (chief), Yangobi, had been consulted. As the Fuma lived a whole day's journey farther north, and my men meanwhile had nothing to eat, we were obliged to take the matter into our own hands, and during the night freely helped ourselves to the maize that was still standing out in the fields.

Having no particular wish to visit Yangobi, whose residence lay quite out of our route, we resolved next morning to continue our way towards the interior, where Gamualla, the central peak of the Ugweno range, rose proudly skywards. The chief of the Gamualla region was Mafurra, and through his territory we hoped to reach the eastern district of Usangi, and thence cross the country to the great bay on the northern side of the mountains, towards which we had already turned longing eyes from Marangu.

The Kahé men being duly rewarded and dismissed, we set out along the valley, trusting to Mwini's knowledge of the language, which really proved to be considerable, to carry us through without a guide. We were attended for some distance by the whole population of the place, who, now that they saw we were likely to slip through their fingers, were ready enough to sell us anything we wanted. Several attempts were made to mislead us as to the road; but we were not to be deceived with the path leading to the foot of Gamualla straight before our eyes.

Fording the marshy Wangobi stream, at the bottom of the valley, we reached the western spur of the mountain and entered the basin of the Kisinga, in which were numerous plantations of sugar-cane. After its junction with the Wangobi, the Kisinga flows in a southerly direction towards the Rufu plains, where it is gradually lost in a series of marshes.

The Kisinga forms the boundary-line between Yangobi and Mafurra, and here we were met by a body of armed warriors, who bade us welcome in the name of their chief. Under their escort we skirted the bare wall of rocky precipices which runs out towards the Rufu plains, and entered a narrow valley rich in sugar-cane and bananas, the residence of Mafurra. Here, as in the valley of the Wangobi, a curious feature in the scene was the apparent absence of dwellings. As a precaution in case of attack, all the huts are so carefully concealed among the trees, that, but for the signs of cultivation, one might almost believe the place to be uninhabited.

On reaching the first plantations, we were immediately requested by our guides to halt; but, as there was no water near the spot they had selected for our camp, we declined to do anything of the sort, and paying no heed to their protests, we continued our way upwards and proceeded to choose ground for ourselves. Naturally there was a tremendous sensation, but all of a sudden the storm lulled—I had set up my theodolite. This queer-looking, shiny, three-legged thing—what was it? Some dreadful engine of sorcery perhaps. And this mighty magician who appeared to hold converse with the sun—who was he? What would he do next? There was a respectful silence and a gradual widening of the circle around me, while the crowd uneasily awaited the course of events.

Meanwhile Mafurra had been informed of what was going on, and I had scarcely finished taking the midday observation when he made his appearance attended by a small following.

He proved to be a frail old man, nearly blind with age—suspicion of the stranger written on his every feature. His half-grown, half-witted son led him by the hand. The chief's intentions seemed hospitable, however, for he had brought a fine fat-tailed sheep along with him ; seeing this, I made up my mind to be agreeable, and presented him with a brilliant new fez with a piece of cloth and some beads for himself and suite. The clouds being propitious, I also gratuitously informed him that my three-legged familiar promised rain that day, whereupon the fat-tailed sheep at once changed hands, its life-blood (of which we each drank a few drops) sealing the bond which made us " brothers."

The natives now gathered round, eager to sell food—not so eager, however, but that they demanded the most exorbitant prices, asking as much as a *doti* for a single fowl.' With a whole sheep in the larder, we could afford to be pretty independent, and eventually we succeeded in getting as much as we wanted at our own prices. Our prophecy of rain having been duly fulfilled, our reputation for beneficence was greatly enhanced, and we even won the general confidence so far as to obtain the promise of a couple of guides to show us the way up Mount Gamualla and into the neighbouring state of Usangi.

I have already referred to the resemblance between the natives of the Wangobi valley and the Wa-shamba of Usambara. Mafurra's people reminded me very much of another Usambara clan, the Wa-mbugu, of whom we shall have more to say hereafter.

The distrust of strangers, so general among the tribes of Western Ugweno, is not without justification. Their experience of outsiders consists of one long series of raids on the part of the Masai and of Mandara, both of whom have for years been accustomed to look upon Ugweno as a happy

O

hunting-ground for the capture of cattle and slaves. Generations of oppression and ill-usage have taught the Wa-gweno many bad habits, of which perhaps not the least objectionable is that of stealing whenever they think they can do so with impunity. Finding that we had not come to rob or kill, but were apparently inclined to be friendly, they at once began to take advantage of our good-nature, by making off with everything they could lay hands on in the most shameless fashion.

It was therefore with no slight feelings of relief that we left Mafurra's on the 4th of November, and started upwards along one of the southern spurs of Gamualla. The path wound through a thicket of tall brackens, with here and there a few bushes and herbs, but no trees. Having gained the crest of the ridge which forms the boundary-line of Mafurra's territory in this direction, Purtscheller and I set off with the guides to ascend the mountain, a bare rounded peak 6500 feet above the sea-level. When we reached the summit, everything was enveloped in mist; but a breeze sprang up, the mist rolled away, and we had a magnificent view of the surrounding region. We seemed to stand in the middle of Ugweno as on the highest island of an archipelago— the sister peaks of Kiberenge and Lambo in the north-west, the solitary Ngovi in the north-east, and the lofty chain of Usangi in the south, separated from us and from each other by a sea of emerald green. At our feet lay the fertile valley of Wangobi, stretching away towards the distant Lambo, while farther to the north the rich colouring of the valley of Msangeni contrasted pleasantly with the stern grey wall of Ngovi. Southward again, along the foot of the Usangi range ran the valley of Kirongaia, the Jego stream meandering through its midst between smiling fields and the groups of huts which form the village of Kirije, the residence of Naguvu, chief of Usangi.

Beyond the Ugweno country, still farther to the south, loomed the distant mountains of Paré ; to the east, Lake Jipé and the Nika steppes ; to the west, the boundless plains of the Rufu, a shimmering expanse of grey. To the north, high above all and monarch of all, was Kilimanjaro, towering skyward zone above zone, its crown now frosted white as silver with freshly fallen snow.

Pity for our guides, who stood shivering with cold in the keen mountain breeze, made us hasten down to rejoin the caravan, after which we bent our steps in the direction of the charming valley of Kirongaia. All along the path we met merry groups of women, young and old, hurrying along to market at Mafurra's, their loads gracefully poised on their heads, or, with greater appearance of effort, carried on their backs. They replied to our salutations with a curious buzzing sound, which, when uttered by a number of them in chorus, sounded, as Mwini said, exactly like the humming of bees. Their dress consisted of an apron of hide, and many of them were tattooed over the lower part of the body— a token of maternity, as we afterwards learned. Nearly all wore a thick collar of brass round the neck, a form of ornament also occasionally to be met with in Jagga as a relic of a fashion now out of date.

We entered the valley of Kirongaia amid song and mirth, the men all in exuberant spirits. Down the face of the Usangi mountains on our right numberless rivulets flashed and sparkled, leaping from rock to rock in foaming cascades as they hurried to join the brimming Desho, and swell its onward course through the valley of Lasanti to the eastern plains. Everywhere the eye rested only on what was beautiful—charming glimpses of mountain scenery, verdant meadows, cosy huts, curling smoke-wreaths, and rushing water, an exact counterpart of the loveliest districts of Usambara. It only wanted a herd or two of lowing cattle, and I could have imagined myself in some mountain valley of Central Europe.

The huts here were of two kinds. Some, as in Usambara, were of the ordinary beehive or haystack pattern, the roof resting on the top of the walls and reaching within a few feet of the ground ; others, as in Jagga, were perfectly conical, the roof sloping upwards from the earth to a point in the middle.

Reaching the bottom of the valley about noon, we continued our way along the banks of the stream, through plantations of sugar-cane, fields of maize, millet, manioc, and sweet potatoes. The natives were busy tilling the ground with hoe and mattock, and greeted us with a kindly "*yambo*"—a sign that Swahili caravans must sometimes pass that way. On the top of a hill, at a point where the river took a sudden bend towards the north-east, stood the kraal of the chief Naguvu, surrounded with a palisade in the Usambara fashion. The spot is called by the Wa-gweno, Kirije.

In response to a volley from our guns, there appeared a party of athletic young warriors, armed with firearms like ourselves. In the most friendly manner we were conducted to a camping-place at the foot of Naguvu's hill, and there, in the course of a few minutes, pitched our tent under the astonished eyes of the bystanders, and unfurled our little flag to the breeze. The latter was regarded with special reverence as a new kind of *dawa* (medicine) of mysterious import.

From the nature of our reception, which was not belied on closer acquaintance, it was easy to see that the people of Usangi were accustomed to meet strangers on friendly terms. Both Mandara and the Masai are glad to fight shy of Naguvu and his doughty warriors; and living thus secure in manly independence, they have no reason to stint their hospitality either through fear or through suspicion.

In the evening we had a thunderstorm, and in the midst of the rain by which it was accompanied Naguvu came to pay us a visit, the usual body of attendants in his train. The chief had just returned from some distant merrymaking, and, to say the least of it, seemed slightly elevated. His effusiveness was quite overwhelming. " Long ago, when I was a boy," he said, holding out his greasy paw, " a white man came to see our valley" (Dr. Kersten, the companion of Von der Decken), " and now that I am old, here is another. The first *mzungu* went away and returned to his own people, but I want you to stay with us always. With powerful medicines you will make my young men strong to conquer all the land of Ugweno, and in return you shall have as much food and as many wives as you please."

Notwithstanding these tempting inducements to a prolonged stay, I explained that my visit could not be extended beyond another day, but promised to do my best for him in the way of medicines. With this my swarthy friend was obliged to be content, and took himself off apparently well satisfied with the interview.

I have called Naguvu swarthy, but he might more correctly be described as ruddy, for his whole body was covered with a coating of red clay and grease, which shone in the lamplight like polished mahogany. With his protruding eyes and thick sensual lips, the chief of Usangi was by no means handsome, but everything he did and everything he said showed that he was unusually good-hearted. His hospitality was unbounded. In the evening he brought us a present of a goat, and in the morning he added a fine fat cow. In return for these we sent him a supply of cloth, beads, powder, and percussion-caps.

The inherent brutality of the negro nature was strongly brought out in a revolting incident which happened at the slaughter of the cow. When the men tried to lead her away, the animal proved obstinate, and stood with angry eyes and lowered horns ready to dash at any one who approached her. At last, impatient for the coming feast, one of the Swahili crept up in the rear of the maddened brute, and with a single cut severed the tendons of the hind-legs. With a bellow of agony the cow sank to the ground, amid the exulting plaudits of the onlookers. My blood boiled at the disgusting sight, and in a moment I had the miscreant sprawling on his back with a blow from the butt-end of my gun; the next, I had put his victim out of pain by a shot through the forehead. There was a general outburst of amazed indignation, and a rush to open the animal's jugular vein, a Mohammedan rite never omitted by these worthy followers of the Prophet, who, however lax in morals, are strict enough in all matters of ceremonial observance.

The goat, which was exceedingly tame, we kept as a pet, and for many days her funny little pranks furnished us ample amusement. We christened her Adelheid, after a lady friend to whom we fancied she bore a striking resemblance in profile.

On going to return Naguvu's visit, we found his kraal surrounded by a hedge of living dracænas, through which the only opening was a narrow doorway, so low that we had to crawl through it on hands and knees. Within the compound stood four very dilapidated huts of the Usambara pattern, in which man and beast dwelt together in Eden-like simplicity. Naguvu is the happy husband of eight wives, who have the honour of sharing his hut with him by turns—two at a time. He is also the father of fourteen children, who, together with their mothers, gathered to stare at us in round-eyed wonder. It was a charming family group, no doubt, but it had its drawbacks, and we were not sorry soon to tear ourselves away, preferring the humble amenities of our plebeian tent to the filth, the smells, the squalling babies of the royal residence.

The sky being clear, at midday I took an observation for latitude ; the remainder of the day we spent in photographing, collecting, and generally getting up information, especially as regards the native method of obtaining iron from the ore, of which we shall have more to say hereafter. The people were everywhere kind, modest, and obliging, and answered our questions readily.

In the evening I proceeded to give a demonstration of my powers as a medicine-man. The entertainment took the form of a grand display of fireworks, which passed off with great *éclat* and produced an immense effect. By way of close to the programme, Naguvu and I were made brothers. The ceremony was a somewhat lengthy one. The chief and his warriors having squatted themselves in a semicircle round the door of our tent, his son appeared carrying a large pot of pombé made from sugar-cane, while Mwini took a piece of roast-meat and cut it into strips. Naguvu and I then came forward and seated ourselves on either side of the pot, and the former began to repeat a long-winded rigmarole pledging himself to eternal brotherhood and invoking the most tremendous curses on all his enemies and on me, if henceforth and for ever I did not treat his foes as likewise foes of mine. During the whole of this tirade, he kept hammering the pot with a stone, and every time he made a point, he stopped to emphasise it by throwing a piece of meat into the pombé. With Mwini's help, I next went through a similar performance, and acquitted myself to the satisfaction of all present. After I had finished, Naguvu and I simultaneously dipped our right hand into the pot, drew out a piece of meat, chewed and swallowed it. Each of us then spat into the pot, and a number of privileged spectators having done the same, the vessel with its sacred contents was removed, to be treasured up for ever among the chief's most cherished possessions.

As my new brother showed a tiresome inclination to hang about me for the rest of the evening, by way of getting rid of him I made an exception in his favour, and granted his desire to have one of our flags, in whose magical virtue as a charm against all evil he profoundly believed. This was the only occasion on which a native chief received the national flag at my hands, and I must beg my readers to understand that I have no sympathy whatever with those travellers who, wherever they go, seem to make it their mission to leave the German colours streaming in their wake. In East Africa, which has been partitioned out by international agreements, the practice is superfluous, if not indeed ridiculous.

To Naguvu, however, the flag had no significance except as a charm; and on seeing the evident delight with which he and his subjects received it, I could not help wondering at the persistency with which these savage races believe in the power of magic, although, from repeated experience of its inefficacy, one would think they would gradually learn to take it at its true worth. The trait is not confined to savage races only, for superstition mingles inextricably with the religions of all; unless indeed an exception is to be made in favour of Christianity—a question I must leave my readers to settle for themselves.

We had decided to leave Kirongaia the following day, and early in the morning Naguvu came to see us off, bringing with him two young men to act as guides as far as Ngovi, a mountain lying in the extreme north of Ugweno. Making towards the lower end of the valley, we passed along the bush-clad mountain-slopes, and crossed the Jego, now no longer a mere rivulet, at a point where it makes a sudden bend eastward. Here the river enters the ravine of Lasanti, where it is joined by the Junguli from the north, and flows onward between huge boulders of gneiss, in the direction of the steppes.

We now bade good-bye to Jego, and followed the course of the Junguli northwards up another deep ravine. Far beneath us on our right foamed the brawling torrent, which we could hear, but could not see, for a thick mist hung over everything. As we stumbled along the slippery pathway, we caught occasional glimpses of fertile valleys opening up on either hand, all carefully tilled and planted with sugar-cane and sweet potatoes, and watered by irrigation channels as in Jagga. The native name of this district is Wambuguni, and the inhabitants are known as the Wa-mbugu. In language and appearance they are identical with the Wa-mbugu of Central Usambara.

The mist lifting for a moment, we had a peep downwards through the ravine of Lasanti to the south end of Lake Jipé, or Ipé, as it is pronounced in Ugweno. A winding belt of green standing out against the red of the steppes marked the course of the Jego-Junguli until it was lost in a wide swamp not far from the margin of the lake, with which it possibly has communication in the rainy season. For a moment, too, the snowy peaks of Kibo and Mawenzi appeared above the clouds, but we had no clear view of the whole of Ugweno until after we had forded the Junguli—the boundary between the districts of Usangi and Ugweno proper—and climbed Mount Sungo, which, standing isolated like Gamualla, commands an outlook over the whole northern region. Here, while I was taking bearings, the men set to work to collect what they could of the iron ore that lay scattered in fragments over the ground, but not in any great quantity.

We now entered the wide valley of Msangoni. At first I thought we were going to have rather a warm time of it,

for instead of the friendly natives and friendly greeting
to which we had lately been accustomed, armed warrior
sprang up around us on all sides, and, with wild yelling an
leaping, did their best to prevent our farther progress. Th
Somál had their hands on their guns in a twinkling, bu
Mwini proudly pointed to the wound on his breast, whic
bore witness to the bond of brotherhood, while the guide
told how I too had made brothers with Naguvu, and that th
chief desired that the *mzungu* should be permitted to clim
the mountain of Ngovi in peace. The effect was magica
At once the threatening din changed to shouts of delight, an
the path lay open to us, though the whole noisy crew cam
trooping after us nearly all the way to Ngovi. Here, in th
shadow of the grey walls of gneiss, we camped by the side c
a running stream, the Monya, and soon were exchanging ou
cloth and beads for the ample supplies of provisions brough
to us by the friendly inhabitants.

Next morning we ascended to the summit of the mountai
the height of which is 5580 feet. Thence we descended t
the plains on the other side, through patches of gallery fore
and a series of ravines, reaching the bottom in time to dete
mine the latitude and catch a splendid side-view of the whol
of Ugweno. A projecting spur hid the great bay on th
northern side of the range, but in the south the massive pea
of Kindorogo, one of the Usangi chain, was plainly visible a
the highest in the region. Eastward lay Lake Jipé, with i
schools of tumbling hippos, its basking crocodiles, and flock
of large white birds hovering overhead. Of the streams whic
flow from the mountains of Ugweno, none ever reach th
lake; all lose themselves in a series of pools and marshes n
far from the foot of the hills. Its only feeder is the Lum
which, flowing from the east of Kilimanjaro, enters the lak
at its northern end, where it has gradually formed a delt

and a small island, the haunt of the hippos already alluded
to. As far as we could see, there is no iron ore on Ngovi.

The mist came down on us again as we turned to go
back, and before we reached camp had changed to drizzling
rain. It rained the whole afternoon and evening, and next
morning, when we set our faces towards Taveta, the mist still
lay round us like a shroud. The path was wet and slippery,
and led steeply downwards along the precipitous face of the
wall of cliffs which forms the eastern aspect of the mountain.
In some places it was little more than a foot broad, and every
now and again I felt a sudden thrill of alarm as one or other
of our laden porters seemed on the brink of toppling into the
gulf below.

We had not gone very far when a great hubbub arose in
our rear, and, halting to see what it all meant, we were overtaken by messengers of the chief, Yangobi, who demanded
that we should at once go back to pay our respects to the lord
of the land. As I had not the slightest intention of doing
anything of the kind, I refused point-blank, and the only
reason I had to regret the incident was that our guides at
once struck work and turned back with the chief's envoys.
It was no great loss, however, for there was little fear of our
losing our way with the lake in sight all the time, and only
one path leading downwards towards the plains.

Near the foot of the mountain we again came upon iron
ore, and from the slag and cinders lying about, it was evident
that the iron had been smelted at the place where it was
found. By-and-by we saw signs that we were approaching
the region of thorny vegetation, and soon we found ourselves
once more upon the level arid plains, with their patches
of grey-green grass and thorn scrub, and their dry twisting
creepers.

Before we bid farewell to the Ugweno country, let me say

a word as to its general aspect and the character of its inhabitants. The prevailing rock formation is gneiss, which is overlaid by the volcanic products of Kilimanjaro in the north as far as the Rufu, in the west as far as the Mrushunga, and in the east as far as the middle of Lake Jipé. The highest mountain chain is the Usangi range in the south-west, in which the principal peaks, proceeding from north to south, are Gamualla, Jego, Kimbale, Kindorogo, and Jomvu. Kiberenge and Lambo in the north-west, and Ngovi in the north-east, come next in importance. Like Usambara and Paré, Ugweno may be compared to an island rising abruptly from the surrounding sea of the steppes, its sides unfurrowed by ravine or valley. The beds of gneiss are of immense thickness, and strike generally from north to south. On the eastern side they dip to the plain at an angle of about 25°.

The principal river is the Junguli, which, rising on the eastern slopes of Lambo, traverses the whole of Eastern Ugweno, and finally enters the plains shortly after its junction with the Jego, the main stream flowing from the mountains of Usangi. Other important streams are the Wangobi, from Kiberenge and the western side of Lambo; the Monjo, flowing from Ngovi towards the west; and the Boru, which drains the whole southern district. The watershed between north and south is thus formed by the comparatively low range of hills between Lambo and Ngovi, which form the face of the great bay at the northern extremity of the region.

None of the streams above mentioned are of any considerable volume. In its middle course the Junguli is only some 18 inches deep and 18 feet wide, while the Jego, close to its confluence with the Junguli, is about the same depth and only some 10 feet wide. According to the natives, the volume of water does not vary much, even in the height of the rainy season. With the occasional exception of the Junguli, none of the rivers enter the Rufu or Lake Jipé. The same system of irrigation being practised here as in Jagga, many of the streams are never permitted to reach the plains, and the few that do are lost in the chain of marshes running along the foot of the mountains.

The inhabitants of Ugweno—the Wa-gweno—mostly resemble the Wa-mbugu of Central Usambara, except in the western district, where they appear to be more closely allied to the Wa-shamba. Among the " Wa-mbugu " of the Junguli valley, who still keep up the old tribal name, the race is preserved in its greatest purity. Formerly these Wa-mbugu were an independent community, governed by an independent chief, by name Kirara, who resided in the north-east of Gamualla. Some years ago they were conquered by Naguvu, their chief slain, and themselves confined to the valley of the Junguli, where they now devote themselves to the cultivation of sugar-cane and bananas, of which a large share goes to Naguvu as tribute.

Though not over middle height, the Ugweno are muscular and well-knit. The round spot tattooed in the middle of the forehead, as the tribal mark of the natives of Usambara, is replaced among their kinsfolk of Ugweno by a black streak running from the middle of the forehead to the nose. Like the Wa-shamba, they file the two upper middle incisors to a point, while the corresponding lower teeth are broken away close to the gum—a practice supposed to impart a ferocious expression. They also cover the whole of the upper part of the body with hundreds of small marks, partly as a charm, partly by way of ornament. The method of tattooing peculiar to the married women has already been referred to.

A farther adornment, according to native ideas, is the layer of grease and red clay with which the unmarried warriors delight to plaster their bodies, after the manner of the Masai. The Masai fashion of dressing the hair is also generally in vogue, pleasingly varied according to individual taste. A few cut away the hair on the crown, others shave it off entirely, and a yet greater number wear it hanging down the neck in a thatch of little pig-tails stiffly plaited with grass. The commonest way of all is to twist the hair into thin strings, which hang down all round the head, and above the eyes are cut away into a regular "fringe." Here and there a dandy of the tribe screws up the strings into rows of rigid lovelocks, while another draws a handful down either cheek, and ties them together under his chin, finishing off this elaborate coiffure with a sprinkling of coloured beads.

The men further follow the Masai in carrying a large spear and shield, and the rite of circumcision is universally practised. Their only clothing is a piece of cloth or hide hanging down across the breast, while the women wear a garment of hide fastened round the waist. In this they copy the Masai, as well as in the spirals of iron wire which they wear as arm and leg ornaments. Their other ornaments include very pretty, large ear-rings of beads like those of the women of Usambara ; thick necklets of brass, and wooden ear-stretchers decorated with iron, by which the lobe of the ear is distended to as much as three inches across.

As far as we could learn, there is no native name for Ugweno as a whole. Ugweno, the name in general use at the coast and on the maps, originally applied only to the most northerly state—that ruled over by the chief Yangobi. This district is familiar to the Wa-Jagga as the nearest to Kilimanjaro, and one upon which they have made frequent raids ; and from them the name has probably been picked up, and by common usage extended to the entire region.

Thanks to the periodical ravages of Mandara, the whole of the north-western district as far the Wangobi valley is

uninhabited. In the north, Yangobi, whose father fell fighting against Mandara, manages to hold his own against the
marauding warriors of Jagga, while the little district of the
aged chief Mafurra acts as a sort of buffer for the districts
farther to the south-west. The southern and eastern districts,
ruled by Naguvu of Usangi, are the most densely populated.
They are in a state of high cultivation, and from the way in
which advantage is taken of every available morsel of ground
along the slopes of the valleys and hollows, we may gather
some idea of what the rest of Ugweno must have been like
before it was laid waste and pillaged by Mandara's marauding
bands.

We have already spoken of the huts, which are sometimes
of the Wa-Jagga, sometimes of the Usambara type. Bananas
are the staple article of food, with beans, maize, millet, manioc,
and sweet potatoes, while pombé is made from the juice of
the sugar-cane. In constant dread of Mandara and the Masai,
the natives are afraid to rear either sheep or goats, and Naguvu
alone is the happy possessor of a very few cattle. As in
Jagga, the animals are all stall-fed, contrary to the custom
of the Wa-mbugu of Usambara, who rear a fine breed of cattle,
which is owned by the chiefs, and regularly driven to the
open pastures.

As one result of the unequal distribution of the population, Ugweno is very irregularly wooded. Anything approaching a forest is only to be met with in the uninhabited
district in the north-west, along the mountains on the outskirts of the region, on the side facing the plains. Elsewhere
everything has been burned down for clearings, or, as on the
higher zones of the mountains, the slopes are covered with
low bush, grass, or ferns.

We had heard great accounts of the skill of the Wa-gweno,
and especially of the Usangi, in smelting and working iron,

but what we saw of it turned out to be rather disappointing. The process of forging we were not permitted to see, though, so far as I am aware, there is no special reason why it should be kept a mystery. No secret is made of the method of extracting the metal from the ore. In the Jego valley the iron is contained in the layer of black sand deposited by the river all along its banks, and here I saw the natives busy at work washing the sand in holes, till scarcely anything was left but the pure particles of iron. The iron is probably carried down by the river from the quartz veins by which the gneiss is everywhere intersected, and which we so often found to be rich in ore. On Mount Sungo, in the west of Ugweno, in the Usangi chain, and on the lower spurs of the mountains of Eastern Ugweno, the ore occurs in lumps, as the result of the weathering of the gneiss, and it is usually worked on the spot.

After the ore has been collected, it is mixed with charcoal and left to roast for several days in a rude sort of earthen furnace, in which the melted metal gradually falls to the bottom. The collecting is the only part of the work intrusted to the women; all the rest is done by men, or rather by a certain set of men called *fundi* (masters), who make the smelting and forging of iron their special business. The wood for the purpose is charred in conical heaps, and is stored up in long faggots covered over with grass.

The bellows consist of a couple of goat-skins, each forming a sack, in which an opening is left above and below. When the bellows are pulled out, the air rushes in by the upper opening and fills the skins. This opening is then held fast, the bellows are squeezed together, and the air is forced out by the lower opening through a clay nozzle thrust into the charcoal furnace. A similar apparatus is used in Jagga, but the articles turned out by the Jagga smiths—spears, axes, knives, spades, arm and neck ornaments—are far superior to those made in Ugweno. One reason of this may be that the Wa-jagga for the most part work with European iron wire, while the Wa-gweno use the native iron, which, with their primitive methods of smelting and hammering, is of comparatively poor quality. The metal is wrought only in small quantities, Mandara and the Masai once more acting as a check to production. "Our cattle have had to go already," said Naguvu, when I mentioned the matter to him; "is it likely we are going to tempt Mandara with a store of tools and spears?"

If it were not for the proximity of Mandara, Ugweno, which has an average elevation of 4500 feet, would not be far behind Usambara. It has a healthy climate, a fertile soil, and industrious inhabitants; and, although, even with universal peace in the Kilimanjaro region, it would never come up to the favoured land of Jagga, it may still be regarded as a valuable colonial possession, and might safely be said to have a very fair future before it, if only communication with the coast were properly established.

Having reached the foot of the mountains on the eastern side of Ugweno, we continued our way across the steppe towards Jagga. For two hours we held on in a northerly direction, and were gradually approaching the "gallery" forest of the Rufu, when we were met by a small band of natives, whom even at a distance we recognised as Wa-taveta, from their fearless bearing. They were on their way home from collecting a quantity of honey, and the meeting proved to be most opportune, for without them we should never have been able to find our way across the great papyrus swamp lying along the banks of the Rufu to the north of Ugweno.

I have seen a good many swamps in my travels, in Java and

P

the Philippine Islands, in Japan and the Transvaal, but nev
anything to equal the papyrus swamp of the river Rufu. T
Wa-taveta had crossed it only two days before, and they nc
found the way back by following their recent tracks.   Clo
behind the narrow belt of trees which bordered the river v
had to push our way through a perfect jungle of gigant
papyrus grasses, in which at every step we sank up to tl
knees in the soft grey mud.   A little farther on we reach
a place where the papyrus had been trodden down by hipp
potami, and here progress was a little easier, the mud havi
been dried by the sun.   We managed to get along by leapi
from space to space between the deep footprints left behi
by the hippos.

Next came a creek of stagnant water, dark and motionle
as the Styx.   We made shift to cross it by an impromp
bridge of papyrus stems, but every man that passed ov
caused the bridge to sink deeper and deeper, and those wl
came last waded up to the neck in water.   Here and the
were tiny islets of mud overgrown with bush and trees, b
they were too far apart to be of much service to us.   Wh
with cutting down the papyrus, fording the creeks, here hel
ing with a load, there dragging out a man who was in dang
of sinking, it was two hours and a half before we had a
struggled through the belt of mud, everybody and everythir
dripping wet.   From time to time we were startled by tl
snorting of a hippopotamus, or warned by the strong odour
musk that we had almost stumbled into the jaws of a croc
dile.   On all sides rose the tall papyri with their bunches
broad leaves, and stems as thick as a man's arm, many
them twelve or fourteen feet in height.

At length we once more reached *terra firma ;* the papyr
jungle passed into a narrow belt of trees along the river-sid
and in a few minutes more we had pitched our camp beyor

the wood under a group of tall mimosæ. Troops of monkeys
barked and frolicked in the trees, and in the marsh we caught
some fish of the Silurus family (sheat-fish), which, though
rather oily, proved not at all unpalatable. Some of them
weighed as much as eighteen pounds. During the night not
one of us could close an eye for the swarms of mosquitoes,
which rose in myriads from the swamp. The buzzing of their
wings mingled with the flutter of bats and nightjars, and
formed a continuous treble to the deep grunts of the hippos,
the hoarse barking of the monkeys, and the sharp cry of the
leopard as it roamed the steppes in search of prey. It was a
chorus of sounds peculiarly wild, peculiarly African, peculiarly
attractive—a weird symphony never to be forgotten by any
who have once listened to it in the appropriate setting of
its own peculiar surroundings.

Tired and unrefreshed, we struck camp next morning at
dawn. At a rounded hill not far from the camp we reached
the boundary-line between the gneiss and the volcanic rock
formations, and crossed the path that leads to Taveta. Here
our guides took leave of us and turned towards home, while we
continued our way across the steppes, not following any path,
but making for the Makessa group of the Wajimba Hills,
which formed a conspicuous landmark at the foot of Kilimanjaro. The mountain was shrouded in mist, and away to the
right the smoke of Taveta curled slowly upwards from among
the trees. The sun above and the earth beneath glowed like
a furnace, and by midday we were all half dead with thirst, for
none of us had thought it worth while to carry a supply of the
muddy water, which was all that was to be had at the swamp.

Shortly before we reached the path which leads to Moji,
we were suddenly confronted by a large rhinoceros, which,
with tail erect and ears pricked up, stood gazing at us with a
petrified stare, not thirty yards away. After a few moments

of indecision, the brute began slowly to advance, and seemed to be making straight for Purtscheller, who was totally un-armed. All of a sudden it changed its mind and made a dash for Mwini, who, with the rest of the men, had taken refuge in the bush. Just in the nick of time Mwini sprang quickly aside; and the rhinoceros, apparently quite satisfied with having routed the caravan, trotted off with an ease of motion I should scarcely have thought possible for such an unwieldy animal. This little episode served to keep the men in amuse-ment long after we had reached our camp at the Habari, where we were soon bathing and drinking to our hearts' content under the shady trees by the side of the rushing stream.

The nine miles between our camp and Marangu were covered next morning amid the usual fun and merriment. We had not been expected for some days, and our appearance came upon every one as a surprise. During our absence much anxiety had been caused by the rumour which had reached Mareale's that the Wa-gweno had opposed our advance, and that we had had some hard fighting. We were received, accordingly, with expressions of the wildest delight. But the Ugweno expedition did end in blood after all, for in the jubilant firing of guns which succeeded our arrival, two of the newly-returned porters got so severely wounded in the thigh, that they were still unable to travel when we started for the coast three weeks later.

As usual after our return from an excursion, the next few days were spent in writing, reading, arranging our collections, and generally putting our affairs in order. A fresh batch of letters arrived from home, containing nothing but good news. A few days afterwards we had a visit from Dr. Abbott, who had been elephant-shooting in Arusha, to the south of Kahé, and had had a narrow escape of being trampled to death. Immediately he had gone came the missionaries from Moji; and so time flew past, each day bringing something new. As my vegetable garden was now in splendid condition, I had always plenty of good things with which to entertain my guests, who, on their part, were kind enough to replenish my stores of coffee and salt, two useful commodities of which we had begun to run short.

At this time my services as a physician were much in demand, especially among the children, many of whom were brought to me by Mareale himself. The poor little creatures suffered greatly from large ulcers in the legs, which arise without any apparent cause, and do not readily heal up—not at least under the native treatment, which consists in a liberal application of fresh cow-dung. Not infrequently the sores measured five or six inches long.

But the routine of camp life was not without its more pleasant variations. Often in the evening we were called away from our more serious occupations by the pleasant tinkling of bells, which announced the approach of a wedding procession. With nothing in the way of bridal array save a tiny apron and a few strings of beads, the bride was conducted to her husband's house by a troop of maidens and young married women, all shining like herself in a fresh coating of grease and red clay. Put into words, the scene savours almost of the ludicrous, but I only wish it could be transported to Europe in all its natural simplicity and fitness to the unconventional surroundings, that from it scoffers might learn to respect the customs of Africa as they deserve.

We were now warned by the weather that if we had any more work to do on Kilimanjaro, the sooner we set about it the better. Every day we had strong winds from the south-west, and almost every night the rain fell in torrents, while above, the peaks of Kibo and Mawenzi were hardly ever free

from clouds. It had long been one of our cherished projects
to visit the southern and western sides of Kibo, and now or
never we must put our plan into execution. We made our
preparations accordingly, and soon everything was in readiness for this our last trip before leaving the region.

BRIDGE ACROSS THE RIVER DEHU.

CHAPTER VII.

WESTWARD HO!

WHEN the enterprising missionary Rebmann first visited Kilimanjaro in 1848, he was not contented with the mere discovery of the snow-capped mountain, but, bent on a systematic survey of the whole region, pushed westwards as far as the Jagga State of Majamé. He was followed in 1861 by Baron Von der Decken, and although since then the Majamé district has been visited by many Europeans, none have materially added to the Baron's interesting account of what is, perhaps, the most imposing aspect of the great African giant.

HOODED VULTURES IN MAJAMÉ.

As already said, a visit to the western side of Kilimanjaro had all along formed part of my programme, and now, in the beginning of November, I found myself in a position to carry it out. Circumstances, however, were unfavourable. Mandara of Moji and Sinna of Kiboso were at war, and willy-nilly all the smaller states were drawn into the feud, so that the whole

of Western Jagga was in a state of turmoil. I was, therefore,
unable to proceed direct to my destination, but, starting from
Marangu, was obliged to proceed to the western foot of Kibo
by way of the neutral path running along the mountain-side,
through the grass-lands above the forest zone.

We set out on the 14th of November. The heat was terrific,
and we were unable to start before midday, for the two guides
provided by Mareale could not be induced to move a moment
sooner, and there was nothing for it but to submit. For the
fifth time we directed our steps upwards through the open
bush and shady banana plantations. Leaving the fields and
the fern zone behind us, we camped for the night at the
little meadow by the murmuring Rua, now gay with orchids, as
when we saw it for the first time. Our caravan consisted of
twenty men—quite as many as we expected to require. Unfortunately, neither Purtscheller nor I were in very good condition for a journey. After our return from Ugweno, I had
had a touch of fever, and Purtscheller was suffering from an
attack of indigestion brought on by eating the Jagga bananas,
which, strangely enough, when ripe, always similarly disagreed
with our porters. We were in good enough spirits, however,
for we counted on the mountain air soon to put us all right.
We felt better even after a single night on the mountain-side,
for in our camp at the Rua, 6430 feet above the sea, the temperature during the night fell to 41° F., and the bracing atmosphere was a splendid tonic. All night long the stream
crooned softly to itself as it flowed along, the cicadæ chirped
among the dewy reed-grass, and from time to time the trumpeting of an elephant awoke the echoes in the neighbouring
wood.

The next morning broke clear and bright. In the forest
many of the plants had now exchanged their sombre livery of
grey-green moss for a rich array of blossom. Here and there

a ray of sunlight strayed downwards through the leafy canopy overhead, and fell athwart the deep blue flowers among the undergrowth, high above which rose the tall dracænas, with their glossy leaves and fair white blooms, and the sumach trees with their clusters of brownish red.

By midday we were out of the forest and had emerged upon the grassy downs above, bright with the crimson flowers of amaryllis and everlasting. As we followed the path westwards along the mountain-side, the clouds began to roll up from the south-east, and before we could reach the shelter of the huts at our old camp by the Mué, we were overtaken by a tremendous thunderstorm. The thunder and lightning was accompanied by terrific showers of hail; and so overcome were the porters with cold and fright, that one after another they flung themselves down beside their loads, and we had to resort to the strongest measures before they could be got to move on again. The storm continued for two hours, and half an hour after it was over hailstones as large as coffee-berries still lay on the ground to a depth of nearly an inch. The fowls we had brought with us from Jagga all died of the cold; nevertheless we had solemnly to go through the ceremony of cutting their throats, that we might eat with a clear conscience, the letter of the law being fulfilled.

The stormy afternoon was succeeded by a clear, cold night. At break of day I awoke and roused the caravan, but to a man the porters refused to stir, even under threats of a general flogging. The fear of the cold outweighed even the respect usually paid to my uplifted stick, whose virtue as a stimulant had never before been known to fail. For once I gave in, however. The temperature was three degrees below freezing-point, and as I looked at these overgrown children, shivering in their scanty clothing, I could not help feeling rather sorry for them, and made up my mind to wait till after sunrise.

As soon as it was warm enough the little caravan was in motion, and the journey westwards along the neutral path was resumed.

We had scarcely got well under weigh when there was another little hitch. All of a sudden our guides came to an abrupt standstill, professing that they did not know the way, and advising us to turn back if we did not want to fall into the hands of the men of Moji and Kiboso, now on the war-path. The rascals had evidently been laying their heads together overnight, and I saw at a glance that the whole thing was a cock-and-bull story, invented partly because they were really afraid to proceed on account of the war, and partly because they wanted to make off with the half of their pay, which, as usual, they had received before starting. A glance towards my Somál was enough. As I laid my hand quietly on the shoulder of the guide who seemed the more intelligent of the two, he was promptly seized from behind and made prisoner; his companion had suddenly disappeared. I then made him a most impressive speech, enlarging upon the supreme wisdom of the white man and the folly of trying to impose upon him; after which, seeing that I judged his fear of Mandara's warriors to be genuine, I gave him our flag to carry as a sure charm against all evil, and bade him once more take his place at the head of the caravan. My harangue was backed up by a bloodthirsty threat that I would shoot him down the moment he showed the least sign of trying to escape. After that Mkumbo, as the man was called, gave us no further trouble, but stuck religiously to his flag till he was once more back in Marangu. He proved to be quite an acquisition, for he was possessed of a great fund of humour, and when he liked, could keep the whole caravan in a roar. His very appearance was mirth-provoking. A battered clerical hat, a faded overcoat of Count Teleki's, and an old pair of shoes, which had once been mine, these, with a spear in one hand and the flag in the other, made up a rig-out that put the fool's traditional motley to shame.

The thunderstorm of the day before had covered both Kibo and Mawenzi with a dazzling mantle of newly-fallen snow, against which the dark patches of rock stood out in bold relief. The sun beat down upon us with scorching radiance, and from the appearance of the sky it looked as if we might expect another storm in the course of the day. As we left Mawenzi behind, and gradually approached Kibo, we crossed a considerable number of tiny rivulets, most of them rising in the region between the plateau and the forest. In their deeply-eroded ravines we noticed a great many *Senecio* trees, some of the already familiar species, *Senecio Johnstoni*, others of a new, many-branched variety, with smooth slender stems.

Our way now lay over a high grassy ridge of lava and through a wide depression, from the edge of which we had a splendid view of the volcanic cone of Meru, towering upward from out the blue haze of the western plains. We could clearly distinguish the large central cone and the jagged western walls of its great crater, which opens towards the east.

We now entered the upper district of Kiboso, and here, in the well-watered sheltered hollow, the belt of trees and shrubs stretched much farther up the mountain than it does farther east. As we continued to ascend, we could trace the tiny brooks gradually becoming more and more thread-like, until at last they dwindled each into a mere series of pools along the rocky channels, cushioned with moss and hoary with grey *Senecios*. Gay-plumaged sunbirds flitted from flower to flower, sucking the nectar from their waxy cups, and every now and again we startled one of the small grey antelopes of the new species discovered by Dr. Abbott. Once we saw a beautifully-marked leopard, which I watched with admiration as it gracefully bounded away with long, agile springs. We had constantly to be on the look-out for game-pits, of which there were a great number close to the pathway. The pits vary from 12 to 15 feet in depth, and are artfully covered over with bushes, so that to the unwary traveller they form a source of no inconsiderable danger.

In the broiling sunshine we toiled onward and upward across the heath-clad slopes, and gradually approached the base of Kibo. Meanwhile towards the south-east the sky began to look so lowering, that at midday I thought it advisable to camp by one of the water-channels, sorely against the will of our guide, who feared that the smoke of our fire might attract the attention of the Wa-kiboso. The Wa-kiboso as well as ourselves had soon something else to think about, however, for presently the storm broke in all its fury, and what that means only those can know who have themselves experienced a tropical thunderstorm among the mountains. While it lasted, the rattle of the hail and the crash of the thunder went on without a moment's intermission, and afterwards rain fell in torrents during the whole afternoon and evening. The porters took refuge among the rocks and under the blocks of lava, and passed the night in a wretched plight, soaked to the skin and half-dead with cold and hunger. For this crowning misery they had themselves to blame. Extra rations had been served out to them before they left Marangu, but as they had made quite certain of reaching Majamé in three days, they had eaten up the food on the march to save themselves the trouble of carrying it.

If such a thing had happened three months before, I should have stormed like a madman, but now I was able to take the matter coolly, although it obliged us to descend again into the cultivated region, instead of continuing our journey upwards, as I should have liked. The only consolation was, that as the rainy season had now fairly set in, with its daily thunderstorms and thick afternoon mists, we could not hope to do much in the way of mountaineering. As it happened, we had chosen the very best time of the year for the ascents we had made from the saddle, and now we were fast approaching the very worst. Accordingly, although, for the principle of the thing, I promised the delinquents a flogging as soon as we were back in Marangu, I did not feel it so much of a sacrifice as otherwise it might have been when I had to change my plans, and give orders to descend next day into the state of Uru, the chief of which was on friendly terms with Mareale.

In the morning there was no need either of threats or persuasions to get the caravan under weigh for an early start. The famishing porters almost raced down-hill, and in three hours we were back again at the camp by the Mué. Here I stopped to take some photographs, after which we continued our way downwards beneath the dripping branches of the forest, while the porters sought to stay their empty stomachs with impromptu pæans in praise of the good things awaiting them in Uru.

The nature of the forest and the conformation of the ground differ widely on this side of the mountain from what is to be seen above Marangu. There we have shelving slopes and wide stretches of ground unbroken by ridges and ravines, and no abrupt change from one form of vegetation to another. Above Uru, on the contrary, the ground dips suddenly at an angle of from 20° to 25°, and has been cut and carved by the combined agency of wind and weather and running streams into a perfect network of jutting crests and deep gullies, such as in the south-east are only to be seen towards the foot of the mountain. Between 9100 and 9500 feet the wood is

composed almost entirely of arborescent heaths, in girth
and general appearance strongly recalling the pine, a genus
which is not represented on Kilimanjaro. As a rule, the
trees attain a height of from 18 to 20 feet, while the stems
average about 18 inches in girth, and are plentifully draped
with greybeard moss. At 8500 feet the heaths abruptly
give place to the typical tropical forest, with its tall trees, its
rich variety of species, and its luxuriant undergrowth of herbs,
bushes, ferns, and moss. Rain is here of daily occurrence, and
as the undergrowth prevents the evaporation of the moisture,
this zone constitutes the immediate source of the water-supply
on this side of the mountain. The ground is soft and clayey,
the path slippery, and often difficult to trace. Below 7500
feet there is less moisture, and the forest becomes less dense.
Instead of the herbaceous undergrowth, there are thickets of
shrubs and creepers, and, instead of greybeard lichens, the
stems and branches are covered with brown moss. As we
proceed downwards the ravines gradually deepen, and along
the banks of the streams tall tree-ferns, with their crowns of
spreading fronds, rise grandly by the side of the clear, cool
water. At 6550 feet the forest suddenly thins away, and
terminates abruptly in a belt of dense bush. At 6400 feet
the bush with equal abruptness passes into a zone of brackens,
which at 5900 feet suddenly ceases on the edge of a steep
terrace, at the foot of which we reach the first banana plantations of Uru, lying at an elevation of 5700 feet.

The forest, and especially the dry region, is a favourite
haunt of the elephant, to judge from the number of uprooted
and broken trees and the deep footprints everywhere to
be seen. It was here that I came upon the largest elephants
I ever saw in Africa. Impeded by the nature of the ground,
the men had lagged a long way behind, and leaving them
to the care of the Somál, I pushed ahead, accompanied only

by Mkumbo and one of the Asikari carrying my gun. As I emerged from a small ravine overgrown with rank vegetation, there was a sudden crashing and crackling of branches, and looking up, I saw a herd of elephants at a distance of about forty yards. With a warning cry of *tembo*, Mkumbo disappeared into the bush—my gun-bearer after him. Left with nothing but a stick in my hand, I was fain to take refuge behind a tree, while the animals, having got scent of us, stood doubtfully sniffing the air, with ears erect and waving trunks. Altogether the herd may have numbered about fourteen, almost all full-grown. I had not long to count, however, for at that moment the head of the caravan appeared in sight, whereupon the elephants took to flight, climbing the sides of the ravine with wonderful rapidity, and trumpeting loud and long as they disappeared in the thicket.

By the time the midday thunderstorm again broke over the upper parts of the mountain, we were beyond the region of rain and hail, and by four o'clock we had reached the plantations of Uru. A little lower down we pitched our camp on a hill between two deep ravines, and the starving porters were at liberty to make up for their long fast by gorging themselves to their hearts' content. But first there were the usual preliminaries to be gone through. As we were the first whites who had been seen in the district since the time of Rebmann, and as no caravan had ever been known to enter the State by the way we had come, the natives were inclined to be a little suspicious. They thawed somewhat when Mkumbo, in a long harangue, explained who and what we were, and the calico and red beads which the porters offered in exchange for their bananas fairly "fetched" them. Towards evening messengers arrived from the chief, Salika, and when I sent them back as the bearer of my salaams to their royal master, with a present of brilliant bandanas and brass chains for themselves, they sang as they went the praises of the great *mzungu* (white man), who, as they said, had descended from the clouds.

The next day the caravan remained in camp, while I went down the mountain to pay my respects to the chief. The way lay over long bare ridges and through three deeply-eroded valleys, and it was two hours before I reached Salika's kraal—a rabble of inquisitive natives at my heels. Within an enclosure surrounded by a high fence, and further fortified by a deep ditch, stood some half-dozen beehive huts for the women, children, and cattle, and a more commodious square house for the chief himself. Announcing our arrival with the customary salute of two guns, we crossed the ditch by the tree-trunk which did duty as a bridge, and, to our profound surprise, were received at the low doorway which gave entrance to the compound by a group of shabby-looking Swahili. No Jagga court seems to be complete without two or three of these rascals, who hang about in the expectation of picking up slaves, a commodity of which a supply is constantly forthcoming as the result of the frequent feuds and forays between the different petty states.

Surrounded by a bevy of young wives, Salika stood within his tidy compound, arrayed in all the glory of a bran-new scarlet cloth. He was a short, thick-set youth of about twenty, and seemed dreadfully embarrassed by the arrival of his white visitors. Cordially shaking hands with him, I told him where I had come from and whither I was going, and hinted that I had some fine presents in store for him. By degrees the awkwardness began to wear off, his tongue loosened over a flowing bowl of pombé, and soon we were chatting pleasantly of Zanzibar and Europe, of which he had heard fabulous accounts from his Swahili. He made no secret of his ruling passions—wine, or rather beer, and women. I never tasted better banana-beer anywhere, and his wives were the pick of Jagga. Of the presents I had brought him, the one that seemed to strike his fancy most was a hideously-painted mask. As a charm of supreme virtue, it was the only thing he kept to himself; all the rest—cloth, beads, looking-glasses, chains, knives, and so forth—were handed over to his headman or steward.

On reaching Salika's, I sent one of the Asikari back to our camp with orders that it should be shifted farther down the mountain, to a lovely little spot we had passed in the morning. By the time we got back, attended by a goodly following of natives, the tents were up and everything in order. Never before had we camped among such charming surroundings. The tents stood under a shady tree on the crest of a high grass-clad ridge, on either side of which flowed a babbling brook. All along the slopes the rich plantations of maize and bananas were watered by many a gliding runnel of clear cool water. Upward the eye ranged over rock and forest to the dazzling snows of Kibo, and westward over wood and steppe to the volcanic peak of Meru. To the south lay the boundless plains—everywhere a glorious panorama of unrivalled extent and peculiar beauty. All the way from Marangu to Moji there is nothing to equal the state of Uru, either for actual loveliness or for extent of view, and from no other point do the exquisite outlines of Kibo show to such advantage—not even from the west, where the mountain, though more impressive, is certainly less beautiful.

From Uru the whole south-western sweep of the mountain, from crater to base, shows the characteristic curve of the typical volcano. The base runs out far into the plains, for on this side the lava streams from Kibo flowed without let or hindrance over cone and parent mass alike, whereas in the east they were dammed back by Mawenzi and

Q

the saddle plateau. The ice-cap, ribbed with countless
ridges of dark brown rock, stretches down almost to the
base of the cone, and is separated from the forest only by a
comparatively narrow strip of grass-land. The forest, as we
had already remarked from Kiboso, here extends much farther
up the mountain than on its south-eastern side, while at the
same time the wooded region below, in common with the
base, runs out much farther into the plains. The Jagga district of Kibongoto (*i.e.*, *Kibo-ngoto*, the state below Kibo)
seems to lie entirely on the wooded plains, while in Kiboso
(*i.e.*, *Kibo-so*, the state up Kibo) the cultivated zone stretches
up the mountain-side to a height of almost 6500 feet.

This extension of the forest on the south of Kibo is easily
accounted for when we consider the heavy rainfall on this side
of the mountain. Every day we could see the clouds rolling
up from the south towards the heights above, where they
broke in rain and hail and snow, and passed away towards
the south-west in the direction of Meru.

All the afternoon I was busy with my usual observations,
while the men impatiently awaited the arrival of the present
Salika was sure to send in return for mine; for in Africa
everything is done on the pernicious principle of *do ut des*.
It was not until after dark that the expected donation made
its appearance in the shape of a couple of goats, which the
Swahili lost no time in killing and cooking. We considered
this an extremely stingy offering, for the chief had plenty of
cattle, and by all the laws of African etiquette he ought to
have sent me at least two cows, that being about the value
in native currency of my gifts to him. Accordingly, without
further delay, I resolved to move on to Majamé.

Next morning messengers came from Salika to bid me
once more to the presence of the chief, but I treated the

request with lordly disdain, and gave orders to quit this inhospitable land forthwith. Nothing loath, now that they were
thoroughly gorged, the porters were soon on the road, Mkumbo,
the guide, leading the way. The path followed the gentle
slope of one of the lower spurs of the mountain downwards,
between endless groves of bananas. The irrigation of the
plantations was effected by means of an unusually complicated
system of canals, through which the water was frequently
brought from miles away, while on either side they were regularly planted with trees to shade them from the sun. Lower
down, where the news of our arrival had not yet had time to
spread, every native we met immediately turned tail and fled
incontinently.

After a rapid march of two and a half hours, we suddenly
found ourselves on the edge of an enormous dry ditch about
fifty feet deep, which marked the southern boundary of Uru.
There could be no doubt that it was intended as a means of
defence—a very effectual one too, I should say, for any unsuspecting enemy. For a moment or two we were at a loss how
to proceed, but after hunting about in the bush for a little, we
came upon two natives—sentinels, as one might say—who, in
answer to my demands, threw two long poles across the trench,
and on these we made our way to the other side. It was no
easy work; a single false step might have cost us a limb, if
not our life, and it was a whole hour before we were all safely
across. Meanwhile, Salika had had time to hear of what was
going on, and the last man had scarcely reached neutral ground
when the chief made his appearance on the scene, looking
very much disgusted to find that he had arrived too late.
The brunt of his wrath fell on the unlucky sentinels, whom he
blamed for allowing us to escape out of his hands. From the
opposite side of the bridge I gave him a piece of my mind,
however, and speedily had him reduced to a state of abject

submission. He promised that, if we would visit him on our
way back, we should have an ox for nothing, and meantime he
sent one of his followers to accompany us, at once as guide
and hostage.

From this man we learned that Uru and Majamé were on
friendly terms, and had joined with Mandara in the league
against Sinna of Kiboso. The new acquisition to our caravan,
who was armed with an old flintlock, seemed to be of rather a
jealous disposition, and was evidently not inclined to make
friends with our Marangu guide. I cannot say I was sorry
on that account, for the two were less likely to make common
cause against me, in the event of anything occurring which
might tempt one or other to play us false.

Below the cultivated region of Uru was a belt of bush, which
stretched downwards and out into the plains, and through it
we had to push our way westward, creeping rather than walking. About ten o'clock we crossed the narrow valley of the
Rau river, which rises in the forest region on the southern
side of Kibo, and, flowing downwards, is here a rapid stream
thirty feet wide. In the vicinity of the water the vegetation
flourished with true tropical luxuriance. Particularly remarkable were the trees of a tall, straight-stemmed *Ficus*
species, many of which were over 180 feet in height, presenting the most marked contrast to the belt of bush on
either hand, with its low glossy trees, thorny shrubs, and rank
grasses. The bush here was similar in character to that below
Marangu, and occurred at about the same distance up the
mountain. Here, however, the elephant tracks were more
numerous—the elephant in this region being, for the most
part, allowed to roam unmolested.

As we approached the eastern frontier of Kiboso, the
guides began to manifest increasing signs of fear, and as the
feeling of uneasiness gradually communicated itself to the

rest of the caravan, the accustomed fun and merriment died away into a dead silence. At the slightest sound every man held his breath and stopped to listen, ready to take to his heels at a moment's notice. The appearance of half-a-dozen Wa-kiboso would have routed the whole cavalcade to a man. As a rule, the Swahili are the most cowardly crew on earth, especially if they know they have to do with an enemy capable not only of swagger and bluster—accomplishments in which they themselves are not deficient—but, if need be, of fighting in good earnest, like the Masai, and to some extent also the Wa-jagga. Although, for his own satisfaction, each of my men was provided with a gun and ammunition, I was very well aware that if they really had occasion to use them, they would fling their weapons down and run after the first shot. The main reason for bringing a bodyguard of Somál with me on the expedition was that I knew the Swahili were not to be relied on in an emergency. Three of this body-guard accompanied me on the present occasion, which meant that there were five among us who might be depended upon to stand to their guns—a force quite sufficient to hold its own against fifty times the number of savages.

But our courage was not to be put to the proof. At the Ngomberé river we passed a camp which had all the appearance of having just been deserted ; but although we supposed the warriors must be somewhere in the neighbourhood, we saw nothing of them. If it had not been that we had come straight from the enemy's country, I should have turned aside into Kiboso and paid a visit to its powerful young chief, with the certainty of meeting with a cordial reception, for Sinna had ere now shown himself friendly to the Europeans who had visited him. Under the circumstances, however, it was useless to think of it, for nothing would have induced my men to follow me, and it was impossible for Purtscheller and me to go alone.

The Ngomberé forms the western boundary of Kiboso.
Leaving behind us the narrow strip of gallery forest which
borders the stream, we kept on among the bush through the
small states of Kindi and Kombo, and crossed three sluggish
streams, the Maëmbe, the Manjoka, and the Nseri. Still keeping below the cultivated zone, we continued westwards along
the mountain-side at an average elevation of 3600 feet, and
about three o'clock reached the vicinity of Naruma. Here we
quitted the unbroken, undulating tract of bush, and entered
a bit of closely-wooded country, through which the path led
gradually upwards in a north-westerly direction, till at length
we came in sight of the banana plantations of the Wa-naruma.
Presently, between the trees, we had a peep of a trim little
village, lying cosily ensconced behind hedges and fences, but
all we saw of its inhabitants were a few old men, who watched
us pass by with apparent indifference. An hour's march
brought us out upon the clearings at the other side of the
wood, and before us lay the deeply-eroded valley of the Weri-
Weri, the river which forms the eastern boundary of Majamé.
The men being very tired, we here pitched our tents on the
Naruma side of the stream, for once setting aside the usual
rule in travelling, to cross the stream first and camp afterwards.
The altitude was about 3900 feet.

In the afternoon, as a token of his good-will and friendship, Ndelongo, the chief of Naruma, sent us a present of some
wild honey—a delicacy we soon disposed of with due relish.
In the evening a small band of Masai passed our camp on
their way out of the state, where they had been bartering
cattle for beans, maize, and bananas. They scarcely took the
slightest notice of us, but kept quietly on their way down the
mountain in the direction of the plains.

The crossing of the stream next morning was a stiffish
bit of work for our laden porters. The rushing river flowed

swiftly along the bottom of a ravine, whose palm - clad
sides rose steeply on either hand to a height of nearly 200
feet. Crossing the stream at a point where the water was
breast-high, we scrambled up the banks on the other side, and
almost immediately found ourselves in a Majamé village. The
natives were very anxious to detain us, in the hope of being
able to exchange the fruits of the soil for some of our coveted
cloth and beads. To that end they came forward with a story
that the chief had sent orders for us to await him there, as he
wanted to make brothers with us before we proceeded farther
into his territory. The concoction was too palpable, and with
a laugh I brushed the speaker aside and quietly took my way
up the mountain. We were followed by a hubbub of threats
and protests, but there the matter ended, no one venturing
seriously to oppose our progress.

All day Kibo remained wrapped in clouds, and we saw
nothing of it; but we had a magnificent view of the whole of
Western Jagga. Here there are no hills or lava ridges, as in
Uru, but all the way from the forest to the plains, the cultivated zone slopes gradually downwards in unbroken regularity.
The plantations are in a much higher state of cultivation than
farther to the east, but here too the custom prevails of leaving
a tall tree at intervals to shade the fields, so that the aspect of
the country is park-like in the best sense of the word. As a
rule, every man has his own little croft, with its group of cosy
huts, surrounded by banana plantations, and separated from
the fields of adjoining proprietors by a hedge. Villages, in
the usual sense of the term, there are none, except along the
southern frontier, where the risk of attack is greatest, and
where accordingly the village frequently serves the purpose of
a fort. As we gradually approached the residence of the chief,
the necessity for some more effectual means of defence became
more and more apparent. In many a green banana grove the

charred remains of what was once a group of huts spoke
sadly of the recent ravages of Wa-kiboso warriors, and everywhere there were traces of rapine and plunder. Strangely
enough, to our way of thinking, the banana plantations had
been entirely spared, and seemed to be all in the most
flourishing condition.

After a climb of three hours through shady groves and
waving fields, with many a murmuring brook between, we
reached the former kraal of Ngamine. Now nothing remained
of it but a pile of ruins surrounded by a stockade—the Wa-
kiboso had been at work here too. Ngamine's new abode
was not far distant, however, and we pitched our camp in a
shady spot that seemed to offer a suitable site. In answer to
our guns, we were soon surrounded by a lively crowd of inquisitive natives, all eager to see the strangers, and get a chance
of driving a bargain. Supplies were cheap and plentiful, and
goods were exchanged with mutual satisfaction. The greatest
good-humour prevailed, and trade went on briskly amid all the
din and chatter, the singing and dancing, the bustle and merriment of a village fair. I seized the opportunity to take a
number of instantaneous photographs, and also succeeded in
obtaining several shields and spears of the small sort which
were once generally in fashion throughout Jagga, but have
now been replaced, in the eastern districts, by the large
shield and long-bladed spear of Masai pattern.

About midday we had a thunderstorm, and the rain fell
in torrents. No sooner had it passed off than our headman
announced the arrival, not of the chief, but of the chief's
brother. He was accompanied by some of the elders of
the tribe, and came to make brothers with me before I
went to pay my state visit to Ngamine. As he had brought
a goat with him, I concluded that the ceremony would consist of the usual interchange of presents, and immediately

offered him some cloth and beads. To my surprise my gifts
were rejected.

"We cannot accept your presents until you have taken
the oath," said my visitor.

"The oath! what oath?"

"The oath of friendship. You must swear it on the head
of this goat."

"Am I not an *mzungu* (European), and is it not enough
that I come as the friend of friends of yours? The guide
from Uru is a witness that I speak the truth."

"We know that you are an *mzungu*, but the ways of the
mzungu are not as our ways, and it may be that you have
bewitched this man of Uru. You come to us from the east.
How are we to know that you do not come from our enemy
Sinna, and would destroy our land with your powerful magic?
Swear then that we may know that you are indeed our
friend."

"I admire your wisdom. You speak well. Let the goat
be brought hither."

The goat was led forward accordingly. Taking the animal
by the horns, the brother of the chief (by the way, he was
the only negro I ever met who stammered) spat lustily on
its forehead and said—

"An *mzungu* has come into our land. He says that he
is our friend. If he lies, may he utterly perish, he and all
his caravan." This brief but solemn invocation concluded,
the goat received another vigorous squirt of saliva between
the eyes.

And now it was my turn. Following the example of my
swarthy friend, I took the goat by the horns, and, having
duly expectorated on the proper spot, repeated the necessary
formula—-

"If I practise any evil against Ngamine, him or his people,

his cattle or his land, may it so be that I utterly perish, I
and all my caravan." Whereupon there was another expec-
toration, and that part of the ceremony was over.

The head of the goat was next cut off, "that blood and
saliva might mingle," and a strip of skin was cut from the forehead. Two slits having been made, the strip was divided into
two portions, one of which was given to each of us, and the
bond was sealed by our slipping our skin rings over the
middle finger of the right hand. Highly satisfied with the
result of their mission, the ambassadors withdrew, having
received my promise that next day I would move my camp
farther up the mountain, nearer to Ngamine's.

Early in the morning the tents were struck, and crossing
the Kikafu, the stream flowing through the narrow valley
behind the camp, we climbed the grassy slopes on the opposite side, and took up our quarters under the shade of a
group of trees on the margin of a tiny murmuring brook.
At our feet, 250 feet below, the rushing Kikafu tumbled
noisily along among the rounded blocks of lava, its banks
the favourite playground of sprightly troops of baboons,
which frisked and gambolled among the trees by the water's
edge the whole day long. The great cloud masses still brooded
heavily on the heights above, and Kibo remained invisible.

In the course of the forenoon, accompanied by Herr Purtscheller, the Somál and the guides, I went to see Ngamine.
The chief's kraal lay in the midst of a grove of shady bananas,
and here we found him awaiting us at the door of a small hut
made of plaited banana leaves. He was surrounded by about
a dozen elders and warriors, of whom the latter were armed
with guns. In spite of his shabby dress, which consisted
solely of an old piece of blue cloth (*Kaniki*), we were immediately struck with Ngamine's appearance. His steady eye
and thoughtful manner of speaking proclaimed him at once as

a youth of superior intelligence, a judgment fully borne out by the unusual respect with which he is universally regarded by his subjects.

Assured of our friendly intentions by the sight of the bulky package carried in our rear, Ngamine invited us to enter the inner sanctuary, whereupon we patiently crawled after him through the four ridiculously low doorways in the series of concentric wooden palisades which guard the more private portion of the chief's residence. Only a favoured few were permitted to accompany us—the rest of the attendants remained outside. Under the shelter of a low shed the package was unwrapped and we produced our gifts—knives, files, beads, and tobacco-pipes, with other trifles dear to the savage heart. A "gold" chain and a Waterbury watch with the well-known noisy tick were the crowning splendours, and produced an immense impression. Everything having been duly admired and liberally spat upon in token of appreciation, the pombé began to circulate freely, while I made myself agreeable to Ngamine's favourite wife, and helped her to bestow the whole collection of ornaments on various parts of her person. She had a tough struggle with a thick necklet of brass, which she mistook for a leg ornament, and insisted upon pulling it up around her thigh, till I came to the rescue and explained the mistake. At the same time I could not but be struck with the amount of taste displayed by this negro queen of the harem in the disposal of her adornments. I noticed too that she had extremely delicate hands and feet—even more delicate than the wives of Mandara, whom I had thought peculiarly favoured in this respect.

On our return to camp, we were accompanied by the chief, who was going down the mountain to visit a small Swahili caravan from Pangani, which had taken up its quarters in the neighbourhood for some weeks, and "by mistake" had kid-

napped one of Ngamine's subjects. The *Manki* (chief) seemed
very much interested in all our belongings, so much so, that
after he and his following had taken their leave, we discovered that one of our drinking-cups had mysteriously disappeared—perhaps also "by mistake."

I was on the point of taking the midday observation when
I found to my dismay that one of my two pocket-chronometers
had stopped, so that for the rest of the expedition I had to
depend solely on the other. If I had been careful before of
the theodolite, I guarded it now like the apple of my eye, for
if anything had gone wrong with it, the main object of the
expedition—to make as complete a survey as possible of the
whole Kilimanjaro region—would have been defeated.

As we had seen nothing of Kibo for two days except as a
ghostly phantom shimmering in the pale moonlight, I began
to be alarmed lest, owing to its being the rainy season, we
might have to wait for weeks before we got a view clear
enough to be of any practical value. The third day began
like the others—nothing but drifting clouds where ought to
have been the snowy summit of the mountain. As the sun
rose, however, the clouds gradually rolled away, and at last
the peak stood out in all its beauty, and I was able to gratify
at once my artistic sense and my scientific zeal by taking
a number of photos and a round of bearings.

Without doubt Kibo is most imposing as seen from the
west. Here it rises in solitary majesty, and the eye is not
distracted by the sister peak of Mawenzi, of which nothing is
to be seen but a single jutting pinnacle. The effect is enhanced by the magnificent flowing sweep of the outline, the
dazzling extent of the ice-cap, the vast stretch of the forest,
the massive breadth of the base, and the jagged crest of the
Shira spur as it branches away towards the west. Rising from
the plains, the whole mountain is visible from base to summit

in one unbroken line—beautiful in its absolute simplicity and serene grandeur, yet with a beauty which depends for its impressiveness on exquisite proportion and harmonious balance of parts, rather than on the more picturesque elements of varied form and colour. It is the beauty of the symmetrical, the severe, the sublimely solitary. To recall what some one has said of the Matterhorn—Kibo is not a mountain, but a genie.

In viewing the mountain from this side, the first feature that strikes the beholder is the glittering ice-cap, here tinted a vivid grey. Towards the south-west, it reaches from the summit to the foot of the cone proper, a distance of 6550 feet, and continues in almost the same extent all round the south side of the peak. On the upper half the ice forms a compact sheet, but towards the bottom, to a height of about 1000 feet, it is split up by longitudinal ridges of lava into four great tongues or glaciers. Above these ridges the steepness of the slope has farther caused the ice to split transversely, so that between the main mass of the summit and the four great tongues below there is a broad zone of fragments and crevasses.

Beyond the westmost tongue, which is also the broadest of the four, there is another great glacier, which issues from a stupendous fissure with precipitous walls, by which the cone is here cloven from head to foot. The glacier is formed partly by the ice which issues from the Kibo crater through the great notch on its western side, and partly from névé in the fissure itself. In a vast sheet over 1500 feet thick, the glacier descends like a cascade from a height of 18,700 feet to below 13,100 feet—the lower limit of the adjoining "tongues"—and finally gives rise to the Weri-weri, the most important river that rises on Kilimanjaro.

There is a still lower extension of the ice-cap beyond

the great fissure ; here the ice again forms a compact mass, and is prolonged downward in another long tongue, directly facing the west. Here, below the cone, and running along the upper third of the parent mass of the mountain, we have the rugged line of the Shira spur, which, when seen from a point farther to the east, appear to form an independent range. Beginning in the forest region, the chain continues upward across the belt of grass-land, and terminates in a bare jagged wall of cliffs, in which the vertical veins of light-coloured rock seem to point to a former independent cone of eruption. In all probability the great lava sheets forming the states of Shira and Kibongoto partly issued from this western cone.

A considerable number of streams rise to the south of the Shira hills and join the Weri-weri, but none flow towards the plains to the north. The western side of Kibo, like the north, is covered with sheets of ashes and overgrown with grass : there is absolutely no forest, and the lower limit of the ice-cap slants northwards and upwards towards the crater rim, meeting it at the point where we had reached it a month before.

Our labours were interrupted by the appearance of the chief. He had heard that we intended to depart next morning, and came to bring us a fine cow, in place of the tough old billy-goat his worthy brother had tried to palm off upon me in the morning, and which I had scornfully rejected. The animal being killed, Ngamine was careful to secure a substantial joint for himself, with which, as is usual in Jagga, he retired to the woods, there to devour his tit-bit in private, for the *Manki* is supposed to be a superior being, and may not be seen indulging in the carnal delights of the common herd.

Ngamine was the proud possessor of eleven guns of all

sorts and sizes, and for the most part useless. By way of making up the dozen, I added a new species to his collection, in the shape of an old single-barrelled Lancaster, which I happened to have in my possession. My kind intentions appeared to have been misunderstood, or perhaps the chief had a weakness for odd numbers; at any rate, when the guns were fired in the morning to announce our departure, my headman's revolver was found to have mysteriously followed the gun. Of course nobody could tell me anything about it; but when I threatened the whole kingdom with fire from Kibo if the revolver were not forthcoming, strangely enough it was immediately discovered hanging from the branch of a tree.

A few hours later we had another proof of the native passion for foreign weapons. Descending the mountain in the dull grey morning, we had just reached our old camp at the Weri-weri, when we were overtaken by our Uru guide, who had remained behind to buy bananas. He was in a state of the greatest excitement over the loss of his precious old flint-lock, which he said had been taken from him by force. I was on the point of turning back, when Mkumbo, the Marangu guide, came forward with the other side of the story. It seemed that some time before, Salika, the chief of Uru, had sent for two of the natives of Majamé, who were in great repute as clever surgeons; they were wanted to circumcise Salika's son, who had now arrived at the proper age. The operation had been duly performed, but the operators had been sent home without the stipulated fee, and they had seized this opportunity of securing payment by making off with the guide's gun, which was of course the property of the chief. Had I not interfered, the guide would have retaliated by laying violent hands on one of the unsuspecting children standing about, that he might carry him off to Uru as a hostage.

After the delay occasioned by this incident, the march was

resumed. Despite the fact that their loads were increased by
the weight of the plentiful supply of meat we had received
from Ngamine, the men hastened downhill with the alacrity
always displayed on the return journey. In the afternoon we
reached the Ngomberé, where we camped in the midst of heavy
rain. There being neither crocodiles nor rocks to prevent it,
the whole caravan indulged in the luxury of a bath, after
which I took some photographs of the left bank, which displayed most interesting sections of the volcanic agglomerates.
All unknown to me, a self-appointed guard of natives kept
watch and ward over us during the night, in case the camp
should be attacked by the Wa-kiboso. Needless to say the
precaution was quite superfluous, for the Wa-Jagga dread the
night as much as any other negroes.

Before sunrise we were up and on the way. The path led
eastward through the belt of trees, with stiff, glossy foliage,
and across the strip of jungle, in which we noticed abundant
traces of elephants. Elephants are the only big game to be
met with in these tracts of jungle ; the other large animals
usually seek the regions where the vegetation is scantier and
more open, as affording the smallest chance of being taken by
an enemy unawares. The elephant seems to possess a marvellous and most exceptional power of adapting itself to different
conditions of life. It is equally at home on the open grass-
lands or in the bush, on the wooded steppes or in the primeval
forest, on the burning plains or on the cool mountain-heights,
and at any elevation from 2000 to 10,000 feet. Occasionally
I have even seen elephant-tracks as high as 13,000 feet, but
higher than that I should think the animals are not likely to
go ; food becomes too scanty, and the rugged lava ridges do
not offer an inviting foothold.

We reached the path which branched upward towards Uru
about noon. To save time, I had made up my mind to return

to Marangu by way of Moji, and accordingly, much to his dismay, I now dismissed the guide with a present, and a message
to his master, Salika, assuring the chief of my good-will, and
expressing regret that I was unable to call for the ox he had
promised to have ready against my return. A little later we
reached the magnificent gallery forest of the Rau, and crossing
the river, kept on towards the east by the path which runs
along the bottom of the mountain. In the course of an hour
we came to the by-path which branches off towards Moji, where
we arrived in the afternoon, and again took up our quarters
with Dr. Abbott in the cosy little station.

Having sent a present to Mandara (which, by the way, the
chief did not reciprocate), Purtscheller and I paid a visit to
the English missionaries, and had a delightful time chatting
with our friends and revelling in the enjoyment of many
unwonted luxuries. What a treat seemed the bracing douche,
the wheaten bread, the cigars and coffee after lunch, the trifling
over the pages of an illustrated paper! At home all these
things are commonplace enough—we take them as a matter
of course. Roughing it in a country like East Africa is the
surest way to teach us the true value of our little comforts,
and we first discover how much we appreciate them when we
think we have begun to learn to do without them.

In the afternoon we wandered a mile or two up the mountain-side, where everything was beginning to look fresh and
green, and we ended our stroll in the lovely little glen of the
Saranka. At the head of the glen a foaming cascade falls
from a height of 180 feet into a wide cup-shaped basin,
brimming over with clearest water, temptingly inviting for a
bath. On either hand the dark lava rocks peeped out grimly
from a sunny drapery of green mosses and creepers, dwarf
palms and wild bananas mingling in tropical profusion. It
was indeed the beau-ideal of one of those idyllic spots which

R

the Northern imagination always conjures up at mention of
the word "tropical." Alas for the traveller in the tropics
that in reality they are so rare !

We passed the evening in a homely atmosphere of tobacco-
smoke illumined by a petroleum lamp, recalling the names of
all the Europeans—travellers, missionaries, sportsmen, colonists, and adventurers—who had ever been known to visit
Jagga. We counted forty-nine in all, and what we remembered of them I have told in the introductory chapter.

Next morning we made an early start for Mareale's, and by
midday were once more in sight of the flag which waved over
the camp at Marangu, for the path was in better condition for
walking than when we had traversed it two months before.
"Camp all well" was Ali's cheering announcement, delivered
with a military salute and a most unmilitary grin.

The next few days were occupied with the preparations for
our final departure from Jagga. We had still much to do
before we were ready for the start. There were former collections of plants and insects to be looked over, and new ones to
be made, and I also took a series of photographs in and around
the camp. Next came the packing. The plants and insects
were stowed away in air-tight tin boxes, the negatives were
enclosed in cases of zinc, and the geological and ethnological
collections were sewn up in raw hides, which, as they dried,
formed an elastic, water-tight envelope, than which nothing
better could be imagined for our purpose. Most of the goods
still remaining of the stock we had brought with us from the
coast I exchanged for a supply of beans sufficient to carry us
over the journey back. The beans were divided into twenty-
four loads and sewn up in bast sacks and matting.

As soon as the natives realised that we were going away
for good, they too seemed anxious to make the most of their
opportunities, and offered provisions and Jagga "curios" at

unusually low prices. Mareale visited us daily, attended by his usual band of followers. He seemed quite overwhelmed when, in addition to gratifying his desire for one of my tin boxes, I made him a parting gift of a complete tweed suit, a pair of lacing boots, a lamp, a large enamelled wash-hand basin, some table and pocket knives, and a quantity of cloth and powder. To show his appreciation of my kindness, he arrayed himself in the unwonted garments there and then, and proudly strutted about to the envy and admiration of the bystanders. He really did not look at all bad, which is saying a good deal for a negro in European clothes.

Mareale's return gifts were a fine Jagga shield, painted with patterns in the Masai style, and an equally handsome spear, which, as a mark of special friendship, the chief had partly fashioned himself. When I thus say that the spear was partly Mareale's own handiwork, my readers must not suppose that in Jagga, as in Germany of old, it is considered the proper thing for the chief to be an accomplished smith. On the contrary, among the Wa-jagga, as among other negro tribes, the smith-work is the monopoly of what we might term a special guild, the *fundi*, and no one dreams of dabbling in the favoured craft as a mere amateur. From the custom common among all savage races of keeping the forge away from the village from fear of fire, the blacksmith's art has become invested with a certain mystery, which extends to all its branches. Thus Mareale was the only man in Jagga whom I was ever privileged to see at work. The workshop was an open shed, in which several men wrought together. The bellows were identical with those used in Ugweno, and the process of manipulating the iron was the same. The iron wire being made up in bundles and bent to the required length, was thrust into a furnace of charcoal, and beaten into shape with stone hammers on a stone anvil. The final polish was produced by rubbing the weapons for two days with pieces of quartz.

The spears and shields now in favour among the Wa-jagga are of the same pattern as those used by the Masai, and are far superior to the small kind formerly in vogue, a few examples of which we picked up in Majamé. In thus adopting a foreign fashion in their weapons of war, the Wa-jagga afford another instance of the tendency so common in Africa, by which oppressed tribes seek to ape the ways of their oppressors, in order that they may appear equally terrible, and in turn play the oppressor to tribes weaker than themselves.

Except where they have been copied from the Masai, the Wa-jagga weapons and ornaments present little variety of design or adornment. A sprinkling of blue and red beads, or a few lines and flourishes, such as may be seen on the pottery of the New Stone Age, are the only embellishments. The art of the Wa-jagga has no distinctive style of its own; it is conventional rather than original, utilitarian rather than decorative, as may be judged from the prevailing forms of the huts, tools, and household utensils.

The last days of our stay in Jagga were so mild, so clear, and beautiful, that the regret we naturally felt at leaving it was increased a hundredfold. Every tree and herb was now decked in its summer garment of emerald green, and the birds trilled and twittered in the trees "from morn to noon, from noon to dewy eve." With the early dawn the bush awakened with the sweet chirping note of a tiny songster, and till far on in the gathering twilight the woods resounded with the deep monotonous cry of the crested turaco. Then when night had drawn around, and the watch-fire flickered redly across the moonlit camp, from all around came the sound of song and shout as the natives danced and made merry in the light of the moon. From these Wa-jagga gatherings our exclusive Swahili held themselves severely aloof, but on the homeward journey they were not above imitating the Jagga songs and dances. A great favourite was the Ula dance, in which a single performer stands on tiptoe and swings his body from side to side, while his dress streams out before and behind, and the rest of the company stand round in a circle singing in chorus and keeping time by clapping the hands and stamping the feet. The movements are no more indecent than in any of the other negro dances I have seen.

The single performer keeps it up for perhaps a quarter of an hour, when his place is taken by another; a new tune is struck up, the dancing begins afresh, and so the thing goes on hour after hour. Nothing pleased Mareale better than to lead off the Ula among his Asikari, and he prided himself on being able to keep it up longer than any of them.

The date of our departure was fixed for the 29th of November. The loads had all been made up and distributed, the tents were struck, every man stood ready for the road— the air was filled with shrieks and shouts and laughter. Scarcely one of my men but had had intimate relations with one or other of the Jagga damsels, but these children of nature are not sentimental, and we had no parting tears. Amid a salute from our guns, the flag, which for the last two months had waved above our camp, was hauled down, and with a second volley we set our faces towards the residence of Mareale, that I might bid the worthy chief a last farewell. "Good-bye, good-bye," he said with a mournful smile, "good-bye, and come again next year." I replied with the comforting "*Inshallah, Bwana, inshallah!*" and, with a

warm pressure of the hand, for the second time bade farewell
to a worthy friend, whom in all probability I shall never see
again. He has my best wishes for his welfare. Of all the
sovereigns of Jagga, he is the only one I ever met who was
at once intelligent, courageous, modest, and amiable—the
very type of all a young prince ought to be, his swarthy
skin notwithstanding.

A HERD OF ELEPHANTS.

CHAPTER VIII.

HOMEWARD BOUND.

" HOMEWARD BOUND ! " To what varied emotions the words gave rise among the different members of our little caravan. To us Europeans home was still too far off, and every other feeling was merged in regret at leaving the land where we had done so much, but where there still remained so much to do—the fairest land in all East Africa, with its kindly, hospitable people. To our men—Somál, Swahili, and Asikari —the words meant all the dear delights of the coast and Zanzibar, and they could think of nothing but the silver harvest of

LION AND KUDU ANTELOPE. rupees, the old sweethearts, and the delicious life of *dolce far niente* awaiting them at the end of their journey. If they had been allowed to follow their own inclinations, I verily believe they would have marched day and night to put behind them that broiling stretch of arid wilderness which still lay between them and their sensual paradise.

We did not in the first place proceed to Taveta direct, but, by way of breaking new ground in south-eastern Jagga, struck eastward through the adjoining friendly states of Mamba, Msai, and Mwika. Leaving the recently-cleared fields of Marangu behind, we crossed the Una, a stream which rises on the slopes of Mawenzi, and unites with the Ngona from the west to form the river Himo, an important tributary of the Rufu. Some distance farther on we crossed the deep ravine of the river Jorro, which we found to be quite dry, the water having apparently all been drained off at a higher level for the purpose of irrigating the fields.

We had now entered the state of Mamba. Close by the wayside we came upon a party of native warriors evidently enjoying themselves over a huge pot of pombé. We were cordially invited to join in the carouse, but I pleaded haste, and the caravan moved on again, and almost immediately entered the monotonous belt of bush through which the path runs all the way through Msai to Mwika. In the course of the march we crossed several watercourses, all dry like the Jorro, and for similar reasons. One of these, the Mwambo, is worthy of special mention. Though quite dry at the point where we crossed it, a number of springs arise in the bed of the stream lower down, and form the source of the Habari, whose cool clear waters had so often refreshed us in the course of our journeyings to and fro.

The little state of Mwika, which we had now entered, is watered by a single small stream, by the side of which we pitched our camp towards noon. We were soon on friendly terms with the chief, Sombararia (the "So," as in Somiriali, is a particle prefixed to denote the rank of chief). This young man seemed to have been partaking rather liberally of pombé, and was somewhat excited in consequence. He listened with ecstasy when I told him of the wonders of Uleia—of the railways, the steamboats, the telegraphs, and repeating rifles—and interrupted my narrative with shouts of delight and wonder. His followers—rather a dull-looking lot—did not seem to share the chief's enthusiasm, but stood listening with passive indifference to all we had to tell.

During the night it rained, and the temperature fell to 47° F., unluckily for the men, who had elected to sleep in the open rather than be at the trouble of running up huts. It was still raining when we quitted Mwika, and therewith Jagga, and hurried downwards past the conical Wajimba or Fumvu hills, behind which lay Rombo, the territory of the chief Wajimba. Still keeping on towards Taveta across the plains, now green with springing grass, we reached the Makessa hills at the foot of the mountain, where the gneiss once more began to show through the volcanic conglomerates. A rapid march of four hours brought us to the forest, where, by the aid of our glacier rope, we succeeded in swimming the swollen Lumi, and took up our quarters with our hospitable American friend, Mr. Chanler.

The next day, December 1st, was Sunday, and we spent it in the orthodox fashion as a day of rest, preparatory to our trying march to the coast. There were great rejoicings in Taveta, for the natives had again effectually repelled the Masai, who, in the course of the last few weeks, had made repeated attacks on the little forest fastness. At this season of the year pasture was plentiful everywhere, and the Masai were free to indulge their roving propensities by wandering in all directions. We thought it extremely probable, therefore, that we might meet with them, or with traces of them, on the steppes before many days were over.

In the evening the Wa-taveta celebrated their victory by a grand dance, which was held in the open space in front of our camp. In the interval which elapsed before all the company had arrived, the warriors amused themselves with a series of warlike evolutions, accompanied by the shrill music of the war-cry. After a sufficient number had assembled, the men formed themselves into a long line; the girls, who so far had played the part of spectators, ranging themselves opposite. Three of the warriors then stepped to the front, and commenced a succession of uncouth leaps and bounds high into the air, while they wildly tossed their long, greasy, clay-plastered manes, and waved their spears and shields. Meantime the bystanders repeated a measured chanting chorus, and the girls kept time with a hopping movement, encouraging the male performers to renewed exertions with all sorts of feminine coquetries. No sooner was one set of dancers exhausted than another was ready to take their place, and so in the moonlight the revel was kept up until far on into the night.

But the Sunday had yet another treat in store for us. Just as I had finished writing up my diary, Ali came to tell us that the post had arrived from the coast with mail-bags for Moji, and a thick packet of letters for us. It was late before we had exhausted the lengthy budget of home news, while around us the snoring of the porters, the buzz of the mosquitoes, and the far-off howling of hyenas recalled to mind the weary distance that still separated us from the friends whose faces looked at us from between the lines.

Good news also came to me from Zanzibar. When in Africa in 1888, I had sent on a hundred loads of goods to the Victoria Nyanza, under the charge of the trader and carrier, Mr. Stokes, intending to pick them up later on, when I arrived in the region with my large caravan. The proposed expedition unfortunately came to grief, and I had long ago given up the goods for lost; but now, to my intense satisfaction, I learned that the greater part had been sold through the agency of the Lake missionaries. In the same letter I read the wonderful announcement that Stanley was with Emin Pasha and Casati in Usagara, and was expected in Zanzibar within a fortnight. We hoped to be at the coast ourselves about the same time, and I looked forward with pleasure to the prospect of meeting three such distinguished personages, and hearing from their own lips the story of the famous Emin Relief Expedition.

Less reassuring was the information brought by the post-runners that the Masai had been seen at the *ngurungas* of Lanjoro. This startling piece of news was the only topic of conversation next morning when we were preparing to start, and, with much outward bravado and many inward qualms, every man looked ostentatiously to his rifle and rammed home an extra charge. Well I knew that, in the event of any real danger, scarcely one among them would be capable of pulling a trigger.

Meantime it was as much as we could do to get away from Taveta. As a result of the general alarm, the narrow aperture which afforded the only means of entrance or of exit was blocked by huge tree-trunks, and all along the path through the wood similar barricades had been placed at frequent intervals. It took us two hours and a half to get through the quarter of a mile of forest between us and the plains, and we had to make up for the delay by an unpleasantly rapid march as soon as we had gained the open. Guinea-fowl and francolins flew across our path, but we did not dare to shoot any for fear of attracting the attention of the Masai. There was no merry talk and laughter to-day, but on and on we steadily tramped, the silence unbroken save by the sound of our footsteps and an occasional word of warning when a hole, a stone, or a thorn threatened the men's defenceless feet. In the northwest the peaks of Kibo and Mawenzi showed here and there between the clouds, and we had a farewell glimpse of the mountains of Ugweno across the pale grey line of Lake Jipé.

We had been marching eastwards for about four hours, when all of a sudden our leader Mwini came to an abrupt standstill. We had come upon the track of the Masai at last! Right across our road was a newly-trodden path, on which we could clearly distinguish the footprints of men, cattle, and donkeys, and above the trees in the direction of Lake Jipé circled ominous flocks of vultures and storks, which always follow in the wake of the Masai, feeding on the offal of their cattle. The men lost not a moment in hurrying on again. Although there was plenty of water at Lanjoro, none thought of a prolonged halt, but, having filled their calabashes, pressed onwards into the wilderness of Taita.

The wilderness was wilderness no longer, for summer had come and the steppes were gay with flower and leafage. The greens and yellows of the leaves, the greys and browns of stems and grasses, the warm red of the soil, the sunny blue of the sky, the lilac and white and violet of the blossoms, combined to form a picture of matchless richness and variety of colouring, in which the old level uniformity was lost. Countless animals of all descriptions gave life and music to the scene. The air was full of the hum of insects and the song of birds, and the game of every kind, no longer confined to isolated patches, but free to rove in boundless liberty, seemed to share in the general renewal of life and vigour. They were all quite safe as far as we were concerned. Even had there been no Masai in the neighbourhood to spoil sport, the porters were too heavily laden to carry an additional burden of flesh or fowl; and leaving the peaceful denizens of the steppes to browse unmolested, we rapidly continued our way till the path began to disappear in the gathering darkness. We pitched our camp under a solitary baobab, and slept peacefully by the smouldering watch-fires throughout the night, undisturbed by the roaring of a couple of lions which seemed to be scouring the neighbourhood in search of prey. At this season of the year the lion can afford to be dainty. He hunts only the larger sorts of game, leaving the small fry to the lesser beasts of prey; the smaller antelopes fall to the leopard, the hares, the rodents, and ground game to the jackals and civets.

As on our journey inland two months and a half ago, the mist was lying in the hollows when we resumed our way next morning at dawn. Just as it was beginning to grow light, I suddenly observed in the distance a line of moving red and white specks, and almost at the same moment Mwini announced the approach of a caravan from the coast. Soon our men were exchanging greetings with their friends in the new caravan, which proved to be bound for Taveta *en route* for Masai Land. The party consisted of about fifty half-breed Arabs and a large number of Swahili porters, with donkeys and draught oxen all heavily laden. It also included some twenty or twenty-five slaves, who presented a woeful spectacle as they toiled painfully along, loaded with chains and carrying heavy burdens of iron wire, the main article of barter in the Masai country. In crossing the steppes the poor wretches had attempted to escape, and had been put in irons as the heaviest punishment their masters could think of under the circumstances.

Among other things, the Arabs informed us that about nine miles farther on we should find water, at a spot where they had camped overnight. Accordingly, after the prolonged halt occasioned by the meeting, we hastened on again, and after a hot march in the morning sun, came in sight of the blue smoke-wreaths which still curled lazily skywards from the deserted Swahili camp-fires. Our approach scared away a flock of ostriches which had come to drink at the slimy pool, or rather puddle, which was filled with a thick, lukewarm, greyish liquid, trampled into mud by the foot of man and beast. Still, it had once been water, and that was enough, so we filled our calabashes and pressed forward. No one pretended to think it refreshing, and our pet goat Adelheid, accustomed to the crystal streams of her native valley, could not be induced to touch it.

An hour later we passed one of our old camping-grounds. A few charred pieces of wood still remained to mark the spot, and at the foot of a tree the Somali Mohammed found a knife which he had happened to leave behind. He very nearly had to pay dearly for the recovery of his lost property, for as he was feeling about on the ground a puff-adder darted out at him, and he narrowly escaped being bitten. This poisonous viper is nocturnal in habit, and in the daytime is scarcely to be distinguished from the grass and stones among which it lies concealed, and which it closely resembles in colour and general appearance. The danger therefore lies in treading on it unawares, for otherwise it does not readily attack man, like the asps and other small snakes. It is of a sluggish nature, and withdraws very slowly when alarmed, so much so, that several times I first became aware of the animal's presence when my foot was almost upon it and it began to wriggle out of my path. Taught by one or two lessons of this description, I soon took to the native habit of making a random cut with my stick whenever anything stirred among the grass or undergrowth, though just as often as not the unseen enemy turned out to be one of the harmless snakes or long-tailed lizards with which the steppes abound.

About noon we came in sight of the mountains of Taita, dimly visible on the horizon through the veil of shimmering haze. No native footpath was ever known to run straight from one point to another, and as we followed the tortuous

windings of the "great caravan route," the mountains appeared to lie now on this side, now on that, and sometimes they were straight ahead. As we gradually approached the inhabited region, there was a marked falling off in the size and numbers of the herds of game. Giraffes, however, were more plentiful, the tall mimosæ of the region being more to their taste than the comparatively low shrubs of the steppes farther west. As we had no great distance to go, and the men really deserved a treat after their toilsome march, I fired from the pathway at one of the unsuspecting animals, scattering the whole herd; but unfortunately I only succeeded in bringing down my game after four shots. In a quarter of an hour the men had it skinned and cut up, and were once more hieing merrily onwards laden with the choicest parts of the flesh, while the carcase remained to feed the flocks of vultures which were soon hovering over the scene of the exploit. It almost seemed as if we were going to have a surfeit of game that day, for a little farther on, while my attention was occupied with the remarkable vegetable forms exhibited among the tree-euphorbias in the neighbourhood of the Bura stream, all of a sudden the head of an enormous rhinoceros appeared looking out at us from the surrounding thicket. Immediately a report rang from four or five guns, and although none of the shots took effect, the lumbering brute promptly turned tail and fled, taking refuge in the thorny bush, where it was impossible for us to pursue it.

Our roast giraffe, though rather tough, proved to be not at all unpalatable, and we washed it down with our second and last bottle of claret. But when we retired to rest for the night, we had forgotten that there were other *gourmets* in the world besides ourselves—not lions and hyenas this time, but those exasperating little imps of darkness, the ants. Scarcely had we got ourselves snugly tucked in, when there was a sudden rush and scuffle outside, and a general cursing and swearing all round, in which the only word I could distinctly make out was *Siafu* (black " driver " ants). In a twinkling I was out of bed, bent on defending my citadel, but already the invading hordes were at the door, and in a few minutes they were swarming over everything in numbers such as I have never seen anything to equal. As they crept up over our legs and arms and nipped our skin with their sharp mandibles, we were soon heartily echoing the strong language of the Swahili, and were glad to save ourselves by flight. The men did their best to smoke out the enemy with gunpowder and burning branches, but in vain ; they were complete masters of the field, and we were glad at length to leave them in undisturbed possession and betake ourselves to a spot a short distance off, where we passed the night rolled up in our rugs.

This was not by any means the first time I had been driven from my tent by the driver-ants (*Anomma arcens*), which always carry on their marauding expeditions during the night, or when the weather is dull and cloudy, On bright sunshiny days they keep out of sight among the grass and leaves, or tunnel out a shelter in the earth, if nothing else is to be had. Often when on the march I have watched these singular insects in the early morning before sunrise, or when the sky was overcast, as they crossed our path in a serried file, while, warned by the cry of " *Siafu*," the men skipped lightly over the advancing column. In the Lilliputian army there are three distinct classes or "castes." It is officered, as it were, by the largest and strongest class, the members of which are distributed at stated intervals throughout the procession. They are provided with sharp, horned mandibles as long as the insect's body, and their work is to seize and, if possible, slay every living thing that comes in their way. The booty is next torn to pieces by the larger of the two classes which make up the rank and file, and which are provided for the purpose with sharp straight mandibles, about half the length of their bodies. The pieces are then taken up and carried away by the third and smallest class, which have their mandibles quite short. If the passing procession is stirred up with a stick, the offending article is immediately pounced upon by the first two castes and attacked with the greatest fierceness, while the third skurry off with their burdens as fast as they can. The driver-ants prey largely upon insects, and are the great check upon the increase and development of insect life throughout the land. At the same time they do not hesitate to attack harmless reptiles, and even some of the smaller mammals. On the morning after they had overrun our camp, when we examined the pieces of meat they had left behind, we found, curiously enough, that their ravages had been mostly confined to the fat and sinews, while the juicy muscular parts were almost untouched.

Our next day's tramp of four hours, through the luxuriant valley of the Matate to the mountain of Javia, was almost like a pleasant constitutional, compared with the trying marches which had preceded it. It was more enjoyable to the booted Europeans than to the porters, however, for many of the latter were suffering from blistered feet, and limped painfully along over the rocky débris which strewed the path.

As I turned to take a farewell look backwards in the direction of the Taita wilderness, a scene of unexpected loveliness met my eye. High above the masses of cumulus clouds which drifted slowly over the steppes rose the snowy dome of Kibo, solitary, serene, majestic, yet soft and shadowy as a mirage. Involuntarily the Masai name of *Ngaje Ngai* (the house of God) rose to my lips, as I gazed in rapture on the phantom shape hanging thus suspended in mid-air. Only once in the

s

Himalayas, looking from Darjiling towards Kanchinjinga, have I seen anything to equal it at once for beauty and impressive grandeur. Through the glass we could see the Kaiser Wilhelm's Peak standing out darkly against the snowy background as distinctly the highest point. But soon the dream-like picture began to fade away as slowly the veil of cloud spread itself out over the mountain's hoary head, until at length it was blotted from our sight, never to be seen again until it reappeared in "counterfeit presentment" in our distant Northern home.

Once more we pitched our tents at the old camping-ground in the valley, which soon resounded with the usual din and bustle of a native market. As I stood listening to the shrill voices of the women, and saw how keen the Wa-taita were over a bargain, I could not help thinking how unfavourably they compared—morally, mentally, and physically—with the Wa-kwafi of Taveta and the Wa-jagga of Marangu. Yet cunning and suspicious as the Wa-taita are, they are still far above the inhabitants of the steppes, the Wa-nika, the Wa-duruma, and the Wa-kamba, in whom constant war with man and nature has developed and exaggerated all the natural defects of the Bantu races.

Our camp at Matate had been made memorable to some of our porters as the scene of a severe flogging. Such harsh lessons in discipline were now no longer necessary. All the men were remarkably obedient, willing, obliging, and capable. On the whole, we had lived together almost as one large family; the men had the greatest confidence in me, and I in them; and now that the end of the expedition was so near, I felt genuinely sorry at the thought of parting with them.

As we gradually approached the coast with its lurking fevers, we were careful not to neglect the precaution of taking arsenic pills at meal-times, and with the best results, at least as far as I myself was concerned. The nights were still delightfully cool and refreshing, but the days were growing more and more sultry, the showers more and more frequent. It was raining when we quitted the Matate valley and continued our way towards Ndara, and the rain no longer fell in short intermittent showers, as on the plains, but in a persistent drizzle, which we attributed to the proximity of the mountains.

Wet to the skin and red as Masai warriors with the mud through which we had been tramping, we reached the rocks below the mission-station at Sagala after a six hours' march. We camped under the sycamore trees which bordered the course of what was now a foaming mountain torrent, where formerly had been a mere waterless rocky channel. Soon the rain cleared off and the sun shone out again, but our friend the missionary was not to be induced to quit his cosy station, although we fired our guns repeatedly to intimate our presence. We had other visitors, however, who were not quite so welcome. These were the Swahili from a small coast caravan which had taken up its quarters at our old camping-ground by the pool. The caravan had been fitted out at Mombaza by our old acquaintance Siwa Haji, and was proceeding to the Victoria Nyanza by way of Sogonoi, this route having been selected in preference to that by Unyamwezi, which was at present considered dangerous. Thirty-four of the porters had already deserted, and, with so many extra loads to carry, it had taken the rest a whole month to travel from the coast to their present camp at Ndara.

At Ndara the locusts had recently been making sad havoc among the fields and plantations, and provisions were in consequence very dear. We had our Jagga beans to fall back upon, however, so that we were not badly off; and the natives were much disappointed when they found they were to have no opportunity of trading with us. The Somál were urgent in their representations that it was time for me to pass sentence on our pet goat; but I was resolved to give the privileged favourite yet a few days respite, and so, for the present, Adelheid was spared. Virtue had its reward. In the night I was awakened by a plaintive bleating, and striking a match to see what was wrong, was just in time to seize my ice-axe and sever the head of a large grey-green snake, which was slowly wriggling itself into my tent. The snake was evidently bent on seeking shelter from the rain and cold outside, and though I have often known these reptiles to approach our camp-fire, attracted by the warmth, as the birds and moths by the light, this was the only occasion on which I ever remember one trying to enter my tent.

Next day I gave my men a holiday and climbed the mountain with Herr Purtscheller, at once to see our dilatory friend the missionary and to learn the extent of the ravages wrought by the locusts. Our visit proved to be not very opportune, for Mr. Wray was in the midst of packing his household gods, preparatory to his departure for Europe. Naturally, he was looking forward with somewhat mingled feelings to the prospect of leaving the station, where he had lived and laboured for eight years, though Taita is by no means an African paradise. And just at present it was far from looking its best. The locusts had been busy on all sides, and many of them were still to be seen hovering about in the fields they had laid waste. Only a week before they had come in enormous clouds from the Paré region, and had settled down *en masse* on the plantations of Ndara, so that in some places the natives were wading through them ankle-deep. For a day and a half the air was literally black with the approaching swarms, and in a single day they had devoured every green blade and leaf in the region. When everything was eaten up, they departed in a body towards the north-east—that is, in a direction obliquely to the prevailing winds—leaving behind them the immediate prospect of a famine in the land.

Next morning at dawn we resumed our way coastwards, carrying with us various letters and messages from Mr. Wray to the central mission-station at Freretown. At the foot of the southern spur of Ndara, which rises from the plains like a miniature African Matterhorn, the gigantic baobabs were now gay with waxy blossoms, hanging from the bare spiky branches like the pendant drops from a Christmas-tree. Among the young grass the guinea-fowl were diligently scratching up the soil in search of food. In the neighbourhood of Ndara guinea-fowl abound in such large numbers, that one of the usual camping-grounds takes its name from them—*Marago ya kanga* (Guinea-fowl camp), and here it may be said there are "*toujours perdrix.*" We took advantage of the opportunity to bag a brace or two for dinner, and were able fully to endorse the opinion we had already formed, that the guinea-fowl is the most palatable of all African wild-fowl, as the Kudu antelope is of its larger game.

The birds were now in full song and plumage, and many species had assumed the most gorgeous colours, although in the dry season, when the leafless trees afford them no protection from their keen-eyed enemies, they masquerade in sombre suits indistinguishable from the greys and browns of trunk and branches. It has been said that East Africa has no singing-birds to speak of. The author of this remark can scarcely have known the country during the wet season, when the air resounds with the most varied twittering and piping, and every grove and field has its melodious band of choristers. The concert is at its best in the cool of the morning, for as the sun rises and the heat

becomes oppressive, a sultry silence gradually creeps over
the land. From time to time the penetrating "ay, ay, ay!"
of the hornbill breaks the stillness, accompanied by the
rapid rush of wings and the humming sound caused by the
vibration of the air in the creature's hollow beak; or one
is startled into momentary forgetfulness of the surroundings
by a cry so exactly resembling the melancholy bleating of
a lamb, that it is difficult to believe that it comes from the
osprey soaring far away into the upper air; or again, a
curious sound like the drumming of a snipe resounds from
overhead, and we know it comes from the missel-thrush as
it stands beating its pinions like a kingfisher ready to dart.
Here and there one of the smaller birds of prey may be seen
flying before a flock of small singing-birds, which pursue
the common enemy in a body, vigorously attacking him with
claw and bill until he manages to make good his escape and
find refuge in a thicket. For the rest, Nature takes her
noonday siesta, and silence reigns supreme.

With the approach of sunset the concert of the morning
recommences, the soft cooing of pigeons mingling with the
love-notes of a thousand other warblers. None of the many
songsters can equal in range and richness of tone our own
nightingales, larks, and redbreasts, but many of them would
compare favourably with such birds as our finches. Nothing,
for instance, could rival the sweetness of the minor duet-like
melodies, in which the two parts are taken by males and
females of the same species, the male leading off first with
three notes, the female following with three notes a third
higher, both voices succeeding each other with such exact and
harmonious precision, that it is difficult to believe the whole
is not sung by one bird. At night the silence is unbroken
save for the occasional monotonous hoot of the nightjar as it
hovers noiselessly around our tent, attracted by the light of

the camp-fire, like the moths and insects for which it is on the watch. As enthusiastic entomologists, we are the nightjar's only rivals ; but our work is easy, for we have only to draw our nets down the outside of our lamp-lit tent to gather in a rich and varied harvest.

Any one who had never seen the East African steppes except in the rainy season might easily be deceived as to the fertility of the region. Marching eastwards towards the coast, it is difficult to believe that scarcely three months ago this fair green grove, all sweetest song and perfume, was nothing better than a howling wilderness. It is only when we begin to turn our attention to the true character of the vegetation and consider the lessons it has to teach, that we are able to realise what must be the adverse conditions of soil and climate which have succeeded in producing such peculiarly arid and forbidding vegetable forms.

Among other welcome changes which we noticed as we passed along, was the increased supply of water obtainable at all the usual caravan stations. At Maungu, where formerly we had been obliged to content ourselves with the turbid contents of an *ngurunga*, there was now a stream of limpid water, and everywhere throughout the region the same happy abundance prevailed. The effect of this discovery on my men was to fire them with a sudden ardour for travelling, which took the form of a clamorous demand that we should continue our way coastwards without delay. The way in which I answered it considerably increased the right I had acquired to the title of "*Bwana kelele*," or "silence," the nickname by which I was popularly known among the men. Neither the Somál nor the Swahili attach any significance to European names, and both are alike clever in the art of inventing nicknames, hitting off little physical or mental idiosyncrasies with great exactness and often with considerable humour. In camp, when retiring for the night, we were often much annoyed by the noise made by the men outside as they sat laughing and chattering around the fires. On these occasions I used to give vent to my feelings and order them off to bed with an imperious *kelele;* hence my title of "*Bwana kelele,*" which had been bestowed on me during my first journey, and had stuck to me ever since. The Somál, however, called me *Dakta*—their way of pronouncing the word "doctor."

Purtscheller's nickname was "*Bwana lolo,*" or "the stammerer," from his habit, in talking Ki-swahili, of repeating his words, so as to make quite sure they were properly understood. The Somál had another title for him, too ; by them he was known as "*angadir,*" or "the vulture," because of his unusually healthy appetite. Another of my acquaintances was called "*Bwana fimbo,*" or "the pole," from his height and slimness ; a second, "*Bwana mambe,*" or "the crocodile," from his pointed teeth ; and a third, "*Bwana tumbo,*" or "the paunch," because of his striking rotundity in the region indicated. Needless to say, these titles were for "private circulation only." As head of the expedition, to my face I was always addressed as "*Bwana mkuba*" (great master), and Herr Purtscheller, as second in command, as "*Bwana mdogo*" (little master).

We were now on the point of crossing the wilderness of Maungu, but, with the prospect of plenty of water ahead, the wilderness was robbed of its terrors. We resumed our journey in the pale light of the waning moon, and had tramped on steadily for about two hours, when just at sunrise we were met by a party of Wa-taita, who, in view of the coming famine, had been buying maize in Samburu. They told us that we should find plenty of water everywhere, and at the end of three hours we reached the first pool, at a spot where three months before there had been nothing but the dry earth.

Yet every rainy season (*masika*) the place is transformed into a marsh, and the pools are black with the spawn of fishes, and with large numbers of small grey frogs which pass the dry season underground, where moisture is always to be met with in the deeper layers of the soil.

Filling our calabashes, we pressed onward between the thorny trees, almost forgetting where we were in the delicious perfume of the blossoms, which filled the air with rich odours of jasmine and heliotrope. At noon we passed our former camp, and from the higher ground of the bush tract had a view southwards toward the pyramidal mountain of Kisigao.

By and by the clouds came rolling up from the east, the sky became black as night, and we were overtaken by a thunderstorm such as is only to be seen in Africa in the wet season. We had had nothing like it as yet in the course of the expedition. Before the thunder could be heard we could see the lightning playing across the horizon in forked flashes. An intense silence fell upon everything—not a leaf stirred. Gradually the clouds came nearer and nearer, the thunder rolled and rumbled, and we could hear the rush and splash of the falling rain, though as yet the storm had not reached us. Then came a sudden puff of wind, followed by another and another; the rushing and the splashing came nearer, and suddenly the windows of heaven were opened, and the rain came down with a force that made every drop seem hard as a hailstone. All around and overhead the lightning glared and the thunder crashed, and the storm-fiends shrieked and howled in fury. In five minutes the path had become a rushing rivulet, through which we splashed wearily onward, ankle-deep in water. The chilly atmosphere seemed to pierce beneath our skin, and while we were white, the men were *grey* with cold. Ten minutes after the storm was over, the ground was almost as dry as before, every drop of water being thirstily absorbed by the cracked and porous laterite soil.

In about a quarter of an hour we had another storm, and in the course of the afternoon two more, but none raged with such tremendous violence as the first. What it meant to the porters to carry the loads, and especially the slippery tin boxes, in such weather, may easily be imagined; but my own work of route-surveying, the constant handling of compass, aneroid, watch, and lead-pencil, was no less arduous and exasperating. Tired to death after a fourteen hours' march, we camped at nightfall in the forest, where we flung ourselves down at once on our soaking rugs, while the Swahili, with greater patience and much skill, got together a supply of dry firewood by cutting down branches and chipping away all the wet outer layers of bark and wood. By the aid of some percussion caps they soon succeeded in making a fire, round which, after they had warmed and dried themselves, they were not long in going to sleep, heedless of a lion we could hear roaring not far off, as he sallied forth in search of his nightly prey.

We awoke next morning to find everything shrouded in mist, in which many of the humbler members of the animal world seemed to find themselves peculiarly at home. Shining *Achatina* snails, whose light-grey empty shells are so common everywhere during the dry season, crawled slowly along among the damp grass by the wayside. Here and there a clumsy land-crab or a sluggish tortoise went creeping and groping about among the loose sand, while all along the pathway huge millipedes, small scorpions, and supple snakes crawled or darted or wriggled, according to their nature.

A march of two hours brought us to near the foot of the long Taro hill, where the *ngurungas* were now surrounded by a tangle of long luxuriant creepers. Here we met a detachment of the Swahili caravan, the main body of which we had passed at Ndara. A little farther on, at the *ngurungas* on the hillside, we met another party of about twenty, the leader of whom informed me, with a broad grin, that at the present rate of progress they might expect to reach the Victoria Nyanza in about two years and a half. Fifty Wa-taita had been hired to supply the place of the deserters, and now another hitch had occurred because the loads were too large for the Wa-taita to carry in their usual fashion, that is, strapped on their backs by a band passing round the forehead.

The hour of our arrival at Taro sounded the death-knell for our faithful Adelheid. With the usual irony of fate, she fell beneath the knife of her most trusted friend —the Somál cook. The forelegs were set aside for the Somál, but a quarrel arose over the division of the spoil, and before I could interfere, the passionate Bulhan had stabbed the cook in the arm. The offender was immediately pinioned, but the cook seemed inclined to view the matter from a fatalistic standpoint, regarding his wound as a "judgment" he had brought upon himself by the treacherous slaughter of his confiding pet.

Now that the inhospitable wilderness of Maungu lay behind us, the men seemed inclined to take things a little more easily. On leaving Taro in the morning we broke at once into our regulation-pace of 106 steps to the minute, whereas in crossing the wilderness the rate to the minute had been 114. As we passed along, we saw frequent signs of the havoc wrought among the trees by the recent storms. Many a fallen trunk and broken branch lay across the pathway, soon to be cleared away by the termites—those wonderful insect-scavengers—which were everywhere busy assisting Nature in carrying out the law that whatsoever has sprung from the earth

to the earth it shall return. As the termites are not a light-
loving race, they first set to work to build covered roads connecting every dead branch and tiny twig of the tree to be
disposed of with the tall conical red ant-heaps, honeycombed
with galleries and chambers, in which the young are hatched
and food is stored up. Under these covered roadways they
bore their way with their sharp mandibles into the very pith,
and soon nothing is left but a hollow tube. In some places
the whole wood was red with these protecting tunnels, and
sometimes the dead though still standing trees were entirely
covered with them. More than once, in sitting down and
leaning back against what seemed to be a tree of ordinary
solidity, I found I had been trusting to a mere hollow
cylinder of bark, held together and partially filled with a
plastering of red earth. The first blast of wind would have
brought it to the ground; and whatever is lying on the
ground, if there is anything left of it to gnaw, the termites
soon make short work of. By an oversight on the part of some
of the porters, one or two of our wooden boxes and the sleeping-sacks we had used on Kilimanjaro were left overnight on
the bare ground. The termites found them out and completely
ruined them. The all-devouring insects even tried their mandibles on the stocks of the men's guns, and in a single night
managed to do considerable damage.

But although one might sometimes wish the termites to
be a little more discriminating in their ravages, there can be
no doubt that on the whole they are an immense benefit in a
country like East Africa, where there is so much waste timber
always to be got rid of. Moreover, by virtue of their incessant
building operations they are of great service in the important
work of turning over the soil, in this respect playing the part
of the earthworm in more temperate regions.

The excessive multiplication of the termites is kept in check by the ant-bear, or aard-vark, an extraordinary animal, which tears its way into the ant-hills with its strong claws, and sweeps the insects into its mouth by means of its long extensile gluti-nous tongue. Wherever there are ant-hills, the burrow of the ant-bear (which resembles the "kennel" of a fox) is sure not to be far off, but I have never succeeded in seeing the animal itself, as it is nocturnal in habit and exceedingly shy.

Shortly before midday we reached the outlying plantations of the Wa-duruma of Samburu, in the midst of an oppressive heat which made us cast a longing look backwards to the more bracing air of the steppes farther inland. Here we met a large party of Wa-duruma on their way home from an expedition under the command of Mr. Joseph Thomson's former associate, Martin, who had been sent out by the British East Africa Company to establish a station in Ukamba. We pitched our tents by the great *ngurunga*, at the place where three of our porters had deserted on the journey up-country. Before very long the natives were on the spot with goats and fowls for sale, and once more we heard the now unfamiliar word "*fethá*" (money). It seemed like the beginning of the end; though as yet there was little in the landscape to show it, we had reached the region of the coast, and our journey was fast drawing to a close.

In the evening we had a sharp thunderstorm, and in the midst of it the post-runners from Jagga, whom we had met at Taveta on their road to the mission-station, came in to seek shelter for the night. We started with them next morning at dawn, and continued our way eastward at a rapid rate. Shortly before noon we passed a very distinct trail of the Masai, a relic of a descent made by a large band of warriors upon the hapless Wa-duruma villages about two months before. Later in the day we passed the lonely *boma* (stronghold, *lit.* fence) of the Arab highwayman Mbaruk, who about three years ago made himself the terror of the surrounding neighbourhood, and levied toll on every passer-by.

At the rate at which we were going we might have reached Rabai that night, but a thunderstorm came down upon us at the Moaje, and the fording of the swollen stream would have been too much for the porters at the end of a long march. The post-runners, accordingly, went on alone, while we pitched our camp at the foot of the mango trees, whose half-ripe fruit was eagerly devoured by the Swahili, as a foretaste of the good things awaiting them at the coast.

Now that there was no further need to husband our supplies, Purtscheller and I celebrated the occasion with a little private banquet, indulging ourselves with all the delicacies which still remained either from our own stores or from those kindly furnished by Dr. Abbott and the missionaries. We had no bread as yet, but our imagination revelled in the thought that we should have it to-morrow, and meantime the festive board was graced with barley - groats, sugar, Swiss milk, jam, mixed pickles, and Worcester sauce—luxuries which I should think do not often come back to the coast with an expedition.

After dinner I made rather an unpleasant discovery. I was going my rounds as usual before turning in, when I came upon a young lad whom I did not recognise, sitting outside the door of Abed's tent. By his features I knew him at once for a native of Jagga, and in reply to my questions was informed by Abed that he came from Moji, and was going to the coast to seek his father, who had run away from Jagga some time before. Of course I did not believe a word of this story, but concluded that the lad was a slave, whom my headman had bought on his own account from Mandara, and whose presence in the caravan he had been clever enough so far to conceal. For the present I pretended to believe the tale, however, thinking it would be time enough to interfere when we reached Rabai.

The distance from the Moaje to Rabai is short. In rather less than two hours after striking camp next morning, we came in sight of the dead, leafless Borassus palms, which stand up tall and conspicuous like finger-posts a short way inland from the cocoa-groves of the station, now likewise visible on the horizon. "*Mnazi, Bwana, mnazi*" (cocoa-palms, sir, cocoa-palms), said one and then another of the porters with a grin, hailing with delight those harbingers of the coast. We ourselves were scarcely less excited than the Swahili, and stepped along briskly, full of pleasant anticipations and countless questionings. Would the missionaries be at home? What news would there be from the coast and from Zanzibar? How long should we have to wait before there was a chance of leaving Mombaza?

No sooner were we in sight of the first huts than one and all the men commenced to fire their guns, bringing a group of natives to every door. So far from attempting to repress these wild demonstrations, I joined in them myself; and when a mission-boy appeared on the scene with a polite "Morning, sir," I seized his hand and shook it as if he had been an old friend.

And now before us, lying snugly ensconced among the trees, was the little white cottage of the mission-station, once the home of Krapf and Rebmann. The clock in the belfry of the little church was striking ten, and the children in the schoolhouse were singing sweetly as we crossed the well-kept gravelled court before the house, where Mr. and Mrs. Burness stood waiting in the doorway to welcome us. As we sat down to the plentiful breakfast which Mrs. Burness—with due appreciation of a traveller's appetite—had hospitably provided for us, I felt most amiably disposed to all the world, and only regained my African hardness of heart when I heard of the alarming accident to Emin—an unfortunate termination to the Pasha's long list of misfortunes, which it required all my philosophy to accept calmly. As long as I was in the austere mood, I went to the rescue of Abed's slave, staggered my headman by telling him serenely I would help the boy to look out for his father myself, and handed over my protégé to Mr. Burness to be sent back to Moji with the post-runners.

With my boisterous band of Swahili I thought it as well not to remain overnight at the mission. Accordingly, after a short rest, we went on towards Bandarin, intending to pitch our tents at the spot where in September we had camped for the first time on the African mainland. On reaching the edge of the plateau, our eyes were greeted by a wide expanse of glittering grey, and ecstatic shouts of "*Bahari! bahari!*" (the sea, the sea) broke from the whole body of the Swahili, as "*Thalatta*" of old from the remnant of Xenophon's army.

At Bandarin we got one of the mission-boats, and accompanied only by the Somál, rowed over to the central station of the Church Missionary Society at Freretown, while the rest of the caravan went round by road. By the kind permission of the inspector, we pitched our camp under the magnificent mango-trees at the station, and there spent the few remaining days of our sojourn in Africa, putting the finishing touches to our maps, and winding up a number of other little odds and ends. The expedition was now practically over, and its results guaranteed.

From Freretown I went down to Mombaza to pay a visit to Mr. Buchanan, of the British East Africa Company, and found him looking exceedingly well. At his house I had the pleasure of meeting Mr. Pigott, who had not long since returned from the Upper Tana, where he had established the station of Korokoró.

At Mombaza, after prolonged negotiations, I concluded a bargain with the owner of an Arab dhow, and was very glad to have the day of our departure fixed at last. It was high time my men were back in Zanzibar, for they were getting fairly beyond control. A free fight under the horrified eyes of the mission ladies was their latest outrage on the feelings of the little community at Freretown.

We glided out of Mombaza with the ebbing tide on December 15th. Scarcely were we well out to sea when the breeze fell away, and there was nothing for it but to take to the oars. All night and all the next day the calm continued, although by the drifting of the clouds over the distant mainland we could see that there a fair wind was blowing from the north-east. The sailors whistled and piped in vain. Then the captain fell foul of the Somál for playing cards, but although the cards were put away the *upepo* (wind) still was coy.

Any one who has never sailed in an Arab dhow does not know what sailing is; and those who have sailed in an Arab dhow without getting sea-sick may consider themselves proof to sea-sickness for ever. Fortunately, I am one of the happy few; nevertheless it was as much as I could do to stand the combination of sickening smells that now greeted my nostrils— the effluvia from the perspiring skins of some seventy negroes, the pestilential stench from the stagnant bilge-water, and the villainous odours from all sorts of filth of the worst description. Crowded as we were, and destitute of any shelter from the broiling sun and drenching rain, I look back on this three days' voyage in the Arab dhow as one of the most trying experiences of the whole expedition.

At the end of the third day we came in sight of Kokotoni, the north-western extremity of the island of Zanzibar. As we approached the coast we came within reach of the breeze

T

which blows all day towards the land, and hoisting our sails, flew merrily southward along the palm-clad shore. Slowly the white walls and towers of Zanzibar arose from the sea. The men laughed and shouted gleefully, and playfully dug each other in the ribs, unable to find adequate expression for their delight. My own feelings were strangely mingled. It was pleasant to think that my work had been successfully accomplished, that I had returned from the expedition safe and well, and that soon I should be back again in the midst of my friends. But the feeling of satisfaction produced by these considerations was largely mixed with regret that the busy, active, unconventional life of the last three months was at an end, that I could no longer be absolute master of my own actions, and that my rôle of petty Cæsar was played out. The laughing Zanzibaris at my side knew nothing of these feelings; for them the past was already dead and buried, and the future promised nothing but enjoyment.

At length we cast anchor in the roads, among craft of all kinds, large and small. Many an inquiring eye was bent upon my noisy crew of porters as they stepped ashore; and many a smile greeted our appearance as we passed through the streets in our tattered, weather-beaten garments. Before long I was exchanging greetings at the Consulate with my friend Steifensand, whose guest I remained until my departure for Europe.

It now only remained to pay my porters and disband the caravan; the Somál alone continued in my employment a few weeks longer. It was with feelings of sincere regret that I said good-bye to Mwini Amani and many others who had done their best in the interests of the expedition. One and all they received a substantial honorarium in addition to their stipulated wages, and, if they wished it, a written certificate of character. " Good-bye, sir," they said, on taking leave; " good-bye. And if ever you go on another expedition, remember we are ready to go with you." In the course of the next few days I occasionally met one or other of them in the streets, doing the grand in snow-white *kanzus*, and flourishing the inevitable little dandy cane. A few almost immediately enrolled themselves at the office of the English Mission for an expedition which was to set out in two days for Tanganyika and the Victoria Nyanza. Such is the life of the East African porter, which, with its constant changes and adventures, has as much charm for the free-born Zanzibari as for the Arab slave.

I had at one time intended to organise an expedition to Kenia as soon as I had returned from Kilimanjaro, but I immediately gave up the idea when I found, on arriving in Zanzibar, that although the tents and other furniture had come back from Ceylon, nothing had been heard of the guns and ammunition. For the present, Kenia must wait.

In Zanzibar, with its relaxing climate and frequent social and convivial gatherings, which I could not have avoided even if I would, I soon began to lose the vigorous health and spirits I had enjoyed in the interior. Twice before, the increasing languor had ended in fever, but this time, fortunately, I escaped. Purtscheller, however, had a severe attack, and the malaria hung about him more or less for months, even after he was back again in Germany.

The main topic of conversation everywhere was, of course, Emin, whom the African furies seemed to have overtaken just as he was on the point of escaping from their clutches, and every item of news from Bagamoyo was eagerly looked for and discussed. I should have gone to see him, but visitors to the sick man were strictly forbidden, and I had to content myself with expressing my sympathy by letter. Stanley I met at the English Consul-General's, and had an interesting conversation with him on the subject of Ruwenzori, which had been the goal of my expedition in 1888.

I spent several pleasant evenings at the Imperial Commissioner's and on board the German men-of-war, where we heard a great deal about recent naval and military operations on the east coast. I was almost sorry when I heard that Bushiri had been captured and hanged, though I had more reason than any one to bear him a grudge. Doubtless the execution was necessary as a matter of policy and military justice, but for my own part I could have wished he had been spared, for, everything considered, he treated us very well while we were his prisoners. I should like to know if the English missionaries who shared my misfortunes and my ransom cherish an equally kindly recollection of the daring Arab chief?

The 24th December came round with all the tropical accompaniments of sunshine, thunder and lightning, and rain. There was little to remind us that it was Christmas Eve, and at first it looked as if the day were going to be allowed to pass without any of the usual festivities. In the evening, however, we had a Christmas tree—an araucaria playing the part of the customary pine ; and when the candles were lighted and we had all received our presents—when the roast turkey made its appearance and pine-apple punch began to circulate— Zanzibar and our tropical surroundings were forgotten, and we drank the toast of " absent friends " amid a chorus of uproarious " Hochs ! "

On Christmas Day I had a private audience with the Sultan. He received me in all the cool comfort of his loose house-dress, while I was stifling in my ceremonial dress-coat —the proper thing for the occasion. Pointing me to a chair close to his own, the Sultan commenced a series of interrogations about the Bushiri affair, about my recent work on Kilimanjaro, and about his " slave " Mandara. Since my last interview his Majesty seemed to have grown much more thoughtful and serious, but at his best he was never a very imposing personage, and on his sudden death early in 1890, his subjects cannot be said to have sustained an irreparable loss.

With the end of 1889 our stay in Zanzibar came to a close. We brought in the New Year sitting on the flat roof of the German Consulate, the moon shining overhead and peacefully reflected in the slumbering sea, while here and there an oil-lamp glimmered dimly in the silent streets, and to our ears came the music from the men-of-war, strangely mingling with the *Wacht am Rhein* from the Usagara house, and the chanting of the Sultan's Hymn in the Goanese quarter.

On the 3rd of January I embarked with Herr Purtscheller and the Somál on board the steamer *Amazon*, of the Messageries Maritimes, bound for Marseilles *viâ* Aden and Abok. Slowly the town and island of Zanzibar sank below the horizon, and silently we bade East Africa farewell. It was now the period between the two monsoons, and we had a pleasant voyage through the Indian Ocean in the enjoyment of congenial society, and all the comforts which a well-appointed vessel had to offer. We called at Aden during the night, so that the parting with my faithful Somál was cut shorter than it otherwise might have been. Ali would willingly have accompanied me to Europe, but I had tried the experiment of bringing a black servant home before, and my experience made me firmly resolve never to try it again. The silly way in which a negro is petted and fussed over by people in Germany, would spoil the best " boy " I ever knew.

The heat in the much-abused Red Sea was not so intense as it had been in July, and when we entered the Mediterranean a north wind was blowing which made us thankful to draw to our warm clothing again.

We reached Marseilles on January 21st, eighteen days out from Zanzibar. Here Herr Purtscheller and I parted company, he going to Italy to recruit, while I took the night express for Paris, and thence a few days later went on to Leipzig, reaching home on the Emperor's birthday, after a seven months' absence.

In the course of a few days I was called upon to give my report to the Emperor, and his Majesty was graciously pleased to accept at my hands the topmost pinnacle of the Kaiser Wilhelm's Peak, which I had not forgotten to bring along with me in my pocket. The pinnacle now lies on the imperial writing-table : over the Peak waves the imperial flag, and I close my record of how these things were accomplished with the wish that, whether in Europe or in the dark recesses of Inner Africa, the name of the Emperor Wilhelm II. may carry with it to his subjects the light of German thought and the blessings of European civilisation.

LEAVING MOMBAZA—AN ARAB DHOW.

CHAPTER IX.

GEOGRAPHY AND COMMERCIAL PROSPECTS OF THE KILIMANJARO REGION.

A GLANCE at the orographical map of Africa shows that the backbone of the continent lies towards the east, the bulk of the land, with its great river systems, stretching westwards towards the Atlantic. From the Gulf of Suez the East African highlands run south-east through Nubia, and south through Abyssinia, Enarea, and Kaffa to the Kenia and Kilimanjaro district, whence they extend into the region of the South African lakes, and bending towards the west, form the watershed between the Congo and the Zambezi. In the position and direction of the watershed the east of Africa is thus a reflected image of the west of South America; but here the parallel ceases, for whereas South America is traversed by the lofty, continuous range of the Andes, in East Africa, from lat. 25° N. to lat. 15° S., we have an elevated plateau, which only occasionally rises into mountain peaks and ranges. Wherever this is the

SURVEYOR'S INSTRUMENTS.

295

case—as in Abyssinia and at the equator—the mountains are of volcanic origin.

But although volcanic agencies have here and there modified the surface features of Africa, they have not entered largely into the formation of the continent as a whole. In fact, except in the eastern plateau region, the evidences of volcanic activity are all comparatively recent, and are confined to small and well-defined areas in the Sahara, the Canaries, the Gulf of Guinea, the coast of Benguela, and the Comoro Islands.

The occurrence of volcanoes is everywhere an indication of serious disturbances in the earth's crust, and wherever the volcanoes form a chain it points to the existence of a line of weakness. Thus in East Africa a line of weakness runs from the southern extremity of the Red Sea all the way to the Kilimanjaro district, and there are even indications that it continues as far south as Lake Nyassa and the basin of the Zambezi. It attains its greatest breadth in Abyssinia, whence it gradually tapers away as it runs southward through Kaffa, and in the Samburu region—recently explored by Count Teleki and Lieutenant von Höhnel—it forms a deep trough between two parallel ranges of mountains. The trough is marked by a long series of salt lakes and marshes without an outlet, and gradually widens out again in the region of Meru and Kilimanjaro. From the south end of the Red Sea the same line of weakness is continued northwards through north-western Arabia and southern Syria, forming the great Erythræan trough in which the Red Sea lies, and the trough of the Dead Sea.

Ruwenzori, Gambaragara, Mount Gordon-Bennett, and other ancient volcanoes to the west of the Victoria Nyanza, apparently lie along a parallel line to the west of that we have just been describing, and a third runs from the islands in the Gulf of Guinea through the Cameroons to Adamawa and Lake Tsad. All three lines of weakness have a general trend from north to south.

Most of the East African volcanoes belong to the Tertiary period.; but a few are still in a state of activity—notably one in Abyssinia, one at Lake Samburu, and a third in the vicinity of the natron lake of the Guaso Nyiro Gelei. Solfataras are more numerous.

In Africa, as in other parts of the world, the greatest manifestations of volcanic activity are to be met with near the equator. There we have Kenia (18,400 feet, according to Von Höhnel), Ruwenzori (18,500 feet, according to Stanley), and Kilimanjaro (19,700 feet)—all of them close upon the average volcanic maximum, for there is no volcanic mountain on the earth's surface which attains a greater elevation than 23,000 feet. According to these figures, Kilimanjaro is the highest volcano in Africa.

" Kilimanjaro " is the name given to the mountain by the Swahili, and means " Mountain of the spirit Njaro." Njaro is a male spirit, a sort of African " Rübezahl," who also inhabits another mountain in Bondei, which is likewise called " Kilimanjaro." The inhabitants of Kilimanjaro, the Wa-jagga, have no name for the mountain as a whole, but call the ice-covered western peak " Kibo " (the bright), and the dark rocky eastern peak " Mawenzi " (the dark). The Swahili have adopted the name Kibo, but, following the analogy in Ki-bo and Ki-limanjaro, Mawenzi has become corrupted into Ki-mawenzi.

Like Kenia, Kilimanjaro rises from the eastern boundary of the great East African trough, while Meru (16,070 feet) occupies a position within the trough to the west of Kilimanjaro. The western side of the trough is lower than the eastern, and here we have a series of lakes having no outlet—Manyara,

the natron lake formed by the Guaso Nyiro, Naivasha, Elme-
teita, and others. The Kibo peak of Kilimanjaro lies in lat.
3° 4′ S., and long. 37° 15′ E.

Kilimanjaro is a twin volcano, formed by the union of the
more ancient Mawenzi in the east with the larger and more
recent Kibo in the west. The major axis of the mountain thus
runs east and west, and is considerably longer than the minor
axis, which runs generally north and south. The plains surrounding the mountain slope from north to south, and have
a mean elevation of 2600 feet above the sea. From the
plains the mountain rises in beautiful curves, which, like
those of Mount Etna, are at first very gentle, but gradually
increase in steepness, till, in the region of the summit, the slope
is almost precipitous. The gradient from the plains (2600 feet)
to Jagga (4600 feet), for a distance of five or six miles, is 5° to
6°; from Jagga to the base of Kibo (14,100 feet), a distance
of about twelve miles, 8°; from the foot of Kibo to the summit
(19,700 feet), 21°. From east to west—from the Lumi to the
end of the Shira ridge—the base of the mountain measures
about fifty-five miles; from south to north—from the parasitic
cones in the Kahé steppes to the belt of marshes in the Nyiri
plain, the distance is nearly forty miles. On the east and
south-east the base of the mountain virtually forms the limit
of the volcanic rocks, for towards Taveta and in the plains of
the Rufu to the north of Ugweno there are only slight and
occasional traces of volcanic activity, evidently of a later date
than that which resulted in the upheaval of Kilimanjaro. In
the north-east, north, and west, however, the volcanic agencies
have again come into free play over a large area.

The parent mass of Kilimanjaro rises from the plains to a
height of 14,400 feet. Here there is a plateau from which the
two cones spring abruptly upwards—Mawenzi, in the east, to
a height of 17,570 feet; Kibo, in the west, to a height of

19,720 feet. The distance between the bases of the two peaks is about five miles. The diameter of Kibo at its base (14,100 feet) is 5200 yards; that of Mawenzi at the same elevation, 3600 yards. At 19,700 feet, Kibo still has a diameter of 2200 yards; but Mawenzi at its summit is crowned by a narrow jagged crest of rocks 2200 yards in length (see Map III.).

Across the plateau, between the south end of Mawenzi and the eastern side of Kibo, runs a series of five volcanic hills, ranging from 100 to 300 feet in height. The two lying nearest to Mawenzi are the oldest and most weathered; they are composed of lava, and from each a long stream of lava descends towards the south. The other three belong to a more recent phase of volcanic activity, and are in a better state of preservation; they are mainly composed of volcanic ashes, and do not give rise to any lava streams. A line of dislocation traverses the major axis of the line of hills, cleaving them from top to bottom, and causing great displacement of the strata. Along the continuation of this line, the eastern side of Kibo is marked by a gigantic ridge of lava, corresponding to which, on the western side of the peak, is an enormous fissure terminating at the lofty Shira ridge (11,480 feet), itself almost worthy to rank as an independent mountain. To the east, Mawenzi sinks down as a sheer precipice in the crater-like abyss we have described elsewhere. Thus, to all appearances, a great fault runs from the base of Mawenzi across the hills on the plateau to the western slope of Kibo, and it is not improbable that it continues westward in a slightly curving line as far as Meru, whose crater opens towards the east. The same fault is continued eastward from Mawenzi to the volcanic mountains of Julu on the River Tsavo.

Leaving the Shira ridge out of account, the western half of Kilimanjaro, which owes its origin to the activity of Kibo, is characterised by more smooth and regular outlines than the eastern half. The latter has been built up by the lavas which once flowed molten from Mawenzi. From the base of the peak (14,100 feet) to the plains (2600 feet) the flanks of the mountain are traversed, or, as it were, buttressed, by several long narrow lines of hills. Some of these are to be regarded as having been formed by the outflow of great streams of lava, but the greater number are parasitic cones indicating where the volcanic products have found their way to the surface through vertical fissures. In most cases the cones are as perfectly preserved as when they were in eruption—a fact which testifies to their comparatively recent origin. The most important series of these parasitic hills is that which runs from the southern base of Mawenzi (14,100 feet) south-eastwards through the Jagga districts of Msai and Mwika, including the Wajimba chain and the Makessa group lower down, and terminating in the hills to the north of the papyrus swamp on the Rufu. A second important series are the Lasso hills between Kilema and Kirúa ; and a third, the line of hills between Uru and Majamé.

Wherever the flanks of the western or Kibo half are deeply furrowed, the ruggedness is due to the action of running water, and especially of the streams which flow from the glaciers.

Parasitic cones, mostly in perfect preservation, and varying from 60 to 500 feet in height, are to be met with all along the southern foot of Kilimanjaro ; and here again they occur most numerously towards the Mawenzi half of the mountain. The girdle of parasitic "foot-hills" extends round the east and west sides of the mountain, but on the north the hills abruptly cease without completing the circle. At the foot of the mountain, between the base of Kibo and that of Mawenzi—a distance of twenty miles—the marshy belt of country in the Nyiri plain is entirely destitute of these foot-hills.

The slopes of the mountain rise in a series of terraces formed by alternate layers of lava and beds of other ejected volcanic materials. The terraces are most marked towards the higher zones of the mountain, where the viscous lavas which were the last to ooze from the crater have hardened into abrupt walls and precipices. Towards the foot, on the other hand, the more liquid lavas of the earlier stages of eruption have spread themselves out in broad flat sheets of enormous extent.

The northern face of the mountain is much steeper and more abrupt than the southern—a fact which may partly be accounted for by the slope of the plains on which the base of Kilimanjaro rests. As the ground rises slightly towards the north, the lavas would here be dammed back, while to the south, where the ground falls, there was nothing to prevent them from spreading gradually outwards. The much greater extent of the southern base of the mountain is also partly to be explained in this way, although here other and more important causes have come into operation. In the first place, it is tolerably certain that from the most remote periods the accumulations of snow and ice have always been greatest on the southern side, and with every fresh eruption the suddenly melted masses combined with the ejected volcanic products and swept downwards towards the plains in the form of vast torrents of mud. A further contribution was forthcoming from the parasitic cones, which, as we have already said, are mostly confined to the south side of the mountain; and this again may have been added to by showers of dust and ashes ejected from the main crater, and carried southwards in the current of the prevailing north-easterly upper trade winds.

Of the two peaks, Kibo at once proclaims its volcanic origin by its shape, which is that of a truncated cone. Of the summit of Mawenzi, on the other hand, nothing is now left but a long median ridge or crest from which radiate numerous smaller ridges separated by heaps of débris. The largest talus is that which slopes away down the middle of the western side of the peak, from a great notch in the central crest that forms one of the distinctive features in the side view of the mountain. The tremendous steepness and jaggedness of the central and minor ridges are probably without parallel. The most precipitous slope occurs in the middle of the eastern side, where the central crest drops down abruptly at an angle of 65° to a depth of nearly 7000 feet. This tremendous abyss is probably to be regarded as forming part of the ancient crater, but from the prevailing dip of the beds of lava it would seem that the centre of the crater must have been further to the south-west of what is now the highest peak (17,570 feet). The latter forms the crown of an imposing wall of rock 1800 feet high which lies on the north side of the central crest. From this peak the line of the crest extends towards the south, and is broken up into five lower but equally jagged masses.

In contrast to Mawenzi, as we have already said, Kibo displays the more regular outlines of the typical volcanic cone. As the result of denudation and secondary eruptions the sides are deeply furrowed by valleys and ravines, many of which are cut out to a depth of over 300 feet in beds of lava of enormous thickness. Relatively to the enormous size of the mountain mass, however, these furrows are too small to affect the general impression of smoothness, the only really striking fissure being the great rift on the south-west side of the cone. At the summit of Kibo is a gigantic open crater 6500 feet in diameter and over 600 feet deep. The rift just referred to starts from the western side of the crater or *caldera,* and forms an opening through which the ice and water accumulated within the latter find their way down the mountain-side. From the bottom of the crater, towards the north, rises a flattened parasitic cone about 500 feet high, the base of which almost touches the crater walls on all sides, with the exception of the south, where a layer of volcanic mud intervenes. The bottom and sides of the crater are for the most part covered with ice, but there is no ice on the upper part of the central cone, from which we may infer that the cone still to a certain degree retains its original heat. In other parts of the world — in equatorial South America and in the South Polar regions, for instance—it is not uncommon to find the summits of the snow mountains similarly clear, and the phenomenon is doubtless to be explained in the same way.

Kilimanjaro has been built up out of many different kinds of volcanic material, but primary formations are nowhere represented. The fact that the lavas have been poured out at different periods, first by Mawenzi and then by Kibo, is the main cause of their wide difference in character. On Mawenzi the prevailing rock is a felspathic basalt, while on Kibo it is a nepheline basanite. (See Appendix.)

In the shattered precipices of Mawenzi the display of lavas of varying colours and varying degrees of thickness is perfectly bewildering. In this respect one of the most interesting features is presented by the veins of compact lava, 10 to 30 feet broad, which everywhere fill up the vertical fissures in the face of the cliffs, and have the appearance of supporting and holding together the whole crumbling structure. Describing an analogous phenomenon characteristic of the lavas of Mount Etna, Sartorius von Waltherhausen compares it to the injection of the venous system in anatomical preparations, and a more graphic simile could scarcely be imagined. Kibo, again, appears to be composed of a compact mass of solid lava, and all traces of secondary eruptions along its flanks have been removed by denudation. Along the edge of the crater the original lava has been transformed in the course of repeated eruptions into a glassy obsidian; elsewhere, as, for instance, on the Kaiser Wilhelm's Peak, we found vesicular lavas similar to those of the central cone (leucitic basanite).

On the saddle plateau greyish-yellow mud and ashes prevail. The former appears in its greatest extent to the north of the plateau hills, where a broad sheet stretches from the north-eastern base of Kibo to far below the north of Mawenzi, and is strewn with enormous boulders as if it had been a playground of the Cyclops. Where sheets of lava extend to the south of the hills, as is the case especially in the direction of Mawenzi, the action of the atmosphere causes the blocks gradually to crumble into fragments, until the sheets are hidden beneath a layer of volcanic sand and mud.

The basalts of the plateau region are distinguished by beautiful large crystals of olivine; from the plateau downwards the basalts gradually become more and more compact and finely crystalline. As the result of secondary eruptions wide sheets of breccia occur in several places at the bottom of the mountain. Still more numerous, in and around the neighbourhood of the foot-hills, are vast streams of volcanic mud, richly interspersed with fragments of rock of various size. As shown in the cuttings formed by the river channels (*e.g.*, the Himo, the Ngombere, and the Weri-weri), the fragments are all rounded and worn, from which we may infer that they had already been long exposed to atmospheric action before they were caught up and imbedded in the advancing stream of mud.

From the form and structure of the mountain, from the nature and distribution of the volcanic rocks, we are able to trace the geological history of Kilimanjaro with tolerable accuracy. The first to make a successful attempt in this direction was Mr. Joseph Thomson, whose sketch we shall here endeavour to supplement in certain important details.

There can be no doubt that of the two peaks Mawenzi is the more ancient. Already Kibo is hoary with age, and has weathered the storm for thousands of years ; but Mawenzi was hoary before Kibo came into existence, and through the action of rain and frost and snow it has crumbled away, until now it is but the skeleton of its former self. Mawenzi was at first upheaved from a transverse fissure running east and west across the line of the great trough which traverses eastern Africa from north to south. It probably originated at the same time as Meru, which, from its shattered summit, is evidently of much greater antiquity than Kibo. As eruption succeeded eruption Mawenzi gradually increased in size and grandeur, until at length its height was so great that it baffled the attempts of the subterranean forces to raise the lava to the surface.

Meanwhile the flanks of the mountain had given way in various places, and the volcanic energy found temporary outlet in numerous small eruptions. At length, concentrating all its powers on the western extension of the Mawenzi fissure, it there found final vent, and a new volcano—Kibo—began its existence on the western slope of the older cone. In the course of centuries it began to rival its neighbour in size, and gradually became one of the chief agents in its destruction, battering Mawenzi's venerable head with showers of stones, undermining its lavas with explosions of steam, and furrowing them with torrents of mud. From time to time the direful siege would cease for a while, and Mawenzi had time to draw around its galled and weary shoulders a protecting mantle of snow and ice, until with a fresh eruption the ice was transformed into devastating floods, which the crumbling rock had no longer power to withstand.

U

Neither in Mawenzi nor in Kibo were the volcanic out-
bursts characterised by extraordinary violence ; the strata are
nowhere greatly disturbed, and the sheets of ashes and streams
of lava have not extended to any great distance over the surrounding plains. More or less quietly the volcanic products
welled up over the crater rim, adding layer after layer to the
flanks of the mountain by a constant alternation of lava sheets
and beds of agglomerate. The lavas first ejected were the most
fluid, and extended farthest out into the plains ; those which
came later were more viscous in character, and hardening more
readily, have resulted in the terraced appearance which has
been already spoken of as distinguishing the higher zones of
the mountain.

At first Kibo was in all probability a perfect cone, the apex
of which may have been some 1500 feet higher than the present summit of the peak. If we may presume that Kibo was
ever convulsed by any tremendous paroxysm, it was when the
explosion occurred which resulted in giving the cone its present truncated form. From the large fragments of characteristic Kibo rocks with which the plateau and the flanks of
Kilimanjaro are strewn, it is not improbable that such an
explosion actually took place. It is still more likely, however,
that the apex of the cone fell in, at or after which event the
disturbance took place along the line of the great transverse
fissure, whereby the western wall of the crater was cleft in
twain, and the long lofty ridge of the Shira hills was upheaved. With this final outburst the great eruptions of lava
probably ceased. The pent-up gases in the bowels of the
mountain were no longer able to force their way to its
lofty summit, and were compelled to find an outlet lower
down.

In the course of successive minor eruptions the flattened
cone at the bottom of the crater was gradually built up, and

in the hollow between Kibo and Mawenzi three cinder cones arose on the side towards Kibo. The two lava hills nearest to Mawenzi had already been long in existence, and the cinder cones may accordingly be regarded as the most recent volcanic formations in the loftier regions of Kilimanjaro. Lower down the volcanic agencies continued to manifest themselves for some time longer, spending their strength in the production of the parasitic cones along the flanks and at the base of the mountain, most of which have given rise independently to small streams of lava. These cones vary in height from 100 to 400 feet.

Gradually, by the agency of the melting snow, assisted by an occasional outflow of mud, the notch in the western side of the crater was widened into a great *barranco*, while heat and cold, wind and rain, set to work slowly but steadily to eat away the solid rocks below and around. The work of denudation still goes on, and the story of Mawenzi is being repeated.

The volcanic activity of Kilimanjaro is now a thing of the past; there is no trace even of fumaroles. Nevertheless, the mountain evidently retains sufficient internal heat to keep the summit of the cone within the crater free of ice and to raise the temperature of the springs in certain places. I myself have never met with any of these warm springs, nor could I learn that they were known to the natives; but Mr. H. H. Johnston mentions one he discovered at an altitude of about 13,000 feet, which had a temperature of 92° Fahr.

Kilimanjaro lies within the region of the permanent trade winds. In summer the southern half of the mountain comes under the influence of the south-east trades, which vary a point or two to the south -or south-west, according to local conditions. The northern half of the mountain is then in the lee of the wind, but in winter the northern half comes under the influence of the north-east trades, and the southern half is sheltered. The summit of the mountain soars far into the region of the upper trade winds, and there accordingly the wind in summer blows from the north, in winter from the south.

We need hardly say that an immense isolated mountain mass like Kilimanjaro must considerably modify the prevailing direction of the wind. As the atmosphere gradually becomes heated during the day, and cools again during the night, corresponding upward and downward currents set in all over the lower zones of the mountain. In the south, where the broad base and the numerous ascending terraces present a larger superficial area to be acted upon, the currents are particularly strong. Thus in Moji, in the month of October, during the storm which came down on us every evening between eight and ten o'clock, I estimated that the force of the wind corresponded to 8 of Beaufort's scale, or a "fresh gale." To the north again, where, owing to the steepness of the slope, the superficial area is diminished, the force of the upward and downward currents is sensibly weaker.

On the saddle plateau, at a height of from 14,000 to 14,500 feet, we found, both in July 1887 and in October 1889, that in the early morning the wind blew from the south-east as a "light breeze" with a velocity of 2–3. Towards midday, as the whole upland region gradually became warmed up, the wind veered round towards the south, and blew as a "moderate breeze" with a force of 3–4. Towards sunset there was an interval of calm, usually lasting for about an hour; then, at our Kibo camp, a north-westerly wind set in from Kibo, and continued to blow until after midnight, beginning as a "fresh breeze," and increasing to "strong" (velocity 5–6), while at our Mawenzi camp, a north-easterly wind set in from Mawenzi, and blew with increasing force (4–5) until near midnight. Once or twice on Kibo the usual north-west wind was replaced by a wind from the north-east (vel. 4–5), possibly the upper trade wind, which the contrary local current had not been able to overcome.

The fact that the rainfall depends on and is regulated by the winds is every day strikingly illustrated on Kilimanjaro.

After sunrise, when the heated air begins to rise from the mountain slopes, the air from the steppes, laden with moisture brought by the trade wind from the Indian Ocean, rushes in to supply the place of the ascending current. As the air rises, it is gradually cooled; and when it reaches the lower part of the forest region (5900–7500 feet), the moisture condenses into cumulus clouds, which, in the course of the day, continue to ascend and increase in volume, until at length they form a broad layer, reaching as high as the saddle plateau (13,000 feet), and completely concealing the two peaks from the eye of the observer below. Thanks to the agency of the upper trade wind, which in summer blows from the north and north-west, the peaks themselves remain clear all the forenoon. At length, in this upper region also, the atmospheric layers in contact with the ground become sensibly heated; but almost immediately they begin to rise above the earth, the moisture is condensed into light wreaths of vapour. At first these are caught up by the upper trade wind, and carried away towards the south-west; but as the day goes on, the mist rises with increasing rapidity from the ice-fields of Kibo and the jagged rocks of Mawenzi, and before midday both summits are completely enveloped.

After midday the upward current from below, with its masses of cumulus, begins to encroach more and more upon the region of the upper trade wind, and finally both Kibo and Mawenzi are concealed by an enormous dome of snowy clouds, which have the appearance of being absolutely motionless, although from the upper layers detached masses are constantly being wafted away to the south-west by the current above, while just as constantly their place is being supplied by fresh masses from below.

All the afternoon the upward currents from both sides of the mountain meet at the saddle plateau, when their accompanying cloud masses are suddenly whirled skywards, and, coming within the influence of the upper trade wind, are broken up and float away towards the south.

Later on, as the temperature falls and the force of the currents diminishes, the clouds in the region of the summit descend in rain and snow, and gradually the peaks reappear. But as the temperature here falls much more rapidly than in the lower zones of the mountain, it frequently happens that, at sunset, the cool downward current which has set in meets the warm upward current half-way, or just above the forest, with the result that a narrow band of stratus cloud spreads itself out all round the mountain. As the lower zones gradually become cooler and cooler during the night, the current from above makes its way further and further down, always carrying the cloud-belt to a lower level, hence the almost regular nightly rains which occur in Jagga. At last, towards morning the clouds disappear, and everything is clear until an hour or two after sunrise, when the daily cycle commences anew.

In the rainy season, which, on Kilimanjaro, occurs during November and May, the above phenomena are accompanied by others of an electrical nature that also seem to be dependent on the direction of the wind. The great thunderstorms which in November daily descend on the mountain at midday, all occurred above the forest zone (9500 feet). They were accompanied by heavy showers of hail and tremendous electrical discharges, and they passed off along the southern side of Kibo, leaving the peak covered with a layer of newly fallen snow. On Mawenzi we had only two thunderstorms, both during the night. They came from the east, and left not only the peak but the saddle plateau white with snow.

One of the most striking physical facts in connection with Kilimanjaro is the contrast which exists between the north and south sides of the mountain in respect of humidity. In seeking to account for this remarkable phenomenon, three things must be borne in mind—first, the south-east trade wind, which blows across the southern side of the mountain, carries with it a greater supply of moisture than the north-east trade wind, which has already travelled across a wide tract of dry land before it reaches the north side; secondly, owing to the vast extent and gentler slopes of the south side, the rainfall is more widely and evenly distributed, and the conditions favour the growth of the forest to a degree impossible on the precipitous northern face; thirdly, the rainfall being greater and the drainage system more complete, there is a corresponding increase in the quantity of moisture constantly being evaporated. Travelling along the base of the mountain from south to east, and thence round to the north and west, we find as we proceed that the streams diminish in size and number, and that the belt of forest gradually dwindles away. The north-west side is the driest and most sterile, for neither of the trade winds ever reaches it directly, and even on the rare occasions when the south-east trade wind veers round towards the south-west, it is effectually prevented from reaching the north-west side of Kilimanjaro by the intervening barrier of the Shira chain. On the north-west side there is not a single stream.

On the more favoured aspects of the mountain the clouds descend on the forest and grassy uplands, in rain more or less heavy; on the saddle plateau in rain or snow, according to the season and the local temperature; and on the two peaks in snow. Far more common than either rain or snow is the raw, damp "Scotch mist," which imparts to the landscape during the warmer part of the day an air of dull, grey, depressing monotony. Below and on the saddle plateau (13,000–14,500 feet) the snow is sometimes soft and flaky, sometimes granular; but the névé I observed on the two peaks between 14,500 and 19,700 feet was invariably granular.

Although Kilimanjaro lies near the equator the extent of its ice and snow varies with the season. The southern summer (December to May) is also the rainy season in the Kilimanjaro region, and it is then that the accumulations of ice and snow are greatest. In the southern winter (June to November) there is a comparative dearth of moisture, the snowfall is proportionately slight, and the process of melting goes on more rapidly; hence, by the end of the season, the accumulations of ice and snow are at their smallest.

A word, first, as regards the extent and distribution of the snow and ice during the rainy season. In July 1887 we found the first isolated patches of snow under the blocks and in crevices in the lava at the "Schneequelle" (12,960 feet). In increased size and numbers the patches occurred at the south-eastern base of Kibo, the south-western base of Mawenzi, and to the south of the hills on the plateau (14,100 feet). Except in unusually favourable situations, the patches never exceeded six feet in size. In the months of April and May they may probably have formed part of one wide sheet, but already all trace of connection had vanished, and from the nature of the snow it was evident that they would all disappear during the ensuing dry season—a surmise we were able to verify during our visit in October 1889. A peculiarity of the snowfields on the steep slopes of Kibo was the piles of stones ranged along their lower margins, almost like a moraine. They had apparently fallen from the rocks above, and slid downwards over the smooth surface of the snow. Later on we saw the same thing repeated on the tali of Mawenzi.

Although these snowfields are none of them permanent, their position is not a mere matter of chance, but is determined by local peculiarities in the structure of the mountain. Since they disappear during the dry season, they cannot be taken into account in fixing the snow-line, but they are important as indicating the limit of the snowfall, which, on the south side of the mountain, we found to be 12,140 feet. On our ascent of Kibo in October 1889—the end of the dry season—the snowfields, up which, in July 1887, we had made our way to the lower limit of the ice-cap, had all melted away. Only the compact mass of ice and névé at the summit remained, with here and there a descending tongue or streak along some deep rut or fissure of the underlying rock. A few large isolated patches of snow occurred below the limit of the ice, but they were due to some recent storm, and would probably not lie more than two or three days. On Mawenzi, in the same month, frozen snow was found here and there in the deeper crannies and hollows, but these accumulations were too insignificant to be taken into account, the largest of them measuring not more than 3 feet deep, and 15 feet long. Thus, in the hot season, Kilimanjaro may be said to be practically free of patches of névé.

The compact mass of névé and ice is thus rendered all the more conspicuous, the lower edge of the ice-cap rising like a bright blue cliff, 15 to 260 feet high, all around the summit. The line of this cliff is extremely irregular. On the north side it keeps close to the summit, meeting the solid rock at an elevation of 18,700 feet. To the north and north-east it forms a jagged zigzag, the " Hans-Meyer Notch " occurring at an altitude of 18,860 feet. On the south-east, again, it divides into two broad tongues or peninsulas, of which the more easterly is the Ratzel glacier. Both of these tongues fill up the hollows of valleys, and extend down the mountain side as low as 17,550 feet. On the south side the ice stretches suddenly downwards. For a considerable distance the vast sheet remains continuous, but afterwards, owing to the extremely rugged and precipitous nature of the slope, it is broken up into a series of tongues and streaks divided by bare dark ridges of rock. In the south this interrupted zone occurs between 16,400 and 13,100 feet, and further to the south-west between 15,750 and 12,470 feet. As it remains in connection with the ice-cap, and the presence of the ice is not due—like the snowfields we have referred to above—to structural peculiarities of the mountain, this zone is of importance in fixing what, to be accurate, we must on Kilimanjaro call the "ice-line." Towards the west, on the further side of the great fissure, the ice-cap extends downwards as a many-tongued peninsula to a level of 13,800 feet. Its appearance is admirably shown in the series of views which were taken by Höhnel in the course of the Teleki expedition.

Thus the limit of the ice on Kibo would be defined by a line passing round the mountain at the following altitudes : south, 13,100 feet; south-east, 12,500 feet; west, 13,800 feet; north-west, 18,500 feet; north, 18,700 feet; north-east, 18,860 feet; east, 18,700 feet; south-east, 17,550 feet.

And here the question arises : Why does the limit of the ice and névé vary so greatly at different places, and why should it be lowest in the west and south, and highest in the east and north ? The primary cause is, of course, the unequal distribution of moisture on the northern and southern sides of the mountain, into the particulars of which we have already entered. But on Kilimanjaro, as everywhere else, even more depends on local peculiarities which favour the preservation of the snow than on physical conditions which favour a large snowfall. On the south, south-west, and west sides of the mountain the former are favourable; on the north-west, north, and east they are quite the reverse.

At the end of the wet season the accumulations of snow on Kibo reach a maximum, after which, for months, the north side is exposed only to the dry north-east and north-west upper trade winds, and to the warm upward currents from the arid northern plains. These continually melt the snow on this side, but only to carry it further in the form of vapour, and deposit it again as snow on the southern side—the one side thus gaining what the other loses. Again, the northern side is exposed to greater heat than the southern—firstly, because the plains on this side lie at a higher level, and the heat which radiates from them is not modified by any intervening layer of vapour as on the plains to the south; and secondly, because during the dry season the sun is to the north of Kilimanjaro, and its rays fall more directly on that side of the mountain.

On the east side, again, the influence of the dry north-east monsoon mostly accounts for the comparative absence of snow and ice; but here another important factor is the intense radiation of heat from the saddle plateau, where the dark rock is sometimes heated to such a degree that the radiation may be directly felt, and even seen in the vibration of the atmosphere over its surface.

Wherever the slope is unusually steep the ice cracks, and great masses become detached and fall to the base of the cone (13,100 feet), where the incline is more gradual. Here, on the north side, they rapidly disappear under the combined influence of heat and drought, while on the south side, where there is more moisture and the heat is less intense, they rapidly unite with one or other of the great tongues of ice.

The various factors above enumerated have determined not only the distribution but the nature of the névé and ice on Kilimanjaro. In the great snowfields, which in July partially covered the slopes of Kibo from the ice-cap to the saddle plateau, the snow near the base was soft and flaky, whilst higher up it was dry and granular. In October, when all the snowfields had disappeared, there was likewise comparatively little snow to be met with on the ice-cap. Over large areas the surface of the ice was covered with granular morsels, half-way between ice and snow, the surface of which was slushy during the day and afforded excellent footing. Newly formed névé occurred only in the hollows. Where the slope was steep, the surface was composed of a sheet of brittle cellular ice, which, under the axe, broke into splinters like glass. In the sections shown in the crevasses, the outer wall of the ice-cap and the terraces within the crater, all the gradations from névé to clear compact ice were to be seen in perfection. On the north side, where the ice forms a wall fifty feet high, I counted as many as twenty-eight distinct layers, all differing from each other in structure and colour, passing through every imaginable shade of grey and blue, from the silver grey of the névé at the top to the deep ultramarine of the solid ice at the bottom.

As may readily be understood, the névé and ice of Kilimanjaro have very little in common with the glacial formations of the Alps. They resemble rather those of the great American equatorial volcanoes, as they are described by Reiss and Stübel, Whymper, Güssfeldt, and other travellers. There is no real reservoir for névé, unless we accept the highly improbable supposition that in summer the crater becomes choked with snow and ice, and, overflowing, becomes the source from which the ice-cap has originated and is maintained. It would be much more reasonable to suppose that the rocky rim of the crater is the real reservoir. Broadly speaking, however, the Kibo ice-cap is simply the result of the accumulations of snow which form on the sides of the peak, and gradually sink downward by their own weight till they reach the limit at which they begin to melt. Thus, immediately before the commencement of the rainy reason, the higher parts of the ice-cap are to a certain extent thinned away, not only from the action of the sun and winds, but through this gradual downward tendency of the ice.

Owing to the smooth symmetrical slope of the cone, crevasses and fissures are not numerous, except on the south side. It is only where the mountain is furrowed with ravines that the ice assumes the appearance of a glacier of the second order. The compact mass then becomes split up by longitudinal and transverse fissures, and the glacier advances with a short tongue at its lower extremity, from beneath which the water flows, or rather trickles, in tiny rivulets that soon disappear among the porous lavas. The Ratzel glacier on the eastern side of Kibo is a glacier of this type, as are also the tongues in the south-east and west. They probably nowhere extend below 14,750 feet. The only example of a glacier of the first order, running as one long, continuous stream down a gentle incline, is the great stream of ice which issues from the notch on the south-west side of the crater. Even it, however, does not reach below 12,450 feet, stopping short when still a long way above the upper limit of the forest (10,500 feet).

Another important cause militating against the formation of glaciers is the porous nature of the volcanic rocks, which check the accumulation of ice by absorbing the water that flows from the melting snow before it has time to freeze again. The entire absence of ice on Mawenzi is to be explained on similar grounds—the extremely precipitous slope of the mountain, and the porous character of the rock of which it is composed.

Superficial moraines are nowhere met with, as there are no rocks above the level of the ice from which fragments could fall. Terminal moraines are of frequent occurrence, however, as the result of the action of the ground ice. Glacial markings are also common on the rocks lining the sides of the ravines. In the great ravine in the south-east the markings may be observed far below the present limit of the Ratzel glacier, and the confused network of lava veins is polished and scratched to a height of over thirty feet from the ground, the striæ running parallel to the course of the valley.

In certain respects the ice within the crater differs considerably from that of the ice-cap. The extent of the havoc wrought by sun and wind on the sheets of ice and névé lining the sides and bottom of the vast cauldron far exceeds anything of a like nature to be seen among the ice on the rim above. The weathering is most marked in the south and east, the ice in many places looking as if it had been ploughed. The furrows run parallel, and are frequently as much as six feet deep, and the ridges and points and pinnacles between are so firm and sharp that I can only compare them to a "*Karrenfield*" in the limestone Alps. As a rule, they follow the downward slope of the subtending rock, so that they probably owe their origin to the combined action of the wind and of the water produced by the influence of the sun's rays. At the shelving bottom of the crater, which is well sheltered from the wind, the furrows disappear, and the ice assumes the undulating, laminated appearance which may be seen, though to a less degree, in the snowfields of Europe. The *nieve penitente*, described by Dr. Paul Güssfeldt in his work on the Andes, seems to be exactly similar in character. On the sides of the crater where the ice is thickest it rises in steep terraces like the outer rim of the ice-cap, and, as in the latter, the transition from névé to ice of different degrees of solidity is distinctly traceable.

The greatest accumulations of ice are to be met with on the north side of the crater. Here the bottom of the crater is highest, and the hollow between the central cone and the succession of terraces which rise upwards to the rim affords an excellent reservoir for névé. On the south side, which is directly exposed to the dry north upper trade wind, and to the rays of the sun during the dry season, the ice is largely melted away; and in October the dark rock was everywhere laid bare. It is probable, however, that in the wet season the south side also is covered with ice, and the whole crater is transformed, for the time being, into a vast reservoir, its icy contents being discharged through the great notch in the western wall. Even in October we could see that the ice-masses all tended towards the western *barranco*, and that the water drained off in the same direction.

As far as could be seen from Majamé, the ice from the vast *caldera* falls as a mighty cascade into the great western fissure, where it unites with the accumulations in the fissure itself, and bending towards the south flows downwards to the south-western base of Kibo as the glacier of the first order, to which reference has already been made. The lower end of the glacier (12,500 feet) terminates in a broad cliff, from beneath which issue the head waters of the Weri-weri. Our attempt to pursue our explorations on this side of the peak were frustrated by the approach of the rainy season, but there can be no doubt that here many interesting problems still remain to be solved.

The extent of the rainfall and the distribution of the ice naturally determine the distribution of the springs, streams, and rivers on Kilimanjaro. On Kibo and Mawenzi, the water from the ice is rapidly absorbed by the porous rock, making its way downward by underground channels, to appear again at the bottom of the peaks. In the loftier regions the only water we saw was a small lakelet on the north of Mawenzi, at a height of 15,420 feet, and a group of springs on the west of the same peak at a height of 15,250 feet. South of the hills on the plateau, and below 14,100 feet, the springs begin to multiply, and the flanks of the mountain are furrowed by the deeply eroded channels of several tiny rivulets flowing in the direction of the forest zone. Fed by the rich supply of moisture afforded by this region, the rivulets rapidly increase in size and number, and unite to form streams, which make their way towards the plains through ever deeper and wider valleys. In their lower course many of the streams attain the magnitude of rivers, but after draining off the water from a number of marshes that occur at the bottom of the mountain (north of Kahé, south of Pokomo), they all fall into the Rufu or Pangani.

In contrast to the southern side, the north side of Kilimanjaro is extremely poor in springs and water-courses, and even the west has but one solitary stream, the Ngare n'Erobi, which rises in the Shira chain and is finally lost in the plains. In the north-west not a single stream descends from the mountain. The water from the ice and from the narrow belt of forest on the north, unites with the water which drains from the bare rocks of Mawenzi in the north-west, and finds its way to the great depression in the northern plains, where it forms four large and several small marshes (Nyiri). The belt of marshes has no outlet, but the balance is maintained by evaporation. Of the four large marshes the two to the west are supplied from Kibo, the others from Mawenzi, whose greater rainfall and broader belt of forest on this side sufficiently account for the size of the eastmost and largest marsh of all. Nearly all the water finds its way to the marshes underground, trickling through the porous superficial layers to the solid rock beneath. Only a few insignificant rivulets are to be met with, and scarcely a ravine furrows the smooth slopes of the mountain.

The north side of Mawenzi forms the watershed for the Indian Ocean. Thence the head waters of the Tsavo and Sabaki flow north-east and east. In the east rises the Rombo, which at first follows a southerly course, but after spreading out into the marshy Lake Rombo (Tsavo), suddenly makes a bend and flows towards the east. The Lumi also rises on the same side of the peak, and flows so close to the Rombo as almost to form a fork. The Lumi, however, maintains its southerly direction, and may thus be said to represent the upper course of the Rufu or Pangani. From this it follows that the watershed between the Sabaki and the Pangani lies between the Useri (a tributary of the former) and the river Lumi. The Pangani receives the drainage from the whole of the south-eastern side of Kilimanjaro, and is the outlet for the crater lake of Jala, while Lake Jipé is only a sort of backwater of the Lumi, from which the river issues again as the Rufu. After receiving all the tributary streams which flow from the south side of Kilimanjaro, and which increase in number and volume towards the west, the Rufu takes a south-easterly direction, and finally falls into the Indian Ocean.

It is not necessary that in the following pages I should devote as much space to the botany, zoology, and ethnology of Kilimanjaro as I have already given to the consideration of its physical features. The former have received ample justice at the hands of my predecessors, most of whom,

x

however, did not penetrate into the lofty regions which formed
my own special sphere of observation. The most important
contributions to our knowledge of the flora have been made
by Von der Decken, Johnston, and Von Höhnel. Count
Teleki, Willoughby and Harvey, and, above all, Dr. Abbott,
have devoted themselves to the study of the fauna; and
every traveller who has visited the region has helped more or
less to familiarise us with the natives and their peculiarities
of race and custom. I shall only attempt, therefore, to throw
new light on the general character of the vegetation by
considering it in relation to the geography of the mountain,
and for the rest must refer my readers to the narrative portion
of the book and to the Appendix.

As the flora of a district depends on the climate and the
nature of the soil, we should naturally expect the very greatest
variety on a snow mountain lying near the equator, where the
greatest extremes both of soil and climate meet. Still, the
character and distribution of the plants to be met with on
Kilimanjaro are not difficult to understand if the following
points are kept in view : that the soil is derived from volcanic
rocks; that the extent of the mountain is much greater
towards the south than towards the north, and that here too
its slope is more gentle ; that the southern side is well watered,
while the north is extremely arid ; and that the southern face
of Kibo is covered with ice from 19,700 to 13,000 feet (the
limit of the snowfall being 1500 feet lower), while in the dry
season the ice on Mawenzi entirely disappears.

According to Mr. Chanler, the belt of tree-steppe at the
bottom of the mountain stretches upward to a height of from
2460 to 2950 feet in the south, and to 4900 feet in the north,
the trees gradually increasing in luxuriance as they ascend.
Along the course of the streams (in Arusha, Kahé, and Taveta,
for example) belts of wood run out into the surrounding

steppes, and as the streams on the south side are extremely numerous, the wooded strips frequently unite and form more or less extensive forests. In these the trees are of the characteristic tropical type, and, favoured by the greater warmth of the steppe region, they occasionally excel those of the true forest zone in luxuriance of growth.

Between 2950 feet and 3600 feet the tree-steppe gradually passes into thick bush. At 3600 feet the bush reaches the lower limit of the mist zone, and gives place to the hilly country of Jagga—the cultivated region of Kilimanjaro—which extends to an elevation of 6200 feet. On the north side the fields of Jagga are represented by a grassy plateau, which runs along the mountain side at the same elevation, and affords a permanent home for the Masai and their cattle.

From 6200 feet—the lower limit of the cloud zone—the primeval forest, well watered and well drained, stretches upward along an increasingly steep subsoil of solid rock, till it reaches the thermal limit at about 9800 feet. In the north the forest is limited to a strip between 7200 and 9100 feet, and in the north-west it disappears altogether, and is replaced by shrubs and grass. From the primeval forest on the south side, belts of wood run upwards along the more sheltered watercourses and hollows, but even these cease at 10,500 feet, which may be stated as the maximum limit of the growth of trees.

Above the forest the grass-lands rise to about 12,800 feet; they are at first studded with shrubs, but these gradually disappear with the increasing elevation. Above the grass-lands proper comes a region where the grass and herbs appear only in clumps and tufts—the region of the highest flowering plants on Kilimanjaro. Both on the south and on the north side the flowering plants combine to form a tolerably close belt of vegetation up to a height of 14,100 feet. Above that they appear only in isolated strips and patches, where peculiarly favoured by local conditions. Above 15,400 feet on the east of Kibo, and 15,550 feet on the west of Mawenzi, they disappear entirely, the last representatives being a sparse sprinkling of low, creeping herbs. Above the limits mentioned the existence of flowering plants becomes impossible, owing to the periodical accumulations of snow, the low night temperature, and the inhospitable nature of the ground, which consists solely of bare volcanic rocks or barren blocks of lava. The region of the summit is reserved solely for the lichens, of which several species continue up to the ice-line, while two go beyond it, and occur even on the rocks of the Kaiser Wilhelm's Peak.

Omitting the cultivated zone of Jagga, which ought properly to be included in the bush region, the vegetation of Kilimanjaro thus naturally divides itself into the six following zones :—Tree-steppe, 300 to 2950 feet ; bush, 2950 to 6200 feet ; forest, 6200 to 9800 feet ; grass-land, 9800 to 12,800 feet ; flowering plants, 12,800 to 15,500 feet ; lichens, 15,500 to 19,700 feet. Of these, the two first gradually pass into each other, whilst between all the others the transition is sharply defined. In the case of the forest, man as well as nature has been at work, so that its limits have been determined as much by the hoe and the firebrand as by temperature and moisture. All the others are the result of natural conditions, and above all, of climate.

The effects of climate are more strikingly seen above the ice-line, where the ice at once records the work of heat and cold, than in the regions further down the mountain, where the vegetation is affected more gradually by extremes of temperature. To show on what data my conclusions have been based, I here submit a table showing the minimum temperature of the atmosphere within the different zones of

vegetation, and the temperature during the day of some of
the streams in the same regions :—

Locality.		Min. Temp. of Atmosphere.	Temperature of Water.	
Dehu (1800 feet) . . . ⎫		67.1	71.6	⎫
		66.2	70.7	
Habari (3170 feet) . . ⎮		63.5	65.3	from
Himo (3020 feet) . . . ⎬		64.4	65.3	Mawenzi.
		66.2	68.0	
Moji stream (2820 feet) ⎮ Tree-steppe at foot	of mountain.	64.4	65.3	
Ngombere (2950 feet) . ⎭		62.6	65.3	
		50.9	64.4	⎫
		51.8	64.4	⎮
Weri-weri (3930 feet) . ⎰ Bush		50.0	63.5	from Kibo.
		55.4	63.5	
Kikafu (4440 feet) . . ⎱		54.5	63.5	
		54.5	60.8	⎭
		42.8	52.7	⎫
Rua (6430 feet) . . . Lower limit of forest ⎰		46.4	53.6	
		47.3	53.6	
		46.4	52.7	from
Mue (9480 feet) . . . ⎫		32.0	45.5	Mawenzi.
		32.9	46.4	
⎮ Upper limit of forest		26.6	44.6	
		27.5	44.6	⎭
		26.6	44.6	
Kiboso (9940 feet) . . ⎭		28.4	44.6	⎫ from Kibo.
		29.3	45.5	⎭
		17.6	42.8	⎫
Snow-spring rivulet (12,710 feet) ; Grass-land ⎰		19.4	41.0	from
		22.1	41.0	Mawenzi.
		19.4	41.9	⎭

Kilimanjaro is thus a mountain on which every con-
ceivable climate is to be met with. The inhabited zone is
limited to Jagga, however, a belt of country occupying the
southern side of the mountain between 3600 and 6200 feet,
and having an area (exclusive of the fern zone) of 300 square
miles. Below Jagga, owing to the barrenness of the steppe,
the country is not habitable except along the banks of the
streams, as in Taveta, Kahé, and Arusha ; above Jagga there
are the eternal mist and rain of the forest, and above the forest
the cold and snows of the Alps. On the north side the want
of streams makes agriculture impracticable, but the pasture-

land is good, and hence it has been taken possession of by the Masai and their great herds of cattle.

But although confined to such narrow limits, Jagga is a splendid country ; indeed it would be one vast garden if it were not for the endless wars waged between the various petty states. The absorption of the smaller states by the larger has already begun ; and if only that these continual feuds might be put a stop to, it is highly desirable that the process should continue.

From a European standpoint, the commercial value of the products of Kilimanjaro so far is *nil*. The timber is worthless, indiarubber is scarce, the orchilla lichen certainly not common, and minerals are almost absent. At the same time, the south side of the mountain offers all the essential conditions by which the country might be turned to good account. The soil is exceedingly fertile, water is abundant, and the climate equable. Coffee, tea, cinchona, cinnamon, and vanilla might be introduced with the greatest advantage. The inhabitants, moreover, are friendly, and are accustomed to obey their chiefs implicitly, and (an unusual thing among negro tribes) the men as well as the women are used to agricultural labour.

As compared with the other mountainous countries of East Africa—with the best of which, Usambara, I am well acquainted —Jagga is the only district which approaches the tropical high-lands of southern India, Ceylon, Java, and the Philippine Islands, of which I can also speak from experience. In fertility it far exceeds the narrow strip of coast-line which is included in the German sphere of interest, and the mountain climate gives it a further advantage over the latter. It has the advantage over Usambara, Paré, and Ugweno in its soil, in the certainty and regularity of its rainfall, the number and distribution of its streams, and its comparatively large population ; yet each of the districts I have named is a little mountain paradise in the unending waste of barren, almost uninhabited steppe, savannah, and bush, which constitutes eighty per cent. of our East African Protectorate.

In order rightly to understand the contrast between these mountainous districts and other parts of East Africa—in order justly to appreciate their value—it becomes necessary to take a brief general survey of the physical peculiarities of the whole region.

The German sphere of interest is a tropical region with definite alternating dry and wet seasons. It is mostly included in the southern hemisphere, and as the rains always occur between the winter and the summer solstice, the wet seasons accordingly extend from October to January, and from the middle of April to the end of May. Throughout their whole extent the East African steppes are entirely dependent for their supply of moisture on these periodic rains, and in the intervals between are exposed to the most intense heat. As we should naturally expect, these wide extremes of climate produce a marked effect on the soil and vegetation of the region, and entirely determine its fertility.

In the dry season a high temperature during the day is followed by a low temperature during the night: the ground is rapidly heated to an unusual degree and then as rapidly cools down, as the result of which the rocks split up, and the soil is dried and cracked to a considerable depth. On the sudden commencement of the wet season, the rain descends in torrents, and penetrates through the soil to the underlying rock. The surface layer of loose earth it partly washes away, and its chemical action on the rock below is no less destructive. Under the action of sun and wind the ground rapidly dries again, and from being light and porous gradually becomes of a clayey and cellular character, and being impregnated with oxide of iron, assumes the brick-red colour which has won for the " red soil " of Africa the name of " laterite."

Under these conditions—which correspond exactly to what Pechuel-Loesche describes as characteristic of West Africa also—there can be no accumulation of humus, and the effect on the vegetation may easily be conceived. The whole period of growth, from the first shooting of the seed to the ripening of the fruit, is compressed into the brief interval of the rainy season, and passes over the land like a gladsome wave of green, only to be succeeded by a dull, dark wave of grey. Leaf and flower and fruit follow each other in rapid succession, and the grass in many places springs to a height of over six feet; but on the approach of the dry season the verdant thicket just as quickly turns to grey, dry touchwood, to be gradually cleared away by the natives as they burn it down before preparing the ground for fresh plantations.

Considering the wonderful change which comes over the aspect of the land, it is easy to understand how two travellers who had visited the region at different seasons of the year might be led to form the most opposite conclusions, as to its fertility. It is not enough to judge by appearances however; the true index to the nature of the soil and of the climate lies in the type and structural peculiarities of the vegetation, dependent as these are on the character of the environment.

Generally speaking, the vegetation of central East Africa consists mainly of scanty, tufted grass, interspersed with the stunted forms typical of the arid bush and tree-steppes, with a sprinkling of deciduous trees and shrubs of extremely hardy character. The woods are confined to narrow strips along the margin of the streams, or to the vicinity of lakes and marshes, and there is nowhere any approach to the vast stretches of primeval forest such as are found in South America and the Indian Archipelago. The flora bears equally little resemblance to the carefully selected, well-arranged collections of tropical plants brought together in our greenhouses and botanic gardens. From these, as a rule, we should form as erroneous an impression of tropical vegetation in its natural state as if we were to judge of the character and civilisation of the natives from the artistic sketches and groups of weapons, ornaments, and household utensils commonly displayed in our exhibitions and museums.

Important modifications take place in the prevailing character of the East African climate and flora in regions which, owing to elevation above or proximity to the sea, enjoy a local rainfall independent of the regular wet season. As every one knows, when the heated air rises from the slopes of a mountain or plateau region, the colder air rushes in to supply its place, and thus an atmospheric current sets in towards the mountain. If the elevation of the ground is so great that the wind thus established is sensibly cooled as it reaches the higher altitudes, or if the wind already contains sufficient moisture to be condensed on coming into contact with outstanding obstacles, clouds are formed and the moisture falls again in the form of rain. These rains are strictly local, the wind parting with all its moisture among the mountains before it reaches the surrounding country.

The same thing happens in the neighbourhood of the sea or of great lakes. During the day a current sets in towards the land, and the moisture is deposited all along the shore across a belt more or less broad, according to the conformation of the land. Here, too, the clouds are sucked dry before they can penetrate beyond the mountains, and the wind, blowing inland, carries with it nothing but drought.

In the regions subject to these local rains—which provide an unfailing supply of moisture even during the dry season—the laterite soil is replaced by a layer of humus, and the flora of the bush and tree-steppes is exchanged for the richer vegetation of more favoured tropical lands. Thus, in Africa, fertility goes by the rule of contraries—the broad plateau lands are sterile, and fertility is limited to the edge of the plateau, the coast, and the isolated mountain regions. In these districts tropical products of all kinds may be raised. Here, accordingly, and along the banks of the streams, we find the only settled population, while the steppes are left to nomadic tribes who constantly roam from place to place, wherever there is sufficient pasture for their cattle.

The greater part, not only of the German sphere of interest, but of all Equatorial Africa, is a sterile, thinly-populated wilderness, which is barely capable of supplying the frugal wants of the negro, and has no natural products of value to Europeans. From the nature of the soil the latter could not be raised even if they were introduced. "One-fifth of German East Africa is good land," says Wissman; "the rest is a barren waste"—a remark which is in curious contrast to the optimistic statement of Dr. Peters, "that for extent and fertility it will stand comparison with any tropical colony in the world." I myself have visited many of the more important tropical colonies, including India, Ceylon, Java, Cuba, and the Philippine Islands, and I am sorry to say I cannot endorse Dr. Peters' opinion.

But the greater part of tropical East Africa is not only sterile—it is unhealthy. Fever is everywhere common, and though the attacks are more frequent and more severe at the coast and near the rivers, the plateaux and the habitable mountain regions by no means escape. Europeans and negroes alike seem liable to be attacked, as I know from experience among the members of my caravan; and even the natives are not altogether exempt, both Mandara and Mareale having been repeatedly obliged to draw upon my stock of quinine. These remarks are corroborated by the statements of Dr. Kohlstock, who, as surgeon-major of the native troops, has had a wide experience. Those travellers suffer least who are constantly on the move, and who do not stay long in any one place, but not one in a thousand escapes scot free, or if he gets off easily with fever, he is all the more likely to fall a victim to dysentery. The coolness of the nights, consequent on the cloudless atmosphere, is hailed by Europeans as a welcome relief after the heat of the day ; but the abrupt changes of temperature interfere with the action of the skin and other organs, causing rheumatism, and generally diminishing the power of the organism to resist disease.

In East Africa it is impossible for Europeans to live continuously for any length of time, as in the healthier climate of the northern and southern parts of the continent ; and, on the other hand, money cannot be made so rapidly during a short stay as in the fertile regions of tropical South America, the West Indies, and the Sunda Archipelago, which are also unsuitable for a prolonged residence. All apparently successful examples of acclimatisation have been short-lived, none ever extending beyond a single generation. This fact would be less hotly contested if the representations of enthusiasts and interested parties were taken for what they are worth, and if people would only learn to distinguish clearly between North, South, and Central Africa. At present, in the minds not only of the ignorant many, but of a large proportion of the cultured few, " Africa " means a confused jumble of " niggers " and " savages," with heat, lions, deserts, palm-trees, and plantations as an appropriate setting ; and he would indeed be a notable exception who remembered that the word Africa includes a whole continent, extending through 70° of latitude and embracing every imaginable climate, and that, therefore, remarks and observations which are perfectly true of the south or north, may be utterly inapplicable to the more central regions. This criticism may seem severe, but it is absolutely true.

Before Germany awakened to a sense of her need of colonies, the most desirable parts of the globe were already taken up, and there was nothing better than Equatorial Africa to fall back upon; and the greatest service that Dr. Peters has rendered to his country has been the bringing of this large extent of territory under her sway. Other nations have sought to share it with us partly because they too had the desire to extend their dominions, and were naturally unwilling that one should absorb what had hitherto been free to all; partly because they saw their vested interests threatened both within the region that is now German and in others adjoining it. In the furore created by the glowing representations of our early pioneers, the more measured language of their predecessors was forgotten, and it was generally believed in Europe that in annexing East Africa we had succeeded in carrying off a prize. From the outset, however, a very different opinion prevailed in Africa, as I myself can bear witness. I happened to be at the South African gold-fields at the very time when, emulating the example of Dr. Peters, our agents and explorers were busy hoisting the German flag in every direction. I was astonished to find that in the Transvaal the events which were creating such a lively sensation in Europe excited little or no attention, whilst colonial projects regarding other parts of Africa were discussed with the keenest interest. The moral and national significance of our colonial policy could not, of course, be appreciated by foreigners; the matter was looked at purely in its practical aspect, and it was generally considered that we had been anything but "practical." Equally little importance was attached to Stanley's sensational journeys, which in Europe were said to have opened up the interior of Africa as the land of the future for European enterprise. The reason for this apparent want of enthusiasm was not far to seek. Among the daring hunters and traders of Natal, the Transvaal, and the Orange Free State, there are dozens who have undergone greater hardships and overcome greater difficulties than any Stanley and many more of our popular heroes ever had to face; and they judge accordingly by a very different standard from that which is applied by the romantic arm-chair explorers and unthinking hero-worshippers of Europe. For similar reasons their views on the subject of the partition of Central Africa are equally common-sense and practical, and broadly speaking, the only regions whose value was supposed to correspond at all to the popular estimate were Uganda, and what was formerly known as the Equatorial Province.

My own opinion concurred exactly with the views current in South Africa as regards the East African plateau regions. We ought all along to have made a point of confining, our operations to the coast; and although, for political reasons, that is no longer possible on an extended scale, the same course should be pursued within our own sphere of interest, for here, as in West Africa, it is the seaports and the coast region that are most capable of development. The whole history of the exploration and exploitation of Equatorial Africa—by the Portuguese, Spanish, Dutch, French, and English—points to the same conclusion. From the latter half of the fifteenth century downwards, these colonising nations, not without frequently coming into collision, have set themselves, with untiring perseverance and enormous expenditure of capital, to develop the resources of this part of the continent, but wherever they have endeavoured to push their commercial conquests far into the interior, the attempt has been rendered abortive either through the unhealthiness of the climate or the unproductiveness of the soil. The same history is being repeated at the present day. Look where you will throughout the more central regions of the dark continent—at the trading stations on the Congo, or the mission stations on Lake Nyassa and the Victoria Nyanza— all alike breathe the air of a churchyard, all alike wear the " Hippocratic face."

To come now to the trade between the interior and the coast. As an opening for commerce, Africa has frequently been called " a second India." A more misleading metaphor could scarcely be imagined. There is little or no resemblance between the Africa of to-day and the India which lay ready to the hands of the English traders a hundred years ago ; and the resemblance between our modern trading companies and the old East India Company is scarcely greater. India, when the English Company first began to open it up, was already densely populated and in a high state of civilisation, easy communication had been established between the interior and the coast, the climate was tolerable, the natural resources were enormous—advantages every one of which are in Central Africa conspicuous by their absence. Seldom or never does the East African negro come down to the coast, bringing with him the produce of his fields or the spoils of the chase ; partly he is too lazy, and partly he has a very reasonable fear of being robbed. Nowhere does nature sow her treasures with unsparing hand, but scatters them thinly over wide tracts of country, whence they must be carried by Arab and Swahili traders, who are content to work under conditions which a European would consider intolerable. Their caravans either consist solely of slaves, or are composed of small independent dealers, each trading for his own profit. To them it is a matter of indifference whether the expedition returns within the time calculated or extends over six months or a year longer. Time is of no value to them, and the Indian to whom they dispose of their wares at the coast or Zanzibar, and who has them completely in his power by an elaborate system of money-lending, knows that he can always find a ready and profitable market among the European commercial firms.

Yet small as is the expenditure of capital required under these conditions, a profitable trade in certain articles, such as oil-seeds, orchilla lichen, cotton, copal, and the like, is only possible throughout a limited area, extending inland to no great distance from the coast. Here these articles have their natural geographical limit, and immediately it is passed, the cost of transport exceeds the commercial value of the goods, except in the case of a few special products, such as india-rubber and ivory. The traffic in the latter is the monopoly of the great Arab traders, who penetrate to the interior and travel over enormous tracts of country, stealing not only the ivory but the natives, whom they utilise to carry their merchandise to the coast. This is the only way in which the ivory trade can be made a source of profit, and it is simply nonsense to think that it might be developed by making roads and railways, for all the ivory that could be collected in the course of a year might be brought to the coast by a single train, and the other products are not of sufficient value to make a railway pay. Roads in most places would be practically valueless, since they could not follow the course of the rivers, and therefore, at least during the dry season, would be unsuitable for oxen, which in South Africa, in spite of the tsetse fly, make excellent substitutes for horses. Neither horses nor camels can stand the Central African climate; elephants are too dear, unless the native species could be tamed; and donkeys offer no essential advantage over the ordinary porter.

In short, until we are prepared to leave " commercial

prospects" in the background, and advance solely in the name of Christianity and civilisation, we may as well abandon all our Utopian schemes for the opening up of inner Africa. Even then I should not care to prophesy too hopefully of the result, for what have we to show to-day for all the money and all the lives and all the earnest labours of many devoted missionaries that have been spent in the endeavour to shed a ray of light across the darkness of African heathendom? How is it that around the mission stations we find the natives as a whole totally unaffected by the preaching of the Gospel, the only converts being a few individuals who find it to their material advantage to enter the service of the missionaries, or slaves whom the latter have bought and freed? How is it that such an amiable missionary as Mackay of Uganda, in reviewing the results of his twelve years' toil, should bitterly sum up with the conclusion that every effort would prove in vain until the backbone of native indifference had been broken? The spiritual teachings of the Gospel are utterly unintelligible to the darkened mind of the Bantu negro; the practical doctrines and ceremonies of Islam appeal to him much more readily; yet I doubt if the negro would ever make even a good Mahommedan.

Apparently the African colossus is not to be overthrown by the pigmy race of men; nature claims the land for her own undisputed sway. But as Edward Dicey pertinently observes, speaking of the present epidemic of "African fever," the effort after the ideal and the unattainable has exercised a magic charm over the minds of men in all times and in all ages; and undertakings of inconceivable magnitude draw the multitude like a magnet, if only they are placed in the proper perspective. The search for the North Pole, and the projects for submerging the Sahara and cutting the isthmus of Panama, are striking illustrations of the truth of this remark. His

Majesty the King of the Belgians has sacrificed his millions
to one of these Utopian dreams, and Stanley notwithstanding,
he will one day wake to find he has been chasing an illusion,
as already all must see who can read colonial history, and do
not look at Africa through rose-coloured spectacles.

The limits of the German and English spheres of interest
have now been determined by international agreement, and
while in East Africa England has decidedly had the best of
the bargain, we, on the other hand, have had the advantage
in Europe in obtaining Heligoland in exchange for Vitu and
the Somál coast. England has secured for herself the backbone of the African Continent, and free communication
between her possessions in the north and in the south,
although possibly the value of the latter concession is more
imaginary than real. She has Mombaza, the best harbour on
the east coast, and Taveta, the only good caravan station in
the Kilimanjaro region. In the Tana she gets the most
important river, and in Somál-land a tract of country which is
comparatively fertile. She further retains the right-of-way
to the Upper Nile, and in Uganda she possesses at once the
most highly cultivated and the most densely populated region
in Equatorial Africa, and the key to the Súdan and Egypt.
The latter is already half English, and it cannot for ever remain
in the state of turmoil created by the recent Mahdist movement. In the south, by securing the free passage of the
Zambezi, England establishes the communication between
Nyassa and the Matabele country on the one hand, and between Nyassa and the Indian Ocean on the other. But the
greatest gain of all has been the proclamation of a British
Protectorate over Zanzibar and Pemba, by which England
acquires not only the right over two large and productive
spice islands and the main seat of African commerce, but
also the control of the Sultan and of the great proportion of

the Arabs, who, as extensive borrowers from the Indians—the capitalist class in East Africa—are completely in the latter's power.

Yet in England, notwithstanding these advantages, there is a daily increasing number of intelligent and far-seeing men, who, through the medium of the press and of the platform, take every opportunity of bidding their countrymen beware of the many apparently plausible schemes for the opening up of inner Africa, and even urge that England should wash her hands of the region altogether, and endeavour to exchange it for the German colony of New Guinea. The cry is a warning to Germany as well as England. Good as are the effects of our patriotic and colonial ardour in many ways, it is apt to blind us to the real value of the possessions we have acquired. The wine of enthusiasm must be mixed with the water of fact if it is to stimulate yet not intoxicate, and in this modern drama, of which Africa is the theatre, we have need of dispassionate and sober-minded judges to act as chorus, however thankless the rôle may be.

Broadly speaking, our only practical plan in East Africa is to limit all our schemes for the development of trade and the cultivation of the soil to the region of the coast and the mountainous districts in its immediate vicinity—more especially the tract of country between Usambara and Kilimanjaro. From a political point of view it may be looked upon as advantageous for Emin Pasha and Wissman to establish stations in the interior—they will always be useful to hold the Arabs and our neighbours in check; but unless for the purely philanthropic object of putting down the slave trade, it is a mistake to suppose that we shall derive any benefit from schemes such as that for placing steamers on the great lakes for example, for except slaves the region of the lakes neither does nor could produce any articles of sufficient commercial value to defray the cost of maintaining the steamers and of transport to the coast.

True, on each of the great lakes—Nyassa, Tanganyika, and the Victoria Nyanza—the English have already either a steamboat or a sailing vessel; but these belong to the English Missionary Societies, and are not expected to "pay" in the commercial sense of the word. It is proposed further to supplement this inland fleet by another steamer for the Victoria Nyanza; but the project has the practical end in view of completing the line of communication through English territory to the Nile and Upper Egypt, and of establishing a connection between the British Protectorate of Uganda and the terminus of the recently inaugurated railway between Mombaza and Kavirondo. I doubt very much, however, whether this railway will ever get far beyond the cutting of the first sod, a ceremony which has been duly performed with a view to attracting additional shareholders. In any case, for the reasons we have so often repeated, it can never be made to pay, except as far as Taveta and Kilimanjaro, the trade with which England would thus absorb entirely. At the same time, to start an opposition German line would be utter folly, for the trade would barely be equal to the support of one, and the initial expense caused by the difficulty of laying the line through German territory would be much greater. To the west of the Usambara and Paré chain the ground is rough and in many places marshy, and to the east, although the ground is level, there is the Rufu swamp to be considered. Even then we should not be able to run the line as far as Taveta, the latter being English, and Taveta, owing to its natural advantages, is the only really suitable site for a terminus. Arusha could never be utilised for this purpose, as all around the ground is too marshy; and besides, it is too far from Kilimanjaro.

My own conclusions on the subject of East African colonisation are these :—Instead of wasting time and money in trying to open up the interior by railways and other unsuitable means, let us confine our operations to the coast, and leave the natives to bring their produce to us after their own time-honoured fashion, which would seem after all to be the one best suited to the nature of the country. Let us devote all our energies to the improvement of our harbours at Tanga, Pangani, Bagamoyo, and Dar-es-Salaam, among which the last possesses great natural advantages over all the others. Let us forcibly prevent the *export* of slaves, though, since the whole internal economy of the country is based on the principle of slavery, we ought not as yet to demand its entire abolition. A moderate house-tax might be imposed, and light export and import duties, the burden of which would mostly fall on the Indians; and the unscrupulous system of money-lending practised by the latter, which gives them such enormous power over the Arab and negro sections of the population, should be rigorously repressed.

Meanwhile we may begin to develop the natural resources of the region by introducing European methods of cultivation into Usambara, whence, if they prove successful, we may proceed further along the same line in the direction of Paré and Ugweno. As we gradually make our way from station to station a light tramway might be laid down, which then, and only then, might be expected to pay from the profits on the produce of the cultivated districts between. In the cultivation of the more valuable products—tobacco, vanilla, tea, and cocoa—free native labourers under European overseers might be employed—an experiment which has already been tried with success in several districts between the coast and Usambara. For the less important articles of export—ground-nuts, cocoa-nuts, and oil-yielding plants generally—

in the raising of which European superintendence may be dispensed with, the system of compulsory labour in vogue in the Philippine Islands might be introduced with advantage. By this system, as in the "boss" system practised in South Africa, the natives are not paid for their labour, but with the consent of the chiefs are compelled to cultivate certain products, which the white traders pledge themselves to buy at a definite, pre-arranged rate.

The result of such a system to the negroes themselves is invaluable. Without being enslaved, they acquire the habit of regular work, and thus make the first step in the direction of a higher plane of civilisation. It is not to be expected that the civilisation which has gradually become part and parcel of the European in the hundreds of years it has taken to develop is to be suddenly slipped on to the shoulders of the negro, like some new garment which would be sure to fit. This fact is so self-evident that it savours almost of a truism, yet apparently it cannot be too often repeated. Again and again we hear it said that the negro is only a child, and all that he needs is to be trained like a child. A child indeed he is, but of most sanguine temperament and immature instincts. He will never be taught merely by good example and fine precepts, as the English missionaries would seem to believe; he must be trained in the school of hard work, and he must be forced to work if he cannot be prevailed upon to do so voluntarily. Moreover, as colonists we have to do not with the education of an individual, perhaps a peculiarly intelligent and well-disposed individual here and there, but with the education of whole tribes and peoples whose moral and spiritual training must necessarily be a work of generations. *We* have to work, and why not the negro also? The true riches of Equatorial Africa lie, not in its mineral treasures, not in the wealth and variety of its animal and vegetable products, but in the latent capacity of its people for labour.

"Slowly but surely" must be our motto, for a colony, like Rome, is not built in a day. In a colony like East Africa especially, where the natural resources are comparatively poor, there must be years, nay, decades of patient toil and patient waiting, before we can hope to reap the fruits of success. Then, too, a new era will commence for Kilimanjaro. The area open for cultivation must always be confined to the region between the arid soil of the steppes and the perpetual mist and rain of the primeval forest; but in Jagga there will be ample room for every one for a long while to come, and by the time that we are in a position to take up all the ground at our disposal, it is to be hoped we shall have come into possession of Taveta also, when the most fertile region in East Africa will lie open to German capital and German enterprise.

Meanwhile, Kilimanjaro, like the Nile, "is settled." The African giant is vanquished—his hoary head has been laid bare. But still for many future years the mountain will prove an ample field for detailed exploration. To scientists of all kinds it offers unexampled attractions; to the botanist and the meteorologist especially its loftier slopes promise an almost undreamed of harvest. And still in the future as in the past the "Ethiopian Mount Olympus" will remain the wonder of all beholders; and until the time when it too shall dissolve and pass away, its majestic grandeur, its beauty and its solitude, shall quicken the fancy and excite the feelings of all who in the silent language of nature can trace the voice of an eternal Godhead.

APPENDIX.

APPENDIX.

I.

COPY OF THE AGREEMENT BETWEEN THE INDIAN MER-
CHANT SIWA HAJI AND DR. HANS MEYER ANENT THE
ENGAGEMENT OF A CARAVAN.

I. Siwa Haji hereby undertakes to engage for Dr. Hans Meyer a caravan
consisting of two headmen and sixty-two porters, each of whom shall carry
a load of 60 lbs. weight. These shall accompany Dr. Hans Meyer or his
representative to Kilimanjaro, and shall pledge themselves to obey him or
his representative under all circumstances.

II. Siwa Haji undertakes to have the whole caravan in readiness to start
from Zanzibar at any date after August 20th, on receipt of ten days' notice
from Dr. Hans Meyer.

III. Dr. Hans Meyer undertakes to pay Siwa Haji for the hire of the
said sixty-four men at the rate of eleven dollars per head per month, reckoning from the date of registration of the contract to the date of the return to
Zanzibar.

IV. Throughout the journey Dr. Hans Meyer will supply the men with
the necessary food and medicines, and will pay the toll for right of way
(*hongo*).

V. Siwa Haji will refund to Dr. Hans Meyer any extra expense incurred
by the latter in supplying the place of deserters.

VI. Siwa Haji undertakes all risk of death, sickness, or desertion among
the porters, and pledges himself to keep the caravan up to its full strength
of sixty-two men. To this end Siwa Haji will send ten men over and above
the stipulated number, who will act as Asikari (soldiers), so long as they are
not required as porters. For each of these Dr. Hans Meyer will pay Siwa
Haji at the rate of eleven dollars per month, dating from the day on which
the man begins to act as porter.

VII. If a man deserts, leaving his load or his gun by the wayside, so
that the load or the gun is lost, or if a man deserts, taking his load or

his gun with him, Siwa Haji undertakes to pay to Dr. Hans Meyer an average indemnity of twenty-seven dollars for a load, and three dollars for a gun. Siwa Haji does not hold himself responsible for any loss which Dr. Meyer may sustain in any other way.

VIII. If a man dies, or deserts, or has to be left behind on account of sickness, Dr. Hans Meyer will pay the monthly hire due up to the date of the casualty.

IX. Dr. Hans Meyer will pay in advance the hire of the entire caravan for three months. From this sum Siwa Haji will pay to each man such a proportion as shall have been previously agreed upon.

X. Dr. Hans Meyer will defray the cost of the passage of the caravan from Zanzibar to the coast, and from the coast back to Zanzibar.

XI. Dr. Meyer will obtain the consent of the Sultan for the formation of the caravan.

XII. Dr. Meyer undertakes to engage the caravan for a period of not less than three months.

(Signed)   DR. HANS MEYER.
,,   SIWA HAJI.

ZANZIBAR, *August* 20, 1889.

Witnessed at the German and English Consulates.

Note.—The point of most importance to me in the above Agreement was that Siwa Haji undertook all risk of desertion (Art. VI.). The point of most importance to Siwa Haji was that I paid him the sum of eleven dollars per head per month (Art. III.), while he paid to the soldiers and porters only the customary hire of six dollars (Art. IX.).   H. M.

II.

NOTE ON THE GEOLOGY OF THE KILIMANJARO REGION.

BY DR. C. A. TENNE, BERLIN.

THE geological collection submitted to me by Dr. Hans Meyer and his companion, Herr Ludwig Purtscheller, as the result of their recent expedition to Kilimanjaro, includes 331 specimens, and extends over three districts, namely, the region between the coast and Kilimanjaro, the Ugweno Country, and Mount Kilimanjaro itself.

In Sadebeck's geological map of East Africa [1] five formations are shown as occurring between the coast from Takaungu to Pangani and Taveta. Immediately behind the alluvial deposits there is a belt of carboniferous

[1] Alexander Sadebeck, *Geology of East Africa*, reprinted from Von der Decken's *Travels.* Leipzig and Heidelberg, 1873.

sandstone, followed by a band of purely carboniferous strata, to the west of which are metamorphic sandstones and schists, and finally the more recent volcanic rocks.

From Dr. Meyer's specimens it would appear that the shales in the vicinity of the Bandarin camp contain ironstone nodules. On the road to Maungu, immediately the Rabai rivulet is crossed, there is a succession of arenaceous limestones, fine and coarse sandstones, and quartz-felspar conglomerates, probably derived from the gneiss region of Ndara, where certain strata are rich in bisilicates (biotite and hornblende), whilst in others these elements are almost entirely absent. In the steppes between Ndara and Taveta the gneiss is overlaid by sandstones and limestones, but occasionally crops out and rises into hills, such as the Javia Hill, between Matate and Bura. The steppes also contribute a few fragments of minerals probably derived from pegmatitic veins in the crystalline rocks, the presence of which is indicated by the specimens of quartz from between Bura and Taveta.

From Lanjoro Mdogo comes a specimen of red friable soil (laterite ?), said to overlie gneiss, and probably to be regarded as the product of the weathering of the same rock.

The above remarks on the formations of Ndara are supplemented by a note on the label attached to one of the specimens, to the effect that the beds of biotitic gneiss (rich in granitic elements) on the west side of the mountain strike north and south and dip towards the west.

The Ugweno Country.—In Sadebeck's map the strata of the Ugweno Country are classified among the crystalline schists. Dr. Meyer sends thirty-seven specimens which fully bear out this classification. They are mostly derived from the western, southern, and eastern slopes of the mountains, but a few come from Gamualla in the north-west, and one or two from the summit of Ngovi at the north-eastern extremity of the range. All these are varieties of gneiss in which orthoclase felspar and quartz, with hornblende, biotite, and occasionally augite, predominate. The gneiss in the vicinity of the Mrushunga contributes several specimens of specular iron, while in the neighbourhood of Naguvu the decomposition of the ore has resulted in the formation of a deposit of ferruginous sand. As in the region between the coast and Taveta, formations resembling laterite also occur. These are the result of subaërial action, and they contain ironstone nodules (rich in hydro-oxides of iron), from which, together with the ferruginous sand above referred to, the natives " obtain by smelting as much iron as they require." The collection includes several fragments of the clay tubes through which the blast is conveyed to the furnace; these are encrusted with a coating of oxidised iron.

Throughout the region the strata are said to strike generally north and south ; in the west they dip at a high angle towards the west (8o° in the specular iron between the Mrushunga and Wangobi) ; in the east they dip

towards the east (gneiss from Ngovi, occurring at an altitude of 5400 feet,
and from between Ngovi and the Rufu swamp at an altitude of 4900 feet).
On Mount Gamualla, however, the strata (augitic gneiss) strike N.N.E. 15°
S.S.W., and dip E.S.E. at an angle of 53°, while the amphiboline gneiss
occurring at an altitude of 5600 feet between Naguvu and Ngovi strikes
N.E. 35° S.W., and dips at an angle of 45° towards E.S.E.

Kilimanjaro.—The geological collection made by Dr. Meyer during his
former visit to Kilimanjaro, which now forms part of the mineralogical
collection in Leipzig, has already been the subject of a thorough investigation
by J. S. Hyland, Esq., of Liverpool.[1] Besides several examples of pegmatite,
one of gneiss, and one of amphibolite from between the coast and Kilimanjaro, Mr. Hyland found representatives of the following types of rock :—
Felspathic basalt (7 localities), Tephrite (3 loc.), Nepheline basanite (5 loc.),
Leucitic basanite (1 loc.), Nepheline basalt (1 loc.), Limburgite (6 loc.),
Basaltic obsidian (1 loc.).

In the present collection, which includes 248 specimens, the same types are
represented, and, so far as my examination goes, there are none that are new.

According to Mr. Hyland, *felspathic basalt* occurs on the Lumi at Taveta,
on the shores of Lake Jipé to the south of Taveta, and again below Marangu.
Specimens from these districts have not reached me ; but in the new collection felspathic basalt is shown to occur farther to the west of Marangu,
between Marangu and Moji, at an altitude of 4260 feet, "on the paths and
in the river-beds, and also cropping out at the surface." I am therefore
able to corroborate Mr. Hyland's opinion that the plagioclase basalt originated
from Kibo, from Mawenzi, and from the two cones on the saddle lying
nearest to the latter peak.

On Kibo the typical rock seems to form a stream running from the
crater towards the south-east in the direction of Dr. Meyer's camp at the
Mué, specimens from the latter place occurring in the collection examined by
Mr. Hyland. From the Mué—judging from the specimens in the new collection—the stream continues downwards to an elevation of 12,470 feet.
The rock appears at the surface only up to a level of 18,700 feet ; the specimens found below 12,470 feet at the Weri-weri, and at the junction of the
Nasere and the Kikafu, have probably been brought down by the streams.
The rock is distinguished by large plagioclase crystals, the faces of which, on
lateral cleavage, appear as rounded discs the size of a shilling ; on basal
cleavage the crystals are seen to be elongated, with rounded ends and many
parallel striæ. On the label attached to a specimen from the eastern lava
hill on the saddle (14,800 feet) there is a note to the effect that the strata
strike north and south and dip towards the south at an angle of 23°. From

[1] J. S. Hyland, *Ueber die Gesteine des Kilimandscharo und dessen Umgebung.* Tschermak's Mineralogische und Petrographische Mitteilungen X.

this it would appear that the stream of lava has flowed from the crater and spread out in the form of a wide sheet.

From the west side of Mawenzi comes a single specimen of felspathic basalt, said to have occurred at an elevation of 16,700 feet. The north side is well represented, however, and the felspar crystals are of the typical plagioclase form. Here, at an elevation of 16,400 feet, the strata are said to be " 150–250 feet thick," and again strike north and south, dipping towards. the north-west at an angle of 25°. Lower down, at an altitude of 15,750 feet, the strata strike south-east and north-west, and dip towards the south. Here also the lava streams have spread out into sheets, having flowed from a rent on the northern side of the Mawenzi crater.

Mr. Hyland mentions specimens of *Tephrite* as having been obtained from three different points—two from near the Schneequelle (spring in the snow), and the third from the lava hill on the saddle, which lies nearest to Mawenzi. None of the specimens I have examined have been obtained directly from the solid rock, but are derived from loose blocks on the path between Marangu and Moji, from between Uru and the Weri-weri, and from the Kikafu. From the Weri-weri specimens were also obtained by Von der Decken.

The rock for the most part is considerably weathered, and the external layers are of a dark brown colour, which passes insensibly into the light grey of the nucleus.

By far the largest number of specimens are *nepheline basanite*, but they are derived almost exclusively from the Kibo region. The main mass of the type of rock in question seems to have originated to the north of the stream of felspathic basalt, which has flowed from the south-east side of the crater. Thence it has spread far out into the region of the Mué along the eastern and south-eastern slopes of the mountain. The sides of the rent in the wall of the crater, which constitutes the valley of the Ratzel glacier, are composed of this rock, as is also the north side of the crater wall. Many of the labels bear notes to the effect that nepheline basanite occurs more commonly and more extensively than any other rock. It is further said to be stratified, from which we may infer that several consecutive eruptions have taken place at the same point.

Nepheline basanite also occurs at the *boma* of the chief of Majamé, in the neighbourhood of the Kikafu, which rises in the south-west of Kibo; but here, as at the Rau and the Weri-weri, the specimens have been derived from loose blocks and boulders brought down by the stream.

In colour and texture the specimens of this rock resemble the basalt, but they may be distinguished from the latter at a glance by the development of the felspar crystals, which on transverse cleavage plainly show the typical form of the rhomboid porphyries. In this class must also be included certain specimens of vitreous rock in which the glassy base, while in a liquid state, has surrounded the typical felspar crystals, so that the true nature of the rock is now only to be judged from the detached crystals of felspar disseminated through it.

As compared with nepheline basanite, *leucitic basanite* is confined to a very limited area. In the collection examined by Mr. Hyland it was represented by a single specimen derived from the sheet of volcanic ash to the south-east of Kibo. In the collection submitted to me all the specimens came from the crater.

The rock consists of a grey base, through which are disseminated large crystals of felspar and small crystals of leucite, both of a whitish colour.

Nepheline basalt, mentioned by Mr. Hyland as occurring in Marangu, is described in the present collection as derived from the region of nepheline basanite between the Mué and Kibo (11,500–13,000 feet), but the beds are not of the same extent and thickness. Some of the specimens come from the eastern lava hill on the saddle between Kibo and Mawenzi, where the strata strike north and, south, and dip towards the south at an angle of 23°. Besides appearing in the stratified form, this rock occurs in large blocks between Marangu and the Rua (5900 feet), and on the Himo (2600 feet) in the form of erratic blocks and boulders from the ravine of the Kikafu.

The rocks of this type are easily distinguished by the presence of olivine, and the absence of the long felspar crystals.

It only remains to mention the presence of *Limburgites*, which, according to Mr. Hyland, appear in the sheet of volcanic ash on the south-east side of Kibo, while a third variety (distinguished by the presence of augite) comes from the lava stream of the hill nearest Mawenzi. The specimens of limburgite submitted to me have likewise been derived only from these two localities. From the remarks on the labels—"From a projecting rock on the sheet of ashes," and "East of Kibo: many loose blocks between 12,800 and 13,500 feet"—I am led to the conclusion that the limburgites have originated prior to the eruption of the felspathic basalts and nepheline basanites from a lava stream issuing from the same rent as these latter. The lava hill nearest to Mawenzi possibly originated at the same time, and the felspathic basalts and nepheline basalts of the region may be derived from masses of lava which issued later from the rent.

In their weathered condition (most of the specimens consist of small fragments, of which the outer layers are much weathered) the limburgites are easily distinguished, the large crystals of augite and the somewhat smaller glittering crystals of olivine standing out conspicuously from the reddish brown (or, in a fresh section, black) base. In fresh specimens the vitreous lustre of the base is a noteworthy feature.

In the formation of Kilimanjaro an important part has been played by the great line of dislocation which runs from the summit of Kibo across the hills on the saddle plateau and the peak of Mawenzi. From the fissure thus caused the various rocks have flowed as molten masses of lava, and its existence will be of importance in determining the order in which the different types have originated. By the kindness of Dr. Meyer the whole of his magnificent collection has been placed in the mineralogical department of the Natural History Museum in Berlin. The petrological peculiarities and the extent to which the strata are developed in different localities will form the subject of a separate monograph.

III.

ON A COLLECTION OF LICHENS FORMED BY DR. HANS MEYER DURING THREE EXPEDITIONS TO EAST AFRICA (1887-89).

By B. STEIN, Breslau.

THE collection of lichens formed by Dr. Meyer in the course of his three expeditions includes 124 species. Of these, 23 come from Usambara and 49 from the steppe region between the coast and Kilimanjaro—an abundance which shows the rich harvest here presented to the student. The steppes are studded with old single trees and groups of trees, and with these lichens are invariably associated, so that, as we should expect, the species characteristic of wood and bark predominate.

The lichens of Kilimanjaro are even more fully represented, yet the 74 species included in Dr. Meyer's collection probably constitute not more than 10 per cent. of the lichens to be met with on the mountain. These examples serve to show, however, that the same rules apply to the lichens of Kilimanjaro as to those derived from other volcanic regions. Basalt and lava are the only rocks which need be taken into account. On both of these the lichens most widely distributed on the plains are able to maintain life at the most extraordinary altitudes, in their typical form, and not in any way modified to suit their alpine situation. The best-known illustration of this phenomenon occurs at the celebrated vein of basalt in the " Kleine Schneegrube " among the Silesian Riesengebirge. There, at an altitude of about 4270 feet, while the granite and the superimposed layer of soil are covered with lichens of subalpine character, the basalt is mainly clad with the forms typical of the plains—common species exactly similar to those of the Silesian lowlands. Intermingled with these are a number of arctic forms and an immense variety of indigenous species. A similar mingling of forms may be seen on the volcanos of Southern Europe— Vesuvius and Etna—and on the lavas of Madeira and Teneriffe.

Nor is it otherwise on Kilimanjaro. Of the 74 species included in Dr. Meyer's collection, 25 belong to the forms characteristic of the plains, and on Kilimanjaro, at an elevation of from ten to sixteen thousand feet, appear in the guise familiar to us on the plains of Northern Germany Only twelve common tropical species are represented, and these are derived mostly from the forest zone. Fifteen arctic-alpine species are known to occur on the mountain, to which may be added the subalpine species *Usnea cornuta* (absent in the polar regions) and *Parmelia Kamtschadalis* (absent in the Alps). The only typical Cape forms are *Parmelia subconspersa* and *P. molliuscula*, but many of the other widely distributed species also occur at the Cape. *Stereocaulon Vesuvianum* and perhaps *Buellia trachytica* are characteristic Kilimanjaro lichens which are also found on the volcanic rocks of Vesuvius, and *Stereocaulon Meyeri* is nearly allied to the various species of *Stereocaulon* common on the volcanoes of the Canary Islands. The lichens of Kilimanjaro thus include representative forms from all parts of the world. Further research may add new species to those already known, but the knowledge we possess of the general characteristics of this branch of the flora can scarcely be materially altered.

The number of new species which I have felt compelled to assign to Kilimanjaro and the neighbourhood may be a matter of some surprise. There are ten in all :—

STEREOCAULON MEYERI.
RAMALINA MEYERI.
PARMELIA MOLLIUSCULA var. KILIMANJAROENSIS.
GYROPHORA UMBILICARIOIDES.
LENORMANDIA GRIMMIANA.
PLACODIUM MELANOPHTHALMUM var. AFRICANUM.
RINODINA PURTSCHELLERI.
URCEOLARIA STEIFENSANDII.
LECIDELLA ATROBRUNNEA FORMA MINOR.
L. KILIMANJAROENSIS, to which may be added USNEA DASYPOGOIDES var. EXASPERATA *Müll. Arg.*

This number might have been considerably increased, for many of the specimens were characterised by minute distinctions. The list of lichens peculiar to Kilimanjaro will probably be diminished in the future, as new species are discovered in the alpine regions of other volcanic peaks ; but, on the other hand, it is certain to be added to, as fresh indigenous species crop up in the collections of future explorers of Kilimanjaro. In justice to myself I ought to state that in many instances I have been compelled to found my classification on single specimens, some of which were extremely small. It is therefore necessarily somewhat arbitrary, and may be even altogether incorrect characteristics being regarded as specific and essential which in reality are accidental. Relying on the future observations of others to rectify such errors as I may have made, I thought it better to utilise even the smallest specimen in drawing up the following list, rather than set it aside in the hope that it would be more largely represented in subsequent collections.

My greatest difficulties in this respect have been in connection with the lichens derived from the bark of the trees on the steppes. Twigs no thicker than a quill, and only an inch or two in length, often exhibited as many as half a dozen different species.

The collection includes scarcely any representatives of the lichens to be found on soil in the Kilimanjaro region, the surface of which would be sure to afford a number of interesting specimens. A region that has produced *Lenormandia Grimmiana* and *Urceolaria Steifensandii* cannot but yield many other natural curiosities, whose acquaintance, it is to be hoped, we shall soon be able to make.

In the following list, the figures 1, 2, 3, placed after the locality from which the specimens have been derived, indicate on which of Dr. Meyer's journeys the latter were obtained. (1) indicates Dr. Meyer's first ascent of Kilimanjaro in July 1887; (2) his Usambara journey in August and September 1888; (3) his residence on the mountain from September to November 1889. The species marked with an asterisk, thus *, are new.

The collections made during the first two journeys I have already described in the *Proceedings* for 1888 of the *Schlesische Gesellschaft für vaterländische Kultur* in Breslau, in which magazine the description of the new species will shortly appear.

In the compilation of the list I have availed myself of the corrections and alterations of names supplied by Professor J. Müller in *Lichenes Africæ tropico-orientalis*, 1890, *Flora*, vol. iv.

1. Usnea longissima *Ach.* South Usambara, Hundu, 2. Filaments over a yard long; exactly corresponding to European variety.

*U. longissima f. Ebersteini, *Stein.* Wooded steppes between Rabai and Taro; not numerous, 1.

2. U. trichodea *Ach.* South Usambara, 2.

3. U. angulata *Ach.* South Usambara, 2. Filaments long, beardlike; fructifications scanty. Between Moadje and Moji, on old trees, not rare, 3; f. ferruginea *Krplh.* South Usambara, 2.

4. *U. dasypogoides *Nyl.* var. exasperata *Müll. Arg.* Kilimanjaro 9850 feet, 3. Specimen fully a yard long; whitish yellow; sterile.

5. U. articulata *Ach.* Kilimanjaro, 1, 3. Above 9850 feet; numerous; in the grass-lands between 9850 feet and 13,000 feet, on shrubs; f. gracilis, on arborescent heaths at 13,000 feet; f. erecta, upper limit of forest *; f. erubescens, with yellowish red folia (a colour often met with in African Usneæ); appears on young shoots between mosses in the upper grass-lands at 13,000 feet; as a variety with long filaments at the upper limit of the forest (9850 feet); as a blackish variety (not unlike *Bryopogon bicolor*) on the surface of the ground in the grass-lands (13,000 feet).

6. U. aspera *Eschw.* South Usambara, 2. Old trees in Moji and the Ugweno mountains; not rare, 3; only sterile specimens collected.

z

7. U. strigosa *Ach.* Wooded steppes between Rabai and Taro; numerous, 1. South Usambara, 2. Between Samburu and Taveta, on old trees (mimosæ), numerous; also in Moji, and between Moadje and Moji, 3; fructification abundant.

8. U. cornuta *Kbr.* On stones at upper limit of forest and in grass-land; 9850–13,000 feet, 1; var. densirostra (*Tayl.*) *Müll. Arg.* (var. Weyeri *Stein*). On stones in upper grass-land; 14,000 feet, 1, 3.

9. Cladonia verticillata *Hoffm.* One small specimen from Kilimanjaro; 9850 feet, 3.

10. C. pyxidata *L.* var. neglecta *Flke.* Kilimanjaro; old trees; 9850 feet, 3.

11. C. crispata *Flot.* var. subsimplex *Müll. Arg.* Extremely small specimens from upper limit of forest; 9850 feet.

12. C. Floerkeana *Fr.* Kilimanjaro; forest; 5900–15,000 feet; apparently widespread, 3; var. intermedia *Hepp.* f. melanocarpa *Müll. Arg.* Upper limit of forest; 9850 feet. A specimen, the reproductive spores of which had become black in drying, I took to be C. isidioclada *Mtg.*

13. Cladina peltasta (*Spreng.*) *Nyl.* Kilimanjaro; forest; 5900–15,000 feet, 3.

14. *Stereocaulon Meyeri *Stein.* Kilimanjaro; on lava blocks; 9850–16,500 feet, 1, 3; specimens of 1887 sterile, of 1889 fertile. Stereocaulon Meyeri approaches most nearly to the American species S. strictum *Th. Fr.* and S. Vulcani Bory of the Mauritius, but is different from both. Th. Fries, author of the monograph on Stereocaulon, to whom I showed a specimen, described S. Meyeri as "optima species nova," so that I feel justified in retaining the name, although Müller is of opinion that the species should be included under S. ramulosum. In the latter, however, the spores are much broader.

15. Stereocaulon Vesuvianum *Pers.* var. confluens *Müll. Arg.* (as species) (var. Kilimanjaroense *Stein*). (Jahresbericht der Schlesischen Gesellschaft, 1888.) On lava blocks at the Senecio (9850 feet) and on the grass-lands (13,000 feet), 1, 3.

16. *Ramalina polymorpha *Ach.* v. Meyeri *Stein* (as species). (Jahresbericht, 1888.) Kilimanjaro; on stones; 13,800 feet, 1.

17. R. Eckloni *Sprgl.* var. membranacea *Müll. Arg.* (lævigata, Jahresbericht, 1888). South Usambara; on trees; a single specimen, 2.

18. R. complanata *Ach.* var. denticulata *Müll. Arg.* var. canaliculata *Nyl.* et var. fallax *Müll. Arg.* (R. rigida *Pers.* var. africana *Stein.* Jahresbericht, 1888). Three localities in Usambara and from Tumakanya; widespread; on trees, 2; on trees, living and dead, in Ugweno, between Moji and Marangu, Moji and Moadje, and Samburu and Taveta; evidently widely spread, 3.

19. R. calicaris *Ach.* var. subpapillosa *Nyl.* Between Matate and Taveta, 3.

20. *R. pusilla *Le Prev.* var. Meyeri *Stein*, 1888. R. pusiola *Müll. Arg.*, 1890. South Usambara and Tumakanya; on trees; apparently widely spread, 2 ; between Matate and Taveta, 3.

21. Tornabenia flavicans *DC.* on trees; Tumakanya, Usambara, 2 ; between Matate and Taveta; on tree trunks in the steppes and in Ugweno, 3 ; f. cinerascens; folia ashy-grey ; Usambara, 2, and Ugweno, 3. One of the most common and widely spread lichens in the region ; mostly occurs in large patches.

22. Sticta retigera *Ach.* et var. isidiosa *Müll.* Kilimanjaro; on trees ; forest ; 5900–9850 feet, 3.

23. S. Garovaglii *Schaer.* Kilimanjaro ; forest ; 5900–9850 feet, 3 ; on trees ; one example ; sterile.

24. Stictina umbilicariformis *Hochst.* Kilimanjaro; on trees ; 9850 feet.

25. Parmelia latissima *Fée.* Kilimanjaro; on mossy rocks and old tree trunks ; 5900–14,800 feet ; numerous but sterile, 1, 3 ; Ugweno, 3. Between Matate and Moji, and between Moji and Marangu, 3 ; South Usambara, 2. Principally f. sorediata *Nyl.*

26. P. perforata *L.* South Usambara, 2 ; wooded steppes between Rabai and Taro ; widely distributed at 9200 feet, 1. Between Moadje and Moji, 3.

27. P. perlata *Ach.* Ugweno, 3. Kilimanjaro, 5900–9850 feet, 3.

28. P. proboscidea *Tayl.* On mimosæ in the steppes, 3.

29. P. abessinica *Krplh.* South Usambara, 2 ; between Moji and Marangu, 3.

30. P. urceolata *Eschw.* Ugweno, 3 ; between Matate and Taveta ; 3. v. nuda *Müll.* (P. Hildebrandtii *Krplh.*), between Samburu and Taveta, 3.

31. P. Schweinfurthii *Müll. Arg. ?* Kilimanjaro ; forest, 3 ; a single rust-coloured, sterile specimen.

32. P. tiliacea *Ach.* var. scortea *Nyl.* (var. eximia *Stein*) (Jahresbericht, 1888). A beautiful light whitish-grey variety, powdered with brown. South Usambara, 2.

33. P. praetervisa *Müll. Arg.* (P. revoluta v. ambigua *Stein*). On old trees in Moji; not rare. South Usambara, 2.

34. P. carporhizans *Tayl.* On trees in the steppes between Taita and Taveta, 3.

35. P. Borreri *Turn.* var. rudecta *Ach.* Kilimanjaro; on trees ; 5900–9850 feet, 3.

36. P. sinuosa *Sm.* Wooded steppes between Rabai and Taro, 1.

37. P. saxatilis *L.* Kilimanjaro; on trees at the upper limit of the forest ; 9850 feet ; between patches of Stereocaulon, 14,800 feet, 1 ; fertile ; on mossy rocks at the same altitude, 3.

38. P. physodes *L.* Kilimanjaro; on an arborescent heath ; 9850 feet, 1.

39. P. Kamtschadalis *Eschw.* var. fistulata *Tayl.* Kilimanjaro; at the bottom of old tree-trunks between 5900 and 9850 feet.

40. P. molliuscula *Ach.* Kilimanjaro; between 9850 and 18,000 feet; on rocks and stony ground; widely spread, but apparently always sterile, 1, 3. Three main varieties.

α typica.

β robusta.

*γ kilimanjaroensis.

α and β appear to be regularly distributed between 9850 and 13,000 feet; the alpine var. γ first appears on basalt and lavas above 15,750 feet. Between the three varieties there are transitional forms of every imaginable kind.

41. P. conspersa *Ehrh.* On quartz at the summit of Gamualla, 6550 feet; one small specimen, 3; var. subconspersa *Nyl.* (as species) Kilimanjaro; on rocks between 9850 and 15,750 feet, 3.

42. P. caperata *Dill.* Kilimanjaro; on trees at the upper limit of forest; 9850 feet, 1.

43. P. fahlunensis *L.* Kilimanjaro; on blocks of basalt and lava. A single sterile specimen from the south of Mawenzi, 14,750 feet, 3.

44. Physica (Anaptychia) leucomelas *Ach.* Ugweno, and on old trees near Moji, 3; var. angustifolia *Mey. et Flot.* South Usambara, 2; Kilimanjaro; upper limit of forest; on tree-trunks between 9850 and 11,500 feet, 1; and on mossy rocks, in large, extremely fertile patches, at 14,750 feet, 3.

45. Ph. (Anaptychia) subcomosa (*Nyl.*). On old trees; between Taveta and Samburu, 3; in a variety of forms.

46. Ph. hypoleuca *Ach.* Tumakanya, 2.

47. Ph. speciosa *Wulf.* On old trees between Moadje and Moji, 3.

48. Ph. picta *Sw.* On mimosæ between Moadje and Moji, 3; Kilimanjaro; upper limit of forest; 9850 feet, 1, 3; var. sorediata *Schaer;* on old trees between Moadje and Moji, 3.

49. Ph. erythrocardia *Tuck.* (Ph. picta var. coccinea *Müll.*). On old trees between Moadje and Moji, 3; Kilimanjaro, 1; two sterile specimens from the tree steppes and the upper limit of the forest.

50. Pyxine Cocoës *Sw.* On the thallus and fruits of Parmelia urceolata; between Samburu and Taveta; numerous young, sterile specimens, 3; on old trees between Taveta and Moji, 3.

51. Peltigera canina *L.* var. membranacea *Ach.* Kilimanjaro; forest; in several mossy spots between 5900 and 13,000; in the higher altitudes also fertile, 3.

52. P. spuria *DC.* Kilimanjaro; on humus soil at upper limit of trees; 11,500 feet, 1.

53. *Gyrophora umbilicarioides *Stein* (Jahresbericht, 1888). Kilimanjaro; on stones in the upper grass-lands; 13,000 feet, 1; to the south of Mawenzi from 14,750 feet upwards, and on Kibo up to the ice-cap, 3.

54. *Lenormandia Grimmiana *Stein, n. spec.* Kilimanjaro; on humus soil and decaying vegetation, 13,000 feet, 3. Although the single specimen

is very small, its peculiarities are so marked as to justify its being classed as a new species.

55. Pannaria pannosa *Sw.* Kilimanjaro; on tree-trunks between 5900 and 9850 feet, 3.

56. Gasparrinia elegans (*Lk.*). Kilimanjaro; in 1887 a single specimen found on a lava block at 18,050 feet; in 1889 found on Mawenzi from 14,450 feet upwards to the summit; on Kibo between 14,450 feet and 19,700 feet—flourishing and fertile on the very summit of the mountain. The Kilimanjaro lichen has the same beautiful orange-red colour as in the Alps and in the Arctic regions.

57. Acarospora fuscata *Turn.* var. smaragdula *Wbg.* Kilimanjaro, at a lava block on the Mué, 9350 feet.

58. Gyalolechia epixantha *Ach.* (G. subsimilis *Th. Fr.*). Kilimanjaro; 16,400 feet; encrusting mosses, 1; on the under surface of lava blocks on Mawenzi; 15,000 feet, 3.

59. *Placodium melanophthalmum *Ram.* var. africanum *Stein.* Kilimanjaro; on the west side of Mawenzi, from 15,000 feet to the summit; widely distributed between 15,000 and 16,000 feet, 3.

60. Candelaria vitellina *Ehrh.* Kilimanjaro, south and west of Mawenzi, between 14,750 and 16,000 feet, 3.

61. Callopisma aurantiacum *Lghtf.* var. corticicolum. On mimosae between Moadje and Moji, 3.

62. C. ferrugineum *Huds.* var. saxicolum *Mass.* Kilimanjaro; lava blocks on Mawenzi, 15,000 feet, 3; var. obscurum *Th. Fr.* Kilimanjaro; lava blocks south of Mawenzi, 14,750 feet; on basalt on Kibo from 11,950 feet to the ice, 3.

63. *Rinodina Purtschelleri *Stein,* nov. spec. Ugweno mountains; on quartz rocks at the summit of Gamualla, 6560 feet. The fourth lichen bearing a resemblance to Rhizocarpon geographicum (Catocarpus chionophilus, Buellia effigurata, Buellia austrogeorgica), but the first Lecanora lichen of this type.

64. R. trachytica *Mass.* Kilimanjaro; probably widely distributed on lava blocks in sunny situations; on Mawenzi from 15,000 feet upwards; on Kibo from 11,800 feet to the ice.

65. R. metabolica *Anzi.* On mimosae twigs between Samburu and Taveta, 3.

66. Lecanora subfusca *L.* var. coilocarpa *Ach.* South Usambara, 2. On mimosae between Moadje and Moji, and between Moji and Marangu, 3; Kilimanjaro, on trees at the upper limit of the forest, 9850 feet, 1; var. lainea *Fr.* Kilimanjaro, on lava at the western base of Mawenzi, 14,750 feet, 3.

67. L. cinereocarnea *Eschw.* The most widely distributed bark Lecanora of the region; on mimosae between Moji and Marangu, and between Moadje and Moji, 3.

68. L. pallida *Schreb.* var. sordidescens *Pers.* On trees between Matate and Taveta, 3.

69. L. Hageni *Ach.* var. nigrescens *Th. Fr.* Kilimanjaro; on lava blocks at western base of Mawenzi, 15,000 feet, 3; var. lithophila *Wallr.*, on lavas and basalts in same locality.

70. L. poliophaea *Wbg. ?* A single fruit found on Mawenzi at an altitude of 16,100 feet, on a fragment of folia about ½ qcm. in size, apparently belongs to this species, but I was unable to determine exactly, 3.

71. L. helva *Stizenberger.* On trees between Moadje and Moji, 3.

72. L. varia *Ehrh.* On trees between Moadje and Moji, 3.

73. L. polytropa *Ehrh.* Kilimanjaro; lava blocks on Mawenzi, 15,000 feet, 3.

74. Aspicilia cinereorufescens *Ach.* Kilimanjaro; basalt blocks on Mawenzi, 15,000 feet, 3; var. diamarta *Ach.* On lava of Mawenzi, 16,000 feet.

75. A. complanata *Kbr.* Kilimanjaro; lavas of Mawenzi from 14,750 feet upwards.

76. *Urceolaria Steifensandii *Stein* (Jahresbericht, 1888). U. scruposa *L.* var. cinereo-caesia *Müll. Arg.* Kilimanjaro; turfy ground of the upper grass-lands, 13,000 feet; on Kibo at 15,750 feet, 3.

77. U. scruposa *L.* var. bryophila *Ehrh.* Kilimanjaro; on fragments of moss at 14,000 feet, 3.

78. Haematomma puniceum *Ach.* On old trees between Moadje and Moji, and between Mwika and Taveta, 3.

79. Pertusaria corallina *L.* Kilimanjaro; a single sterile specimen from basalt at the Kifinika stream, 8500 feet, 3.

80. P. communis *DC.* f. areolata *Ach.* Sterile crusts on Kilimanjaro, 14,750 feet; and on quartz at the summit of Gamualla, 6550 feet, 3.

81. P. melaleuca *Duby.* On dead branches; between Moadje and Moji, 3.

82. P. leioplacoides *Müll.* On mimosa stems; between Rabai and Moji, 3.

83. P. leucodes *Knight ?* Kilimanjaro; on branches in the tree-steppes between Rabai and Taro, 1. The specimen agrees fairly well with the New Zealand variety.

A sterile Pertusaria (?) thallus, of a whitish-grey colour, which is not altered by alkalies, was found on lava blocks at the Mue at an altitude of 9500 feet, 3.

84. Thelocarpon spec. Ugweno mountains; summit of Gamualla, 6550 feet; numerous on thalli of Pertusaria communis and Lecidella lapicida; perhaps identical with Th. epithallinum *Nyl.*

85. Bacidia endoleucoides *Krplh.* On old trees between Moadje and Moji, and between Moji and Marangu, 3.

86. Biatora coarctata *Sm.* Ugweno mountains; on quartz at the summit of Gamualla; 6550 feet, 3.

87. B. erythrophaea *Flke.* On mimosæ between Moji and Marangu, 3.

88. *Bombyliospora Meyeri *Stein* (Jahresbericht, 1888). Patellari Meyeri *Müll. Arg.* On barks in Hundu, Usambara, 2.

89. *Lecidella atrobrunnea *Ram.* f. minor thalli areolae minutae leproso albo-marginatae. Kilimanjaro; on lavas of Mawenzi up to 16,400 feet, 3.

90. L. Mosigii *Hepp.* Kilimanjaro; on lavas of Kibo up to 16,400 feet, 3.

91. *L. Kilimanjaroensis *Stein, n. sp.* Kilimanjaro; on lavas of Mawenzi, 15,000 feet, 3

Externally resembles Lecidea fuscocinerea *Nyl.* and many forms of Biatora uliginosa.

92. L. lapicida *Ach.* Ugweno mountains; on quartz at summit of Gamualla; 6550 feet, 3.

93. L. pungens *Kbr.* Ugweno mountains; on quartz at summit of Gamualla; 6550 feet, 3.

94. L. latypea *Ach.* Kilimanjaro; lavas on the south of Mawenzi; 14,750–16,000 feet; var. aequata *Flke.* and var. pulverulenta *Th. Fr.*; same locality, 3.

95. Diplotomma alboatrum *Hoffm.* Kilimanjaro; lavas of Kibo, 18,370 feet; Mawenzi, 15,000 feet, 3.

96. Catocarpus chionophilus *Th. Fr.* Kilimanjaro; basalt of Kibo up to 16,400 feet, 3.

97. Rhizocarpon geographicum *L.* f. contiguum *Fr.* Kilimanjaro; lavas of Mawenzi, from 14,750 feet to the summit; on Kibo from 11,800 feet to the summit; apparently very widely spread.

98. R. Montagnei *Fw.* Kilimanjaro; lava of Mawenzi up to 15,000 feet, 3. In the specimen the thecae were two-celled; plant therefore to be classed with f. geminatum *Fw.*

99. Buellia spuria *Schaer.* β minutula *Hepp.* Kilimanjaro; lavas of Mawenzi from 14,750 feet upwards. Ugweno mountains; summit of Gamualla, 6550 feet, 3.

100. B. lecidina *Fw.* Kilimanjaro; lavas at western base of Mawenzi, 15,000 feet, 3.

101. B. cinereo-cincta *Müll. Arg.* On mimosæ between Matate and Taveta, 3.

102. B. parasema *Ach.* var. vulgata *Th. Fr.* Branches of mimosæ between Moadje and Moji, 3.

103. Celidium stictarum *Tul.* Kilimanjaro; on Sticta retigera, between 5900 and 9850 feet, 3.

104. *Helminthocarpon Meyeri (*Stein*) Müll. Arg.* (Phlyctis Meyeri *Stein*, 1888). On a twig at Tumakanya, 2.

105. Opegrapha Bonplandi *Fée*, var. abbreviata *Müll.* South Usambara; on barks, 2.

106. Graphis lineola *Ach.* On twigs in South Usambara, 2. On mimosæ twigs between Moadje and Moji, 3.

107. G. subimmersa *Mass.* On trees between Moadje and Moji, 3.

108. G. conferta *Zenk. ?* On mimosæ between Moadje and Moji, 3.

109. Phaeographina caesiopruinosa *Fée.* Tree-steppes between Rabai and Taro, 1. On mimosæ between Matate and Taveta, 3; var. bispora Thecæ always two-spored. On mimosæ twigs between Moadje and Moji, 3.

110. Graphina curta *Fée ?* On barks between Samburu and Taveta; a single imperfect specimen, 3.

111. G. (Chlorographis *Müll. Arg.*) spec. On branches of tree-steppes between Rabai and Taro, 1.

112. Arthonia Antillarum *Fée.* On mimosæ between Moadje and Moji, 3.

113. A. serialis *Müll.* On mimosæ twigs between Moadje and Moji, 3.

114. Melaspilea cicatrisans *Ach. ?* On banks in forest region of Kilimanjaro, 3. The dwarfish fruits, and the size and shape of the spores, appear to agree pretty closely with the South American species; but the specimen was too small to form an exact opinion.

115. *M. coccinea *Stein, n. sp.* On branches of old trees between Moadje and Moji, 3.
The remarkable characteristic of this species is the bright red powder on the edges of the fruit, from which I feel justified in classifying it as new, although I had only a single specimen.

116. Glyphis favulosa *Ach.* β intermedia *Müll. Arg.* On branches in the tree-steppes between Rabai and Taro, 1.

117. Arthothelium macrotheca *Fée.* On dead trees between Taita and Taveta, 3.

118. Anthracothecium pyrenuloides *Mull. Arg. ?* Kilimanjaro; a few fruits on a twig, from an altitude of 11,500 feet, 3. From the variable size of the fruits, possibly to be regarded as new.

119. Arthopyrenia Persoonii *Mass.* f. minuta. On a smooth-barked species of mimosæ between Moji and Mawenzi, 3. Perhaps also new.

120. Melanotheca cruenta (Mtgne.) *Müll. Arg.* (Pyrenula Gravenreuthii, *Stein,* Jahresbericht, 1888). Kilimanjaro; and on young branches on the tree-steppes between Rabai and Taro, 1. Not very numerous.

121. Tichothecium pygmaeum *Kbr.* var. microcarpum *Arnold.* Kilimanjaro; on the folia and fruits of Gasparrinia elegans; 17,700 feet, 3.

122. T. gemmiferum *Tayl.* Kilimanjaro; on the crustaceous thallus of Buellia spuria; south of Mawenzi, 15,000 feet, 3.

123. Leptogium tremelloides (*Fr.*). South Usambara, on barks, 2; forest region of Kilimanjaro, between 5900 and 9850 feet, 3.

124. Synechoblastus Robillardi *Muell. Arg.* South Usambara, on barks, 2; between Moadje and Moji, 3.

IV.

THE MOSSES OF THE KILIMANJARO REGION.

BY DR. CARL MÜLLER, HALLE.

It is now four years since the first examples of the mosses of the African Mont Blanc arrived in this country. In 1886 the collection made by the late Bishop Hannington between Mombaza and Kilimanjaro was submitted to Mr. William Mitten of Hurstpierpoint, who found that it included thirty-eight species. As far as it went, the collection was a noteworthy contribution to science, for the distribution of the mosses and other cryptogams is of great importance in relation to the geographical distribution of plants in general. These plants have never been cultivated, and therefore, like the higher orders, they are more likely to be met with in their original habitat, and thus form an index to the natural character of the flora of the region—and not only an index, but a means of comparing the various botanical regions one with another. Viewed from this standpoint, Hannington's successor, Dr. Hans Meyer, has rendered the scientific world no small service in bringing back with him from his two splendidly successful journeys to the mountain the collection of mosses which has just been submitted to me. This collection derives additional importance from the fact that it comprises mainly species from above the forest zone, where the vegetation assumes an alpine character, and we are thus enabled to compare the alpine mosses of Kilimanjaro with those of other alpine regions.

Dr. Meyer's first collection included twenty-five new species, nearly all alpine. Inspired by this success, he and his companion, Herr Ludwig Purtscheller, on their journey of 1889, devoted particular attention to the mosses, and with the most gratifying results. The second collection is not only fuller than the first, but it again includes a large number of new species, from which it appears that the mosses on the other side of the mountain are totally different from those on the side first explored. The new species number thirty-three.

A further important addition to our knowledge of this division of the vegetable kingdom was contributed by Count Teleki and Von Höhnel on their expedition to the Kilimanjaro region in 1887. The collection made by Von Höhnel I had the pleasure of examining on his return. It comprised not only specimens from Kilimanjaro, but also from Kenia and the foot of the Aberdare range in Lykipia. Setting the latter aside as apart from the region at present in question, I found that Von Höhnel had discovered 11 new species, which, with the 58 contributed by Dr. Meyer, makes a sum total of 69. Bishop Hannington had already made us acquainted with 38, so that there are now 107 species altogether, known as occurring on Kilimanjaro. For certain reasons, however, I am inclined to regard 24 out of the 38 species discovered by Hannington as doubtful; but even omitting these, we have still 93 about which there can be no doubt whatever—a number quite sufficient to enable us to gain a fairly accurate idea of the distribution of these plants on the mountain.

The first zone, as including the forest, may be said to be entirely tropical; it extends upwards to a height of 9850 feet. Here the mosses are of the type familiar to us as accompanying the tropical trees of all lands. They approach those of Madagascar on the one hand, and the subtropical forms of the Cape on the other, without being exactly similar to either. Above 9850 feet there is a boundless extent of grass-land; and here, as we gradually ascend, the cryptogamous vegetation more and more loses its tropical aspect, and assumes the characteristics of temperate, and even arctic zones. Here we meet with types common to the higher altitudes of our own mountain peaks: *Andreæa, Distichium, Polytrichum, Campylopus, Scopella, Rhodobryum, Eubryum, Argyrobryum, Senodictyum, Sclerodictyum, Philonotis, Eubartramia, Syntrichia, Anœctangium, Hedwigia, Ulozygodon, Eugrimmia,* and *Bracythecium.* Between these two extremes is an intermediate zone, where we are to some extent reminded of the forms to be met with on the higher mountains of Mascarenhas. Here occur types resembling *Leucoloma, Leptostomopsis, Philonotula, Plicatella, Leptodontium, Braunia* and *Pterogonium.*

But while on the upper regions of Kilimanjaro we thus meet with such types as might be expected from analogy with corresponding altitudes in other lands, it is to be remembered that entire species are peculiar, or assume the characteristics of species totally different. Thus *Campylopus procerus* was found at an altitude of 9850–15,750 feet, and bore the most deceptive resemblance to *Campylopus altissimus* (C. Müll.), from the alpine regions of Paramos Antioquas (United States of Columbia, South America). It is certainly most remarkable that this moss should continue to flourish up to such an unusual height, but it is not unlikely that the further exploration of Kilimanjaro may afford other examples of the same phenomenon. On the other hand, many species which externally bear an extraordinary resemblance to many widely distributed alpine types, are found, on closer examination, to differ materially in structure. Thus *Bryum ellipsifolium* apparently closely resembles our European species *Bryum argenteum;* but while, in the latter, the leaves are hairy and acute, in the former they are obtuse and arranged in whorls, peculiarities which completely distinguish it from *Argyrobryum.* Another interesting case is that of a *Funaria* which flourishes on Kilimanjaro between 4900 and 9850 feet. Externally it is exactly similar to the European variety *Funaria hygrometrica,* but it differs from the latter in its cellular structure, so that I have felt bound to classify it as a distinct species, *Funaria Kilimanjarica.* Examples might easily be multiplied. Thus *Andrœea, Distichium, Grimmia,* and other types all recall our European mountain species, but they are found mingling with others characteristic of tropical mountain regions.

Taking the mosses of Kilimanjaro as a whole, then, we see that in this respect the flora of the mountain is much like that of other tropical alpine regions, comprising, as it does, many European types under a tropical disguise, and others characteristically tropical and peculiar to the district. There is no moss on Kilimanjaro which attains a development in keeping with the vast size of the mountain ; even the longest—*Polytrichum Höhneli*— once more recalls such a European form as *Polytrichum juniperinum.* Kilimanjaro has nothing to show equal to the *Spiridens* species of the mountains of the South Sea Islands, New Guinea, and the Malay and Philippine Islands; or the *Dawsonia superba* of Australia; or the arborescent *Dendroligotrichum* of New Zealand, Chilé, and Terra del Fuego. Had it been otherwise, such remarkable forms could scarcely have escaped the observation of the various travellers who have visited the district. It is frequently to the European types that we have to look for the strange and wonderful ; and here, as in the highest altitudes of the Alps, we find such species as *Bryum bicolor* occurring between 9850 and 15,750 feet in a form of Lilliputian minuteness which in its way is as remarkable as the gigantic species alluded to above. The universal geographical law that the higher we ascend the more dwarfed and scanty becomes the vegetation, applies to the mosses of Kilimanjaro as to those elsewhere—the more so that here they subsist on bare earth and rocks. Within the forest zone they attain their greatest luxuriance, many species, as in other tropical forests, appearing as long "beards" hanging from the branches. As in Europe, these "beards" are either composed of species resembling *Neckera (Distichia platyantha)* or of a confused web of long delicate many-branching stems (*Orthostichella imbricatula*), in the interstices of which a whole army of other mosses find a congenial habitat.

We have alluded to certain points in which the mosses of Kilimanjaro resemble those of other tropical alpine regions, and also shown in what respects they may be said to be deficient. It now only remains to refer to the forms which are confined to this mountain alone. Dr. Meyer has brought back at least one moss, the discovery of which ought to rank as one of his greatest achievements. There is nothing specially remarkable about the plant itself ; not one of the specimens bore any fruits, and the tiny patches reminded me of a delicate green mould more than anything else. Yet this moss is the most remarkable of all the species known to exist on the mountain. I have named it *Erpodiopsis Kilimanjarica*, and classed it with the *Cleistocarpæ*, as forming at once a new family, genus, and species. For further particulars as to its structure and development, I must refer the reader to my article in the botanical magazine *Flora*, which contains a detailed description of Dr. Meyer's collection. The names of the different species are systematically arranged in the following Catalogue :—

CATALOGUE OF THE MOSSES INCLUDED IN DR. MEYER'S COLLECTION.

(New species marked with an asterisk [*].)

I.—CLEISTOCARPAE.

Group: *Erpodiopsideae.*

1. *Erpodiopsis Kilimanjarica *C. Müll.*

II.—SCHIZOCARPAE.

Group: *Andreaceae.*

2. *Andreaea firma *C. Müll.* | 3. *Andreaea striata *C. Müll.*

III.—ACROCARPAE.

Group: *Fissidenteae.*

4. *Fissidens caloglottis *C. Müll.*
5. — undifolius *C. Müll.*

Group: *Distichiaceae.*

6. *Distichium Kilimanjaricum *C. Müll.*

Group: *Funariaceae.*

7. *Funaria Kilimanjarica *C. Müll.*

Group: *Mniaceae.*

8. *Mnium Kilimanjaricum *C. Müll.*
9. Rhizogonium spiniforme *Brid.*

Group: *Polytrichaceae.*

10. *Polytrichum nano-globulus *C. Müll.*
11. *Polytrichum pungens *C. Müll.*
12. * — Höhneli *C. Müll.*

Group: *Dicranaceae.*

13. *Leucoloma dichotomum *Brid.*
14. * — drepanocladium *C. Müll.*
15. *Campylopus procerus *C. Müll.*
16. — Höhneli *C. Müll.* ·
17. — Johannis Meyeri *C. Müll.*

18. *Campylopus acrocaulos *C. Müll.*
19. * — leucochlorus *C. Müll.*
20. *Dicranum (Scopella) acanthoneuron *C. Müll.*

Group: *Bryaceae.*

21. *Rhodobryum minutirosatum *C. Müll.*
22. * — rosulatulum *C. Müll.*
23. * — spathulosifolium *C. Müll.*
24. *Leptostomopsis Meruensis *C. Müll.*
25. *Eubryum bicolor *C. Müll.*
26. * — nano-torquescens *C. Müll.*
27. * — inclusum *C. Müll.*
28. *Brachymenium capitulatum *Mitt.*
29. *Argyrobryum ellipsifolium *C. Müll.*
30. * — argentisetum *C. Müll.*
31. *Senodictyum afro-crudum *C. Müll.*
32. *Apalodictyum minutirete *C. Müll.*
33. *Sclerodiotyum compressulum *C. Müll.*

Group: *Bartramiaceae.*

34. *Philonotis tricolor *C. Müll.*
35. * —gemmascens *C. Müll.*
36. *Eubartramia strictula *C. Müll.*
37. *Plicatella Kilimanjarica *C. Müll.*
38. * — subgnaphalia *C. Müll.*

Group: *Calymperaceae.*

39. Orthotheca aspera *Mitt.*

Group: *Pottiaceae.*

40. *Syntrichia Meruensis *C. Müll.*
41. *Senophyllum pygmaeum *C. Müll.*
42. *Leptodontium Johannis Meyeri *C. Müll.*
43. * — pumilum *C. Müll.*
44. * — repens *C. Müll.*
45. — radicosum *Mitt.*

Group: *Zygodonteae.*

46. *Anoectangium viridatum *C. Müll.*
47. — pusillum *Mitt.*
48. *— paucidentatum *C. Müll.*
49. *Ulozygodon Kilimanjaricus *C. Müll.*
50. Stenomitrium erosum *Mitt.*

Group: *Orthotrichaceae.*

51. *Orthotrichum serrifolium *C. Müll.*
52. *— undulatifolium *C. Müll.*

Group: *Grimmiaceae.*

53. *Grimmia immergens *C. Müll.*
54. *— calyculata *C. Müll.*
55. *— obtuso-linealis *C. Müll.*
56. *— argyrotricha *C. Müll.*
57. *— campylotricha *C. Müll.*

Group: *Brauniaceae.*

58. *Hedwigia Johannis Meyeri *C. Müll.*
59. *Hedwigidium teres *C. Müll.*
60. Braunia Schimperania *Bryol. Eur.*

Group: *Erpodiaceae.*

61. Erpodium Johannis Meyeri *C. Müll.*

Group: *Hypopterygiaceae.*

62. Rhacopilum Africanum *Mitt.*

Group: *Hookeriaceae.*

63. Hookeria (Callicostella) versicolor *Mitt.*

Group: *Mniadelphaceae.*

64. Daltonia patula *Mitt.*

Group: *Cryphaeaceae.*

65. Cryphaea Welwitschii *Mitt.*
66. *— scariosa *C. Müll.*

Group: *Neckeraceae.*

67. *Porotrichum subpennaeforme *C. Müll.*
68. *— ruficaule *C. Müll.*
69. *— pterops *Rehm.*
70. *Distichia platyantha *C. Müll.*
71. *Pilotrichella chlorothrix *C. Müll.*
72. *Orthostichella imbricatula *C. Müll.*
73. *— tenella *C. Müll.*
74. *— profusicaulis *C. Müll.*
75. *Eriocladium cymatocheilos *C. Müll.*
76. *Papillaria serpentina *C. Müll.*
77. *— breviculifolia *C. Müll.*
78. Prionodon Rebmanni *Mitt.*
79. Calyptothecium Africanum *Mitt.*
80. Trachypus serrulatus *P. B.*
81. Leptodon Smithii *Mohr.*
82. *Pterogonium Kilimanjaricum *C. Müll.*
83. *Entodon (Erythrodontium) rotundifolius *C. Müll.*

Group: *Hypnaceae.*

84. Anomodon devolutus *Mitt.*
85. *Microthamnium glabrifolium *C. Müll.*

86. *Cupressina Höhneli *C. Müll.*
87. *Hyocomiella bartramiophila *C. Müll.*
88. *Brachythecium gloriosum *C. Müll.*
89. *— nigro-viride *C. Müll.*

90. *Tamariscella loricalycina *C. Müll.*
91. *Trismegistia trichocolea *C. Müll.*
92. *Helicodontium subcompressum *C. Müll.*
93. Rigodium toxarion *Mitt.*

The new species is described in *Flora* for 1888, No. 27, and 1890, Part V.

V.

THE LIVERWORTS (HEPATICAE) OF THE KILIMANJARO REGION.

BY F. STEPHANI, LEIPZIG.

THE plants mentioned below formed part of the collections made by Hannington, Dr. Hans Meyer, and Count Teleki, which have already been alluded to by my friend Dr. Carl Müller in his paper on the "Mosses of the Kilimanjaro Region." Of these collections, the first is only known to me from the written description and the illustrations by which it was accompanied.

The total number of liverworts brought to Europe by these travellers comprises sixty-two species, most of which were derived from the forest region midway up the mountain; twenty-one species have been collected by Dr. Meyer, of which three are new. As far as my examination goes, very few liverworts were found among the mosses in the higher zones of the mountain, whence we can scarcely look for an abundant harvest in the future, as shade and moisture, the conditions congenial to the life of these delicate plants, are there generally absent. The more hardy nature of the mosses ensures them a wider distribution.

As regards the liverworts, the most interesting discovery made by Dr. Meyer was the existence on Kilimanjaro of our European species *Lunularia cruciata* L. Scarcely less interesting is the presence of the stunted alpine species *Plagiochila subalpina* and *Bazzania pulvinata*, of which the latter in the structure of its leaves and under-leaves closely resembles *Bazzania decrescens* of the Mascarenhas. Most of the species are closely allied to those of the Mascarenhas and Madagascar, and occasionally also to those of the Cape.

As among the mosses, certain cosmopolitan species of liverwort occur here also, such as *Chandonanthus hirtellus*, *Frullania squarrosa*, *Targionia hypophylla*, *Lejeunea flava*, and *Noteroclada porphyrorhiza*; while two species, *Ptycholejeunea striata* and *Plagiochila calva*, are met with among the flora of the Sunda Islands.

Porella Hoehneliana, one of the plants included in the Teleki collection, is a quite anomalous form, but seems to be allied to tropical species. A purely Northern form is *Jungermannia minuta*, first described by Mitten.

The plants mentioned in the following list I have already described in *Hedwigia*, with the exception of the four new species recently furnished by Dr. Meyer, viz., *Bazzania pulvinata, Plagiochila divergens, Plagiochila Jaggana,* and *Plagiochila subalpina*. These will form the subject of a paper to be shortly published in the above-mentioned magazine.

ALPHABETICAL LIST OF THE HEPATICAE OF THE REGION.

(New Species marked with an Asterisk [*].)

Bazzania convexa *Thunb.*
*— pulvinata *St. n. sp.*
— pumila *Mitt.*
Chandonanthus hirtellus (*Web.*)
Cyathodium africanum *Mitt.*
Fimbriaria Boryana? *Mont.*
Frullania angulata *Mitt.*
— brunnea *Sprengel*
— cordata *Mitt.*
— Ecklonii *Spreng.*
— squarrosa *Nees*
— trinervis *L. u. L.*
— Usagara *Mitt.*
Herberta dicrana *Tayl.*
Isotachis Auberti *Schwägr.*
Jungermannia minuta *Dickson*
Leioscyphus infuscatus *Mitt.*
Lejeunea (Acro) emergens *Mitt.*
— — Pappeana *Nees*
— (Archi) xanthocarpa *L. u. L.*
— (Cerato) cornuta? *Ldbg.*
— (Coluro) digitalis *Mitt.*
— (Eu) acuta *Mitt.*
— — flava *Str.*
*— — hepaticola *Steph.*
— (Lepto) adhaesiva *Mitt.*
— (Lopho) atra *Mitt.*
*— (Micro) africana *Steph.*
— (Odonto) Hanningtoni *Mitt.*
— — tortuosa *L. u. L.* (syn : lunulata)
— (Ptycho) striata *Nees*

Lejeunea (Strepsi) brevifissa *G.*
Lepidozia cupressina *Ldbg.*
Lunularia cruciata *L.*
Marchantia globosa? (sterilis)
— *n. sp.* (sterilis)
Metzgeria furcata *L.*
*— myriopoda *Lindb.*
Noteroclada porphyrorhiza *Nees*
Plachiochila Barteri *Mitt.*
— calva *Nees*
*— comorensis *Steph.*
— dichotoma *Web.*
*— divergens *Steph.*
*— Jaggana *Steph.*
*— Hoehneliana *Steph.*
— javanica *N. u. M.*
— Lastii *Mitt.*
— sarmentosa *Lehm.*
— sinuosa *Mitt.*
— squamulosa *Mitt.*
*— subalpina *Steph.*
*— Telekiana *Steph.*
— terebrans *Nees*
Porella capensis *G.*
*— Hoehneliana *Steph.*
Radula appressa *Mitt.*
— Boryana *Nees*
— mascarena *Steph.*
*— Meyeri *Steph.*
*— recurvifolia *Steph.*
Targionia hypophylla *L.*

VI.

SIPHONOGAMOUS PLANTS COLLECTED BY DR. MEYER IN THE COURSE OF HIS EXPEDITIONS TO KILIMANJARO IN 1887 AND 1889.

By Dr. A. ENGLER, Berlin.

THE following catalogue includes the names of the plants collected by Dr. Hans Meyer in the course of his expeditions to Kilimanjaro in 1887 and 1889. In its compilation I have been assisted by Professor Schweinfurt, Dr. Schumann, Dr. C. Hoffmann, Dr. Taubert, and Herr Gurke. The classification of the ferns has been undertaken by Professor Max, and may be looked for shortly. The new species (here marked with an asterisk [*]), and the relations existing between the flora of Kilimanjaro and that of Abyssinia and of the Cape, will be described elsewhere.

Between Samburu and Moji
(*November* 1889).

Asclepias macrantha *Hochst.*
Waltheria americana *L.*
Cassia goratensis *Fres.*
*Ceropegia Meyeri Johannis *Engl. n. sp.*

Steppe Region between Mombaza and Kilimanjaro
(*November and December* 1889).

Acacia leucacantha *Vatke.*
— subalata *Vatke*
*Boswellia campestris *Engl. n. sp.*
*Commiphora campestris *Engl. n. sp.*
*— Meyeri Johannis *Engl. n. sp.*
— Schimperi (Berg) *Engl.*
Gloriosa virescens *Lindl.*
Ormocarpum Kirkii *S. Moore*

Lower Limit of Forest (*July* 1887).

Sparmannia abyssinica *Hochst.* var. Schumanni *Engl.*
Geranium simense *Hochst.*
Trifolium semipilosum *Fresen.*
Crotalaria laburnifolia *L.*

Eriosema cajanoides *Hook. f.*
*Crotalaria jaggensis *Taub. n. sp.*
Rhynchosia caribaea *DC.*
Cassia Kirkii *Oliv.*
*Tephrosia Meyeri Johannis *Taub. n. sp.*
Rubus dictyophyllus *Oliv.*
Lantana viburnoides *Vahl.*
Pentas longifolia *Oliv.*
Thunbergia fuscata *Th. Anders.*
Pentas purpurea *Oliv.*
Bidens pilosus *L.*
Achyrocline Hochstetteri *Sch. Bip.*
*Echinops Hoehneli *Schweinf. n. sp.*
Gomphocarpus fructicosus *R. Br.*
Achyranthes argentea *Lam.*
Rumex alismifolius *Fresen.*
Rhus villosa *L. fil.*

At the Rua rivulet (6200–7550 feet; *November* 1889).

Carduus leptacanthus *Fresen.*
Helichrysum globosum *Sch. Bip.*
*Celsia brevipedicellata *Engl. n. sp.*
Halleria abyssinica *Jaub. et Spach.*
Conyza Newii *Oliv. et Hiern.*

Thalictrum rhynchocarpum *Dill.* et *Rich.*

*Trifolium kilimanjaricum *Taub. n. sp.*

Parochetus communis *Ham.*

*Crotalaria kilimanjarica *Taub. n. sp.*

Rumex abyssinicus *Jacq.* var. Kilimanjari *Engl.*

Ipomaea involucrata *P. Beauv.*

Desmodium Scalpe *DC.*

Adenocarpus Mannii *Hook. f.*

*Begonia Meyeri Johannis *Engl. n. sp.*

Brayera anthelmintica *Kunth.*

Between Marangu and Camp at the Mue (4900–9500 feet; November 1889).

Helichrysum abyssinicum *Sch. Bip.*

Thalictrum rynchocarpum *Dill.* et *Rich.*

Dierama pendula *Baker.*

Helichrysum Kilimanjari *Oliv.*

*Blaeria Meyeri Johannis *Engl. n. sp.*

*Helichrysum Meyeri Johannis *Engl. n. sp.*

Ericinella Mannii *Hook. f.*

Erica arborea *L.*

In and above the Forest (5900–9850 feet; November 1889).

*Dolichos maranguensis *Taub. n. sp.*

Justicia palustris *Th. Anders.*

Justicia neglecta *Th. Anders.*

Achyrocline Hochstetteri *Sch. Bip.*

Erica arborea *L.*

Ipomaea involucrata *P. Beauv.*

*Orobanche kilimanjarica *Engl. n. sp.*

*Pupalia affinis *K. Schum. n. sp.*

Euphorbia monticola *Hochst.*

Sporobolus indicus *R. Br.*

Tricholaena Teneriffae *Parl.*

Sanicula europaea *L.*

*Cluytia kilimanjarica *Engl. n. sp.*

Agauria salicifolia *Hook. f.* var. latissima *Engl.*

Senecio Johnstoni *Oliv.*

*Helichrysum Guilelmi *Engl. n. sp.*

Caylusia abyssinica *Fisch.* et *Mey.*

Halleria abyssinica *Jaub.* et *Spach.*

Brayera anthelmintica *Kunth.*

*Nuxia glutinosa *Engl.*

Artemisia afra *Jacq.*

Cynoglossum micranthum *Desf.*

Combretum racemosum *P. Beauv.*

*Myrica Meyeri Johannis *Engl. n. sp.*

Dierama pendula *Baker.*

*Blaeria silvatica *Engl. n. sp.*

Lantana viburnoides *Vahl.*

Hebenstreitia dentata *L.*

*Bartsia Purtschelleri *Engl. n. sp.*

Helichrysum Kilimanjari *Oliv.*

Senecio discifolius *Oliv.*

Ageratum conyzoides *L.*

*Helichrysum Meyeri Johannis *Engl.*

Ranunculus oreophytus *Delile.*

Hypericum lanceolatum *Lam.*

Albizzia maranguensis *Taub. n. sp.*

*Peponia kilimanjarica *Cogn. n. sp.*

Upper Limit of Forest (9100–9850 feet; July 1887).

Drymaria cordata *Willd.*

Hypericum lanceolatum *Lam.*

Trifolium Johnstoni *Oliv.*

Pseudarthria Hookeri *W.* et *A.*

Desmodium Scalpe *DC.*

Crassula abyssinica *A. Rich.*

Asystasia gangetica *Th. Anders.*

Selago Johnstoni *Rolfe.*

Conyza Hochstetteri *Sch. Bip.*

Helichrysum globosum *Sch. Bip.*

Artemisia afra *Jacq.*

*Cineraria kilimanjarica *Engl. n. sp.*

Erica arborea *L.*

Celsia floccosa *Benth.*

Bulbostylis schoenoides *Kunth.*

Psoralea foliosa *Oliv.*

Hebenstreitia dentata *L.*

Schmiedelia rubifolia *Hochst.*

Striga elegans *Benth.*
*Tillaea obtusifolia *Engl. n. sp.*
Senecio Johnstoni *Oliv.*

Grass and Shrub Region above the Forest (9850–15400 feet; *July* 1887).

Arabis albida *Stev.*
Cerastium vulgatum *L.*
*Geranium kilimanjaricum *Engl.* n. sp.*
Scabiosa Columbaria *L.*
Helichrysum Meyeri Johannis *Engl. n. sp.*
Erigeron Telekii *Schweinf. n. sp.*
Euryops dacrydioides *Oliv.*
Helichrysum Steudneri *Schweinf.*
— abyssinicum *Sch. Bip.*
Helichrysum Kilimanjari *Oliv.*
Blaeria Meyeri Johannis *Engl. n. sp.*
— glutinosa *K. Sch. n. sp.*
Antholyza abyssinica *A. Brongn.*
Asparagus aff. plumoso
Andropogon Schimperi *Hochst.*
Koeleria cristata *L.*
Panicum Hochstetteri *Steud.*
Setaria glauca *P. B.*
Veronica myrsinoides *Oliv.*
Adenocarpus Mannii *Hook f.*
Selago Thomsoni *Rolfe.*

On the Mue (10,170 feet; *July* 1887).

Alectra asperrima *Benth.*
*Galium kilimanjaricum *K. Sch.*
Helichrysum Gunæ *Schweinf.*
Hebenstreitia dentata *L.*
*Protea kilimanjarica *Engl. n. sp.*
Myrsine africana *L.*

At the Spring in the Snow (12,950 feet; *July* 1887).

Geranium simense *Hochst.* var. Meyeri *Engl.*
Sebæa brachyphylla *Griseb.*
*Anagallis Meyeri Johannis *K. Schum. n. sp.*

Between the Mue and the Camp at Mawenzi (9845–14,435 feet; *November* 1889).

Luzula spicata var. simensis *Hochst.*
Kniphofia Thomsoni *Baker.*
Dierama pendula *Baker.*
*Swertia kilimanjarica *Engl. n. sp.*
Alchemilla argyrophylla *Oliv.*
Cnicus polyacanthus *Hochst.*
Hebenstreitia dentata *L.* var. integrifolia *L.*
*Bartsia Purtschelleri *Engl. n. sp.*
*Thesium kilimanjaricum, *Engl. n. sp.*
Cardamine pratensis *L.* forma alpina.
Ranunculus oreophytus *Delile*
*Sedum Meyeri Johannis *Engl. n. sp.*
Alchemilla Johnstoni *Oliv.*
*Rhamphicarpa Meyeri *Engl. n. sp.*
Subularia monticola *A. Br.*

Marangu, Uru, and Majame (4265–4920 feet).

Dodonaea viscosa *L.*
Eriosema parviflorum *E. Mey.*
*Gnidia Meyeri Johannis *Engl. n. sp*
Thunbergia fuscata *Th. Anders.*
Heliotropium kilimanjaricum *Engl.*
Cissus arguta (*Hook. f.*) Planch. var. Oliveri *Engl.*
Nymphaea Lotus *L.*
*Jasminum Meyeri Johannis *Engl. n. sp.*
Striga elegans *Benth.*
Cuscuta Kilimanjari *Oliv.*
Peperomia reflexa (*L. fil.*) *A. Dietr.*
Anthericum rubellum *Baker*
Tricholaena Teneriffa *Parl.*

Cultivated Plants from Jagga (*November* 1889).

Colocasia antiquorum *Schott*
Eleusine Coracana (*L.*) *Gärtn.*
Vigna sinensis *Engl.*

Phaseolus vulgaris *L.* var. sarcozebra *Alef.*

Nicotiana Tabacum *L.*

Ugweno Mountains (November 1889).

Melanthera Brownei *Sch. Bip.*

Stylosanthes erecta *P. B.*

Thunbergia alata *L.* var. exalata *Engl.*

Asparagus aff. plumoso

Adenium speciosum *Fenzl.* var. glabrum *Engl.*

*Dolichos uguenensis *Taub n. sp.*

Erica arborea *L.*

*Hedysarearum *Taub. gen. probabiliter novum*

Helichrysum Kilimanjari *Oliv.*

*Cycnium Meyeri Johannis *Engl.n. sp.*

VII.

THE BUTTERFLIES OF THE KILIMANJARO REGION.

By C. FROMHOLZ, BERLIN.

THE collection of sixty-eight species of butterflies made by Dr. Meyer in the course of his third expedition, and presented by him to the Royal Museum, includes several species which are distributed throughout the whole of Tropical Africa ; such are *Papilio demoleus, Papilio pylades, Pontia alcesta, Eronia buquetii* (also found in Arabia), *Acraea serena, Junonia clelia,* and *Hamanumida daedalus.* Others again are characteristic of West Africa, as *Papilio leonidas, Precis sophia, Precis elgiva, Patula macrops,* and *Cyligramma fluctuosa. Papilio nireus* occurs both in Central and South Africa. *Pieris eriphia, Colias electra,* and *Callosune jalone* are characteristic of South Africa alone, and *Papilio antheus, Acraea lycia, Precis amestris, Salamis anacardii, Eurytela hiarbas, Hypanis ilithyia, Neptis agatha, Palla varanes,* and *Antherea tyrrhaea* are distributed throughout West and South Africa. *Pieris abyssinica* is known both in Abyssinia and at the Cape, and seems to occur all along the East Coast. Except in the west, *Pieris severina* is to be met with everywhere throughout the Continent ; *Idmais chrysonome* and *Idmais dynamene* are found in Arabia.

Of the remaining species, the following occur in Southern Europe as well as in Africa :—*Danais chrysippus* and *Deiopeia pulchella ; Hypolimnas misippus* occurs in India, and *Cupido (Lycaena) telicanus* is met with over the whole eastern hemisphere. *Vanessa cardui* is common all over the world.

Among the rarer species are the following :—*Papilio constantinus* (only found in East Africa), and *Teracolus protomedia* (known also in Abyssinia and Arabia). The following species had already been brought to Europe by Von der Decken :—*Papilio demoleus, Pieris abyssinica, Callosune exole, Acraea serena, Precis amestris, Junonia oenone, Salamis anacardii, Hypanis ilithyia, Hamanumida daedalus,* and *Cupido (Lycaena) jesous.*

CATALOGUE OF THE BUTTERFLIES COLLECTED BY DR. MEYER IN THE KILIMANJARO REGION.

(*New species marked with an asterisk* [*].)

1. Papilio leonidas *F.*
2. — demoleus *L.*
3. — antheus *Cram.*
4. — pylades *F.* var.
5. — nireus *L.*
6. — zenobia *F.*
7. — constantinus *Ward.*
8. — philonë *Ward.*
9. — Pontia alcesta *Cram.*
10. — Eurema var. floricola *Bsd.*
11. — Pieris pigea *Bsd.* (?).
12. — abyssinica *Luc.*
13. — eriphia *Godt.*
14. — severina *Cram.*
15. Tachyris poppea *Cram.* var.
16. — sylvia *F.*
17. Eronia buquetii *Bsd.* var. arabica *Hopff.*
18. Catopsilia pyrene *Swains.*
19. Colias electra *L.*
20. *Idmais chrysonome *Kl.* var.
21. dynamene *Kl.*
22. Teracolus protomedia *Kl.*
23. *Callosune jalone *Butl.* var.
24. — exole *Reiche*
25. — phlegetonia *Bsd.*
26. evarne *Kl.* var.
27. — spec.
28. Danais chrysippus *L.* var. dorippus *Kl.*
29. limniace *Cram.*
30. Mycalesis safitza *Hew.*
31. — remulia *Godt.* (?)
32. Acraea lycia *F.* var. fulva *Doubl.*
33. — natalica *Bsd.*

34. Acraea anemosa *Hew.*
35. — serena *F.*
36. — eponina *Cram.*
37. — oncaea *Hopff.* var.
38. — insignis *Dist.* var.
39. — spec.
40. Vanessa cardui *L.*
41. Junonia clelia *Cram.*
42. — oenone *L.*
43. Precis amestris *Drury.*
44. —. kowara *Ward.*
45. — natalica *Feld.*
46. — elgiva *Hew.*
47. — limnoria *Kl.*
48. — sophia *F.*
49. Salamis anacardii *L.*
50. Eurytela valentina *Cram.*
51. — hiarbas *Drury.*
52. Hypanis ilithyia *Drury.*
53. Hypolimnas misippus *L.* ♀ var. inaria *Cram.*
54. Neptis agatha *Cram.*
55. Hamanumida daedalus *F.*
56. Palla varanes *Cram.*
57. Lycaena (Polyommatus) spec.
58. Cupido (Lycaena) telicanus *Hb.*
59. — jesous *Guér.*
60. — spec.
61. — spec.
62. — spec.
63. Nisoniades spec.
64. Deiopeia pulchella *L.*
65. Isochroa phedonia *Cram.*
66. Antherea tyrrhaea *Cram.*
67. Patula macrops *L.*
68. Cyligramma fluctuosa *Drury.*

VIII.

THE BEETLES OF THE KILIMANJARO REGION.

By H. J. KOLBE, Berlin.

The Coleoptera in the collection presented by Dr. Hans Meyer to the Royal Museum agree, for the most part, with the species known to prevail throughout East Africa. A few, however, are peculiar to the Kilimanjaro region, viz., *Diastellopalpus johnstoni* Waterh., one species of *Onitis*, two species of *Trox*, and a new species of weevil, *Entypotrachelus meyeri*. None of these latter were formerly included in the Royal Collection.

Of the remaining species belonging to Kilimanjaro, *Ateuchus aeratus* Gerst. is hardly known outside the district, while *Anachalcos procerus* Gerst. is known throughout Central Africa as far as the Congo region. *Rhyso-trachelus teani* Gerst. was described a few years ago as occurring in Shoa. *Oniticellus planatus* Boh. occurs likewise in South Africa. Widely distributed species are : *Mylabris amplectens* Gerst. (East and West Africa), *Hybosorus arator* F. (throughout Africa and the Mediterranean region), *Chilomenes lunata* F. (West, South, and East Africa, as far as Abyssinia ; Madagascar and India), *Epilachna punctipennis* Muls. (East, West, and South Africa).

Several species of beetles are common to Ugweno and Kilimanjaro, viz., *Ateuchus aeratus* Gerst., *Mitophorus semiaenus* Gerst., and a species of *Schizonycha*. Other species are distributed more widely throughout East Africa, viz., *Mylabris aperta* Gerst., *Tefflus juvenilis* Gerst., and *Tefflus hacquardi* Chaud. *Ceralces natalensis* Baly, *Diplognatha silicea* M'Leay, and *Silpha micans* F. extend as far as South Africa. A species of Alesia, one of *Goniochilus*, one of *Monochelus*, one of *Phrynocolus*, and one of *Exochonus* appear to be restricted to Kilimanjaro.

The beetles collected on the return journey from Kilimanjaro to Mombaza (end of November and beginning of December 1889) mostly belong to well-known East African species, e.g., *Tefflus hacquardi* Chaud. and *T. juvenilis* Gerst., *Chlaenius maximiliani* Har., *Gymnochila squamosa* Gray, *Anomala kersteni* Gerst., *Sternocera boucardi* Saund., *Amiantus castanopterus* Haag (new to the Royal Collection), *Sepidium muscosum* Gerst., *Dinoscelis passerinii* Gerst., *Microcerus annuliger* Har., and *Systates pollinosus* Gerst.

Certain species first brought home by Von der Decken from the interior and also from the Kilimanjaro district are included among those collected on the return journey : such are *Ateuchus catenatus* Gerst., *Trox baccatus* Gerst., *Micrantereus femoratus* Gerst., *Anomalipus heraldicus* Gerst., *Rhytidonota gracilis* Gerst., *R. ventricosa* Gerst., and *Chaunoderus stupidus* Gerst. Another species new to the Royal Collection is *Sternocera hunteri* Waterh., first discovered in 1889, the typical specimen coming from the same locality. Another remarkable beetle brought by Dr. Meyer from the same region as these last is a species of *Lachnodera*, a genus of Melonthidae hitherto known only to occur in Madagascar.

CATALOGUE OF THE BEETLES COLLECTED BY DR. MEYER IN THE KILIMANJARO REGION.

(New species marked with an asterisk [*].)

1. Tefflus hacquardi *Chaud.*
2. — juvenilis *Gerst.*
3. Chlaenius maximiliani *Har.*
4. Rhysotrachelus teani *Gestro.*
5. Metaxymorphus *spec.*
6. Orthogonius *spec.*
7. Silpha micans *F.*
8. Saprinus splendens *Er.*
9. Hister tropicalis *Mars.*
10. Gymnochila squamosa *Gray.*
11. Ateuchus aeratus *Gerst.*
12. — catenatus *Gerst.*
13. Gymnopleurus splendidus *Dej.*
14. Anachalcos procerus *Gerst.*
15. *Onitis meyeri *spec. nov.*
16. Oniticellus planatus *Boh.*
17. Diastellopalpus johnstoni *Waterh.*
18. Onthophagus picticollis *Gerst.*
19. * — fraternus *spec. nov.*
20. — *spec.*
21. — *spec.*
22. — *spec.*
23. Catharsius *spec.*
24. Phaeochrous beccarii *Har.*
25. Hybosorus arator *F.*
26. *Lachnodera fulvescens *spec. nov.*
27. *Schizonycha *spec.*
28. * — *spec.*
29. * — *spec.*
30. *Monochelus vagans *spec. nov.*
31. Trochalus *spec.*
32. Anomala tendinosa *Gerst.*
33. — kersteni *Gerst.*
34. Pachnoda ephippiata *Gerst.*

35. Diplognatha silicea *M'Leay.*
36. *Goniochilus meyeri *spec. nov.*
37. Trox baccatus *Gerst.*
38. * — montanus *spec. nov.*
39. — *spec.*
40. Sternocera hunteri *Waterh.*
41. — boucardi *Saund.*
42. Melyris pumila *Gerst.*
43. Hapalochrus amplipennis *Har.*
44. Lycus *spec.*
45. Luciola *spec.*
46. Micrantereus femoratus *Gerst.*
47. Phrynoculus ater *Waterh.*
48. * — undatocostatus *spec. nov.*
49. Amiantus castanopterus *Haag.*
50. Sepidium muscosum *Gerst.*
51. Dinoscelis passerinii *Gerst.*
52. Anomalipus heraldicus *Gerst.*
53. Rhytidonota ventricosa *Gerst.*
54. — gracilis *Gerst.*
55. Lagria *spec.*
56. Mylabris amplectens *Gerst.*
57. Mylabris aperta *Gerst.*
58. Lytta *spec.*
59. Macrathrius *spec.*
60. Mitophorus semiaeneus *Gerst.*
61. Systates aeneolus *Har.*
62. — pollinosus *Gerst.*
63. Chaunoderus stupidus *Gerst.*
64. *Entypotrachelus meyeri *spec. nov.*
65. *Peribrotus *spec.*
66. Microcerus annuliger *Har.*
67. — spiniger *Gerst.*
68. Ceratites jaspideus *Serv.*

69. Aspidomorpha *spec.*	74. Exochomus *spec.*
70. Callispa *spec.*	75. Chilomenes lunata *F.*
71. Ceralces natalensis *Baly.*	76 Chilocorus distigma *Gerst.*
72. *Alesia kilimana *spec. nov.*	77. Epilachna scalaris *Gerst.*
73. — *spec.*	78. — punctipennis *Muls.*

IX.

DR. HANS MEYER'S OBSERVATIONS FOR THE
DETERMINATION OF HEIGHTS.

COMPUTED BY DR. ERNEST WAGNER OF BERLIN.

A FEW remarks on the methods employed in computing Dr. Meyer's hypso-metrical observations may prove acceptable, in order that the reader may be enabled to estimate the trustworthiness of the results obtained.

As the readings of the aneroids pointed to great resultant heights, it was deemed inadvisable to work out special tables for their reduction, especially as the climatological materials, as far as Eastern Africa is concerned, are still very imperfect. All heights were computed according to the complete for-mula of Pernter,[1] which is a modification of that of Rühlmann. Pernter's for-mula not only embodies the most trustworthy values of the physical constants, but also enables us to dispense with the correction required by the change of gravity from the latitude of 45° to the latitude of the place of observation. These tables are thus directly applicable to observations made with aneroids. This remark applies also to boiling-point thermometers, the observed tem-peratures of which yield directly the corresponding atmospheric pressure, without its being necessary to apply any corrections whatsoever.

Dr. Meyer took with him three boiling-point thermometers by Fuess of Berlin (Nos. 135, 158, and 159), of which one (No. 159) was broken, whilst the others were brought back to Berlin and verified at the Imperial Physical Observatory at Charlottenburg. The use of these instruments proved in-valuable in checking the index-errors of the aneroids. They were verified both before starting and after returning, and their index-errors were found to be so trifling that the mean readings of both could be confidently accepted as correct. Boiling-point thermometer No. 159 gave almost parallel read-ings with No. 158 up to the time it was broken, and its index-error, as ascertained before starting, thus furnished a sufficient basis for correcting its readings during the journey.

By means of these instruments a general idea of the index-errors of the aneroids could be formed. It should be stated that aneroids No. 1250 and

[1] See Exner in *Repertorium der Physik*, 1888, pp. 161-178.

1255, by Böhne of Berlin, proved exceedingly trustworthy, and this was confirmed by the careful verification to which they were subjected at the Physical Observatory after returning.

It is well known that the index-error of most aneroids is a very variable quantity, and that a full knowledge of it is absolutely necessary if heights are to be determined by their means. Dr. Meyer checked his aneroid readings by boiling-point observations taken at intervals of two or three days, and sometimes even more frequently. He thus determined a number of points in a curve representing the variations in the index-errors of the aneroids. These curves show that the variations were never abrupt, as happens in the case of these delicate instruments after a fall or other accident. They show rather that the variations observed originated exclusively from the principle on which these instruments are constructed. They indicate changes of atmospheric pressure in consequence of the elasticity of the vacuum-chamber, and it is for this reason that imperfections in the materials employed in making the instrument must necessarily affect its readings. Even the best aneroids are not free from these elastic after-effects: their amount depends upon the changes in atmospheric pressure, and the rapidity with which they take place, and must be thoroughly ascertained if aneroid readings are to be utilised for computing heights.

At the Physical Observatory, the aneroids were subjected to pressures corresponding to those experienced when they were in use, and this enabled the computer to determine approximately the variations in their index-errors in all those instances in which they were not checked by boiling-point observations. This method of interpolation is preferable to accepting the index-errors as ascertained before the start and after returning, as the instruments are naturally affected by long sea-voyages under a constant pressure of 760 mm. (30 in.).

A convenient view of the changes of atmospheric pressure, and of the rapidity with which they took place, was obtained by treating the recorded readings of the aneroids as ordinates and the intervals of time as abscissæ. With the aid of a curve of atmospheric pressure thus obtained, and of the index-errors actually determined at the Physical Observatory, it became possible to construct a curve representing the variations in the index-errors for the period intervening between boiling-point observations. For pressures ranging from 760 to 390 mm. (15 to 30 in.) this curve fairly represented the facts of the case, and, although only an approximation, proved sufficient for the purpose. Changes of atmospheric pressure to the extent of 80 mm. (3 in.) were experienced in the course of a few days, which naturally entailed an accumulation of conflicting "elastic after-effects." A skilled observer might possibly succeed in determining these after-effects in a physical observatory, but all that can be looked for subsequently are approximate results.

During very many days the aneroids never rose above 457 mm. (18 in.), an atmospheric pressure which few of these instruments are supposed to record. On Kaiser Wilhelm's Peak the corrected readings of the two aneroids Nos. 1250 and 1255 were 374.9 and 375.1 mm. (14.760 and 14.768 in.) respectively. The true variations in the index-error could therefore be expressed only by a complicated function. Taking due note of the verifications which took place after the return home, and accepting plausible mean values for the variations, we obtain a curve which exhibits frequent abrupt changes, but is nevertheless continuous.

Some idea of the character of these variations may be formed from the following data. On August 30, 1889, aneroid 1250 recorded 762.4 mm., the index-error amounting to + 0.1 mm. On October 7, after a minimum atmospheric pressure of 374.9 mm., the index-error for the same instrument rose to + 3.8 mm. On October 22, in the course of eight hours, the atmospheric pressure increased from 456.9 mm. to 543.5 mm., the index-error rising simultaneously from + 5.5 mm. to + 6.7 mm. (0.22 to 0.26 in.). On January 3, 1890, with an atmospheric pressure of 760.2 mm., the index-error had once more fallen to − 0.9 mm. In the case of aneroid No. 1255 the corresponding index-errors amounted to − 3.3, − 0.5, + 2.3, + 3.9, and − 4.5 mm. It will thus be seen that the index-errors of both instruments moved on nearly parallel curves, although they differed so widely in the absolute amount.

The readings of the aneroids were corrected for temperature in accordance with the results of their examination at the Physical Observatory. In computing the altitude the corrected means of both instruments were taken.

All differences of height were referred to the German war-ships *Schwalbe*, *Sperber*, and *Carola*, the meteorological journals of which for the period in question were kindly communicated by the Admiralty. They were, as a rule, stationed at Zanzibar, but it happened frequently that all three vessels were absent at one and the same time, either off Pemba or at some port of the mainland. The observations made on board the vessels were nevertheless treated as if they had been made at the same place, for within the tropics temperature and atmospheric pressure are but little influenced by short distances, such as those in question here. As the distance between the lower and upper stations frequently exceeded two hundred miles, the correction for the temperature of the intermediate air could only be an approximate one. No correction due to the diurnal range of the barometer was applied, firstly, because it is insignificant as compared with the correction due to differences of temperature, and, secondly, we know but little about this range in the case of lofty mountains lying within the tropics.

On Mount Dodabetta (8630 feet) the diurnal range amounts to 0.083 inches, as compared with 0.118 inches at Madras. Even if we had introduced this value into the hypsometrical formula, it would scarcely have affected the results obtained. For greater altitudes within the tropics we have no observations at all. On Pike's Peak in Colorado (14,130 feet) the diurnal range reaches at most 0.032 inches ; it is therefore probable that it decreases with the height under the tropics also. This, however, is merely a hypothesis. When temperature and humidity were not determined at places where the aneroid was read, values for these elements were interpolated. Dr. Kersten's observations for humidity in 1864 furnished mean values which were accepted, whilst Dr. Meyer's own temperature observations showed that the temperature of the region explored decreased with the height at the following rates. viz., between 6 A.M. and 6 P.M. at the rate of 0.53° C. for 100 metres (1° F. for 344 feet), and between 6 P.M. and 6 A.M. at the rate of 0.6° C. for 100 metres (1° F. for 304 feet).

LIST OF THE PRINCIPAL HEIGHTS DETERMINED BETWEEN MOMBAZA AND KILIMANJARO.

DATE. 1889.	LOCALITY.	FEET.
Sept. 4.	Mombaza (Harbour)	52
,, 5.	Rabai (Mission station)	545
,, 6.	Camp at the Moadje	492
,, 7.	Mkuyuni camp	617
,, 8.	Ngurungas of Gore	590
,, 9.	Samburu camp	945
,, 9.	Taro camp	1,214
,, 10.	Ngurunga at Makanga	1,355
,, 10.	Camp in the steppes	1,503
,, 11.	Maungu camp	2,349
,, 12.	Ndara camp	2,172
,, 14.	Matate camp	2,845
,, 15.	Bura camp	3,100
,, 16.	Marago ya Mzungu	3,219
,, 17.	Lanjoro mdogo	2,815
,, 17.	Taveta	2,444
,, 21.	Habari R.	2,966
,, 21.	Himo camp	3,015
,, 22.	Moji stream	2,831
,, 22.	,, English mission	4,380
,, 22.	,, German station	4,485
,, 25.	Summit of Kirúa	5,154
,, 25.	Hill of Lasso	5,256
,, 25.	Mué stream	4,587
,, 25.	Marangu	4,565
,, 25.	Camp at the Rua	6,430
,, 28.	In the forest	6,880
,, 29.	Camp at the Kifinika	8,707
,, 29.	,, ,, ,, Mué	9,478
,, 30.	Dr. Abbott's camp	12,979
Oct. 1.	Kibo camp	14,200
,, 2.	Talus in valley on S.E. Kibo	16,270
,, 3.	Ice above S.E. ridge	17,983
,, 3.	Crater rim	19,262
,, 3.	In the "red ravine"	14,682
,, 5.	Bottom of S.E. valley	14,659
,, 5.	Cave where we bivouacked	15,263
,, 6.	Lower end of Ratzel glacier	17,392
,, 6.	Upper ,, ,,	18,681
,, 6.	First peak on summit of Kibo	19,676

DATE. 1889.	LOCALITY.	FEET.
Oct. 6.	Second peak on summit of Kibo (Kaiser William's Peak)	19,718
,, 6.	Third peak on summit of Kibo	19,679
,, 11.	Camp at the Schneequelle	12,910
,, 12.	Camp at Mawenzi	14,301
,, 13.	Lower extremity of great talus on Mawenzi	15,256
,, 13.	Commencement of solid rock	16,057
,, 13.	Western ridge	16,687
,, 15.	Cleft in the central crest	16,713
,, 15.	Purtscheller Peak	16,834
,, 15.	Highest flowering plants	15,420
,, 17.	Lower limit of ice-cap on the north of Kibo	18,560
,, 17.	Detached glacier	15,912
,, 19.	Ice below the "Hans-Meyer Notch"	18,914
,, 19.	Bottom of crater	18,928
,, 19.	Ice above "Hans-Meyer Notch"	19,242
,, 19.	Foot of the "Red Hill"	14,616
,, 19.	Summit of the "Red Hill"	14,830
,, 21.	N.W. hills on Mawenzi	14,823
,, 21.	Northern ridge	15,190
,, 21.	Cleft in N.W. ridge	16,132
,, 31.	Kahé camp	2,454
Nov. 1.	Rufu, where we crossed	2,382
,, 1.	Mrushunga camp	3,103
,, 2.	Wangobi camp	4,547
,, 3.	Mafurra	5,180
,, 4.	Summit of Gamualla	6,565
,, 5.	Naguvu camp	4,491
,, 6.	Ngovi camp	4,692
,, 7.	Mt. Ngovi	5,578
,, 8.	Camp at the Papyrus swamp	2,484
,, 9.	,, Habari River.	3,169
,, 15.	Ngona River	5512

(Nos. 1–8 of Nov. bracketed "Ugweno.")

DATE. 1889.	LOCALITY.	FEET.	DATE. 1889.	LOCALITY.	FEET.
Nov. 16.	Camp in Kiboso	9918	Nov. 26.	Nanga stream .	4268
„ 17.	Upper limit of forest	8894	„ 26.	Hill of Kiriia .	5158
„ 17.	{Uru, upper limit of cultivated zone	5686	„ 29.	Una stream	5095
			„ 29.	Mwika camp .	4751
„ 18.	Camp in Uru .	4849	„ 30.	Taveta .	2444
„ 19.	Trench at the boundary	3530	Dec. 2.	Lanjoro mdogo	2812
„ 19.	{Confluence of the Wumbo and the Ngombere	2950	„ 2.	Camp in the steppes	3127
			„ 3.	Bura camp	3100
„ 19.	Maëmbe stream	3632	„ 4.	Foot of Javia Hill .	3474
„ 19.	Manjoka stream	3582	„ 4.	Matate camp .	2845
„ 19.	Nseri „	3563	„ 5.	Ndara camp	2172
„ 19.	Camp at the Weri-weri	4078	„ 7.	Maungu „	2343
„ 19.	River Weri-weri	3927	„ 9.	Taro „	1220
„ 21.	Camp in Majamé	4626	„ 10.	Samburu „	945
„ 21.	River Kikafu .	4439	„ 11.	Moadje „	518
„ 21.	River Nasere .	4446	„ 12.	Rabai „	541
„ 23.	Camp at Ngombere River	3114	„ 12.	Bandarin camp	154
„ 24.	River Rau	2946	„ 13.	Mombaza (Freretown)	20

X.

CARTOGRAPHY.

BY DR. B. HASSENSTEIN OF GOTHA.

A PERUSAL of Dr. Meyer's narrative distinctly reveals the fact that the author has missed no opportunity of supplying materials for a map. During his second expedition this task had devolved upon Dr. O. Baumann; on the present occasion it was undertaken by Dr. Meyer himself, who had provided himself for that purpose with excellent surveying instruments, and had undergone a course of instruction at the Admiralty Office at Berlin. When Dr. Meyer reached Aden on his way home, he offered me the whole of his cartographical materials, well knowing that I held the giant mountain of Eastern Africa in special veneration ever since the earlier materials furnished by Rebmann and Krapf, and by Baron Von der Decken and his companions, had passed through my hands.

The materials brought home by Dr. Meyer turned out to be of exceptional value. I saw at once that the whole of them could not be utilised for the present volume. It appeared to me that a compilation combining Dr. Meyer's work with the surveys of Thornton and Von der Decken, and of Lieutenant von Höhnel (1887–88), as also with other existing materials, was called for. This complete map, together with a memoir, I propose to publish in a geographical periodical.

The following figures, therefore, are merely intended to give an idea of the original materials which were available for the construction of the maps accompanying this volume. With two exceptions, they are results obtained by Dr. Meyer himself in the course of 1889, and fall under the following heads : —

    1. Astronomical determinations of positions.
    2. Route surveys.
    3. Measurements of angles.
    4. Determinations of altitude.
    5. Determination of magnetic variation.
    6. Sketches, profiles, photographs, and the like.

    1. *Astronomical Observations.*—These were made with the aid of a portable transit theodolite by Hildebrand & Schramm, of Freiburg, in Saxony, and of three pocket-chronometers by A. Lange & Sons, of Glashütte, near Dresden. The vertical circle of the theodolite was divided to half degrees, and the instrument was examined by Mr. Neubert, of the German Admiralty, before Dr. Meyer's departure, and again after his return. The watches (described as Nos. 6, 7, and 8) were carefully rated at the Royal Observatory at Leipzig.

Colonel von Sterneck, of the Military Geographical Institute of Vienna, kindly computed Dr. Meyer's observations. The results are as follows :—

Date. 1889.	Stations.	South Latitude by Observation.	Observed Error of Watch on Mean Local Time. Watch No. 8.	Watch No. 7.	Watch No. 6.	Longitude West of Mombasa.	Longitude East of Greenwich.
		° ′ ″	h. m. s.	h. m. s.	h. m. s.	h. m. s.	° ′
Sept. 5	Mombaza	4 2 57	+2 39 20	+0 37 14	+0 4 36	0 0 0	39 41.2
,, 8	Samburu Camp	3 46 40	0 37 39	0 35 10	0 3 34	0 1 54	39 12.7
,, 9	Taro Camp	3 44 48	0 37 10	0 34 35	0 3 35	0 2 21	39 5.9
,, 13	Ndara Camp	3 30 21	0 34 44	0 31 40	0 1 50	0 5 11	38 23.4
,, 16	Bura Camp	3 30 20	0 33 51	0 30 23	0 1 34	0 6 17	38 6.9
,, 18	Taveta	3 24 26	0 31 32	0 27 45	−0 0 32	0 8 54	27 27.7
,, 20	,,	3 24 50	0 31 27	0 27 30	0 0 07	0 8 50	...
,, 24	Moji station	3 18 5	0 30 05	0 25 48	0 0 35	0 10 29	37 3.9
,, 27	Marangu (Mareale's village).	3 18 14	0 30 27	0 25 52	0 0 14	0 10 20	37 6.2
Oct. 2	Kibo Camp (Rock of the Four Men)	3 7 14	0 30 51	0 25 01	+2 42 20	0 10 24	37 5.2
,, 14	Mawenzi Camp (East Lava Hill)	3 6 36	0 31 05	0 23 52	0 46 34	0 11 24	36 50.2
,, 16	,, ,,	...	0 30 55	0 23 34	0 47 10	0 11 24	...
,, 20	,, ,,	...	0 31 09	0 22 58	0 48 9	0 11 24	...
Nov. 3	Kisinga rivulet	3 40 54	0 32 24	+2 32 47	0 49 16	0 11 28	36 49.2
,, 4	Naguru Camp	3 41 47	0 33 36	0 32 46	0 50 31	0 10 21	37 5.9
,, 7	Ngovi Mount	3 34 30	0 34 03	0 32 48	0 51 00	0 10 9	37 8.9
,, 14	Marangu	3 17 30	0 34 27	0 31 36	0 52 47	0 10 20	37 6.2
,, 18	Uru-Salika Camp	3 16 13	0 34 07	0 30 00	+3 03 08	0 10 58	36 56.7
,, 21	Majamé Camp	3 13 16	0 33 33	Watch No. 7 Injured +2 35 38		0 11 46	36 44.7
,, 25	Moji station	3 18 5	0 35 9	...	0 35 35	0 10 29	37 3.9
,, 28	Marangu	3 18 18	0 36 3	...	0 37 13	0 10 20	37 6.2
,, 28	,,		0 36 3	...	0 37 16	0 10 20	...
,, 29	Mwika	3 17 42	0 36 21	...	0 38 05	0 9 41	36 15.9
Dec. 4	Matate	3 30 17	0 40 17	...	0 41 58	0 6 09	38 8.9
,, 6	Ndara	3 30 25	0 41 06	...	0 43 13	0 5 11	38 23.4
,, 10	Samburu	3 46 40	0 44 40	...	0 45 18	0 1 54	39 12.7
,, 13	Mombaza	4 2 57	0 46 44	...	0 47 39	0 0 0	39 41.2

In the preceding table the longitudes given in the last column are referred to the Mombaza Fort, supposed to be 39° 41' 10" east of Greenwich, in accordance with observations made by officers of Her Majesty's surveying vessel *Stork* in 1888, kindly communicated by Captain Wharton, the hydrographer, viz. :—

Zanzibar, British Consulate . . .	! 39° 11' 8" East of Greenwich.
Difference in longitude between this Consulate and Ras Kidomoni (English Point), near Mombaza	30' 8" East of Greenwich.
Resultant longitude of Kidomoni . .	39° 41' 16" East of Greenwich.
Flag-staff of the Fort, Mombaza . .	6" West of Kidomoni.
Longitude of the flag-staff	39° 41' 10" East of Greenwich.

Colonel Von Sterneck, in the letter which accompanies his calculations, states that the latitudes are quite trustworthy, but that owing to the shortcomings of the watches, and especially of Nos. 6 and 7, the longitudes are not satisfactory. " Longitudinal differences between places lying so near each other," he says, " cannot satisfactorily be determined by this method, as unavoidable errors are greater than the differences. Only the telegraph, or a larger number of chronometers, could yield satisfactory results. It would be advisable to recalculate the observations, for the errors of the watches were very considerable, as has been the case with all watches used by African travellers, as far as my experience goes."

As it was most desirable to obtain a satisfactory longitude for Taveta, Dr. Harzer, the Director of the Gotha Observatory, kindly undertook to recalculate the observations. He found, however, that the error in the longitude of Mombaza amounted to 10', whilst at the western stations it reached ± 20'. Dr. Harzer assured me that these errors were due to serious injuries suffered by the chronometers, and I therefore rejected Dr. Meyer's longitudes altogether, and had to trust to his other materials in plotting the general map.

As to Taveta, I accepted the longitude determined by Lieut. Von Höhnel, of Count S. Teleki's expedition, viz., 37° 35' east of Greenwich.[1] A more careful plotting of all Dr. Meyer's observations than that which I have been able to effect for the present volume may possibly show whether the longitude accepted by me is the most nearly correct.

2. *Route Surveys.*— These, as usual, were made by the aid of a watch and of a pocket-compass (of square form, by E. Schneider of Vienna). Dr. Meyer plotted his routes on ruled paper, on a scale of 1 milimetre to the minute (2.4 inches to an hour's march). He took bearings at intervals of about three minutes, and the results proved highly satisfactory. The whole of the route was plotted on sixteen folio sheets, on the scale adopted by Dr. Meyer, and this general map afforded the means of systematically arranging the notes

[1] See Lieut.' Von Höhnel's Report in Petermann's *Mitteilungen*, Supplement, No. 99, p. 43.

on the features of the ground, the direction of the rivulets, the character of the vegetation, &c., which were found in Dr. Meyer's note-books.

Dr. Meyer, on various occasions, determined the length of his paces, and thus afforded a valuable means of plotting his routes. The average length of his pace was 64 cm. (25.2 in.). In the steppe plains between Mombaza and Taveta, and to the west of the latter, he took 110 paces in a minute, the rate of progress amounting to 4.2 km. (2.6 miles) an hour. In the inhabited parts of Jagga and Ugweno he marched at the rate of 102 paces a minute, being equivalent to 3.9 km. (2.4 miles) an hour; in the primeval forest and beyond this route it was reduced to 66 paces, or 2.6 km. (1.6 miles) an hour. Higher up still the progress varied exceedingly, according to the steepness of the ground and the exhaustion of the traveller, and by itself afforded no means of plotting the route.

The caravan route from Mombaza to Taveta was surveyed very carefully, and has been plotted by me on a large scale, with the aid of bearings to the conspicuous peaks of Kilibasi and Kadiaro, and of four trustworthy latitudes. As the scale of map 1 in this volume is too small to show all the details, I propose to publish this map subsequently on a larger scale.

3. *Measurements of Angles.*—Bearings taken with one of Cary's prismatic compasses, and supplemented by profiles facilitating the identification of the objects sighted, constitute by far the most valuable portion of the material contributed by Dr. Meyer towards the construction of a correct map.

These bearings, more than one thousand in number, were plotted by me upon separate sheets of tracing-paper; the adjustment of which furnished a series of forty-seven connected stations, numbered chronologically upon the maps. Having prepared a projection on a scale of 1 : 250,000, and indicated upon it the latitudes of Taveta, Moji, Uru-Salika, Majamé, Mwika, Mawenzi camp, and Kibo camp in the north, as also those of the camps at the Kisinga, the Naguvu, and Mount Ngovi in the south, these bearings enabled me to plot a network of triangles, which is invisible upon the map, but the knowledge of which would enable future cartographers and explorers to form a true estimate of the trustworthiness of the trigonometrical basis of the maps. The object of these lines is to supply the place of that trigonometrical tracing.[1]

Among the stations which afforded the most satisfactory results were those from which both summits of Kilimanjaro were visible, or from which the volcanic cone of Mount Meru, a sharply-defined "volcanic mountain in the

---

[1] I venture to advise future travellers once more to supply themselves not only with the latest maps of the territories they are about to explore, but also to apply to cartographers for series of triangles, lists of positions, memoirs, and lists of desiderata, so that they may be enabled to direct their attention to things actually wanted, and avoid wasting their strength upon work already satisfactorily done by their predecessors.

[It would be advisable if cartographers were to publish these "triangulations" forthwith. In the present instance the principal bearings might have been inserted upon the maps in red, or they might have been shown in a diagram covering half a page of this volume.—*Tr.*]

plain," or the principal summits of the Ugweno mountains could be sighted. The most productive stations in Jagga were Nos. 7, 5, 45, 44, and 47. Three summits in Ugweno (Gamualla, Sungo, and Mount Ngovi) not only yielded bearings towards Kilimanjaro, but also afforded objective points for an excellent survey of Ugweno itself, the delineation of which thus differs considerably from the map based upon Mr. Thornton's bearings. More abundant still were the materials furnished by Stations 12 to 29, which lie on the saddle plateau and on the upper slopes of Kilimanjaro, and which are shown distinctly on Map III.

The topographical details furnished by this latter group of bearings, together with numerous profiles and photographs, as also the personal explanations of Dr. Meyer, enabled me to construct a map of the upper regions of Kilimanjaro on a large scale (1 : 40,000), of which Map III. is a reduction. This map is based upon the observed latitudes of the Mawenzi camp (3° 6′ 36″ S.) and the Kibo camp (3° 7′ 14″ S.), combined with the distance between these two localities. This distance, as deduced from the itineraries and the triangulation, amounts to about 5, certainly not under 4 km (2½ miles). Dr. Meyer, who apparently trusted to his astronomical observations, did not measure a base-line, an omission which one of his successors may possibly be in a position to make good.

4. *Altitudes.*—A list of these, as far as they have been computed by Dr. E. Wagner, will be found on p. 378. Further observations, including four series of vertical angles measured with the theodolite, have still to be computed, and will furnish additional materials for a continued map of the region.

5. *Magnetic Variation.*—These observations for finding the errors of the compass were taken with a prismatic compass by Cary, and with a compass of square form by E. Schneider. The results, as calculated by Colonel Von Sterneck, are as follows :—

Date, 1889.	Station.	By Prismatic Compass.			By Square Compass.		
		⊙'s Azimuth.	Reading of Needle.	Error W.	⊙'s Azimuth.	Reading of Needle.	Error W.
Aug. 28	Zanzibar	63° 23′	72° 0′	8° 37′	...	...	...
„ „		60° 16′	70° 30′	(10° 14′)	55° 37′	298° 50′	5° 33′
Sept. 5	Mombaza	34° 42′	41° 50′	7° 8′	...	...	...
„ 13	Ndara	277° 12′	285° 30′	8° 18′	276° 38′	73° 0′	10° 22′
„ 19	Taveta	80° 24′	88° 45′	8° 21′	78° 12′	272° 0′	9° 48′
„ 27	Marangu	270° 24′	279° 0′	8° 36′	270° 23′	80° 30′	9° 7′
Oct. 16	Mawenzi	99° 18′	105° 30′	6° 12′	99° 21′	250° 0′	(10° 39′)
„ 20	„	102° 18′	108° 30′	6° 12′	102° 23′	251° 0′	6° 37′
Nov. 14	Marangu	114° 57′	124° 30′	9° 33′	64° 51′	235° 0′	9° 51′
„ 21	Majamé	243° 41′	257° 40′	(13° 59′)	243° 55′	101° 0′	(14° 5′)
Dec. 14	Mombaza	239° 45′	246° 30′	6° 45′	239° 54′	247° 40′	7° 46′

Colonel Von Sterneck has furnished no explanation as to the great differences between the above results and the variation indicated upon the Admiralty charts. He seems inclined, however, to give the preference to the observations made with the square compass. I have therefore taken the mean of the stations Taveta, Marangu, and Majamé (9° 6' W.) in constructing the map of Kilimanjaro, especially as this result agrees satisfactorily with Lieutenant Von Höhnel's observations. I rejected the results obtained at the Mawenzi camp (6° 30' W.). Bearings taken from Stations 28 and 29 on the northern spur of Mawenzi towards points such as the outlet of the Lumi, the position of which is known, show conclusively that the proximity of volcanic rocks causes a local deflection of the magnetic needle towards the East, amounting to 18 or 19 degrees. At Station 27, whence bearings were taken towards the Nyiri swamps, this easterly deflection scarcely amounts to a degree.

6. Numerous sketches, photographs, and profiles proved of great use in the construction of the map, and a verbal explanation of the photographic views of Kibo and Mawenzi furnished many topographical details which have therein found a place.

XI.

BIBLIOGRAPHY.

LITERATURE OF EAST AFRICA CONTAINING REFERENCES TO KILIMANJARO.

A full catalogue (with critical remarks) of the literature dealing with East Equatorial Africa till the year 1870, is given in Hassenstein's *Uebersicht der Litteratur von Ost-Afrika*, appended to C. C. Von der Decken's *Reisen in Ost-Afrika*, vol. iii., Part 3. The following list includes the names of such works as deal more particularly with the history of travel and exploration in the Kilimanjaro region.

EMERY, Lieut.—Short Account of Mombas and the Neighbouring Coast of Africa. (*Journal of the Roy. Geog. Soc.*, 1833, vol. iii. pp. 280–282.)

COOLEY, W. D.—The Negroland of the Arabs Examined and Explained; or an Inquiry into the Early History and Geography of Central Africa. London, 1841. (*Journal of the Roy. Geog. Soc.*, vol. xii., 1842.)

COOLEY, WM. DESBOROUGH.—The Geography of Nyassa; or the Great Lake of Southern Africa. (*Journal of the Roy. Geog. Soc.*, vol. xv., 1845, p. 185; vol. xvi. p. 138.)

FROBERVILLE, EUGENE DE.—Analyse d'un Mémoire sur les Langues et les Races de l'Afrique Orientale au Sud de l'Équateur. (*Procès verbaux des séances de la Société d'Histoire Naturelle de Maurice*, 1846. Appendix, p. 16.)

GUMPRECHT, T. E.—Ueber den grossen südafrikanischen Volks- und Sprachs-stamm. (*Monatsb. der Ges. f. Erdk.*, Berlin, new edit., vol. vi., 1849, pp. 142-191. Conf. also vol. vii., 1850, pp. 239-291.)

GUMPRECHT, T. E.—" Rapport sur les Races Nègres de l'Afrique Orientale du Sud de l'Équateur, observées par M. de Froberville." (*Comptes-rendus de l'Académie des Sciences*, vol. xxx., 1850, No. 22.)

COOLEY, W. D.—Inner Africa Laid Open; or an Attempt to Trace the Chief Lines of Communication Across the Continent. London, 1852.

GUILLAIN, Capt. M.—Documents sur l'Histoire, la Géographie et le Commerce de l'Afrique Orientale. 2 vols., with atlas and 54 plates. Paris, 1856 and 1857.

ROSCHER, Dr. ALBRECHT.—Ptolemäus und die Handelsstrassen in Zentral-Afrika. Ein Beitrag zur Erklärung der ältesten uns erhaltenen Welt-karte. With 2 maps. Gotha, 1857. (Conf. also *Petermanns Mitteil.*, 1857, p. 154.)

MURCHISON. — Ueber die Beschaffenheit der Zentral-Regionen Afrikas. (*Petermanns Geogr. Mitteil.*, 1857, p. 340.)

GUNOT, ARNOLD.—Ueber die Struktur des Afrikanischen Kontinents. (*Geogr. Mitt.*, 1857, p. 383.)

BEHM, E.—Die Völker Ost-Afrika's nach Guillain, Krapf und anderen. (*Petermanns Geogr. Mitt.*, 1858, p. 396 and table.)

MACQUEEN, JAMES.—Observations on the Geography of Central Africa. (*Proceedings of the Roy. Geog. Soc.*, 1859, p. 209.)

BEKE, Dr. CHARLES T.—The Sources of the Nile. London, 1860.

BEKE, Dr. CH. T.—On the Mountains forming the Eastern Side of the Basin of the Nile, and the Origin of the Designation "Mountains of the Moon," as applied to them. (*Edinburgh New Philos. Journ.*, XIV., 1861, pp. 240-154.)

NEUMANN.—Forschungsreisen von Zanzibar und Zentral-Afrika. (*Zeitschr. f. Allg. Erdk.*, new edit., vol. vi., 1859, p. 386.)

ZEITHAMMER.—Rückblicke auf die Geschichte der geographischen Erforschung Süd-Afrikas. (*Mitteil. der k. k. geogr. Ges. in Wien.*, IV., 1860, p. 165.) Review of the literature on South Africa from the time of Ptolemy to 1860, with critical remarks.

JOURNEYS OF THE MISSIONARIES KRAPF, REBMANN, AND ERHARDT.

A chronological account of the journeys of Krapf and Rebmann in East Africa is given in Hassenstein's *Bemerkungen zur Karte der Region des Kilima-Ndscharo und Kenia in Ost-Africa.* (*Petermanns Mitteil.*, 1864, Part 12, pp. 449-456.)

KRAPF, Dr.—Schreiben an Professor von Ewald aus Rabbay Empia über Rebmann's Entdeckung des Schneebergs Killi Mandscharo. (*Zeitschr. der Deutsch. Morgenländ. Gesellsch.*, vol. iii. p. 317.)

REBMANN, J.—Journal d'un Excursion au Djagga, les Pays des Neiges de l'Afrique Orientale. (*Nouvelles Annales des Voyages*, 1849, II., pp. 257, 300.)

GUMPRECHT, T. E.—Die von Rebmann im östlichen Süd-Afrika in der Nähe des Aequators entdeckten Schneeberge. (*Monatsberichte d. Ges. f. Erdk.*, new edit., vol. vi, 1849, pp. 285-297.)

RITTER, E.—Dr. Krapf's Reise von Mombas zu dem Lande der Schneeberge in Ukamba unter dem Aequator, 1849. (*Monatsber. d. Ges. f. Erdk.*, new edit., vol. viii. p. 193.)

BERGHAUS, HEINR.—Killi Mandscharo, das Schneegebirge im tropischen Ost-Afrika, unter $3\frac{2}{3}°$ südl. Br. (*Geograph. Jahrbuch zur Mitteil. aller wichtigern neueren Erforschungen*, von Dr. Heinrich Berghaus, vol. i., 1850, pp. 59-61.)

BERGHAUS, HEINR.—Bergketten und Flusz-Systeme in Afrika. Anschauung derselben im Jahre 1850. Zur Erläuterung der vorgehefteten Karte. (*Berghaus' Jahrbuch*, Part 2, 1850, pp. 1-19.)

KRAPF, Dr. LUDWIG.—Journal seiner Reise nach Ukambani, 1849. *Verhandl. d. Ges. f. Erdk.*, 1851, VIII., p. 193.)

KRAPF, Dr. L.—Journal d'un Voyage au Ouadigo, au Ouachinsi et à l'Ousambára, Contrées de la Côte d'Afrique dans le Sud et le Sud-ouest de Mombaze. (*Nouv. Annales des Voyages*, 1850, IV., pp. 5-143; 1851, I., pp. 51, 283; III., pp. 113; IV., pp. 72.)

BEKE, Dr. CHARLES T.—Ueber die Herleitung des Nils aus dem N'Yassi oder Groszen See von Süd-Afrika und über die Schneeberge im tropischen Ost-Afrika. Schreiben an H. Berghaus. (*Berghaus' Jahrbuch*, Part 3, 1851, pp. 62-66.)

GUMPRECHT, T. E.—Schnee und neue Schneeberge im tropischen Afrika. (*Zeitschrift für Allgem. Erdkunde*, 1853, L., pp. 230-240.)

PETERMANN, A.—The Snowy Mountains of Eastern Africa. (*The Athenæum*, 1853, No. 1348.)

REBMANN, J.—Report of the British Association, 1854. (*Transactions*, p. 123.)

REBMANN.—Briefe aus Ost- und Mittel-Afrika. (*Calwer Missionsblatt*, 28, Jahrg. 1885, No. 19, pp. 78-83.)

KRAPF, Dr. J. L.—Reisen in Ost-Afrika, ausgeführt in den Jahren 1837-1855. Kronthal und Stuttgart, 1858.

ERHARDT, J.—On an Inland Sea in Central Africa. (*Proc. of the Roy. Geog. Soc.*, 1856, p. 8.)

ERHARDT, J.—Memoire zur Erläuterung der von ihm und J. Rebmann zusammengestellten Karte von Ost- und Zentral-Afrika, nebst Bemerkungen von W. Desb. Cooley und A. Petermann. (*Peterm. Geogr. Mitt.*, 1856, pp. 19-32, and p. 483.)

(A German edition of the celebrated map which first appeared in the *Church Missionary Intelligences*, and gave such an impetus to the work of exploration during the next decade.)

KRAPF, Dr. L.—Kurze Beschreibung der Masai- und Wakuafi-Stämme im südöstlichen Afrika. (*Ausland*, 1857, Nos. 19 and 20.)

ERHARDT, Rev. J.—Vocabulary of the Enguduk Iloigob, as Spoken by the Masai Tribes in East Africa. Ludwigsburg, 1857. (*Petermanns Mitteil.*, 1857, p. 222.)

KRAPF, Dr. L.—Die frühere Geschichte der Stadt Mombas, 4° südlich vom Aequator, in Ost-Africa. (*Ausland*, 1858, No. 36.)

KRAPF, Dr. L.—Travels, Researches, and Missionary Labours during an Eighteen Years' Residence in Eastern Africa. London, 1860. (An American edition appeared in Boston in 1860.)

KRAPF, Dr. L.—My Late Mission Tour to the East Coast of Africa. (*Christian Work throughout the World* for 1863. London, 1863, vol. i. p. 193.)

MEINICKE, C. E.—Krapf's und Rebmann's Reisen im östlichen Südafrika. Mit 2 Karten von Kiepert. (*Zeit. f. Allgem. Erdk.*, 1860, new edit., vol. ix. p. 22 *et seq.*)

Die Entdeckungen in Afrika und die Mission. (*Baseler Evangelisches Missions-Magazin*, 1861, January number.)

BARTH, Dr. H.—Dr. August Petermann und die Schneeberge. (*Zeit. f. Allgem. Erdk.*, new edit., vol. xiii., 1862, pp. 342-347.)

BURTON'S TRAVELS.

BURTON, R. J.—Zanzibar, and Two Months in East Africa. (*Blackwood's Edinburgh Magazine*, 1858, No. 134, February, March, and May.)

BURTON, Capt. R. J., and J. H. SPEKE.—A Coasting Voyage from Mombasa to the Pangani River; Visit to Sultan Kimwere. (*Jour. of the Roy. Geog. Soc.*, vol. xxviii., 1858.)

BURTON, Capt. R. J.—The Lake Regions of Central Equatorial Africa, with Notices of the Lunar Mountains and the Sources of the White Nile. (*Jour. of the Roy. Geog. Soc.*, vol. xxix., 1858.)

PETERMANN, A.—Atlas der neuesten Entdeckungen in Afrika. Gotha, 1860.

HASSENSTEIN, B.—Memoire zur Karte von Inner-Afrika. (*Geogr. Mitt.*, Ergänzungsband, 2, p. 1 *et seq.*) Which see also for journalistic literature on Burton and Speke's first journey.

HASSENSTEIN, B.—Bemerkungen zur Karte der Region des Kilima-Ndscharo und Kenia in Ost-Afrika. (*Geogr. Mitteil.*, 1864, pp. 449-456.)

BURTON, R. J.—Zanzibar, City, Island, and Coast. London, 1872.

APPENDIX.

C. C. v. d. Decken's Expeditions, 1860–65.

Decken.—Auszug aus einem Brief des Herrn Baron Carl v. d. Decken an seine Mutter sowie Briefe an Herrn Dr. Barth. (*Zeit. f. Allg. Erdk.*, new edit., X., 1861, pp. 133, 229, 467; XL, 1861, p. 369; and XII., 1862, p. 73.) Brief nebst Auszügen aus den Briefen von Dr. O. Kersten. (*Zeit. f. Erdk.*, XIV., 1863, pp. 41, 348; XV., p. 149; and XIX., 1865, p. 153.)

Kersten, Dr. O.—Briefliche Mitteilung über seine Besteigung des Kilimanjaro in Gesellschaft des Barons v. d. Decken. (*Zeit. f. Allg. Erdk.*, new edit., 1863, p. 141. Conf. *Peter. Geogr. Mitt.*, 1863, p. 99.)

Rose, Prof. G.—Beschreibung der von Herrn v. d. Decken gesammelten Gebirgsarten aus Ost-Afrika grösztenteils vom Fusze des Kilima-ndjaro. (*Zeit. f. Allg. Erdk.*, new edit., XIV., 1863, p. 245.)

Roth, Dr. J.—Beschreibung der von Herrn v. d. Decken aus der Gegend des Kilima-ndjaro mitgebrachten Gebirgsarten. (*Zeit. f. Allg. Erdk.*, new edit., XV., 1863, p. 543.)

Kiepert, Dr. H.—Bemerkungen zu den Karten Baron C. v. d. Decken's: (1) Das Schneegebirge. (2) Skizze seiner zweiten Reise von der Afrikan. Ostküste zum Kilima-ndjaro. (*Zeit. f. Allg. Erdk.*, new edit., XV., 1863, p. 545.)

Thornton, R.—Expedition to Kilimanjaro. (*Proc. of the Roy. Geog. Soc.*, vol. vi., No. 2, p. 47.)

Thornton, R.—Notes on a Journey to Kilimanjaro, made in Company of the Baron v. d. Decken. (*Journal of the Roy. Geog. Soc. of London.*, vol. xxxv., 1865, p. 15.)

Barth, Dr. H.—Das neue Unternehmen des Herrn Baron v. d. Decken. (*Zeit. f. Allg. Erdk.*, new edit., XVIII., 1865, p. 54. Conf. also *Geogr. Mitt.*, 1865, p. 266.)

Kersten, Dr. O.—Die neuesten Nachrichten über die Schicksale der Expedition des Herrn Baron C. v. d. Decken. (*Zeit. d. Ges. f. Erdk.*, I., 1866, p. 97 and 160.)

Kersten, Dr. O.—Ueber Kolonisation in Ost-Afrika. Mit Hervorhebung ihrer Wichtigkeit für Deutschland. (Reprint from the *International Review*, 1867, vol. ii.)

Decken, C. C. von der.—Reisen in Ost-Afrika in den Jahren 1859 bis 1865. Bearbeitet von O. Kersten. In 2 Teilen oder 4 Bänden. Leipzig, 1869–79.

Kersten, Dr. O.—Tabellarische Uebersicht über die Geschichte Ostafrikas (bis 1874). (Von der Decken's *Reisewerk*, vol. iii., Pt. 3.)

Kersten, Dr. O.—Astronomische, geodätische und Höhenmessungen im mittleren Ost-Afrika, nebst kartographischen Bemerkungen. Leipzig u. Heidelberg. 1879. (Reprint from v. d. Decken's *Reisewerke*, vol. iii. Pt. 3.)

BIBLIOGRAPHY. 389

KERSTEN, Dr. O.—Dem Andenken Carl Claus von der Decken's. (*Deutsche Kolonial-Zeitung*, 1890, new edit., III., p. 245.)

JOURNEYS OF THE MISSIONARIES NEW AND WAKEFIELD.

NEW, CHARLES, and WAKEFIELD, Letters from Revs. (*The United Methodist Free Churches' Missionary Notices*, 1864, p. 204 *et seq.*)

WAKEFIELD, Rev. T.—Routes of Native Caravans from the Coast to the Interior of Eastern Africa. (*Journal of the Roy. Geog. Soc. of London*, vol. xl., 1870, pp. 303–339, with map.)

NEW, Rev. CH., and R. BUSHELL.—Letter to Dr. Kirk on an Ascent of Mount Kilima-Njaro. (*Proc. of Roy. Geog. Soc.*, vol. xvi., 1872, No. 3, pp. 161–171. (Conf. *Behm's Geogr. Jahrbuch*, 1872, p. 416, and *Peterm. Geogr. Mitt.*, 1873, p. 193.)

NEW, CH.—Life, Wanderings, and Labours in Eastern Africa. With an Account of the First Successful Ascent of the Equatorial Snow Mountain Kilima-Njaro, and Remarks upon East African Slavery. London, 1874.

NEW, Rev. CH.—Journey from the Pangani, *via* Wadigo, to Mombasa. (*Proc. of the Roy. Geog. Soc.*, vol. xix., 1875, p. 317.)

WAKEFIELD, Rev. L.—Wakefield's Fourth Journey to the Southern Galla Country in 1877. (*Proc. of the Roy. Geog. Soc.*, 1882, vol. iv. No. 6.)

JOURNEYS, BOOKS, AND PAPERS FROM 1870–1880.

GAUME.—Voyage à la Côte Orientale d'Afrique pendant l'Année 1866. Par R. P. Horner. Paris, 1872.

DELITSCH, Dr. O.—Das äquatoriale Tafelland in Süd-Afrika nach dem Stande unserer jetzigen Kenntnis. (*Aus allen Weltteilen*, Oct. 1872, p. 3.)

HILL, CLEMENT.—Expedition up the River Wami. (*Proc. of the Roy. Geog. Soc.*, 1873.)

FRERE, Sir H. BARTLE.—A Few Remarks on Zanzibar and the East Coast of Africa. (*Proc. of the Roy. Geog. Soc.*, vol. xvii., 1873, No. 5, p. 343.) (Conf. *Globus*, XXIII., 1873, pp. 29, 318, 333, and XXIV., p. 73.)

ELTON, Capt.—From Natal to Zanzibar, with Descriptive Notes of Zanzibar, Mombasah, the Slave Trade, Sir Bartle Frere's Expedition, &c. Durban, 1873.

MALCOLM, Capt.—Der Ostafrikanische Flusz Wami. (*Zeitschr. d. Gesellsch. f. Erdkunde.* Berlin, VIII., 1873, Pt. 4, p. 217.)

HORNER.—Reisen in Zanguebar in den Jahren 1867 und 1870. Regensburg, 1873.

BELLEVILLE, A.—Journey to the Universities Mission Station of Magila, on the Borders of the Usambara Country. (*Proc. of the Roy. Geog. Soc.* vol. xxii., 1875–76, No. 1, p. 74.)

Beschreibung der Ostküste von Afrika von der Pangani-Bucht bis Ras
Kimbiji. (*Annal. der Hydrographie und marit. Meteorologie,* 1875,
Nos. 17-20.)

HUTCHINSON, E.—The Best Trade Route to the Lake Regions of Central
Africa. London, 1877.

SCHNEIDER, G.—Die katholische Mission von Zanguebar. Thätigkeit und
Reisen des P. Horner. Regensburg, 1877.

RAFFRAY, A.—Voyage chez les Ouanika, sur la Côte Zanguebar. (*Tour du
Monde,* 1878, No. 905.)

FARLER, F. P.—The Usambara Country in East Africa. (*Proc. of the Roy.
Geog. Soc.,* 1879, No. 2, p. 81. Conf. *Peterm. Mitt.,* 1879, p. 115.)

HILDEBRANDT.—Uebersicht seiner Reisen in den Küstenländern von Arabien
und Ost-Afrika. (*Verhandl. d. Gesellsch f. Erdkunde.* Berlin, 1874,
No. 10, p. 269, and 1877, p. 284.)

HILDEBRANDT, J. M.—Meine zweite Reise in Ost-Afrika. (*Globus,* 1878,
No. 17, p. 269, No. 18, p. 279, No. 19, p. 296, and conf. *Petermanns
Geogr. Mitt.,* 1878, p. 41 and 116.)

HILDEBRANDT, J. M.—Ethnographische Notizen über Wakamba und ihre
Nachbarn. (*Zeitschr. für Ethnographie,* 1878, No. 5.)

KURTZ, F.—J. M. Hildebrandt's Reisen in Ost-Afrika. (*Verhandl. d. Botan.
Vereins der Prov. Brandenburg,* 1878.)

HILDEBRANDT.—Von Mombassa nach Kitui. (*Zeitschr. d. Ges. f. Erdk.,* vol.
xiv., 1879, p. 241 and 321.)

HANN, J.—Einige Resultate neuerer meteorologischer und hypsometrischer
Beobachtungen im äquatorialen Ost-Afrika. (*Peterm. Geogr. Mitt.,*
1880, p. 373.)

JOHNSTON, K.—Map of the Lake Region of Eastern Africa, showing the
Sources of the Nile recently Discovered by Dr. Livingstone. Edinburgh
and London, 1870.

HOOKER, J. D.—The Subalpine Vegetation of Kilima-Njaro. (*Journal of the
Linnean Soc. of London,* XIV., 1873-74.)

JOHNSTON, K.—Notes of a Trip from Zanzibar to Usambara. (*Proc. of the
Roy. Geog. Soc.,* 1879, p. 545.

JOHNSTON, K.—Notes on the Rev. Thomas Wakefield's Map of Eastern
Africa. (*Proc. of the Roy. Geog. Soc.,* vol. xvi., No. 2, p. 125.)

H. H. JOHNSTON'S EXPEDITION.

JOHNSTON, H. H.—The Kilima-Njaro Expedition. (*Proc. of the Roy. Geog.
Soc.,* 1885, VII., No. 3, conf. 137. *Peterm. Mitt.,* 1884, pp. 73, 152,
394.)

JOHNSTON, H. H.—The Kilima-Njaro Expedition, with 6 Maps, London,
1886.

JOHNSTON, H. H.—Die Kilima-Ndscharo-Expedition, mit 6 Karten und zahlreichen Abbildungen. Leipzig, 1886.

JOHNSTON, H. H.—The People of Eastern Equatorial Africa. (*Journ. of the Anthropol. Inst.*, London, 1885, vol. xv. p. 3.)

JOHNSTON, H. H.—British Interests in Eastern Equatorial Africa. (*Scottish Geog. Magazine*, 1885, vol. i., No. 5, p. 145, and *Journ. of the Manchester Geog. Soc.*, 1885, vol. i. p. 160.)

JOSEPH THOMSON'S EXPEDITION.

THOMSON'S EXPEDITION zum Kenia u. s. w. *Petermanns Mitt.*, 1880, pp. 32, 119, 139, 158, 440, and 1882, pp. 315, 390.)

THOMSON, J.—Through the Masai Country to Victoria Nyanza. (*Proc. of the Roy. Geog. Soc.*, 1884, VI., No. 12, p. 690.)

THOMSON, J.—Notes on the Geology of Usambara. (*Proc. of the Roy. Geog. Soc.*, 1879, No. 9, p. 558.)

THOMSON, J.—Through Masai Land. With 2 Maps. London, 1885.

THOMSON, J.—Au Pays des Massaï. With Map. Paris, 1886.

THOMSON, J.—Durch Massai-Land. Mit 2 Karten. Leipzig, 1885.

HOOKER and OLIVER.—List of the Plants Collected by Mr. Thomson on the Mountains of Eastern Equatorial Africa. (*Journ. Linn. Soc.*, vol. xxi. p. 392.)

THOMSON, J.—Altitudes in East Central Africa, compiled by S. S. Snyden. (*Journ. of the Roy. Geog. Soc.*, vol. L p. 268.)

THOMSON, J.—Notes on the Geology of East Central Africa. (*Nature*, 1880, p. 102.)

THOMSON, J.—East Central Africa and its Commercial Outlook. (*Scot. Geog. Magazine*, 1886, vol. ii. No. II. p. 65.)

DR. G. A. FISCHER'S EXPEDITIONS—1880, 1883, AND 1886.

Die Denhardt-Fischer'sche Expedition auf dem Tanaflusz. (*Peterm. Geogr. Mitt.*, 1878, pp. 73, 197, 317; 1879, p. 115; 1880, p. 74; 1884, p. 314.)

FISCHER, G. A.—Ueber die jetzigen Verhältnisse im südlichen Galla-Lande und Wito. (*Mitteil. d. Geogr. Ges.*, Hamburg, 1876-77, p. 347.)

FISCHER, Dr. G. A.—Das Mapokomo-Land und seine Bewohner. (*Mitt. der Geogr. Ges. in Hamburg*, 1878-79, and *Peterm. Mitt.*, 1879, p. 434.)

FISCHER, G. A.—Mehr Licht im dunkeln Weltteil. Betrachtungen über die Kolonisation des tropischen Afrika unter besonderer Berücksichtigung des Sansibar-Gebietes. Hamburg, 1885.

FISCHER, G. A.—Reise in das äquatoriale Ostafrika. (*Globus*, 1884, XLV. No. 1, p. 11, and *Proc. Roy. Geog. Soc.*, 1884, VI. No. 2.)

Fischer's projektierte Expedition zum Samburu-See. (*Peterm. Geogr. Mitt.*, 1882, p. 432.)

FISCHER, G. A.—Bericht über die im Auftrage der Geographischen Gesellschaft in Hamburg unternommene Reise in das Massai-Land. (*Mitt. d. Geogr. Gesellsch.*, Hamburg, 1882–83, Part 1, p. 36 ; and *Peterm. Mitt.*, 1882, p. 432 ; 1883, p. 436 and 465 ; 1884, p. 232.)

Ueber Fischer's Reise nach dem Naivascha. (*Peterm. Mitt.*, 1883, p. 436.)

FISCHER, G. A.—Ueber das Massai-Gebiet. (*Verhandl. d. Gesellsch. f. Erdkunde*, Berlin, 1884, XI. No. 2, p. 94. Conf. *Peterm. Mitt.*, 1884, p. 232.)

FISCHER, G. A.—Das Massai-Land (Ost-Aequatorialafrika). Hamburg, 1885.

FISCHER, G. A.—Vorläufiger Bericht über die Expedition zur Auffindung Dr. Junkers. (*Peterm. Mitt.*, 1886, p. 363. With map. Conf. also pp. 59, 125, 150, 216, 254.)

MISCELLANEOUS—1880–85.

DENHARDT, KLEMENS.—Ostafrikanische Forschungs-Unternehmen. (*Petermanns Mitt.*, 1877, p. 33.)

DENHARDT, KL.—Erkundigungen im äquatorialen Ost-Afrika. (*Peterm. Geogr. Mitt.*, 1881, p. 11 and 130. With map.)

DENHARDT, KL.—Anleitung zu geographischen Arbeiten bei Forschungsreisen. (*Mitteilungen des Vereins für Erdkunde*, Leipzig, 1882.)

PRICE, W. S.—Notes from East Africa. (*Church Miss. Gleaner*, 1882, No. 104, p. 90.)

PRICE, W. S.—Journal in East Africa ; Expedition from Frère Town to Shimba. (*Church Miss. Intell.*, 1882, VII. No. 83, p. 668.)

LAST, J. T.—The Masai People and Country. (*Proc. of the Roy. Geog. Soc.*, 1882, p. 224, and 1883, p. 517. With map.)

Work of the German African Association in Western Equatorial Africa. (*Proc. of the Roy. Geog. Soc.*, 1882, IV. No. 11, p. 678. With map.)

KRAPF, J. L.—Mount Kenia. (*Proc. Roy. Geog. Soc.*, 1882, IV. No. 12. p. 747.)

LEDOUIX, CH.—Explorateurs et Missionnaires dans l'Est de l'Afrique. (*Bull. de la Soc. de Géogr.*, 1883, II. Nos. 6, 10, 11.)

DUTRIEUX.—Souvenirs d'une Exploration Médicale dans l'Afrique Intertropical. Paris, 1885.

PRINGLE, M. A.—Towards the Mountains of the Moon. A Journey in East Africa. With map. London, 1884. (New edition, 1886.)

KELLER, C.—Die tiergeographischen Verhältnisse in Ostafrika. (*Mitt. d. Ostschweiz. Geogr.-Komm.-Gesellschaft*, 1884, No. 1, p. 1.)

GISSING, C. E.—A Journey from Mombasa to Mounts Ndara and Kasigao. (*Proc. Roy. Geog. Soc.*, London, 1884, VI. No. 10, p. 551. With map. Conf. *Peterm. Mitt.*, 1884, p. 431.)

BIBLIOGRAPHY.

WRAY, J. A., and J. W. HANDFORD.—The Taita Mission. (*Church Mission. Intellig.*, 1884, IX. No. 106, p. 641.)

WRAY, J. A., and E. A. Fitch.—The First Year of the Chagga Mission, (*Church Mission. Intellig.*, 1886, XI. No. 127, p. 555.)

COUNT TELEKI'S EXPEDITION—1887 AND 1888.

TELEKI.—Die Expedition des Grafen Teleki in das Gebiet des Kilima Ndschara und Kenia. (*Mitt. d. K. K. Geogr. Gesellsch.*, Vienna, 1888, XXI. p. 353, 441, 471, and XXII. 1889, p. 189. Conf. *Peterm. Mitt.*, 1888, p. 371.)

HÖHNEL, L. VON.—Die Afrikareise des Grafen Samuel Teleki. (*Mitt. der Geogr. Gesellsch.*, Vienna, 1889, XXII. p. 531.)

HÖHNEL, L. VON.—Zur Hydrographie des Samburu-Seen-Gebietes. (*Mitt. d. K. K. Geogr. Gesellsch.*, Vienna, 1889.)

HÖHNEL, L. VON.—Ueber die Hydrographische Zugehörigkeit des Rudolfsee-Gebiets. (*Peterm. Mitt.*, 1889, p. 233.)

CECCHI, A.—Esplorazione Teleki. (*Boll. Soc. Geogr. Ital.*, 1889, II. p. 99.)

WAUTERS, A. J.—L'Exploration du Comte Teleki; un Nouveau Réservoir du Nil. (*Mouvement Geogr.*, 1889, p. 13.)

HÖHNEL, L. VON.—Bergprofilsammlung der Graf Teleki'schen Afrika-Expedition 1887-88. Vienna, 1890.

HÖHNEL, LUDWIG, RITTER VON.—Ostäquatorial-Afrika zwischen Pangani und dem neu entdeckten Rudolf-See. Ergebnisse der Graf S. Teleki'schen Expedition 1887-88. (*Ergänz.-Heft*, No. 99 *zu Peterm. Mitt.*, 1890. With 3 maps.)

JOURNEYS, BOOKS, AND PAPERS FROM 1885-90.

Only those works are mentioned which contribute new matter bearing on the geographical exploration of the region north of Pangani, including the coast as far as Mombaza.

LANGE, H.—Deutsche Forschungsreisen in Ostafrika. (*Geogr. Rundschau*, 1885, VII. No. 4, p. 145.)

LE MONNIER, Fr. v.—Die neuesten Forschungen in Ost-Aequatorialafrika. (*Mitt. der k. k. Gesellsch. in Wien*, 1885, XXVIII. No. 3, p. 135.)

LAST, J. T.—Remarks on East Africa. (*Proc. of the Roy. Geog. Soc.*, 1885, VII. No. 7, p. 452.)

TÖPPEN, K.—Handel und Handelsverbindungen Ostafrikas. (*Mitteil. d. Geogr. Ges.*, Hamburg, 1885-86, Part 3, p. 222.)

COURMONT, R. DE.—Une Tournée dans le Vicariat Apostolique du Zanguébar. (*Missions Cathol.*, 1885, XVII. No. 851 *et seq.*).

HANNINGTON, BISHOP.—Visit to Chagga. (*Church Mission. Intellig.*, August 1885, X. No. 116.)

The Victoria Nyanza Mission and Bishop Hannington. (*Church Mission. Soc.*, 1886.) With Portrait and Map. Extracts from the Diary and Letters of the Right Rev. James Hannington, 1885.

The Story of the Uganda Mission and the Church Missionary Society's Work in Eastern Equatorial Africa. Lond. 1886. With 22 Illustrations and a Map.

HANNINGTON.—The Last Journals of Bishop H., Aug. to Oct. 1886. (*Church Mission. Soc.*, 1886.)

WAGNER, J.—Deutsch-Ostafrika. Geschichte der Gesellschaft für Deutsche Kolonisation und der Deutsch-Ostafrikanischen Gesellschaft. Berlin, 1886.

HOFFMANN, Kapit. zur See, Kommand. S. M. Kriegsschiff "Möwe."—Die Küste des Sultanats Zanzibar von Tunghi bis Saadani. (*Annalen der Hydrographie*, 1886, XIV. No. 7, pp. 304 and 308.)

REISE S. M. Kriegsschiff "Möwe" von Zanzibar nach Aden ; topograph. und hydrogr. Beobachtungen. (*Annalen der Hydrographie*, 1886, XIV. No. 9, p. 341.)

SMYTHIES, RICH.—The Mountain Towns of the Bondei Country. (*Central Africa*, 1886, No. 42, p. 75.)

ENGELHARDT, P., and J. v. WENSIERSKI.—Karte von Zentral-Ostafrika. Berlin, 1886.

WEISZ, K.—Meine Reise nach dem Kilima Ndjarogebiet. With Map. Berlin, 1886.

JÜHLKE, K.—Die wirtschaftliche Bedeutung Ostafrikas. (*Kolonialpolitische Korrespondenz*, 1886, No. 24, p. 148.)

JÜHLKE, K.—Meine Wanderung nach dem Kilima-Ndscharo. (*Köln. Zeit.*, 1886, No. 153 *et seq.*)

EBERSTEIN, v.—Die Besteigung des Kilima-Ndjaro. (*Kolonialpolit. Korrespond.*, 1887, No. 48 *et seq.*)

Küstenbeschreibung und Hydrographie Ostafrikas. (*Annalen der Hydrogr.*, 1887, XV. Part 6, p. 225.)

LANGEMAK.—Rekognoszierungsfahrt S. M. Kanonenboot "Hyäne" an der Ostküste von Afrika. (*Annalen der Hydrogr.*, 1887, XV. No. 4, p. 134, with map.)

TÖPPEN, K.—Eine Reise nach dem Innern von Afrika. (*Ausland*, 1887, No. 33.)

KIEPERT, H.—Polit. Uebersichtskarte von Ostafrika nach den neuesten Verträgen und Besitzergreifungen. Berlin, 1887. (*Petermanns Mitteil.*, 1887, p. 123.)

SCHMIDT, Dr. W. K.—Erlebnisse in Ostafrika ; Reise durch Usambara. (*Kolonialpolit. Korresp.*, 1887, No. 16 *et seq*)

BOETERS, KORV.-KAPT., Kommand. S. M. Kriegsschiff "Möwe."—Beiträge zur Küstenbeschreibung von Ostafrika. (*Annal. d. Hydrogr.*, 1887, XV. No. 12, p. 482.)

SMITH, S.—Explorations in Zanzibar Dominions. (*Suppl. Pap. Roy. Geog. Soc.*, London, 1887, II. No. 1, with map. Conf. *Peterm. Mitt.*, 1887, p. 153.)

Offiz. Karte des Sultanats Sansibar und der deutschen Interessensphäre. (*Petermanns Geogr. Mitt.*, 1887, p. 123.)

STUHLMANN, FR.—Bericht über eine Reise durch Usegua und Ungún. (*Mitt. der Geogr. Ges. in Hamburg*, 1887–88, p. 143.)

STUHLMANN, FR.—Zweiter Bericht über eine nach Ostafrika unternommene Reise. (*Sitz.-Ber. der Kgl. Preusz. Akad. d. Wissensch.*, 1889, No. 33.)

BLACKBURN, J.—The Country between Mombasa and Mamboia. (*Proc. Roy. Geog. Soc.*, London, 1888, X. No. 2, p. 92.)

ROHLFS, G.—Die Araber in Ostafrika. (*Münchener Neueste Nachrichten*, October 1888.)

PETERS, Dr. KARL.—Briefe aus Tanga und Mandabucht. (*Deutsche Kol.-Zeit.* 1888, new edit., I. p. 18.)

BÜLOW, F. v.—Reiseskizzen und Tagebuchblätter aus Deutsch-Ostafrika. Berlin, 1888.

KRENZLER, E.—Ein Jahr in Ostafrika. With Map. Ulm, 1888.

KRENZLER, E.—Sklaverei und Sklavenhandel in Ostafrika. (V.–VI. *Jahresbericht d. Württemb. Vereins f. Handelsgeogr.*, 1888, p. 69.)

RUDOLF HELLGREVE.—Aus Deutsch-Ostafrika. Zwanzig Landschafts- und Staffagebilder und ein Titelbild. Berlin, 1888.

KETTLER, J. J.—Spezial-Wandkarte von Deutsch-Ostafrika. Weimar, Geogr. Institut., 1888-89.

SCHMIDT, Dr. K. W.—Die Bodenverhältnisse Deutsch-Ostafrikas. (*Petermanns Mitteil.*, 1889, p. 81.)

SEIDEL, H.—Die Araber in Ost- und Mittelafrika. (*Globus*, 1889, LV., p. 145.)

REICHARD, P.—Vorschläge zu einer praktischen Reiseausrüstung für Ost- und Zentralafrika. (*Zeitschr. d. Gesellsch. f. Erdk. zu Berlin*, 1889, No. 1.)

DEUTSCHE ADMIRALITÄT.—Skizze der Untiefen und Inseln zwischen Masin und der Comanez-Bai. (No. 109.) Berlin, 1889.

WILLOUGHBY, J.—East Africa and its Big Game. London, 1889. (*Peterm. Mitt.*, 1890, Litteraturbericht, No. 352.)

DILTHEY, R.—Der wirtschaftliche Wert von Deutsch-Ostafrika. Düsseldorf, 1889.

BAUMANN, Dr. Oskar.—Handel und Plantagenbau im tropischen Afrika. (*Oesterr. Monatsschr. f. d. Orient*, 1889, XIV. p. 1.)

KETTLER, J. J.—Handkarte der deutschen Schutzgebiete in Ostafrika. Weimar, 1889.

ENGLISCHE ADMIRALITÄTSKARTEN.—No. 663, Bay of Tanga; No. 664, East

Coast, Zanzibar, and Pemba; No. 665, Mombaza to Patta Island; No. 666, Mombaza Harbour.

EHLERS, O. E.—Meine Besteigung des Kilima-Ndscharo. (*Peterm. Mitt.*, 1889, p. 68; and Baumann, *Mitteilungen des Oesterr. Alpenvereins,* 1889, p. 121; also Purtscheller, *Mitteil. d. D.-Oe. Alpenvereins,* 1890, p. 103 and 169.

EHLERS, O. E.—Einiges über die Wadschagga. (*Deutsche Kolonialzeitung,* 1889, p. 224.)

RAVENSTEIN, E. G.—A Map of a Part of Eastern Africa. 9 pages, London, 1889. (Conf. *Peterm. Mitt.,* 1889, p. 231.)

EHLERS, O. E.—Briefe an die "Kölnische Zeitung," 1890, 14 and 15 Mai.

FÖRSTER, BRIX.—Deutsch-Ostafrika. Geographie und Geschichte der Kolonie. Leipzig, 1890. (Conf. *Peterm. Mitt.,* 1890. Litteraturber. No. 350.)

HOLZAPFEL, P.—Bodenbau und Bewässerung des deutschen Ostafrika. (Inaug.-Diss., Halle, 1890.)

WEISZ, PREM.-LEUT.—Ueber Verkehrswege in Ostafrika. (*Deutsche Kolonialzeitung,* new edit., III., 1890, No. 10, p. 117, and No. 11, p. 134.)

BAUMANN, Dr. OSKAR.—Neueste Reisen in Deutsch-Ostafrika. 1890. (*Peterm. Mitt.,* 1890, Monatsbericht, Part 10, p. 255.)

Die Eisenbahn nach dem Kilimandscharo. (*Deutsche Kolonialzeitung,* new edit., III., 1890, p. 221.)

Der Nordwesten Deutsch-Ostafrikas. (*Deutsche Kolonialzeitung,* new edit., III., 1890, p. 203.)

PIGOTT, J. R. W.—Journey to the Upper Tana. (*Proc. of the Roy. Geog. Soc.,* 1890, p. 129. With Map.)

DR. HANS MEYER'S EXPEDITIONS, 1887, 1888, AND 1889.

MEYER, Dr. HANS.—Meine Besteigung des Kilimandscharo. (*Peterm. Geogr. Mitteil.,* 1887, No. XII.)

MEYER, Dr. H.—Ueber seine Besteigung des Kilimandscharo. (*Verh. d. Gesellsch. für Erdkunde,* Berlin, 1887, XIV., No. 10, p. 446.)

MEYER, Dr. H.—Einiges über Deutsch-Ostafrika. (*Mitt. d. K. K. Geogr. Ges.,* Wien, 1888, XXXI., p. 255.)

MEYER, Dr. H.—Touristisches von meiner ersten Besteigung des Kilimandscharo. (*Mitt. d. Dtsch. u. Oesterr. Alpenver.,* 1888, No. 1.)

MEYER, Dr. H.—Die Schneeverhältnisse am Kilima Ndscharo im Juli 1887. (*Mitteil. des Vereins für Erdkunde,* Leipzig, 1888, p. 277.)

MEYER, Dr. H.—Briefwechsel mit einem ostafrikanischen Fürsten. (*Deutsche Kolonialzeitung,* new edit., I., 1888, p. 92.)

MEYER, Dr. H.—Zum Schneedom des Kilima Ndscharo. 40 Photographien aus Deutsch-Ostafrika, mit Text. Berlin, 1888.

BAUMANN, Dr. O.—Usambara. (*Peterm. Mitt.,* 1889, XXXV., p. 41, with Map.)

BAUMANN, Dr. O.—Reise in Deutsch-Ostafrika. (*Mitt. d. K. K. Geogr. Ges.*, Wien, 1889, XXXII., p. 29.)

MEYER, Dr. H.—Letzte Expedition in Deutsch-Ostafrika. (*Verh. d. Gesell. f. Erdk.* Berlin, 1889, XVI., p. 83.)

MEYER, Dr. H., und Dr. O. Baumann.—Bericht über ihre Reise in Usambara. (*Mitteil. aus d. deutsch. Schutzgebiet*, 1888, I., p. 199.)

HYLAND, J. S.—Ueber die Gesteine des Kilimandscharo und dessen Umgebung. (*Mineralog. und petrograph. Mitteilungen*, hrsg. von G. Tschermak, vol. x., Part 3, p. 203. Inaugural-Dissertation, Wien, 1888.)

STEIN, B.—Flechten vom Kilimandscharo. (*Jahresbericht d. schles. Gesellsch. für vaterländ. Kultur ;* botan. Sektion, 15 Jan. 1888.)

STEPHANI, J.—Lebermoose vom Kilimandscharo. (*Hedwigia*, 1888, Part 2.)

MÜLLER, Dr. KARL.—Die Mooswelt des Kilimandscharo. (*Flora*, 1888, No. 27.)

BAUMANN, Dr. O.—In Deutsch-Ostafrika während des Aufstandes. Wien, 1890. (Conf. *Peterm. Mitt.*, 1890, Litteraturbericht, No. 29.)

MEYER, Dr. H., and L. PURTSCHELLER.—Reise nach dem Kilima-Ndscharo, (*Peterm. Mitt.*, 1889, p. 183.)

MEYER, Dr. H.—Die Besteigung des Kilimandscharo. (*Peterm. Mitt.*, 1890. p. 15. With Map and Views of the Kibo Crater.)

PURTSCHELLER, L.—Die Ersteigung des Kilimandscharo. (*Mitteil. des D. Oe. Alpenvereins*, 1890, p. 85.)

MEYER, Dr. H.—Das Bergland Ugueno und der westliche Kilimandscharo. (Letter to *Peterm. Mitt.*, 1890, p. 46. With Sketch Map.)

MEYER, D. H.—Ascent to the Summit of Kilima-njaro. (*Proc. of Roy. Geog. Soc.*, 1890, June, pp. 331–345.)

MEYER, Dr. H.—Across East African Glaciers. London, 1890. (English edition of "Ostafrikanischen Gletscherfahrten.")

INDEX.

— ❖ —

399

THE END.

GEORGE PHILIP AND SON, LONDON AND LIVERPOOL.

9 780548 307908